TWILIGHT OF THE YOUNG

A PERSONAL REPORT BY

Klaus Mehnert

TWILIGHT OF THE YOUNG

THE RADICAL MOVEMENTS OF THE 1960s AND THEIR LEGACY

HOLT, RINEHART and WINSTON
New York

Hoover Institution Press
Stanford

TO MY ALMAE MATRES IN AMERICA

University of California at Berkeley
(1928/29 and many times later)

Hoover Institution on War, Revolution and Peace,
Stanford, California (1960 and many times later)

Columbia University, Research Institute on
International Change, New York, New York
(1972/73 and many times later)

Published simultaneously in Canada by Holt, Rinehart
and Winston of Canada, Limited.

Hoover Institution Publications No. 182

Library of Congress Cataloging in Publication Data
Mehnert, Klaus, 1906–
    TWILIGHT OF THE YOUNG.
    Translation of Jugend im Zeitbruch.
    Bibliography: p.
    Includes index.
    1. Students—Political activity. I. Title.
LB3610.M413   1977   322.4   76-58520
ISBN 0-03-019476-8

LB
3610
m413
1977

Grateful acknowledgment is made to reprint portions of the lyrics from the
    following songs.
"To Bobby." Words and music by Joan Baez. © 1971 Chandos Music. All Rights
    Reserved. Used by permission.
"It's Alright Ma (I'm Only Bleeding)," by Bob Dylan. © 1965, Warner Bros. Inc.
    All Rights Reserved. Used by Permission.

First published in the United States 1977

Printed in the United States of America

10 9 8 7 6 5 4 3 2 1

CONTENTS

PREFACE

THE years since 1960 have witnessed the outbreak of a youth rebellion which quickly spread to country after country, changing the world—truly a world revolution. It has shaken old traditions (academic, cultural, moral, political) and brought all authority into question; it has convulsed governments, toppling some. And all this while the proportion of young people in the world grew dramatically with the exploding population. Today there live on our earth 2.5 billion people younger than twenty-five years of age.

In the decade following the end of the Second World War, most adults in the Western world (this includes Japan) had come to be, on the whole, satisfied with their lives. Many felt—I was among them—that once again man had survived an ordeal of tremendous dimensions, unimaginable before. In Germany, where total war had brought what seemed nearly total annihilation, we went in droves to Thornton Wilder's play *The Skin of Our Teeth,* perhaps the most popular postwar drama on the German stage, where the title had been rendered as *Wir sind noch einmal davongekommen* (Once More We Have Survived). Peace reigned, apart from some local conflicts; even the war that raged dangerously in Korea was brought to an armistice. Prosperity had returned to the industrialized countries, surpassing anything before. Dozens of new nations, former colonies, had taken their place on the world stage.

Then the young people rebelled, led by the students—the most privileged of all—and mainly by those from well-to-do families. They had nothing but scorn and contempt for the old generation's achievements, and they heaped accusations upon their elders, who had expected praise or at least some understanding acknowledgment. Most adults were nonplussed and hardly believed their ears. But the shrill voices became louder, more numerous, more urgent, until the tumult could no longer be overlooked or made light of as a youthful fad.

Like most of my generation I too was bewildered. But there must be an explanation, I thought, for why many of the most intelligent young people should suddenly find the existing order detestable to the point that they preferred chaos. It became imperative to understand what was going on, for this attack threatened not just the normal order of things but the very foundation of modern civilization. These young people were not hoodlums or criminals (whom society had always known how to handle), nor were they psychopaths (as some adults thought and perhaps still think). They were members of the young elite, the pride of their nations, the students from the most prestigious universities—from Berkeley and Stanford, from Columbia and Harvard, from Paris and West Berlin, from Seoul and Tokyo, even from Warsaw and Prague.

A heavy price was paid in this revolt. Hundreds of young people were killed (the largest number in pre-Olympic Mexico). Hundreds of thousands ran away from home, many turning into flower children, all the way from San Francisco to Katmandu, some of them never to return—victims of misery, disease, prostitution. Millions experimented with drugs (250,000 in conservative Bavaria alone), and millions with new sex relations, often ending up in perplexity and grief.

Sacrifices such as these only make sense (for parents and friends, for all of us) if we can see them in the context of experimentation for the future, as aid—albeit unintended aid—in the exploration and eventual mastering of the new age. Has it not always been the function—if this mechanical word be allowed—of the young to serve as pioneers and explorers of tomorrow? And is it not the merit of the democratic system that it offers to the young—if the old ones are wise and self-confident enough—the means by which they can transform their visions and longings into effective, durable reforms?

When, since the Ice Age, have the conditions of human life changed so radically, and above all so quickly, as in our era, which leaped from the steam engine to space rockets, from the Winchester rifle to the hydrogen bomb? To understand youth's drive and—if it be not too daring a hope—to put this drive to the service of the future: that is the aim of this book.

The time has come for an attempt of this kind. New youth dramas will certainly occur, but the curtain is coming down on the one described in the following pages—from the high-spirited idealism of its earlier phases to the desperate terrorism of recent years.

What youth is this book about? Not the "silent majority" who avoid meetings or, if they attend them, never open their mouths, who even shy away from the small chore of casting their votes in student elections. Not those who only think—on the campus and later—about their own careers. Rather, I have in mind those young people who in the past two decades have led the way, primarily on the campus; who were "involved"; who vigorously affected the ideas and the style of the silent majority, at times even mobilized it into violent action; who took sides on every issue in public life, in international affairs, in the Third World, in war and peace, in the problems of the twentieth century and even of the twenty-first; and who chose directions for their own lives, for active engagement in society or, by submersion in the world of hippies and drugs, for passive withdrawal.

No addition to the mighty wave of literature on youth psychology is intended. "Youth" in the context of this book simply means young people in that period of human life when three supreme tasks must be mastered: working out, with the awakening of sexuality, an appropriate relationship to the opposite sex; developing one's own personality while loosening ties with parents; and finding one's place in the wider social setting.

Unlike the author of an encyclopedia, compelled by the nature of his work to register everything within the scope of his subject, I was free to take my own way and thus, for example, to say more about Japan than about France, more about Marcuse than about Mills and nothing about Sartre, and also to include subjects which some readers might not expect in a book of this kind, such as the "Esperanto of the Rock Generation."

Walter Laqueur has said, in his book about the German youth movement of the early part of this century, to call youth movements idealistic is to state the obvious—they have never had personal profit in mind. They do not represent a trade union or an industrialists' lobby. Almost always they are in favor of change—frequently through reforms, sometimes through revolution. In affirming this view, I do not deny that the silent majority exists—but this majority does not determine the image of its time, either in real life or in this book. My theme is not the young generation in general, in all its groups and manifestations, but the *restless* youth. It is found primarily among that growing proportion of young people who, in contrast to former times, experience in very large numbers a lengthening period in their lives between the end of learning the "three Rs" and other fundamental knowledge, and the taking on of a real job. This book is about the young people whom I have observed in twenty-five years as professor in universities of many countries—young people of UNESCO's "third level" of education (the third after the elementary and secondary levels). The world over, they number today about 30 million.

Thus, the following chapters do not represent a cross section or a statistical average, but a portrait which, in contrast to a photograph, brings out only the characteristic features of the model, as I did in my book *Soviet Man* twenty years ago. There I tried to portray the inhabitants of the U.S.S.R., then largely unknown. Here the subject is the youth of today, difficult for many people to understand because they are baffled by the young generation, by its sudden, noisy leap onto the world stage and by its almost equally sudden disappearance.

Although the various character traits will be considered separately, the reader is asked to keep their relationship to the entire portrait in mind. Obviously, geographic and economic preconditions in the countries mentioned are—and for a long time will be—too different for their problems to be solved in identical ways and with the same results. Yet, having observed developments in many locations, I feel that the similarities are stronger than what may be considered strange or divisive; national peculiarities have therefore, on the whole, been relegated to second place. This awareness grew as I gathered material for this book, which is based both on personal experience and on the study of documents and scholarly literature, including "underground" publications.

Many people today think that youth has definitely quieted down, that "the danger is past." They are not going to read books of this kind. But they must be told that the present quiet may be deceptive. Are millions of unemployable young people going to be content to spend their time riding motorcycles and sitting in front of the TV screen? Might not the unrest of the sixties return—as the result not of prosperity and plenty but of existential anxiety and enforced idleness? Have not new and mortally effective methods been worked out which bring power even to tiny splinter groups—hijacking and kidnapping, for instance? Have not thousands of young blacks taken to the streets in South Africa? Tremors will not be wanting. Thus, it might be wise to know more about the thoughts, sentiments, and behavior of youth at a moment in history when the continuity of our civilization is breaking.

Readers turning their attention to this book may wish to know more about its author. Is he old, or young, and what is his connection with this theme?

I was born—as a German citizen—in 1906 in Moscow under the tsarist eagle. In 1914 my father went to war as a reserve officer of the Imperial German Army; he died in Flanders for his emperor, Wilhelm II. Thus, my roots reach into an era which seems not merely very distant but unreal to the youth of today. Yet there is no development without encounter and opposition between the generations.

There are two personal reasons which brought me to the subject of this book. First, the country where the great unrest broke out was familiar to me. In 1926, as a student, I visited Britain, and in 1928/29 I was a graduate exchange student at the University of California in Berkeley. In the following years I spent several summers in the U.S.S.R.—on my own, which was then possible, since Intourist was still in its infancy—to find out something about Soviet youth. My first two books, published in Germany, dealt with American youth (1930) and Soviet youth (1932), the latter being translated into a dozen languages and published in both the United States and England (they were reprinted in German in one volume in 1973). Of my twenty-five years in academia, I have spent twelve in Germany, twelve in the United States and China, and the remainder as a guest professor in universities of other countries.

The earliest indications of a new kind of youth unrest I found in 1960 in East Asia: in Japan, where demonstrations by tens of thousands of students prevented the state visit of the most powerful ruler on earth, President Eisenhower, and in South Korea, where students caused the fall of Syngman Rhee, the superannuated president and father of the nation.

At that time I did not understand fully the exemplary significance of these two events. But I began to collect information and documents on the unrest of youth—not only in East Asia—and soon it became clear that something new was under way. A visit to the Berkeley campus in 1965; the start of the Cultural Revolution in China in 1966, viewed by me from Hong Kong and described in *Maos Zweite Revolution* (Mao's Second Revolution) before that year was out; the events at West Berlin's Free University in 1967; 1968, the "year of the students," which I witnessed in a dozen countries including (in this sequence) Germany, France, Great Britain, Japan, the United States—all this confirmed that a rebellion of the young generation, mainly on the campus, was in full swing. Of the more than four dozen countries I visited after the fifties, most were affected at one time or another by the fever of the student rebellion; everywhere I had lengthy and often heated discussions with students after my lectures. The reaction of the Communist states to this development interested me especially; *Peking and the New Left* (1969) and *Moscow and the New Left* (1975) were the results.

Six semesters on U.S. campuses between 1968 and 1976 provided welcome opportunities to study the youth rebellion in the country which in many respects is a forerunner of things to come for the rest of the world. One might say without exaggeration: the U.S.A. Monday, Western Europe and Japan Tuesday, the U.S.S.R. Friday, China—perhaps never, at least while it went its separate way under Mao. Within the United States, one might add, California ordinarily is one or two hours ahead. Americans are often the first to encounter new problems, and they have developed methods of research and publication which disseminate data and analyses quickly, thereby making it easy for the observer to observe—if he or she is not overwhelmed with information. Also, speedy access to what is going on may stimulate the actions of those, such as the students, who cause things to happen. Occasional visits and lectures in Great Britain (and Canada) proved the existence of strong mutual influence among the English-speaking nations.

The second motive for writing this book leads farther back into my youth. In the early twenties I was a member of one of the many groups in the German youth movement. I belonged to the *Weisse Ritter* (White Knights), and this group was much concerned with social questions. It contributed to the change of the movement's emphasis from cheerful hiking and camping to more serious matters. But, like the rest, it too was, as the name clearly indicated, a piece of late Romanticism. It had its solemn initiation rites (with candlelight and violins), its dream of a New Man (under the motto of Walter Flex, killed in action in 1914: *Reif werden und rein bleiben*—"Become mature and stay pure"), its hikes through the Black Forest or along the Rhine, and its quick "cell division," so characteristic of all vital movements. I was one of the first to leave it, in 1923 at age seventeen.

The German youth movement of my days was just as independent as that of the sixties (we were not Boy Scouts, led by adults), but it was less aggressive and impetuous. We were critical, but we did not hate; we left the cities, those symbols of decadence (so we saw them), as soon as school was over on Saturday noon, not to return before Monday morning. But we did not contemplate the destruction of the existing regime (then the early Weimar Republic). Nor did we really want to escape it. Alcohol and tobacco were taboo—and we had not even heard about drugs. We believed that the spirit of the youth movement would gradually rejuvenate and unite the whole world. With such background memories, I witnessed the awakening of the new youth movement not merely with interest but, from the start, with utmost fascination.

Today there exist highly specialized computers which, if properly "fed" with thousands of facts, may produce a book. My book too tries to serve the reader with facts and information, but it is rather subjective and will not satisfy everybody. The reader will notice that I disliked some of the things I observed. But I was gripped by the drama of the events and the individual destinies of the students before me. And what I saw became one world, one youth, moved by one storm—as my untranslatable title in the original German would suggest, *Jugend im Zeitbruch*, "Youth at the Break of Time."

It is my hope that the English title conveys something of this flavor: twilight, the hour of uncertainty, of promise and doubt, of transitoriness and evanescence. There is a twilight in the morning and one before nightfall. Only in time will we know which of the two has been the twilight of the young during these past twenty years.

ACKNOWLEDGMENTS

MY thanks to those who helped me with the German edition have been expressed in its *Vorwort*, and I refrain from repeating them here, except those for Mrs. Ruth Henning (of Ludwigsburg) and Mr. Hans Schneider (of Tübingen), who have been helping me diligently and dependably with my books since the fifties.

In the English-language edition my thanks go to the directors of the Hoover Institution on War, Revolution and Peace at Stanford, California, especially to W. Glenn Campbell, Richard F. Staar, Richard T. Burress, Dennis L. Bark, and to my old friend Milorad Drachkovitch, the archivist; to Columbia University's Institute on International Change and its director, Professor Zbigniew Brzezinski, my colleague and host during three semesters, and to the University of California, especially to Professor and Mrs. Chalmers Johnson, my hosts at frequent occasions. They all provided me with first-rate research facilities and librarian aid, plus all the modern technology which makes the scholar's life so much easier today.

The Hoover Institution did more than that. It gave me, for ten weeks in 1976, ideal living and working conditions for the purpose of translating and updating this book for the English-language edition, as well as two invaluable helpers: Mrs. Susan D. Cassell, who typed my translation, assisting me with her own knowledge of the American campus in the sixties (every slight frown signaled to me that something was wrong with my syntax or word selection); and Mr. Jesse Phillips, editor by profession and passion, who provided me with his experience in language and grammar, and his own lexicographic resources, fighting manfully and—I hope—successfully against my Germanisms. My old friends in San Francisco, Mr. and Mrs. John Paasche (as well as their daughters and sons-in-law) supplied me with much useful material from this dynamic city. In London, I was greatly assisted by Mrs. Gertrude Mander. To all these organizations and people who were of help to me, my most sincere thanks.

A number of authors entrusted me with unpublished manu-scripts, among them Professor Stanley Rothman (mentioned in Chapter 25) and Dr. Stephen Pittel (in Chapter 29). Dr. and Mrs. Ed Bacciocco, who built up the New Left Collection of the Hoover Institution, were most helpful, as was Dr. Bacciocco's book on the U.S. New Left. It has been a pleasure to work with the editors-in-chief of the American and British publishing companies, Mr. Thomas C. Wallace of Holt, Rinehart and Winston, New York (who was my editor once before, when we did *Peking and Moscow* together), and Mr. T. G. Rosenthal, of Secker and Warburg, London.

My particular thanks go to many hundreds of students the world over whose interest, criticism, anger, and encouragement are the pepper and salt of this book.

KLAUS MEHNERT

I
THE
STORY

Many countries were theaters of the worldwide youth rebellion. In this book the spotlight will be on the United States in the New World, Germany in the Old World, Japan in the Far East. In America the development was by far the most profuse and varied; it ranged from literary protest (the beatniks) and nonideological violence (motorcycle gangs) to idealistic efforts (on behalf of the blacks in the South) and political campaigns (by the SDS and similar groups, fired strongly by resentment of the Vietnam war). The movement finally withered and disintegrated when the majority withdrew from active participation, while some activists took the only road they believed open to them—that of conspiracy and terrorism. In Europe the prepolitical phase was not strongly developed except among the Angry Young Men in England and the Provos in the Netherlands; in its climax and decline, however, the European movement paralleled the American, even in the terrorism that came simultaneously in Germany—and also, with extraordinary fury, in Japan.

The terrorists were partly inspired by the Latin American guerrillas, who are described in a separate chapter. We note also the events in France, England, and other Western countries and the Third World in a summary survey of 1968, that "year of the students," following the sequence in which they caught the attention of the world, from Belgium to Mexico. Youth's unrest did not bypass the Communist countries, as will be shown in the cases of the U.S.S.R. and Czechoslovakia, as well as Poland, Yugoslavia, Cuba, and China.

The emphasis of this first part is on a narrative description of the events themselves; analysis and commentary are given in the later portions of the book.

UNITED STATES

1
START WITH A HOWL

THE howl was heard by few. Yet it was alarming, a first rumble in the underground. It had to come someday. It came on an October evening in 1955.

In the "Six Gallery," where modern Californian art was usually shown, not far from the Embarcadero in San Francisco, young writers were reading from their works. What witnesses and historians later reported is probably overdone; no one among the six young people on the podium or in the audience of a hundred or more could have known that on that evening a new phase in the American life-style had begun, with consequences for the rest of the world, though some may have sensed that the event was unusual.

The strongest impression was created by *Howl,* a poem of 112 stanzas, recited by its author, Allen Ginsberg. The happy mood of those present was expanded when one of them, after collecting money in his hat, bought a gallon bottle of wine and passed it around. Practically no one knew him. His name—Jack Kerouac. Several writers who were present at that evening's event have their place in the history of American literature, though works by only three of them are readily available in the bookshops today: the poems of Ginsberg, the writings of Gary Snyder, and the novels of Kerouac.

Jack Kerouac was then thirty-six years old, the son of a printer in an industrial town north of Boston. In his veins ran the restless blood of his French-Canadian ancestors, who had come from Quebec to the United States. A seemingly hopeful career as a football player was cut short when he broke a leg. After that he had been everything and nothing; he had tried many jobs, including that of a sailor in the merchant marine during the war, but never settled down; a brief marriage had ended in divorce. Like a madman he chased through the States, by bus or hitchhiking, from coast to coast, a true vagabond, a bum, but with a burning desire to become a writer, one of those many young Americans in every generation who break out, as Huck Finn once did, from the narrowness of their homes into the wide open spaces.

But America had changed since the days of Mark Twain; all that was left of the "frontier" was a dream, and all his life Kerouac chased it. He was, in the words of his biographer, "a child permanently cut adrift in a darkening world."[1] Only in his books did Kerouac realize this dream, mainly in *On the Road* and *The Dharma Bums,* two titles that express his whole life: he was always on the road, always searching for something (for a while he believed that he had found it in the Indian dharma), and always a bum.

Kerouac wrote *On the Road* in 1951, in a creative fever (so far as we know, without drugs). He was so possessed by his work that he hated to take the time to change the paper in his typewriter; a friend brought him a long roll on which he typed the whole manuscript within a matter of three weeks. *On the Road* reads as breathlessly as it was written. Its hero is Dean, a friend of the narrator, in many ways a picture of the author himself.

> The most fantastic parking-lot attendant in the world, he can back a car forty miles an hour into a tight squeeze and stop at the wall, jump out, race among fenders, leap into another car, circle it fifty miles an hour in a narrow space, back swiftly into a tight spot, *hump,* snap the car with the emergency so that you see it bounce as he flies out; then clear to the ticket shack, sprinting like a track star, hand a ticket, leap into a newly arrived car before the owner's half out, leap literally under him as he steps out, start the car with the door flapping, and roar off to the next available spot, arc, pop in, brake, out, run; working like that without pause eight hours a night, evening rush hours and after-theater rush hours, in greasy wino pants with a frayed fur-lined jacket and beat shoes that flap.[2]

The manuscript wandered from publisher to publisher for six long years and did not appear in print until September 1957. In the meantime Kerouac had written books one after another; after the success of *On the Road,* seven appeared in short sequence. During these wild years he was (as he said about his hero, Dean) like "an arrow" certain of its aim. By 1961 he was burned out, consumed by the heat of his literary eruptions—and by alcohol. He died almost unnoticed in the autumn of 1969. But his books are constantly being reprinted.

When *On the Road* appeared, the reviewer in the *New York Times* spoke of a "historic occasion" and an "authentic work of art"; as Hemingway's *The Sun Also Rises* had marked the end of an epoch, *On the Road* started a new one.[3] Bruce Cook, the chronicler of the period, wrote fifteen years later:

> It is difficult, separated as we are by time and temper from that period, to convey the liberating effect that *On the Road* had on young people all over America. There was a sort of instantaneous flash of recognition that seemed to send thousands of them out into the streets, proclaiming that Kerouac had written their story, that *On the Road* was their book.[4]

In 1945, Kerouac had become a friend of the poet Allen Ginsberg, who was then studying at Columbia. Although the all-too-intellectual Ginsberg was not quite his type ("He doesn't do anything but talk," he said in 1960),[5] Kerouac went with him through quite a few adventures and contributed in his way, as mentioned before, to his friend's success in the Six Gallery.

Allen Ginsberg, born in 1926, was the child of Jewish parents in Paterson, New Jersey. His mother, a child of immigrants from Russia, became a Communist and later went insane. In 1944, at the age of eighteen, Ginsberg arrived at Columbia with a modest scholarship from his hometown's Jewish community. But as a student he frequented a world that was anything but academic. His true life began in 1954 when he came to San Francisco; he lived in the North Beach section, the habitat of the California bohemians. There he wrote his *Howl*, not long before the evening at the Six Gallery. The avant-garde publisher Lawrence Ferlinghetti printed it in San Francisco the following year. According to Bruce Cook,

> publication of the book was blocked by an obscenity suit. It took no less than criminal lawyer "Jake" Ehrlich to win the case and get the book into distribution. [...] The notoriety brought to *Howl* by the trial had assured it wide distribution.[6]

After that, Ginsberg roved around the world. Returning to California in 1965, he contributed to the hippie movement. Young

7

people were mesmerized by his ecstatic cosmic love and his "howling" against society, especially in his vision of Moloch, whom he seems to have beheld when, full of peyote, he saw the high-rise Hotel Sir Francis Drake from his window. In his *Holy*, Ginsberg, expressing a frenzied pantheism, demolished all limits, including those of traditional aesthetics, by declaring everything to be holy, including cock, asshole, and typewriter.

If you find everything in everything, you end up without history, as he does: "History is bunk. [...] There's nothing to be learned from history anymore. We're in science fiction now. [...] We're back to magic, to psychic life."[7] The true change occurred in Ginsberg on his long journey through Asia in the first half of the sixties.[8] In Japan, he experienced his satori, a flash of enlightenment, in, of all places, the fastest train in the world. In *The Change* he joyfully describes his rebirth as a second birth from the previously despised mother's womb.[9]

First all-hatred, then all-love. Wildly exaggerated and almost maniacal, both attitudes were enthusiastically adopted by a young generation that was eager to hear such messages. More than most of his fellow writers, Ginsberg used the language of the gutter: "Fuck for Peace" was inscribed on a flag in his apartment; the composer Stockhausen, he said, "put his gigantic electronic fart into the middle of his symphony." Divinity and bliss he defined as "tongues of angels licking honey off his asshole."[10] (We shall return to the phenomenon of the brutalized language in Chapter 18.)

The chronicler of those years has said that with Ginsberg a "new kind of hero" entered the literary scene. To the young he appeared "a sort of self-appointed shaman—intense, voluble, irascible, and obviously convinced of his mission as a poet. He was as far as could be from the going 'cool' style, just as his poetry—naked, gauche, and crudely confessional as it was—seemed the very antithesis of the dry, precise, and calculated verse of the academic poets who were then thought to be the only American poets worthy of the name."[11]

Gary Synder was the third of those men in the Six Gallery who survived the changing fashions. He too had experienced his satori in Japan. In poems and essays he preached to Americans the virtues of Asian religions and the simple life; they should, he suggested, take the American Indians as models, not omitting to make occasional use of their sacred mushroom, with its intoxicating effects. Above all, they should love and honor the earth:

Mankind's mother is Nature, and Nature should be tenderly respected. [...] We not only should but *do* love one another [...] These values seem almost biologically essential to the survival of humanity.[12]

THE BEAT GENERATION

Kerouac, Ginsberg, and Snyder—they were the prophets of the Beat Generation. Much has been written about the origin and the meaning of "beat." Since the early fifties, it had been applied increasingly to the mood of young people who had grown up during the turmoil of the Second World War and experienced difficulties in finding their place: the mood of a "beaten" generation. In 1952, Kerouac's friend John C. Holmes published an article entitled "This Is the Beat Generation."[13] Kerouac, he reported, had used this expression one evening in New York's Times Square. The word "beatnik" originated later: following the impact of the unexpected Soviet sputnik in 1957, the suffix "-nik" came quickly into use, and Herb Caen of the *San Francisco Chronicle* coined the new word, which soon took hold. Naturally, the beatniks encountered much bitter opposition. They had provoked the academically oriented literary Establishment. What Kerouac did wasn't writing at all, Truman Capote said on TV: "It's typing." Serious newspapers called *On the Road* "frantic" and "really mad"; it was the "the romantic novel's last whimper," a book "for those whose lives so far have led nowhere."[14]

The beatniks had also antagonized the conservative elements of America—not by describing parking-lot attendants, about whom any American could happily read, but by bringing in crass sex, homosexuality, decadence, drunkenness, and drug addiction (the latter particularly in *The Naked Lunch,* by William Burroughs, one of Kerouac's friends). Today we have grown used to all this, but in those days people were deeply shocked. For America then, the writers of the Beat Generation were corrupters, of the young, and the protagonists of their works were nothing but anti-heroes.

Protestants and Catholics alike were irked by the admiration the beatniks felt for Asiatic religions. Kerouac's strictly Catholic mother was most unhappy when her son immersed himself eagerly in Buddhist texts and meditations. How could a good Christian (Gary Snyder in this case) spend years studying the Japanese language, enter a Buddhist monastery in faraway Kyoto, write a book under the title *Buddhism and the Coming Revolution,* and finally live in Japanese fashion in San Francisco's Japanese dis-

9

trict? How could Kerouac bring himself to describe all this crazy nonsense in his *Dharma Bums,* which has Gary Snyder as chief hero, under the name of Japhy Rider? When Allen Ginsberg, in a discussion following a lecture in Los Angeles, was asked what it was that he wanted to explain in his poems, he answered, "Nakedness." And when the questioner egged him on, wanting to know what he meant by this, Ginsberg promptly stripped—and this in America, in the Eisenhower years.

But these were also the years of the beatniks. The difficulties of the immediate postwar period had been overcome while Truman was still in office; America was, under President Eisenhower (1953–1961), again the land of prosperity, of unlimited possibilities, of domestic and foreign security, without serious conflicts. Fundamentally unpolitical, Eisenhower ran the country with an easy hand—one might almost say, from the golf course. People felt that was how it should be; in 1956 he received almost 10 million more votes than Adlai Stevenson, a man of far greater brilliance. In spite of Little Rock (1957) and a recession (1957–1959), commentators spoke of an "age of consensus," which was also the subtitle of a book on that period.[15]

A much-read book in the midst of the Eisenhower era, *The Organization Man* (1956),[16] characterized the people of the time in its title; and the title of a popular novel, *The Man in the Gray Flannel Suit* (1955), became an epithet for the typical white-collar American.[17] The young people of the fifties were called the "silent generation" because they did not speak up and simply wanted to be left in peace, accepting society as something given and, on the whole, as something good. Later they were to be labeled as "apathetic, materialistic, and apolitical conformists" and the period as a whole the "dullest and dreariest in all the history of the United States."[18] In 1960 a leading sociologist, Daniel Bell, proclaimed the "the end of ideology": it seemed that no one needed an ideology anymore. The "American way of life" and the "consumer society" were still held in high regard, and Communism, so effectively denounced abroad by John Foster Dulles, was almost unanimously rejected at home. (Had not Nikita Khrushchev himself unmasked his predecessor Stalin as a tyrant and murderer?) The Korean War (1950–53), though located in distant Asia, was fought in a patriotic mood.

This "dullest and dreariest" period was, after the shocks of the sixties and early seventies, to become an object of nostalgia, brought to life in films (e.g., *American Graffiti,* showing teenagers with small problems and big ice-cream cones just before the storm broke), in musicals *(Grease)*, and in a television series *(Happy Days)*. But below the surface of prosperity unrest had set in. "Success," the magic word of American history, was losing some of its splendor. Was it not too costly? The young (and not only they) began to ask: Did one not pay too much for success—with ulcers and divorces? Wasn't there anything more important?

I happened to be in America when Eisenhower died, a little less than a decade after the end of his presidency. The nostalgic way in which the whole of America observed the funeral ceremonies showed that the people, after years of turmoil at home and a "dirty" war in Vietnam, wanted to indulge for at least a few days in remembering Eisenhower and his era. No wonder Kerouac had to wait six years to find a publisher.

Yet there had been critical and warning voices even under Eisenhower. David Riesman, in *The Lonely Crowd* (1950), pictured a nation of manipulated people. In *The Sane Society* (1955), Erich Fromm showed that contemporary society was far from sane. C. Wright Mills focused on society's manipulators in *The Power Elite* (1956). Meanwhile, a still unknown immigrant from Germany, Herbert Marcuse, was sharpening his arrows.

The beatniks did not become politically active in the traditional sense; certainly Kerouac didn't. At heart he was, politically speaking, a child of the era. During the election campaign of 1956 he was for Eisenhower, though he was too restless to wear an "I Like Ike" button. Nor was he happy when, during the sixties, the left-wingers picked him up. "They took over my mantle and twisted my thoughts to suit their own purposes," he said in 1968.[19] He was scared by the drug abuse all around him; he did not doubt that Moscow had promoted the distribution of drugs in order to destroy America from within. He didn't conceal his approval of a man on the Right, William F. Buckley, Jr., and in one of his last interviews, in the autumn of 1969, he explained: "I'm pro-American and the radical political involvement seemed to tend elsewhere . . . the country gave my Canadian family a good break, more or less, and we see no reason to demean said country."[20]

Allen Ginsberg was of a different opinion. His *Howl* was a political confession as well as a piece of literature. Kerouac did not particularly like this aspect of his friend, his "omniscient image mania."[21] Yet the beatniks as a group were considered enemies of society, the more so as their views were echoed in the criticism of

11

American society heard from abroad. Those who remember the tremendous effort of the United States to popularize the American way of life after the war, often in an all-too-sugary form, may understand why the beatniks were received in foreign countries at first with surprise and then with some relief. They obviously didn't think much of the "American myth"; they laughingly disdained success stories and the work ethic. In fact, they created an "anti-myth":

> Instead of American cleanliness, the Beats offered dirt; for industry, sloth; and in place of the official, fundamentally Protestant American ethic, they presented their own, a morality with principles but no rules. This was how the Beats looked to the world at large. Accepting them, it was possible to reject some aspects of American culture and still retain affection for those qualities of the national character that have always been most appealing— informality, enthusiasm, openness to adventure, and a kind of bold, plain-spoken honesty.[22]

ANGRY YOUNG MEN—ABROAD

The howl that emanated from the Six Gallery in October 1955 was heard a few months later on the other side of the world. On May 8, 1956, John Osborne's *Look Back in Anger* was presented in London by the newly founded English Stage Company. Here, too, many critics understood—in words similar to those used by their American colleagues—that something important had happened. They heard "the authentic new tone of the Nineteen-Fifties, desperate, savage, resentful" *(New Statesman)*; they found the play "young, young, young" *(Daily Express)* and "of extraordinary importance" *(Financial Times)*. Others called *Look Back in Anger* "rather muddled" *(Manchester Guardian)*, "neurotic, exaggerated and more than slightly distasteful" *(Daily Mirror)*, and the premiere "a night misconceived and misspent" *(Birmingham Post)*.

John Russell Taylor, in his book about the British drama of that time, believes that "the whole picture of writing" in England had undergone a transformation since the play's first performance. He sees in it "the biggest shock to the system of the British theatre since the advent of Shaw" and in Jimmy Porter, its hero, "the mouthpiece of protest for a dissatisfied generation"[23]—as Kerouac and his heroes were in the United States. Young intellectuals in England were quoting up and down the

5

The

country the words which Osborne, then twenty-six years of age, had put into Jimmy Porter's mouth:

I suppose people of our generation aren't able to die for good causes any longer. We had all that done for us, in the thirties and forties, when we were still kids. There aren't any good, brave causes left. If the big bang does come, and we all get killed off, it won't be in aid of the old-fashioned, grand design. It'll just be for the Brave New Nothing-very-much-thank-you. About as pointless and inglorious as stepping in front of a bus.

The success of John Obsorne's *Look Back in Anger* on the British stage was possible because it expressed the growing criticism among the young of England. The British play was a scream of desperation, more hopeless than Ginsberg's *Howl*; the reconciliation at the end of the play's three hours of mutual torturing was clearly but a brief episode—life would continue as it had been before.

There were signs of fermentation on the Continent too. In France, emotions aroused by the war in Algeria were shaking the Fourth Republic and would lead, before the end of the decade, to its collapse.

Germany was still too busy with postwar reconstruction to produce beatniks or Angry Young Men. There the great and solid Social Democratic Party served as a receptacle and outlet for critically minded youth; it educated young members for constructive opposition, not for a beatnik-style escape from politics, not for anger. The campaigns against atomic weapons in 1958 and 1959 barely registered with the public; yet a young coed who would later be notorious, Ulrike Meinhof, was actively involved.

In the U.S.S.R., since the early twenties, with their Mayakovskys and Esenins, there had been nothing comparable to the beatniks' tumultuous and lively readiness to experiment. Perhaps one might call the early Yevtushenko a Russian—or rather, Siberian—beatnik; his *Station Zima,* published a year after the meeting in the Six Gallery, was certainly no *Howl,* but against the frozen literary background of the Soviet Union it was no less exciting.

Only Japan, which the proud West had considered devoid of originality, was far ahead. Before anybody had ever heard of the beatniks, thousands of students and policemen were battling each other.

A new wind was blowing in large areas of the world in the

second half of the fifties. But what was it that was new about the beatniks and their likes? It was, beyond the limits of literature, a new attitude toward life, a new freedom, an awakened immediacy, a rebellion against middle-class society preoccupied with careers and material goods, a "rucksack revolution" (as Kerouac said in his *Dharma Bums*, using the German word), an opposition to history in general, a readiness for sudden decisions and enlightenments, an inclination toward Asiatic religions and mysteries and toward the simple life (of the American Indians, for example). New also was the open use of four-letter words and the frank irresponsibility—for others in questions of love, for oneself in the consumption of drugs. The wind was blowing away all kinds of conventions.

2
DEVILS AND ANGELS

ON a Sunday morning in 1963 we were driving on a freeway in northern California, not very crowded at that hour. My friend suddenly slammed on the brakes—I was almost thrown through the windshield—and sharply veered into a clump of shrubs at the right. After some fifty yards or so he stopped the car and said, "It's better this way. I've seen the Hell's Angels in the rearview mirror." Now I could hear the hellish roar, and seconds later they were shooting past us, always two choppers side-by-side in tight formation, in a burst of chrome and pipes—black-leathered men, girls with flying hair clinging to them, on thundering, stinking steeds.

The Hell's Angels were the most famous of the West Coast motorcycle gangs in the early sixties; there were also the Satan's Slaves, Coffin Cheaters, Iron Horsemen, Diablos, Road Rats, Galloping Horses, and many more. Others existed at the same time in various parts of the country, and also abroad. But sunny California was particularly suited for this kind of sport, and only there have I witnessed it.

Most of the Angels worked and had their own income from some humdrum job, but the very thought of normal middle-class life made them vomit; they were looking for another life outside society. On weekdays they were tiny screws in the giant machine; on weekends, lords of the road, feared—and loathed—on sight.

The students looked with a certain fascination on these wild and courageous people whom I shall refer to, for short, as Angels. They belonged to the same age-group; they too rebelled against

15

society and the authorities. Could they not become allies in the stepped-up fight against America's involvement in the Vietnam war? The answer was no.

There is no need to go into the habits and rituals of the Angels; they have been the subject of films *(The Wild One, Devil's Angels)* and books (the best description I know is by Hunter S. Thompson, who researched the Angels, at the suggestion of *The Nation,* and lived among them). In our context, they are of interest as one manifestation of protest against society and of the stress of identity crises ("identity" was to be one of the key words of the sixties, and we shall return to it). A minister, G. Mansfield Collins, put it very well when he said, after describing one of the Angels' riots:

> Here's the man who doesn't have any identity. But *tonight* he has the Los Angeles Police Department and the Los Angeles Fire Department upset. He has the National Guard called out. Tonight he is somebody. Tonight he has an identity.[1]

Provoking society is one of the ways of acquiring identity. That is why the Angels liked to wear old German helmets and military decorations, had "Hitler" or a swastika tattooed on their bodies, shouted *Sieg Heil* when drunk, and praised Hitler's henchmen ("There was nothing chickenshit about 'em"). One of them said:

> When you walk into a place where people can see you, you want to look as repulsive and repugnant as possible. We are complete social outcasts—outsiders against society. And that's the way we want to be. Anything good, we laugh at. We're bastards to the world and they're bastards to us. [. . .] We fight society and society fights us.

They enjoyed the publicity that they were sure to get in a country which has always loved its outlaws, its Bonnies and Clydes. But publicity is fickle. When interest waned, one of them, Terry the Tramp, mused on the radical students with some envy because they were into something constructive. He foresaw the Angels' end if they came up with nothing better than just beating up everybody.

WANTED: A POLITICAL IDEA

Terry the Tramp was not the only one who felt that way, and there were some lines of communication with the university students at Berkeley. It turned out, however, that the Angels were less alienated from society than the students who came from families with higher incomes. This became evident on October 16,

16

1965, when students marched from Berkeley to Oakland in a demonstration against the Vietnam War. The Angels violently attacked them, calling them traitors, Communists, beatniks. A mere handful against more than 10,000 demonstrators, they were finally subdued by the police.

Shortly afterward, Allen Ginsberg, in a poem of 210 lines, beseeched the Angels not to stand again in the way of anti-Vietnam demonstrations. It seems not to have impressed the addressees deeply, probably in part because it was written in a language foreign to them.

Before any new Vietnam demonstration could be organized, the Angels called a press conference and declared that they had decided not to "counter-demonstrate at this despicable un-American activity [. . .] because our patriotic concern for what these people are doing to our great nation may provoke us to violent acts [and because] any physical encounter would only produce sympathy for this mob of traitors." Then the "Maximum Leader" of the Angels read the text of a telegram to President Lyndon B. Johnson, volunteering with his friends to do service as a "crack group" behind enemy lines in Vietnam in order to "demoralize the Viet Cong and advance the cause of freedom." He added: "We are available for training and duty immediately."

The Angels had found that just scaring Middle America on the highways was not enough to give them a durable identity; they hoped to find it in a sentiment which has provided a haven for people in search of identity throughout the ages—patriotism. But President Johnson did not accept their service. The Angels went downhill, although from time to time one could still hear about them—in 1969 at Altamont, and in 1975 in Bridgeport, Connecticut, where they killed a Puerto Rican.

Similar gangs also existed and still exist outside the United States, even in Japan. In England the most talked-about were the Mods and the Rockers, who fought each other in bloody battles. In 1969 branches of the Angels were organized in England. The one best known was led by "Buttons," whose real name was Peter Welch. He got his gang name because his leather jacket was beautified with 6,120 mother-of-pearl buttons.[2]

Thompson, the chronicler of the Angels, called their activities a "revolt of the losers." Losers they were, he said, because modern civilization offered no opportunities for people of their kind; they did not go with the times, were early dropouts, and did not like reading. He added:

They are reconciled to being losers but instead of losing quietly, one by one, they have banded together with a mindless kind of loyalty and moved outside the framework, for good or ill. They may not have an answer, but at least they are still on their feet. [...] There is no talk among the Angels of "building a better world," yet their reactions to the world they live in are rooted in the same kind of anarchic, para-legal sense of conviction that brought the armed wrath of the Establishment down on the Wobblies. There is the same kind of suicidal loyalty, the same kind of in-group rituals and nicknames, and above all the same feeling of constant warfare with an unjust world. The Wobblies were losers and so are the Angels ... and if every loser in this country today rode a motorcycle the whole highway system would have to be modified. [Yet the cities are full of people] who would pay all the money they could get their hands on to be transformed—even for a day—into hairy, hard-fisted brutes who walk over cops, extort free drinks from terrified bartenders and thunder out of town on big motorcycles after raping the banker's daughter.

Yet the Hell's Angels are still around. Each May they ride their choppers for a prolonged weekend to Sonora and on to the Calaveras County Fair and Jumping Frog Jubilee (nobody seems to know why these events attract them), exhibiting "noise, sex, speed, drunkenness and quick, isolated outbursts of mayhem." An inhabitant of the invaded area wrote in 1976 that "they behave like cruel, rude, witless children," and concluded: "Their attempt to expand that chaos until it devours the order we have created, painstakingly, in our lives, is the greatest offense of all."[3]

Few as they always have been, the Angels are—and were—"acting out the daydreams of millions of losers." Called a loser, one of them replied: "Yeah, I guess I am. But you're looking at one loser who's going to make a hell of a scene on the way out." He exaggerated. The people who did make a "hell of a scene" did it with totally different methods, and they did it in the Deep South.

"DON'T STRIKE BACK"

The restless sixties began not on January 1, 1960, but on February 1, when four black students took seats at the lunch counter of the Woolworth store in Greensboro, North Carolina. It was "for whites only." The four were not served, but they remained; it was the first sit-in in a long sequence. The next day, thirty students came, and within two weeks there were sit-ins in fifteen southern towns.

The previous years had brought great changes for the blacks,

partly as a result of the Second World War, in which blacks had
fought and died like white Americans. Now they wanted to live
like them. There were the Supreme Court decisions against racial
segregation in schools (1954) and in railway stations (1958), and
the measures taken by authorities to enforce equal rights, with
the school integration battle at Little Rock (1957) as the climax.

Two new things in this latest wave of black protests—the
method used and the television coverage—together caused the
eyes of America to turn southward, not least the eyes of the students. The National Student Association, founded in 1947 by
young war veterans, urged its members in 500 colleges and universities to mount protest demonstrations and boycotts of the
Woolworth chain stores and similar establishments. Some southern restaurants began to serve blacks.

What happened next has been described many times. Here we
are interested in the role of the students, organized by SNCC, the
Student Nonviolent Coordinating Committee. SNCC agreed with
the most popular among the black leaders, Martin Luther King,
Jr., that the struggle must be and must remain nonviolent.

The iron discipline of the young activists of SNCC in following
the rule of nonviolence was their outstanding and—throughout
the world—most admired characteristic. Among the rules which
they had to observe was the following:

> Don't strike back and curse if abused.
> Show yourself courteous and friendly at all times.
> Remember love and nonviolence.[4]

For quite some time the activists observed these rules; it soon
turned out that their behavior was highly telegenic and worked
in their favor whenever they, always "courteous and friendly,"
were mistreated by whites and carried off to jail, while they were
greeted as angels by the blacks. By the first anniversary of the
Greensboro sit-in, 3,000 activists had received jail sentences and
150 Woolworth branches (and many similar enterprises) had
abandoned segregation.

But these successes were confined to the northern part of the
South. To achieve results in the Deep South, the "Freedom Rides"
were initiated, beginning on May 4, 1961. Although the first
Freedom Riders—six of the thirteen were young whites—were
mistreated on their bus trip from Washington, D.C., to New Or-
leans, the rides continued. By October 1961, three railroad companies in the South had desegregated their trains and stations.

Next came the struggle for political equality. SNCC sent white students to overcome the blacks' fear of voter registration and to support young blacks, who were particularly exposed to abuse for attempting to vote. On August 28, 1963, 200,000 people demonstrated in Washington for civil rights. In a symbolic gesture, 83,000 Mississippi blacks (of 400,000 blacks of voting age in the state) nominated a black candidate for governor.

Although the advances in attaining civil rights for blacks were remarkable, they came along too slowly for the activists. The assassination of President Kennedy in November 1963 added to the feeling of disillusionment, and anger was inflamed when three young organizers, two whites among them, were found murdered in Mississippi in August 1964; the suspects were never brought to trial.

NOT WITHOUT "POWER"?

As doubts were voiced increasingly about the effectiveness of nonviolence, the question arose: Was the existing political and economic system of the United States justified? The word "power" was heard with growing frequency. The creation of local "power centers" and other black institutions outside the established system was proposed and debated.

SNCC prepared an energetic—and, as it turned out, a last—big action in connection with the 1964 elections. Again students were mobilized to instruct blacks not only in civics but also in other topics to give them greater self-confidence. Nonviolence was still the order of the day. A SNCC organizer told a group of white volunteers before they departed from Stanford University for the South:

> If you think you're going to hop in your Volkswagen with a guitar and take a vacation South to help the Negro, don't come. You'll cause more trouble than you're worth ... I want you to become totally committed to nonviolence. What about self-defense? There is no place for it. It just fans the fires of hatred. We become no better than the people we're trying to change.

In training sessions volunteers were urged to leave any beatnik habits at home because the blacks were conservative, respectable, churchgoing people. They were also warned to keep their hands off black girls.

Five hundred students, mainly whites, from the North and

West accepted the challenge. They lived simply, often in Negro homes, taught school, disregarded threats, and experienced their first success: the Mississippi blacks sent forty-six delegates to the Democratic National Convention in Atlantic City. But then came the disappointment. The convention refused to admit the black delegates.

A decline of the movement set in. The march from Selma, Alabama, to Montgomery, the state capital, in March 1965 never reached its avowed target, getting only as far as the Alabama River. The hopes connected with the enactment of civil rights legislation were succeeded by disappointments because formal equality was not followed up by actual equality. The names of new black leaders came to the fore, men like Stokely Carmichael, Rap Brown, and of course Malcolm X, the Black Muslim who was skyrocketed to fame by his best-seller autobiography and was murdered early in 1965, barely forty years old. New and tougher slogans were voiced; a new organization, the Black Panther Party, was soon on everyone's lips; and Watts, a black section of Los Angeles, exploded in racial riots.

White students, excluded from this development which led to "black power," turned to issues that touched them more personally than the civil rights movement in the South. SNCC disappeared from the headlines. But the years since Greensboro had furnished important experiences and lessons. It had become clear that a few hundred students, at most a thousand, could capture the imagination and intense interest of the entire nation if they proved courageous and straightforward, if they employed original methods such as sit-ins and Freedom Rides, and if they were able to get the mass media, above all TV, at the right moment to the right place. Within a few years they had accomplished what had seemed impossible before: Restaurants, railroads, buses, hotels, museums, swimming pools had been opened for blacks in the South, irreversibly.

And equally important: The white students who had gone South and their comrades who had observed their struggle on television at home (incidentally, also on TV screens in many other countries) had seen the disparity between ideal and reality in America, at least in the South. The crusaders for civil rights, yesterday proud defenders of the American way of life, returned with doubts in their hearts to the North and to the West—where the next chapter in the history of the American youth rebellion was just being opened.

3
SDS AND FSM

SDS in America and SDS in West Germany have pursued similar aims, but the three initials have different meanings. In Germany the first S stands for Socialist, the DS for German Student Alliance. The name of the American organization is somewhat more general: Students for a Democratic Society. The American SDS, like the German one, was an impetuous and, in the end, discarded offshoot of the moderate labor movement. In 1905, Jack London and Upton Sinclair founded the League for Industrial Democracy (LID), a respectable organization. From its midst grew the Student League for Industrial Democracy, which changed its name to SDS in 1960 and soon became the avant-garde of the New Left.

In the beginning the American SDS was (not unlike its German counterpart) a loyal child of the parent. It had inherited a liberal and antitotalitarian position—a tradition of fighting against fascism and also, especially after Stalin signed his pact with Hitler in 1939, against the Moscow Communists. But SDS was more critical of the American system than the League for Industrial Democracy had been, although this became evident only gradually.

A few weeks before Greensboro sit-in, SDS called a "Conference on Human Rights" at Ann Arbor, the home of the University of Michigan. Other conferences followed, and some of the black students who participated later helped to found SNCC.

Tom Hayden was the leading theoretician of SDS almost from the start. A graduate in journalism at the University of Michigan, he went south in a liaison capacity with SNCC. When he returned, a group of SDS leaders, meeting at Ann Arbor in December 1961, commissioned him to draft a political manifesto for the New Left before the next annual SDS convention. This convention was held in a camp belonging to the United Automobile Workers at Port Huron, Michigan, in June 1962. There Hayden's manifesto was accepted, after some rewriting, and he was elected president of SDS.

The term New Left had taken root quickly after the American sociologist C. Wright Mills, in the autumn of 1960, had published a "Letter to the New Left" in the British New Left Review.[1] Since then the term has had many interpretations. As for me, I mean by New Left the entirety of leftist radical movements and groups in the industrial countries of the West (with Japan included) which seek, with the help of more or less socialist slogans, to change the world politically and also in its life-style, and which keep their distance from the Moscow-led old Left. This aim has been pursued with varying degrees of radicalism. More often than not, the groups started out as moderates, turned increasingly toward radicalism, and then disintegrated. But in saying this, I am ahead of my story.

Various Left organizations which did not belong to SDS sent representatives to Port Huron. A man from a youth organization close to the Communist Party also was there. The presence of a Communist and the insufficient rejection of the U.S.S.R. and its brand of Communism by the SDS caused tensions between it and its parent, the LID, but these were resolved; the complete break came two years later.

In pragmatic America the Port Huron Statement—Hayden's manifesto—aroused attention simply because of its ideological nature. Encouraged, SDS decided to push its ideological efforts. By the summer of 1963, three more programmatic papers had appeared: Students and Social Action, Students and Labor, and America and the New Era. Hayden was still considered the leader of the organization, but frequent changes at the top was one of SDS's principles. Its president now was Todd Gitlin.

The four documents produced thus far, together with a number of articles in a left-wing paper, Studies on the Left (appearing since 1959), encompass the ideology of the SDS of those years; they are also practically the only overall declarations of the ideas of the American New Left.[2] They criticized American society as a whole and particularly the trade-union organizations, the Demo-

23

cratic Party (the Republicans were dismissed as outright enemies), and the liberals. The general satisfaction of Americans with conditions in the country was, the SDS said, due to ruthless "manipulation" from above. There was also criticism of the unequal treatment of races and the steadily growing military budget, which was said to be unnecessary because there was no threat of danger from the U.S.S.R.

The SDS papers developed a program for the future which demanded, for the purpose of radical change in society and in the political structure, a true "participatory democracy," in which all were to take part, and a planned economy. (The well-known problem arising from the contradiction between a participatory democracy and a state-planned economy was ignored.) The papers also demanded greater freedom for students, whose private lives should no longer be of any concern for the university authorities, and called for an alliance with the workers—for which there was little chance given the conservative attitude of the trade-union leaders.

If its program should be rejected by the U.S. Congress, by organized labor, and by the university administrations, the SDS threatened a "new insurgency" of blacks (both on the "plantations" of the South and in the ghettos of the North) and impoverished whites—that is, exactly those "outcasts and outsiders" in whom Herbert Marcuse (as will be noted later) envisaged the revolutionary potential of our time.

The SDS documents were intensely debated by the New Left, but among the students in general they did not then find much of an echo; if activists came forth, they did so in order to volunteer for work in the South. Meanwhile, SDS was trying to do in the North what SNCC had accomplished in the South: It sought the mobilization of the poor in the cities. Hayden advocated a "natural alliance of all the poor."[3] Hence "community unions" were to be organized in the poor sections of the cities, and to coordinate this work the Economic Research and Action Project (ERAP) was founded. Early in 1964 many student organizers—in all, about 125— went to Baltimore, Boston, Cleveland, Louisville, Newark, Philadelphia, and Trenton. The most talked-about effort was in Newark, New Jersey, where the young ERAP people tried not only to look after individual problems but also to tackle the ills of the city in general.

The results were disappointing for a number of reasons. First of all, there was not enough sustained effort; most students participated for a few months and then returned to their colleges. Next, the antagonism between white and black was much too strong to permit a broad alliance of the poor. Furthermore, the workers showed little appreciation of the young intellectuals: The males did not seem to be real "he-men," and they all spoke an incomprehensible jargon. The students, in turn, found it difficult to fit in with worker households—especially those of the poor. Finally, the open hostility of SDS toward the major political parties, big business, and the trade unions made these groups uncooperative or even antagonistic; they put hurdles in the way of SDS in order to ward off possible damage to themselves.

One difficulty lay in the SDS itself (and was characteristic of the New Left in general). Believing in total spontaneity, SDS members felt disdain for any kind of organization. There existed no links worth speaking of, for example, between the ERAP center in Ann Arbor and its local groups. The *ERAP Newsletter*, on July 23, 1965, actually asked how much longer anyone could afford to waste eight hours in debate on each and every point that came up.

ERAP dissolved itself in 1965, though some local efforts were continued. Tom Hayden, in a conversation I had with him in 1969, spoke nostalgically of the community unions, particularly the one in Newark. But while SDS groups were still unsuccessfully trying to fight misery in the slums of some eastern cities, the theater of action had shifted west, to Berkeley.

BERKELEY's 26-FOOT STRIP

In 1928/29 I spent a year at the University of California at Berkeley as an exchange student from Germany. Later I visited the campus many more times, teaching and doing research, including two semesters in 1968/69. Thus I have known the area for almost a half century. In 1928 the rip-roaring days of the old West were just a few decades removed; parents of my classmates still remembered the times when the West was wild. Across the bay, the boisterous, bohemian city of San Francisco had fully recovered from the earthquake and fire of 1906.

In the twenties and for some years afterward, the bravado and high spirits of the Berkeley students found outlets in Big Games and booze. Then the Second World War absorbed their energies. But all the while the city held to its tradition of tolerance for eccentrics, and the stevedores and migrant farm workers of California had long been known for their radicalism: It is not surprising that the Beat Generation should have been born in San Francisco, and the campus rebellion in Berkeley.

In the early sixties, news of the civil rights struggle in the South reverberated in California. Groups were formed by students and others wanting to do their part for the blacks. Though no segregation existed by law in California, its blacks and Chicanos were often felt to be socially inferior and treated accordingly. Here on the West Coast, if you raised the race issue, you soon reached the social problem.

Politically involved students from Berkeley participated in the Woolworth boycott; in 1963 they picketed Mel's Restaurants and the famous Sheraton-Palace Hotel in San Francisco to force management to employ more blacks. The climax came with a big sit-in, Southern style, at the hotel. Mel's and the hotel yielded. But there were confrontations with the police all along, and in the course of ten months more than a thousand students were taken into custody. Still, the mass of the students on California's many campuses paid little if any attention.

The change came in the autumn of 1964. Clark Kerr, the president of the University of California at Berkeley, contributed to it. In his youth a member of that very student league which had been the predecessor of SDS, Kerr enjoyed a wide reputation as a scholar and educator. In a book published just a few months earlier under the provocative title *The Uses of the University*, he had voiced the opinion that the *uni*versity had long ago turned into a *multi*versity. More than that, he explained in precise and cool words, the "knowledge industry" was successfully permeating society and the economy, providing it with a constantly growing number of specialists of ever higher intellectual qualifications:

> The university has become a prime instrument of national purpose. [...] What the railroads did for the second half of the 19th century, [...] the knowledge industry may do for the second half of this century. [...] The university is at the center of the knowledge process. [...] The federal agencies will exercise increasingly specific controls.

Earlier than most of his colleagues, Kerr had discerned rumblings among the students, and in 1963 had warned in a speech that they were beginning to feel as if they were a "class," some of them as if they were a proletariat, and that he sensed a "beginning revolt" against the faculty.[4]

Kerr, of all people, should have known what effect his thesis about the knowledge industry would have on the emerging student "proletariat." The university a knowledge industry, in the service of the state, exploited by business—was it for this that the students had come to Berkeley? The most violent "no" was sounded in an open letter written by a graduate student, Brad Cleveland, at the beginning of the fall semester. Addressed to the undergraduates at Berkeley, the letter took up what Kerr had said:

> The multiversity is not an educational center, but a highly efficient industry: it produces bombs, other war machines, a few token "peaceful" machines, and enormous numbers of safe, highly skilled, and respectable automatons to meet the immediate needs of business and government. This institution, affectionately called "Cal" by many of you, [...] does not deserve a response of loyalty and allegiance from you. There is only one proper response to Berkeley from undergraduates: that you *organize and split this campus wide open!* [Emphasis supplied.]

Cleveland ended by urging "an open, fierce, and thoroughgoing rebellion on this campus."[5] The aims of the revolt: participation by the students in the administration of the university, abolition of examinations and grades, and of course, no more parietal prerogatives for the administration.[6]

This challenge coincided with the administration's decision to prohibit any use of the "26-foot strip" for political activities. The main entrance to the university is from Bancroft Street, which bounds part of the campus. At the entrance is a strip 26 feet wide which legally belongs to the university but also serves the general traffic, especially heavy at this point. Here many student groups—political and nonpolitical—had habitually set up tables from which they recruited members and distributed brochures; pretzels and freshly squeezed orange juice were sold. The new decree affected eighteen groups.

In their negotiations with the administration, no compromise was found. On September 30, five students who had been sitting at their tables on the strip were ordered to appear at 3:00 P.M. in the dean's office. Instead, some 500 students marched there, declaring solidarity with the five. The name of the man who led them was soon to be known throughout America: Mario Savio. In a jubilantly acclaimed statement he charged the administration with intending to get rid of those parts of the multiversity that did not function as required—the critical students. Defense of the

27

right of free speech was, therefore, paramount. Thus emerged the Free Speech Movement (FSM), which during the following weeks was to lead a loosely organized battle against the administration.

The tables reappeared on the strip. Behind one of them sat a former Berkeley student, Jack Weinberg, soliciting for SNCC. He was arrested. But the police car which was to take him away to headquarters was immediately blocked by a vast crowd of students. It couldn't move an inch. Its top served as a podium for Savio and other speakers. On the following day, when 500 policemen tried to break through to the car, it was surrounded by 7,000 students. The negotiations continued. That evening Savio again mounted the car. Kerr, he announced over the loudspeaker, had agreed to release Weinberg. Tremendous enthusiasm! After thirty-two hours, the police car finally left.

The ensuing events, well documented as they are, do not have to be described in detail. Two months passed as negotiations, strikes, and demonstrations continued. On December 2, Sproul Hall, the administration building, experienced its famous sit-in. About four o'clock the following morning, Governor Edmund G. Brown ordered the police to clear the building. A force of 635 policemen arrested 814 protesters; the entire operation took almost twelve hours because many students purposely went limp and had to be carried to the paddy wagons. They were distributed among three jails and soon released on bail.

A few days later the university faculty met in Wheeler Auditorium, besieged by several thousand students shouting slogans in unison. After long and bitter debates, a resolution dispensing with disciplinary measures against offending students was passed by a vote of 824 to 115. Mario Savio and the FSM had won.[7] Eventually Kerr resigned.

Savio had become the FSM's leader without striving for the role. He had experienced his initiation into youth protests during the police action against the Sheraton-Palace sit-in in December 1963. In the summer of 1964 as a SNCC volunteer in the South he was further alerted to injustices existing in American society. With his new insights, he discovered social problems in the Bay Area also. The same rights, he said, were at stake in Berkeley as in Mississippi. That autumn he was elected chairman of a small group, the University Friends of SNCC. When the fight started about the 26-foot strip, he was suddenly catapulted into leadership; millions saw him on TV; he and the FSM became one. After the victory he participated in similar activities, including an effort for fair-housing legislation in Berkeley; these frequently started on the famous strip. Then he moved into the background.

THE CHANGED CAMPUS

Since I had first seen Berkeley, the university had undergone profound changes. Student life was no longer just a pleasant continuation of a joyful childhood, nor was the campus an enlarged playground where one "had fun," taking in stride (and overstepping nonchalantly) its not-too-cumbersome rules, as one had done at home with those of one's parents. The students now asked: Had the university actually become a knowledge factory? Was Brad Cleveland right in saying it was but a tool of a capitalist-run society, busy turning out efficient and obedient slaves for the big corporations? Some who joined the FSM were, of course, just swept along by the intoxicating notion that they would suddenly be lifted from everyday life into an exciting drama and turned overnight from unknown extras into stars on the TV screen.

Clark Kerr never quite got over the events of the last months of 1964. His decision to call the police onto the campus pushed thousands of previously peaceful students into rebellion. In the end he confessed: "We fumbled, we floundered, and the worst thing is I still don't know how we should have handled it."[8]

Whence came those armies attacking the university? Some were pulled in by a "ritual of protest regardless of the cause," as Bacciocco put it. Others came for the fun. One said frankly: "It's a place to see the girls and sometimes we have a great time. It's our way of living." Some were actually overwhelmed by the bewildering jungle of university life and were searching for a way out. Some who had come with great expectations felt disappointed when they had to spend endless hours on studies that to them seemed quite irrelevant. And thousands saw red when the police arrived; blindly they solidarized with the radicals.

There was a certain automatic quality to this process of solidarization. As a matter of fact, the great majority of the students did not hate the university. In a poll taken in November 1964, at the height of the FSM conflict, 82 percent said they were "satisfied" or "very satisfied" with lectures, examinations, and professors; 92 percent even affirmed that the president of the university was "really trying very hard to provide top-quality educational experiences for students." Other studies came up with similar results.

In the last analysis, campus problems as such did not stand in the foreground of the conflict, either at Berkeley or in other universities. The true enemy was "society"—whatever that might mean for the individual—the university simply being that segment of society with which the students happened to be confronted. Hence they concentrated their energies mainly on political aims that had very little to do with their studies and the university itself.

In 1965 the main battle in Berkeley was over a vacant lot in the middle of town, bought by the university for future expansion but thus far unused. Now the voluntary labor of students and hippies transformed it into what was called "People's Park." When the university administration demanded their departure and the now familiar confrontations with the police followed, 80 percent of the Berkeley students immediately declared their solidarity with the small group that had worked for the park. Confrontation also erupted on the campus when job recruiters from big corporations (e.g., the Dow Chemical Company, which produced napalm among other things) were chased off campus. Lectures and seminars on "black" subjects were demanded—more for political than for academic reasons. (Hundreds of universities and colleges quickly included such courses in their curricula, but the enthusiasm has long since waned and the number of students enrolled has dwindled.)

Academic reforms brought about by the rebellion do not seem to have made the Berkeley students very much happier. Between 1964 and 1968 the percentage of students who believed that the university administration took sufficient cognizance of their rights and demands decreased to about one half.[9]

The significance of the Berkeley events lies in the new note that they introduced—in fact, several new notes—soon to be heard in student rebellions all over the world. Until Berkeley, student political movements had been carried along mainly by three ideas—liberalism, patriotism, socialism—whatever may have been the interpretation of these terms at any given moment. But the students of Berkeley did not carry the slogans of liberalism on their flags (from the viewpoint of traditional American liberalism they already possessed all the liberties they could possibly have wished for). Nor were the slogans those of patriotism (rather the opposite; witness the Vietnam War) or socialism (this word did not even appear in the name of the American SDS). Neither was it poverty that drove them to the barricades. In fact, theirs was not a political revolt in the traditional sense at all: Lyndon

Johnson was elected in November 1964 by a landslide to which students over twenty-one contributed heavily; at that time he was held in high esteem on the campus because of his strong stand on civil rights, and Vietnam was still a small cloud on a very distant horizon.

Compared with nations where the students demanded freedom for their people (Hungary, 1956), greater social justice (Korea, 1960), more national sovereignty (Japan, 1960), or removal of a hated regime (Czechoslovakia, 1968), the America of 1964 was in a post-liberal, post-nationalist, highly prosperous phase. Gradually, during the course of that autumn in Berkeley, one thing became clearer: The students were grappling with problems which were new to them, so new that many did not know what the problems were (there will be more on this in later chapters). The university administration was even more confused. It did not understand what was going on, in spite of the great number of outstanding political scientists, sociologists, psychologists, and philosophers on the campus. One of them, the sociologist and philosopher Lewis S. Feuer, emigrated to Canada and let his exasperation be known in a book with a title that is much milder than its content: *The Conflict of Generations*.

But the Berkeley students accomplished one thing: Their victory fired restless spirits on other campuses. Everywhere a deep impression was made by the fact that violent confrontation had begun, of all places, in a university considered to be an almost perfect realization of the American dream, with excellent study and living conditions, and great academic distinction, the quintessence of everything that is grand and glorious about California and about America.

The leaders of SDS, constantly on the lookout for student unrest, recognized the importance of what had happened. They wired their moral support to the FSM; they did not have more to offer.[10] The SDS and its organizations across the country, like its Berkeley branch, lacked the strength to set the torch to other universities.

In the meantime another issue was kindling, at first barely noticed on the campus, an issue that soon was to cause a true prairie fire—Vietnam.

4
VIETNAM AND THE STUDENTS

SDS, always a few lengths ahead of others, had sensed the danger of America becoming involved in the Vietnam war when the Congress in August 1964, after the Tonkin Gulf affair, empowered President Johnson to employ all necessary measures to repel armed aggression and to protect American forces. In December, at a time when the United States had dispatched only military advisers to South Vietnam, the SDS decided to call for a protest march in Washington on April 17, 1965, against military involvement in the conflict. By the time the demonstration was held, many people had been aroused by the landing of the first American marines at Da Nang on March 8 and 25,000 people participated in the protest—the folk singer Joan Baez among them. Washington was not impressed. But SDS had been right in its assumption that a new movement was beginning on the campus, a movement against the Vietnam war.

This movement originated not in Berkeley but in another center of student unrest, the University of Michigan. Here the first teach-in was held, on March 24 (in preparation for the protest in April). It lasted until the following morning; professors and students spoke, information and agitation alternated; songs, coffee, cookies, and a torch parade were also offered; 3,000 came where 500 had been expected. The example caught on, and soon there were teach-ins on more than a hundred U. S. campuses. The spark even flew across the Atlantic. In the summer of 1965, I took part in a teach-in at the University of Lund, Sweden, invited by the student body. It was quite orderly and academic, as these things still were in Europe at that time.

But the SDS did not follow up. When proposals were made that SDS, because of its initiative and effort in planning the April march in Washington, "the biggest peace march in American history" should lead a "National Day of Protest" in August against the Vietnam war the group demurred. It even intimated that its people had something better in mind for that weekend.[1]

What was the reason for this curious attitude? I suspect the answer is hidden in the character of the SDS. Its leaders wanted to do serious intellectual and ideological work; they were less concerned with the pursuit of this or that aim (with the ending of this one war, for example) than with the formulation of a great programmatic concept for achieving fundamental change in "imperialist America." SDS did not think much of organized marches; it preferred spontaneous and spectacular happenings to demonstrations requiring long, tedious planning and staff work. Problems of organization were so uninteresting to SDS that it opened its doors to whoever wanted to come. At Port Huron a Communist was admitted, as we have seen, to an important SDS convention, and the annual meeting in the summer of 1965 (in Kewadin, Michigan) eliminated the paragraph in the SDS constitution which forbade the admission of advocates of totalitarian principles as members.

Michael Harrington, one of the leading American socialists and sometime president of the Socialist Party (which was intellectually respected, though weak in membership), later remarked that a principled opposition against any totalitarianism appeared to the young people in SDS as unreal as a "purple cow."[2] He and his friends were angry that SDS, while loudly defaming American society, had only mild words of criticism for Soviet totalitarianism and protested neither the invasion of Hungary nor the building of the Berlin Wall. Indeed, the American SDS was blind in one eye; above all, it greatly disliked quarrels with groups that were organized along stricter lines.

Naturally, SDS did not abandon the fight against the Vietnam war entirely, and some of its local chapters were still to have roles in the forthcoming peace marches, but it had needlessly given away the leadership of the movement, which was to prove by far the strongest in the latter sixties. Who took it up?

Theoretically, the pacifists might have been the logical leaders. They had a long tradition in America; they possessed a respected spokesman, David Dellinger, and the talents of Joan Baez were at their service. But by their very nature the pacifists are not apparatchiks; they are idealists, often quite impractical, many of them highly individualistic. Theirs is not the temperament that likes to wrestle night after night in smoke-filled committee rooms about the fine points of formulations and the staging of tactical tricks. And the large crowds of pacifists who, for whatever reasons, joined the peace movement and participated in its marches, suffering hardships, beatings, and even jail, might have gone once in a while to committee meetings, but they were without experience in the political business, amateurs who could not stand up to the professionals.

The professionals—they were found above all among those hostile cousins, the Communist Party and the Trotskyists. Who was going to win? To say it right at the beginning: the "Trots."

The Communist Party, U.S.A.—which has some 15,000 members, according to its own count[3]—was hampered in its movements by having to take Moscow's policy into consideration; when the Kremlin wishes to appear reasonable and moderate, the Party must stay away from radical excesses which could frighten middle America. The Socialist Workers Party, on the other hand, with some 2,500 members,[4] belongs to the Fourth International, founded by Trotsky in 1938. Its youth organization, the Young Socialist Alliance, has some 3,000 members. Entirely free in choosing their strategy and tactics, they can always afford to pronounce slogans so radical as to make all other groups appear tame and pale. If their demands are not met, it does not do them much harm; if they are met, an epochal victory can be celebrated.

The Trotskyists proved to be masters in the tactics of unobtrusive infiltration and indirect rule. They knew how to produce ever new organizations of the antiwar movement and supposedly nonpartisan "coalitions," and by stacking them with sympathizers, not readily recognizable by members of other groups, to win strong positions in the leadership of these groups. In nonpartisan conferences they managed to get people who looked and sounded like independents onto important committees, and with their help scored unforeseen voting successes. The Trotskyists were also well trained in wearing down opponents in nightlong meetings and getting them to sign any resolution just to be done with it.

Eventually, other groups became wise to the Trots. One of the leaders of a committee for the coordination of the fight against the Vietnam war summarized his experiences with them in a book with the revealing title *Marching Nowhere*. While the committee, he explained, had tried merely to mobilize as many people as possible for the protest demonstrations,

The Trots were clearly after a socialist revolution. The Trotskyite strategy is essentially this: alliances with anyone (liberals, conservatives, vegetarians, *anyone* who is willing to go into the streets or to a rally because of some particular issue); it is then hoped that once those people *do* go to rallies and listen to Trot speakers, they will come to see the larger "contradictions" in a capitalist society.[5]

OFF TO VIETNAM!

The Trotskyists showed their tactical skill when the Vietnam war suddenly reignited the campus. In the summer of 1967 it became known that the deferment of graduate students from military service would be stopped the following year (the undergraduates remained exempt), affecting about 650,000 male students. The president of Harvard University, Nathan M. Pusey, predicted that in graduate schools one would soon find only "the lame, the halt, the blind, and the female."[6]

Overnight the climate on the campus changed. When students returned for the fall semester, the world had darkened. As described by Steven Kelman, then a young Harvard student,

> A peaceful campus, only marginally concerned with Vietnam, suddenly became desperate. We felt boxed in. We were like the man about to go into the gas chamber, with no way out and the walls slowly but inexorably closing around him.

Until now the campus had remained relatively aloof—others were fighting the war, many of them blacks. But now the mood changed. "Burning frenzy," wrote Kelman, "suddenly enveloped Harvard in the months between September and November [1967]." (Similar reports came from other campuses.) He honestly admitted that

> in many cases it was not our oft-praised idealism and sensitivity—those traits which we frequently and stupidly believe we are the first generation in world history to possess—which led us into mass action against the war. It was something close to self-interest. An enlightened self-interest, nothing to be ashamed of—but nothing to become a self-righteous self-proclaimed guardian of morality over either.[7]

For countless young Americans on the campuses (and for their girl friends and wives), the war in the jungles of Vietnam had now moved very close, at a time when debate about the war, the fight

35

between hawks and doves over whether to step up the war or pull out, was deeply dividing public opinion. The successes of the Viet Cong in the Tet offensive (starting January 29, 1968) was to shake again the credibility of the nation's military leadership. For whatever went wrong, President Johnson was held personally responsible. Not long ago a hero of the students because of the civil rights reforms, he became a hated figure. They called him a fascist, sneeringly shouted *Sieg Heil* when he appeared in person or on the screen, and invented insulting slogans such as "Hitler Lives in the White House," "Hey! Hey! LBJ! How many kids have you killed today?" or the especially vicious "Lee Harvey Oswald—Where Are You? We Need You!"[8] In 1968 hundreds of assassination threats arrived at the White House every month.

The turn came with surprising suddenness. On March 31, Johnson announced that he would not run for reelection. In November, Richard Nixon won his election by promising to bring the boys home, and negotiations between Kissinger and Le Duc Tho in Paris actually produced the first withdrawals of American soldiers. The Vietnam war seemed to be losing its sting. But not for long.

On the last day of April 1970, President Nixon informed the nation that he had ordered the "incursion" of Cambodia. A wave of anger gripped the campus. When soldiers of the Ohio national guard, on May 4, opened fire on demonstrating students at Kent State University, killing four and wounding nine, and when two more students were shot at Jackson State College, a black campus in Jackson, Mississippi, the storm broke. Students at 350 colleges went on strike, ROTC buildings were burned on 30 campuses, the national guard was called out in 16 states, a student at San Diego State College committed suicide by self-immolation as a sign of protest.[9] Several books were written about the shootings at Kent State (the most readable being James Michener's) and Crosby, Stills, Nash and Young even wrote a song about the incident.

In later years, I have inquired about those days on many campuses. I am satisfied that neither the Trotskyists not their hated cousins in the Communist Party were pulling any strings. It was a spontaneous rising. It affected campus sentiment profoundly. In 1965 the war's continuation was considered necessary by 91 percent of the students polled and more than half favored its escalation; on the other hand, in 1970, after the Kent State shootings, 91 percent pleaded for American withdrawal, and more than half for immediate or speedy withdrawal.[10]

But this powerful wave also ebbed. The troups were withdrawn from Cambodia. The presence of American GIs in South Vietnam was reduced as part of a plan which demanded the "Vietnamization" of the war. A last giant demonstration in the nation's capital, on April 24, 1971, went off without incident. The Trotskyists, who had done most of the work in preparing the protest march of almost a half million people, were now masters of the movement against the Vietnam war—ironically, just at the moment when the war was losing its importance in American eyes. In November 1972, Nixon was reelected by an impressive majority.

When, around Christmas 1972, the war flared up once more and North Vietnam experienced one of the most massive bombardments of all time, the shock, it seemed to me, was greater in Europe than in America. Posters went up in German university towns branding Nixon as a murderer (and, for good measure, calling Willy Brandt his accomplice). But on the Columbia campus, where battles had been fought in 1968 because of a far less weighty issue (the building of a gymnasium), I saw no demonstrations—Vietnam seemed no longer anybody's concern. When I visited Kent State in the spring of 1973, students who took me around the campus matter-of-factly pointed out where the national guardsmen stood and fired their shots, where the students were killed—much as if they were taking me over the fields of Gettysburg or some other battleground of long ago.

The losses in Southeast Asia had been tremendous—more than 50,000 young Americans lost their lives there and 300,000 were wounded. Meanwhile, some 100,000 (or more) had become deserters from military service or fugitives from the draft, many of them going abroad. It would be impossible to estimate the numbers of those who, without being wounded, returned psychologically damaged. They came home from a war which lay far outside all accepted notions. A war in swamps and jungles, against an enemy barely seen, slight of build, in physical strength far inferior to the tall athletic GI, and yet an enemy neither to be vanquished nor to be won over to the American way of life. A war in a strange land, among people whose language few understood, where friend and foe could not be distinguished. A war which never seemed to end, the purpose of which was ever less comprehensible, in which one could not fight decently as a man, where goods obtained for a few cents at the PX could buy anything, including girls and drugs. What weighed most heavily on the conscience of the soldiers was the cruelty with which the war was waged—on both sides. Of this, My Lai was to become a symbol.

When the soldiers came home, many found it difficult to live with their memories; some tried the psychotherapist, others the preacher. One of them later reported that, although estranged from the church, he had gone to the confessional in hope of relief. But all the priest wanted to know was whether he had smoked marijuana over there. When the young soldier said that he had, he was admonished not to do it again. The things that truly tortured him were never touched on.

VETERANS—STRANGERS AT HOME

The returning Vietnam veterans found it difficult to readjust to American society. One, who had been decorated for bravery, planted a small patch of marijuana in the cornfields of his father's farm. When questioned by the police, he lost his temper, went roaring through the little town in his car like a madman, and finally landed in a psychiatric ward.[11]

Many upright and patriotic parents were horrified to learn their sons had turned to drugs in Vietnam; they didn't want to hear about the terrible things that happened over there. Perhaps the father had been a soldier in the Second World War and had fought with a good conscience, convinced that he was doing the right thing in destroying Hitler; in his experience, discipline was accepted, the enemy clearly recognizable, the black market more or less irrelevant,and there was no reason to treat civilians cruelly; returning home, he was feted as hero and victor. Such fathers did not want to believe what their sons told them about the war in Vietnam.

Many veterans married quickly, to find a home of their own. But they didn't like to talk to their brides about their experiences, and if they did, they met with shocked disbelief. Almost half of these postwar GI marriages broke up after a short time; if a child had been born, more complications arose. The return to normal work was difficult, too. Employers had heard enough about drug addiction among the GIs; considered to be of low moral habits, unsteady, unreliable, and hot-tempered, they were not particularly cherished as workers. The country that sent them to Vietnam now looked at them with suspicion. The suicide rate among veterans was abnormally high. Feeling that they were being treated as outcasts, some turned against society. Many scars remained.

A final question must be asked: Would there have been such violent unrest on the American campus without the war in Vietnam? We have seen that the initial demonstrations in the South (1960–1963) and in Berkeley (1964) had nothing to do with Vietnam. We also know that in other countries with serious student riots, including Germany, Vietnam became an issue only indirectly—as a means for showing sympathy with the Third World and with American comrades in their "fight against imperialism." It is therefore my assumption that the unrest which existed before America's large-scale intervention in Vietnam was bound to have evolved further, but without the extreme animosity and venom that emerged when the detested war became, for an entire student generation, a matter of life and death.

Early in 1965—that is, before the first great wave of protests against the war—the attitude of the American students had been remarkably conservative. A Harris poll found that they had a great deal of confidence in the pillars of modern American civilization, most of all in research and science, but also (in this sequence) in the medical profession, the banks, the Supreme Court, the universities, and the corporations. Five years later, after Kent State, 75 percent demanded "fundamental changes," and 67 percent urged protest activities by students in order to bring about such changes.[12]

This matches my own observations during frequent visits to American universities: The Vietnam war, especially the change in the recruiting law (1967–1968) and the invasion of Cambodia (1970), contributed to the rejection of the entire American system, just as the ending of the war had a calming effect on the campus.

What did SDS—this student avant-garde which had started out to revolutionize the campus and America—do during that time? SDS lost its way and disappeared. This process—half drama, half danse macabre—we shall now consider.

5
DISINTEGRATION AND END

AFTER observing the terminal crisis of SDS in America, I found three main reasons for its demise.

First: The student population of America, who had once taken society for granted, had become highly critical. After the murders of Robert Kennedy and Martin Luther King, about a million young people were convinced that society could no longer be improved by peaceful, democratic means. In the autumn of 1968 a poll by *Fortune* magazine found that 14 percent of the the students "partially" and 5 percent "strongly" believed a revolutionary mass party to be necessary in America; these together would correspond to about 1.3 million students. According to another poll, after the shootings at Kent State, 1.5 million students demanded a revolution.[1] The activists at SDS headquarters in Chicago thought that the "revolutionary situation" which the Marxists always talked about might have arrived in America; hence they demanded a more radical approach than that of the rank and file of SDS. (In reality, the unrest—despite the new upsurge after Cambodia—had already passed its high-water mark.)

Second: In their conflicts with competitors on the extreme Left, the SDS leaders had witnessed the power which some of their rivals owed to tight organization under a central leadership. As early as 1967 one of the top men in SDS, Greg Calvert, had doubted that one could cope with future problems while leaving all decisions to local groups who practiced direct democracy. "The basic problem with participatory democracy lies [. . .] in its basic

inadequacy as a style of work for a serious radical organization."
Hence he suggested that all SDS branches be tied to a central
steering committee for the purpose of developing "long-range organizing strategies and programs."[2]

Third: Doubts had also arisen with regard to the virtue of a
total absence of dogma in SDS. In fact, this was found to be a
serious handicap in debates with opponents. During the first
years of youthful drive the Port Huron Statement and other early
declarations were quite sufficient for an ideological foundation, or
at any rate had startled other groups. But now the rival organizations, fully recovered from their surprise, were voicing objections
to the SDS idea and demanding answers to many newly arisen
questions. Also, the documents of 1962–1963 had been written in
a language not suited to larger and less sophisticated audiences.
The comrades in the Communist groups were far better equipped.
The compactness of their ideological system was fascinating, and
many non-Communists, including some SDS members, began to
employ Marxist terms and to quote, aside from Marx himself,
Lenin, Mao, Ho Chi Minh, and even Stalin—whose name had,
after all, come to stand for the quintessence of brutal oppression.
Steve Weissman, one of the FSM people of Berkeley, was to say
later that more should have been done to remedy SDS's lack of
organization and ideological clarity and thus halt its disintegration: "It was clear enough that a new Marxist group was taking
over."[3]

What was this "new Marxist group" that had begun to domi-
nate SDS? The reader may have been waiting for their name to be
mentioned. Usually they were called the "Maoists"; officially they
were the Progressive Labor Party (PLP, or simply PL).

Early in 1962 a few people were expelled from the Communist
Party, U.S.A. Shortly afterward they organized the Progressive
Labor Movement, and in 1965, under Maoist banners, the
Progressive Labor Party. After Peking dramatically improved its
relations with Washington (1971–1972), the PLP became more
critical of the Chinese and, while remaining opposed to the
U.S.S.R., gradually adopted a stance that was more Stalinist than
Maoist. (Here, however, we are still dealing with the PLP's
Maoist phase.) In the search for recruits, the PLP early in 1967
turned its attention to the restless campus and founded the
Worker Student Alliance for the purpose of infiltrating student
organizations—especially SDS, which was still confident enough
(or naïve enough) to let anybody in. The Maoists had no difficul-

ties in steadily extending their influence in SDS and forming a faction of their own within its ranks. To avoid misunderstanding and to distinguish the new Maoist wing within SDS from the SDS old-timers, I shall call these latter the "veterans" or the "old core."

What was the conflict in SDS about? The Maoist wing emphasized class struggle and wanted SDS to be an auxiliary to the proletariat; the old core recognized, of course, the importance of the workers, but wanted SDS to remain a youth organization and therefore make its coalitions exclusively with young workers. The whole debate was in a way irrelevant, as the workers showed no inclination to join either wing. But it is a characteristic trait of radical groups that eventually they all end up fighting about details and interpretations of dogma as if they were religious sects. To emphasize its own point of view, the SDS old core, at the Christmas convention of 1968, pushed through the founding of a youth organization called the Revolutionary Youth Movement (RYM).

Meanwhile, President Nixon, in his first year (1969), was proceeding to carry out his campaign promise to restore "law and order." For this he had his voters' mandate, including the support of many who had not voted for him. According to a Gallup poll in the spring of 1969, 82 percent of adult Americans desired the expulsion of student demonstrators from the universities.[4] Attorney General John Mitchell and his deputy Richard Kleindienst (both later swallowed up by the Watergate vortex) were ordered to take energetic measures against political riots. The trial (beginning in March 1969) of those allegedly responsible for the excesses during the Democratic National Convention of August 1968, the "Chicago 8," aroused much attention (Tom Hayden was one of the defendants).

The backlash was unmistakable. The FBI turned its attention to the campus, overstepping its legal authority in a number of instances, as was to become known later. In 39 state legislatures almost 400 draft laws were submitted (100 in California alone) to provide punishment for rebellious students. In the first six months of 1969, 4,000 students were arrested. University administrations also began to employ the powers newly accorded to them. Energetic actions were now being demanded by the majority of professors, 80 percent of whom considered demonstrations to be a threat to academic freedom, while 76 percent called for the expulsion of disturbers.[5] SDS, the main object of these attacks, was forbidden on a number of campuses.

ENTER "WEATHERMAN"

In this tense atmosphere the SDS met in Chicago's Coliseum on June 18, 1969. This was the group's ninth and, as it turned out, last annual convention. I only know it from reports; even the press was excluded, and no verbatim account is known to exist; the events were much too stormy and chaotic for minutes to be taken. The old core had picked Chicago because this city was the SDS stronghold, and hence better suited than any other place for confronting the Maoist members. Another reason: Fifty universities and colleges had refused—a sign of changing times—to furnish accommodations for the convention.

Only members were admitted to the Coliseum, and even these were searched for weapons, cameras, tape recorders, knives, and drugs. Outside the building, the TV broadcasters posted their cameras; there were many curious bystanders and also many policemen, uniformed and not. Within the building many organizations with members in SDS had their tables: Maoists, Trotskyists, anarchists, Moscow-oriented Communists. Every delegate— there were some 1,500 of them in all—received a special edition of *New Left Notes*, which carried, in addition to other convention material, a six-page article "You Don't Need a Weatherman to Know Which Way the Wind Blows."[6]

In the context of the convention, this slogan was both a program and a challenge to the Maoists; it not only enjoined the young people, as Dylan had done, to pay no attention to the old generation because they knew themselves which way the wind was blowing; it was specifically meant to impress the loyal SDS veterans and to tell them: We know which way we are going and therefore do not need any lecturing from the Maoists or any other "meteorologists."

The draft of the Weatherman article was written by eleven people of the old-core group, three of whom we shall hear from again: Bernardine Dohrn, Mark Rudd, and Terry Robbins. What they wanted was finally to give SDS a firm ideological ground to stand on and, with the help of their article, to furnish an intellectual bulwark against Maoist subversion. They set out clearly the distinctions between the old SDS and the Maoists. Summarizing it in my own words, the document:

1. Underlined the complete support of SDS for the fight of the blacks in America, granting them the leading role in the struggle against U.S. "imperialism" and reserving for SDS an essentially supporting function (for the Maoists, American blacks existed only as a segment of the proletariat);

2. Assigned to youth a special importance in this battle because it had a greater revolutionary potential than labor had (this was a reactionary position in the view of the Maoists, who wanted everybody, including youth, to submit to the leadership of the proletariat);

3. Demanded the mobilization of a mass movement in the Third World (which, of course, the Maoists also wanted, but with the proviso that it remained firmly in proletarian hands or, more precisely, in their own);

4. Considered as unavoidable the creation of a conspiratorial organization of revolutionaries under a single general staff (which to the Maoists seemed very close to foolish adventurism).

This Weatherman statement did not really tell the youth of America "which way the wind blows." Instead of arousing them with great goals, it offered them nothing but the function of an auxiliary force for the blacks and the Third World—and under the veil of conspiracy. Any appeal it had was further diminished by the fact that it was written mainly in twisted and doctrinaire language that only insiders could understand.

The convention began on Wednesday, June 18, at 2:00 P.M. Right at the start one of the SDS veterans proposed to admit members of the press, provided they paid a $25 entrance fee and promised to be discreet with regard to matters that might interest the police. A Maoist immediately proposed the opposite: Representatives of the capitalist press were not to be admitted, no matter how much they paid. This counterproposal was accepted by a majority—a first defeat for the veterans, when the convention had barely started. The Maoists, although a small minority, had managed to swing many non-Maoists with their arguments.

A lively debate was kindled by a procedural question: Should the floor be given to a young SDS member who had just returned from China? The Maoists were opposed, claiming that a distorted picture of China would be painted. The veterans taunted this rigid attitude of the Maoists in a demonstration which was intended to be witty. They pulled out Little Red Books, climbed chairs, and shouted in unison: "Mao—Mao—Mao." Although the assembly decided to listen to the China traveler (later on), the majority for this decision was not big. The first afternoon was spent in debates such as these.

On Thursday morning there were meetings of committees and discussions among the leaders of the veterans, and also among the Maoists. In the evening meeting, an incident occurred which was embarrassing for the majority group: a Black Panther who had been asked to speak on behalf of the old core angered the women at the convention with some crude remarks, and the meeting ended in chaos. Now the women were hostile, and the alliance with the blacks had suffered some damage.

Friday passed in sticky debates which led nowhere. In the evening session a Panther suddenly asked for the floor. (The Black Panther Party was averse to a further growth of Maoist influence in SDS because of the Maoists' insistence on subordinating the blacks' goals to those of the class struggle and on proclaiming the leadership of the proletariat. There hardly existed anything in America that one might call a proletariat; but this was beside the point in these hair-splitting doctrinal debates.) The Panther read a declaration prepared by his group and other minorities calling the Maoists "counterrevolutionary traitors" and demanding that they be treated accordingly. There were wild scenes once more: "Power to the *People*," the veterans shouted; the Maoists, "Power to the *Workers*." Led by Bernardine Dohrn, who was proving more and more to be the driving force of the convention, the majority moved to another room of the Coliseum for deliberations that lasted deep into the night and through the better part of Saturday.

Bernardine Dohrn pleaded for the expulsion of the Maoists—a move that was in contradiction to the SDS principle of keeping the doors wide open. Against some opposition, she prevailed. Twenty-four hours after leaving the main conference hall (where the Maoists had continued to meet), she returned with her supporters. For twenty minutes Dohrn enumerated the Maoists' sins over the past few years. She ended by saying that the Maoists— and all those who did not believe in the principles of SDS—were no longer members of the organization. Then she stormed from the hall and out of the Coliseum, followed by hundreds, while the Maoists remained, proclaiming themselves as the one and only SDS.

These experiences of the movement against the Vietnam war (which ended with the movement in the hands of the Trotskyists) and of the SDS (which was eventually captured by the Maoists) clearly show the problems of holding together a movement that has no disciplined organization, no dogma, and no charismatic leader personifying a dogma. Such a movement may organize itself, building its own hierarchy and its disciplined ranks, in which case it develops bureaucratic structures and ceases to be a movement. Or it may remain an open, fluctuating, lively movement, which then must face the emergence within itself of strong factions whose members may have their own dogma, their own leaders, and their own organization outside the movement. In this case the factions may become strong enough either to take over the movement or to destroy it.

SDS had retained its preeminence for seven short years, from Port Huron in 1962 to Chicago in 1969. Now the end had come. Two main groups left the Coliseum, both claiming to be the legitimate SDS. The Maoists had an advantage inasmuch as they stayed in the building to the convention's end. They actually succeeded in capturing the old SDS branches on a few campuses, but to little avail, since the branches soon withered. Toward the end of 1972, at Columbia, I was asked to lecture by a group of students who called themselves ex-Maoists. They explained that they could no longer be real Maoists, now that Mao had given Richard Nixon a great welcome in Peking. There are, of course, still Maoist students on American campuses, some quite active, but their influence has dwindled.

Those who left the Coliseum under the leadership of Bernardine Dohrn hung onto the SDS name at first. But events took a dramatic turn, and soon they were known under a totally different designation—"Weatherman."

6
UNDERGROUND

WITHIN the political youth movement of the late sixties (outside of Latin America), the "Weathermen" were the first group to reach the front page because of terrorist activities. They came by their name in an odd way: originally they had used the word in a negative context ("You don't need a Weatherman. . . ."). But soon the catchy term was adopted by the mass media for the group who had left the Coliseum precisely because it *refused* advice from any weatherman. In the end, even the members of the group began to use this name. (At some point they tried to placate the strong female contingent by using "Weatherpeople.") Who were they?

FIERCER BY DESPAIR
In the epoch of Women's Lib it comes as no surprise that a woman takes the first place. Bernardine Dohrn was born in 1942 of a well-to-do family, her father a Hungarian Jew, her mother of Swedish descent. In school she was not notably different from her classmates. While studying in Chicago she admired the nonviolent tactics of Martin Luther King and was a participant in various humanitarian activities, such as helping poor tenants in legal hassles with their landlords. But she became impatient with the lack of visible progress and moved toward the Left. After graduating from law school she worked for the National Lawyers Guild, which specialized in defending left-wingers and advising draft resisters. Someone who knew her in those days described her thus in *Esquire*'s April 1971 issue:

She was an overwhelming personality. First of all, there was her sex appeal. She had the most amazing legs—every draft resister on the East Coast knew those legs. People would come from miles around just to *see* her. But she was regarded as a good "political person" at the time when other women in the movement weren't given any responsibility at all. Students really turned on to her.[1]

She joined SDS early in 1968. Soon she moved into its leadership. (In addition, she worked for women's rights.) Before her advent, Mark Rudd had been the SDS member most widely known. His parents were middle-class, Jewish, and from New Jersey. During his school days he was not remarkable in any way; he got good grades and was a Boy Scout. But as a student at Columbia University in 1965, he met young radicals. He joined SDS a year later and rose to the top during the riots of 1968. Suddenly he was famous all over America, as Mario Savio had been four years earlier. As noted earlier, he and Bernardine Dohrn were among the eleven authors of the Weatherman document.

The Weatherpeople did not wish to spend their time merely in discussions—they wanted to act. ("One must do something," Ulrike Meinhof was saying in Germany at about that time.) They devoted their lives to the revolution and to the creation of a New Man. Their life was tough and—so it seems to me—joyless. There was no room for any personal life; everything had to be done according to strictest discipline; nobody mentioned "direct democracy" anymore. One girl reported, after leaving the group, that one needed the permission of the others even to read a book. Firm ties between female and male Weatherpersons were frowned upon; instead, by exchange of partners the group was supposed to become all the more closely knit. (Later, police found a copy of Dostoevski's *The Possessed* in a room where Dohrn had stayed briefly. It would be interesting to know to what extent she and the other Weatherpeople were influenced by that novel, which pictures its heroes, a Russian terrorist group, in a not very favorable light.) In the work of the Weatherpeople there was, in addition to the ideology of Marx and Mao, instruction in violence, including karate, and the making and use of bombs and other weapons.

Only a minority was able to stand this kind of life. Those who remained fanaticized each other. The girls proved to be especially radical; they stormed into high schools, threatened the teachers, and preached the need for revolution to baffled students. When occupying a school in Pittsburgh, some of them provocatively bared their breasts (a gesture that was also made about the same time at the University of Frankfurt.)

Wherever they had a chance, the Weatherpeople created demonstrative disturbances, even—at the price of sixteen arrests—during the Davis Cup championship in September 1969. The greater the damage, the more spectacular the effect.

Their biggest action, the last public one, came during the four "Days of Rage" in Chicago. By it they hoped to unleash a revolutionary movement in America. For months they had agitated at colleges and in black and white slums. Thousands were to come, Mark Rudd had boasted in a TV interview, but when they came storming out of Lincoln Park on Thursday, October 8, 1969, at 10:30 P.M., armed with rocks, sticks, bottles and bicycle chains, there were only a few hundred, mostly whites. The blacks, of whom there were hundreds of thousands in and around Chicago, kept their distance. At first the demonstrators enjoyed the advantage of surprise. Running through the streets, shouting through bullhorns, they demolished parked automobiles and smashed windows. Then 2,000 uniformed policemen and many plainclothesmen swarmed upon them. Within an hour, it was all over.

On Saturday, the Weatherpeople went into action again. Once more they attacked unexpectedly, in the business section of the Loop. This time the police needed only fifteen minutes to restore order. During the two events 287 people were arrested—more than half of the active participants, including most of the leaders. All were set free when $2.3 million was posted in bail, mainly by parents. They went underground during the following year before their cases could be tried.

The Days of Rage are comprehensible in the light of the belief—held by many radicals, who may have read Frantz Fanon's *Wretched of the Earth*—that violence is, in and of itself, liberating for those who exercise it, whatever the outcome. There were, to be sure, some Weatherpeople who disagreed and left the group, one of them explaining why with a variation on the words of the Weatherman slogan: "You don't need a rectal thermometer to know who the assholes are."[2]

A semipublic appearance of the Weatherpeople came at Christmas in 1969 when they held a conference at Flint, Michigan. They sang wild songs, including one—fashioned after the Beatles' "Nowhere Man"— about the Weatherman who

> Knows just what he's fighting for:
> victory for people's war,
> trashes, bombs, kills pigs and more.
> the Weatherman.[3]

They waved Viet Cong flags, shouted "Ho, Ho, Ho Chi Minh," and paid homage in unison to the Communist chief of North Korea:

> The most beautiful sound I ever heard:
> Kim Il Sung, Kim Il Sung, Kim Il Sung.

Some of the speakers at that occasion expressed undisguised approval of violence. Mark Rudd: "It's a wonderful feeling to *hit* a pig. It must be a really wonderful feeling to *kill* a pig or blow up a building." John Jacobs: "We're against everything that's 'good and decent' in Honky America. *We'll burn and loot and destroy.* We are the incubation of your mother's nightmare."(Emphasis supplied.) And Bernardine Dohrn (alluding to the murders by the Charles Manson "family," whose most prominent victim was the film star Sharon Tate, eight months pregnant at the time): "Dig it: first they killed those pigs [in this case the "pigs" were not policemen, but Sharon Tate and her friends], then they ate dinner in the same room with them, then they even shoved a fork into the victim's stomach. Wild!" These words of Dohrn's may survive her; Dave Dellinger, one of the Chicago 8, writes in his book about the peace movement that they have been confirmed to him by at least a dozen people who were in Flint that day.[4] John Milton's magnificent phrase "Now fiercer by despair" fits only too well here, as it does in the case of the Baader-Meinhof group or that of the Japanese Red Army.

After Flint the Weatherpeople dissolved into small groups. It was one of these that blew up a town house on Eleventh Street in Manhattan on March 6, 1970, while working on or tinkering with time bombs. Two girls escaped naked, were given clothes by unsuspecting neighbors, and disappeared into the underground. One was the daughter of the owner of the house, Cathlyn Wilkerson, twenty-two years old; the other, Kathy Boudin, was twenty-six; both were graduates of respected universities. Three Weatherpeople died in the explosion: Diana Oughton, twenty-eight, a graduate of Bryn Mawr; Ted Gold, a graduate of Columbia; and Terry Robbins, whose body was horribly disfigured but whose identity was reported by the survivors.

RICH KIDS

Diana Oughton came from a prosperous and respected family in the Middle West; her father was a member of the Illinois legislature. She grew up in a nice home, studied in a girls' college, spent two semesters abroad (in 1961, at Munich), went into social work, lived with a radical boyfriend (the son of a well-to-do family who later turned his attention to another woman), found entry through him into revolutionary circles, and when the wave of the student rebellion ebbed, followed him into the terrorist underground where she met her death.[5]

Her parents had kept her away from everything that was ugly. Thus the real world which she faced after graduation caused a severe shock. She broke with the social group from which she came, worked for two years in a highly "progressive" kindergarten until it folded because—how bitterly disappointing!— precisely the poorer parents wanted their children to go to a normal school and finally learn something. Estrangement from her lover was a further trauma. She threw herself frantically into political work, escalating the demands she put on herself and others, higher and higher, beyond reasonable expectations. This brought some disappointment and finally hatred of all others— and of herself. In desperation and fury she sought relief in such senseless destruction as the burning of automobiles. She lived in endless discord with herself because her actions had become a fiendish caricature, the opposite of what she originally had tried to do for society. In the end she turned to dynamite. Her maimed body could only be identified with the help of the tip of one of her fingers.

This catastrophe didn't alter the course of the Weatherpeople, who now called themselves the "Weather Underground." The underground became their constant way of life. They continued their bombing activities and from time to time they appeared in print. Late in 1974, Jonah Raskin published in New York a booklet of 124 pages which contained a chronicle of the Weather Underground, together with a number of other documents. It began with a "Declaration of War" of May 21, 1970, reproduced several "communiqués" (e.g., about a bombing in the Capitol at Washington), and led up to a declaration of sympathy for the Symbionese Liberation Army (SLA) on February 20, 1974, two weeks after the kidnapping of Patricia Hearst. Some documents were signed by Dohrn; judging by the style, others may have been written by her, too. Far removed from reality, they spoke of millions of young people being with the Weatherpeople in their hearts and showed lack of knowledge of recent revolutionary history.[6] The Weather Underground even came out with its own publication, 152 large pages, sold in left-leaning bookshops for $1.50 under the name *Prairie Fire*, with Bernardine Dohrn mentioned first among the authors. It was dedicated to the three who died in the Wilkerson house, and to a long list of friends in and out of prison.

In January 1974 Attorney General William Saxbe stopped proceedings against those accused in connection with the four Days of Rage. But the Weatherpeople did not use this opportunity to emerge from the underground. In the introduction to his booklet, Jonah Raskin wrote that most of them, if they could choose, would prefer the underground life. This seems to be true for the hard core.

But some could not endure that kind of life. Jane Alpert was one, a highly gifted girl from a prosperous home, who had graduated with distinction in 1967. In 1970 she was arrested for her part in an explosion in New York which injured twenty-one people. Set free on bail, she went underground. After four years, she surrendered to the police; early in 1975 she began a twenty-seven-month prison term. In an interview a few days before, she said that the ideas of the left were no longer relevant.[7]

Susan Stern, an SDS member since 1967, went through the convention in the Coliseum and the Days of Rage, was in jail repeatedly, lived in the underground, and used drugs. She has written the most detailed account about the haunted life in the underground, a constant up-and-down between men and causes, demonstrations and arrests, euphoria and despair. When accused of participating in a conspiracy as part of the Seattle 7, she was triumphant: finally she was somebody and the newspapers were writing about her. After leaving prison in 1971 she found a new man. When this affair ended, she changed over to cocaine, which she got by appearing topless in bars, and wrote a book.[8] She died in 1976 at age thirty-three, of general exhaustion.

Underground and underworld were now curiously intertwined—witness the case of the SLA.

PATTY/TANIA
Apart from the fact that Bernardine Dohrn praised the SLA after its abduction of Patty Hearst for having produced a leap in everyone's consciousness,[9] there does not seem to have been any connection between the Weatherpeople and this "army." Its most important members were:

Nancy Ling Perry. Daughter of a conservative businessman in Santa Rosa, California; graduated from high school with distinction; a student at Richard Nixon's alma mater, conservative

Whittier College, and then at Berkeley, majoring in English literature; briefly married to a black musician (to the parents' horror); made a living by selling orange juice on the Berkeley 26-foot strip. At twenty-six, in 1973, she was possessed by a dreadful self-hatred, full of "poison against herself,"[10] and was living in a commune in Oakland, California, in a house with the curious name of "Peking Man."

Russell Little. Son of a Navy electrical engineer in Florida; graduate of the local university, wrote a thesis on Marx and Sartre (under the influence of a young professor who, during a visit to Germany, had joined the German SDS). After moving to Oakland he lived in the Peking Man commune and had an affair with Nancy Perry.

Joe Remiro. Vietnam veteran (an excellently trained killer, he called himself); expelled from home by his patriotic father, an immigrant from Mexico who didn't want a son who told horror stories about the war; drug addict since Vietnam; peace marcher; briefly in jail because he had a U.S. flag sewn to the seat of his pants; member of a radical group in Oakland; a participant, briefly, on the Indian side in the fighting at Wounded Knee. He had contacts with the people living in Peking Man.

Emily and Bill Harris. She the daughter of an engineer; graduated from high school and also from college with distinction. He the son of a well-to-do businessman; a graduate in drama, a marine in Vietnam, retaining feelings of guilt. In Berkeley she was a secretary on the campus, he a truck driver.

Angela Atwood. Daughter of a trade-union official; university student; Remiro's girl friend; owner of a cat by the name of Vagina.

Camilla Hall. Daughter of a Lutheran preacher at the University of Minnesota; a graduate in art history; had seen much misery while doing social work. She was an employee of Berkeley's Parks Division and had a passionate and intimate relationship, expressed in poems, with Patricia Soltysik.

Patricia Soltysik. Called Mizmoon; dropped out as a student of sociology; a feminist and a lesbian.

They all met by chance, daughters and sons of middle-class families, all (except Remiro) with some university education, all searching for new human relations, for new aims. What united them was their particular interest in reforming the penal system.

Student interest in the fate of prisoners dated back to the execution of Caryl Chessman in May 1960. That case had aroused much attention because of an appeal lasting twelve years; the condemned man had tried to prove his repentance through his writings and thus won himself a great many friends. On the night preceding his execution, students from various universities and colleges held a vigil outside the prison gates, protesting what they called a murder. The movement against the death penalty thus received a new impetus, and in many states this form of punishment was abolished.[11] A participant in the vigil told me of his opinion that Chessman's execution had helped radicalize many students and had caused others to question the validity of all the country's laws.

The reform movement acquired a new dimension with the civil rights struggle, dramatically highlighted by the fires of Watts and Detroit. In most prisons, blacks comprised a high percentage of the inmates—in many, the vast majority. Also, blacks had fought bravely in Vietnam proving themselves often enough as loyal comrades. Hence many young whites felt a need to do something for the blacks to discharge some of the guilt they felt for the sins committed against blacks by their forefathers.

Among the students there was to be found, toward the end of the sixties, an attitude of awe toward blacks. I witnessed it in Berkeley, where white students compared themselves and their own sloppy, haphazard ways with the impressively disciplined appearance of the Black Panthers, who had their headquarters in neighboring Oakland. "They are tough types," the white students would say, "not spoiled brats like us. We should have them for our allies in making the revolution."

But how could young whites prove their sympathy for the blacks? By befriending black prisoners, of course. And where could they find black revolutionary fighters? Also in prison. It followed that they could expect to find recruits for the revolution by looking after blacks in the prisons. During the winter of 1972/73, time and again young people from the Peking Man house would drive to Vacaville. They organized discussions with the prisoners there and taught them, without the administration's knowledge, Maoist and other revolutionary ideas.

One of the black prisoners impressed the young white visitors in particular—Donald DeFreeze, who called himself Cinque Mtume, which was supposed to mean "Fifth Prophet." He had a long prison record, was violent, hated whities (he wanted to eat them for breakfast, he said). But he was also smart: when on trial, he quoted the Bible, sang hymns, and threatened judges with the wrath of God. At this time he was serving a five-year sentence.

In March 1973 he managed to escape. Mizmoon Soltysik hid him at her place. She became his lover but had to share his favors with Nancy Perry and Emily Harris. In Cinque Mtume the group now had a leader, soon to refer to himself as Field Marshal. They called themselves the SLA, or Symbionese Liberation Army. On November 6, some of them murdered Marcus Foster, a black school superintendent in Oakland. In "communiqué number one," which they sent to a radio station in Berkeley, the SLA justified the murder by calling it the "execution of a death sentence" which had been passed because of Foster's alleged surrender of the Oakland schools to police surveillance. Two months later the police found SLA material during a spot check of a car. The occupants, Remiro and Little, admitted their membership in the organization, but their involvement in the murder could not be proved. Charged with participation in a conspiracy, they were given life sentences.

Foster's assassination was not very different from many other killings that were taking place. It was only the kidnapping of Patricia (Patty) Hearst from her Berkeley apartment on February 4, 1974, that brought the SLA into the headlines. Grandfather Hearst, builder of a newspaper empire, was known in his native California as a generous Maecenas (streets are named after him, as is the big stadium in Berkeley), but for young radicals he and his descendants were personifications of hated Big Business. This might have contributed to the SLA's choice of Patty as a kidnap victim.

The rest is all too well known: how Patty was at first assaulted and abused; how she joined her captors' cause—whether from fear or conviction, we do not know, nor perhaps does she—and participated in their outlaw life, staying underground even after the SLA core was killed in a dramatic shoot-out in Los Angeles on May 17, 1974; how she was caught by the FBI on September 18, 1975 (as were Emily and Bill Harris); and was found guilty of armed bank robbery on March 20, 1976. This theme has occupied the American mass media ever since her abduction; books have been written about her, plays and movies produced, souvenirs sold—one of her letters was auctioned in New York for $1,000 (a letter by Charles Manson went for $250; one by the late President Eisenhower, $65).

Reading the material produced by SLA members in the form of "communiqués" or tapes which were sent to radio stations, I was surprised by the low intellectual quality. They did not show any signs that almost all the members had been university students, some even graduates. The language was primitive, the spelling not the best. They read like compositions by schoolchildren playing at revolution.

A statement three pages long gave a verbose explanation of the SLA's coat of arms, the seven-headed cobra. With apparent seriousness it was stated that the emblem was 170,000 years old, that four of the heads represented sun, moon, earth, and water (the others, God and the universe—what was the seventh?), and that they also represented seven human groups: black, brown, yellow, red, white, young and old.[12] The number seven was said to have figured in "pre-Zionist" African religions and in the seven pillars of Egyptian temples.

This half-baked education showed itself in the choice of the overblown name. The group claimed to be addressing "the people" of the world. But who had ever heard the word "Symbionese"? Nobody, because the SLA people had fabricated it themselves. Perhaps to prove their education, they borrowed the term "symbiosis" from biology, where it pertains to the union of dissimilar organisms. They did not even use the regular adjectival form "symbiotic," inventing instead a totally new one, "symbionese." Was this the proper language for reaching "the people"?

The other documents were just as immature.[13] There were confused (as well as megalomaniacal) assertions about a nonexistent "Symbionese Federation," a union of members of various races, nations, and socialist parties in the "Fascist United States of America." From the "Field Marshal" and "Fifth Prophet," who had grown up under extremely adverse social conditions, this mumbo jumbo can be condoned. But it is depressing to find such nonsense coming from a group in which seven of the nine members had attended universities. It may have arisen from a desire to submit to black leaders and humbly endure their lack of education, and from the feeling, held by many, that whites could not lead the revolution in America.

So far as I can see, the courage of the six SLA members who

died in the burning house in Los Angeles called forth respect; some young radicals applauded the words and deeds of the SLA because these people had challenged the authorities and made a laughingstock of the police for a time. But I have not found any show of interest in their naïve program.

Since the end of the SLA, many more acts of terrorism have been committed. But the SLA members were among the first to show that such acts required only a minimum of intelligence and ideology.

THE HOSTILE ENVIRONMENT

Why did they turn to terrorism—the Bernardines and Dianas, the Marks and Pattys, who had grown up as normal American kids, had been adequate or better in their studies, and had professed high ideals? One of the reasons was the environment in which they lived: Isolation and loneliness troubled these young people and many others long before they made the conscious decision to drop out of normal society.

The campus riots evoked abhorrence and even hatred in the great majority of adult Americans. Including those in the lower income brackets, Americans in general were repelled by the riots and by the ideas behind them. The jeering disrespect for all patriotic sentiments, for all symbols dear to the nation (above all, the Stars and Stripes), and the expressions of solidarity with an enemy against whom America was waging war (for example, the hoisting of the Viet Cong flag) angered people just as much as did the New Left's elitist contempt for them as "squares" who had no comprehension of what was going on.

The voice of the people expressed itself with particular pungency on an occasion that might have called for sympathy with the rebels—after the death of the four Kent State students. James A. Michener, who has researched the events before, during, and after the shooting with a staff of assistants, quotes pages and pages of remarks by adults who approved the action of the national guard. All this makes sad reading.

A student with a good record in Vietnam reported that his mother said, "It would have been a good thing if all those students had been shot." When he exclaimed, "Hey, Mom! That's me you're talking about," she answered: "It would have been better for the country if you had all been mowed down." A mother of three Kent State students said: "The lazy, the dirty, the ones you see walking the streets and doing nothing ought all to be shot." Some simply raised four fingers to demonstrate their dislike for the students who were killed. A jingle made the rounds:

The score is four,
And next time more.

Michener found that "this sequence of events had alienated the students not only from their parents, but from all society as they had known it." From some of the "very finest young people" he heard "compelling tales of their alienation." One student (a history major,who had been a respectful son previously) said, "I don't suppose I'll ever be able to talk with my parents again," and added:

After Kent, when I saw how so many people, including my parents, truly feared and hated students, I realized there was no middle ground. Now I'm working against everything my family has worked for, and I will fight them as long as necessary.[14]

This attitude was not just the reaction to the Kent State event; it had grown over the years. It is not surprising that many young people who were not leftist radicals felt deserted by their parents and by the "silent majority."

Disappointment with the blacks added to the feeling of loneliness. The blacks had seemed to many young radicals the ideal complement to the predominantly white SDS—natural allies in a united front against the Establishment. The Black Panthers, founded by Bobby Seale and his friends in Oakland (a few miles from Berkeley) on October 15, 1966, had accepted the alliance with the SDS as long as they felt that it helped them widen their base, even though, at the high-water mark of their confidence in Black Power, the cooperation with the "white kids" did not come easily to them. But after the Coliseum meeting not much was left of brotherly feelings. Within a few weeks, the break came. Seale called the SDS "a bunch of jive bourgeois chauvinists," and the Black Panther chief of staff promised to "beat those little sissies, those little schoolboys' ass."[15]

The most bitter disappointment came from the lack of any response by the workers. The students knew from Marx, if only at second hand, that a victory over the Establishment—over the bourgeoisie, as Marx used to say—was impossible without the workers, and those who had read Herbert Marcuse, or at least heard about him, knew that no rising of the proletariat was to be expected in the near future. The workers were indeed uninterested and hostile—even when the students met them daily, on the campus.

I have observed campus workers, in the midst of student unrest, going about their jobs with aloof expressions—mowing the lawns, fixing clogged toilets, or repairing damage done by student rampages. I found not the slightest trace of sympathy for the New Left when talking with them. Their feelings were quite different: They too might like to be students, to sit in pleasantly air-conditioned libraries, to relax with miniskirted coeds on the grass, but they had to earn money for their families. The lucky students who had all the facilities and intellectual treasures of the university at their disposal, scholarships to boot, acted like fools and destroyed what was built for them with the people's taxes. "The students maintain," I said, "that they are demonstrating and fighting for you. They want to change society to improve the lot of the worker." Not once did I encounter agreement. "They should study," the workers would say. "We do not need protesters, pushers, and fags. We need teachers for our children, doctors when we are sick, and engineers for industry." One remembers the day in New York City when hard-hat construction workers broke up a student demonstration.

Not even the *lumpenproletariat* youth of the slums—called outcasts by Marcuse and considered by him to be mobilizable—could be aroused. Their resentment against society, accumulating over the years, vented itself in small and large crimes, in the formation of youth gangs. They had no stomach for ideology, and if they did organize, then the young blacks fell in with the Black Panthers or the Black Muslims, the Puerto Ricans with the Young Lords, the Chinese with scattered "Yellow Power" groups, and always with an antiwhite direction. (There have been reports that the Weatherpeople who went to live in the slums and agitate there among the young met first with amazement, then with rejection, until finally they were driven out of their chosen turf.)

It goes without saying that socialist slogans were obnoxious to the farmers and the middle class. The only section of the population that applauded the radical students—and only in the beginning—was the intelligentsia. By this term, used first in the Russia of the nineteenth century, I mean those intellectuals who, in addition to exercising an intellectual profession, have political ideas and promote their realization.

INTELLIGENCE AND POWER

The tension between intelligence and power is age-old. More than two millennia ago, Plato tried to overcome this tension when he entered the service of Dionysius of Syracuse, but the great philosopher's effort to reform the tyrant's government was in vain. The intellectual lives in the world of ideas, morals, and principles; the politician works with the practicalities of power and compromise. Occasionally, intellect and power meet, or seem to meet, as in the early days of President John F. Kennedy. But his successor did not have the right knack with the intelligentsia, whose criticism of White House policy increased in direct proportion to the enormous involvement of the United States in Vietnam.[16] *The New York Review of Books,* the favorite of Left intellectuals, was especially hostile; one day it offered on its cover, visible on every newsstand, graphic instructions for making Molotov cocktails.

Some intellectuals jumped into student radicalism as if it were a fountain of youth, among them Norman Mailer (who was forty-four years old at the time) during the peace march on the Pentagon on October 1,1967. This writer, who related everything to his own ego, dived almost voluptuously into the flood of the mass movements, had himself arrested (and, of course, interviewed), and came up with this profound discovery: "The average good Christian American secretly loved the war in Vietnam [. . .], the good Christian Americans needed the war or would lose their Christ."[17]

"Politics is the organization of power and power is the enemy of life," wrote a leading intellectual in 1965.[18] The idea could hardly be formulated more bluntly. American dissidents of the older generation enjoyed the courageous actions of the students. But the young radicals had no more esteem for those liberal intellectuals than their German counterparts had for the Federal Republic's *Scheissliberale* ("shitty liberals"), and showed them brutally what they were—over thirty.

Toward the end of the decade, the young rebels lost even these sympathizers. No praise could be heard for the radicals who built bombs in the underground. Some intellectuals now felt like Goethe's sorcerer's apprentice, who found himself unable to keep his own creations under control; secretly they were glad that the otherwise unloved Richard Nixon was restoring order on the campus.

The Weathermen were not like fish in the water—as, in Mao's impressive comparison, the revolutionaries should be among the populace. On the contrary they found themselves in an almost totally hostile environment. When a wave of riots once more enveloped the campus after the shootings at Kent State, and a favorable situation emerged for a revolutionary leadership, there existed for a week or two the "water" but no "fish" who were able to swim in it. America had no intention of entrusting its fate to Trotskyists, Maoists, and any other breed of Communists; and Weatherman, that last activist descendant of the student movement, had already blown himself to smithereens in the New York town house on Eleventh Street.

7
NEW INTERESTS

TWOand a half years after the sad events on the Kent State campus I came for two semesters to Columbia University. Everything was back to normal. Hardly anyone even mentioned the fifth anniversary of the battle of Morningside Heights or the third anniversary of Kent. The rising of a group of Indians at Wounded Knee and their skirmishes with federal agents were played up by TV, but this did not arouse the campus. Five years earlier, thousands of students all over the country would have marched to express solidarity with their red brethren. In 1973 the Indians stood almost alone.

THE CAMPUS IS CALM
During the entire academic year there were but two small disturbances at Columbia—one, when a group of homosexual students demonstrated to get their own clubroom on the university premises (they did not succeed then, but such facilities have since been provided on numerous campuses); the other during a variety show on the campus, when about a hundred conservative students protested the performance of a striptease and in the ensuing melee the student responsible for the entertainment had his nose broken.

I often asked students: "What happened to the revolutionary energies of the sixties?" What I heard in response came close to the well-known answer a coed gave to pretty much the same question: "They paired off and went to bed, locking the door behind them." I especially remember a young pair who invited me to their small apartment near the campus one evening. They had withdrawn from the world, rarely even stepping outside; they raised their own marijuana in a closet, in a box of soil under a plant light.

Young people were in a mood to horse around. In the good old days the question was how many students could be crammed into a telephone booth. Now they competed, the press reported, to see who could devour the greatest number of light bulbs. Some decades ago a student could seek fame by swallowing more live goldfish than the others; now, by being a streaker. As the political groups lost members, the fraternities gained them. The number of students volunteering for ROTC increased steadily after reaching its nadir around 1970. So did the number of those who called themselves conservatives, while the moderates climbed to 55 percent, the highest point since the American Council on Education began its count.[1] Relationships changed toward parents, and toward the older generation in general. If I asked students what they thought of their parents, I heard words of love and respect; some phoned home two or three times a week (collect); letters had gone out of fashion with silent movies.

The students gave a number of reasons for this extraordinary change in the brief period since Kent State. First and foremost: the end of the Vietnam war (the draft had been abandoned in 1973). Next: resignation (no sense in fighting, the Establishment is too strong). Third: since Mao had invited Nixon to Peking there were no more Left heroes, except dead ones like Trotsky, Che Guevara, or Ho Chi Minh. Fourth: the developments of the sixties had clearly taken a dangerous direction. The dead students at Kent State and Jackson State, the torn bodies in the New York town house, later the flaming death of the SLA group in Los Angeles—these were all powerful and brutal impressions vastly magnified by the TV screen. Even the murders by the Manson "family" (1969) weighed on the consciences of sensitive young people who by their own actions had helped to promote the climate of violence. Others saw before their mind's eye drug-addicted friends whose trips ended in insanity or suicide. Fifth: the economic boom was declining, the number of jobless graduates with excellent records was growing. One student formulated it this way: "As long as you want to become a locomotive engineer or a cowboy, you are an idealist. Later on, you have to make money." Sixth: declining interest in political issues. A student said: "Anybody can demonstrate for the problems of the

world. It is much more difficult to form your own life. That is what
we are concentrating on now." Seventh: The politicians themselves were undertaking measures to safeguard civil liberties and
punish the guilty—a process beginning with the Ervin committee
which led to Nixon's resignation and then to exposure of CIA
abuses. Finally: themes and slogans which were only partly political began to take up the time and energy of those activists who
were not content to withdraw into complete privacy but wanted to
do something for the improvement of life in their country by
working for various causes, two of which will be mentioned here
as examples.

"ECORILLAS"

Revisiting Berkeley in the early seventies, I asked some students
to show me what was new on the campus and in their lives. After
a brief consultation they took me first to a natural-foods restaurant. While I was fed strange dishes, a man in the next room—
white-bearded, clothed in nondescript Asiatic garb—preached to
a crowd of listeners sitting around on the floor: he was telling
them about the happiness created by a simple and good life.

Everybody was into "ecology" that year, thinking of ways and
means to save the world from pollution and destruction, so I was
invited next to the students' house, to see the garden where they
had planted small patches of vegetables. They were particularly
proud of the compost pile, their source of organic fertilizer, something formerly unknown to American city dwellers; a pamphlet
had shown them how to prepare it.

We sat on the floor in their living room and I asked what else
they were doing to clean up the earth. They began by teaching me
a few new words. To do ecology properly, I was informed, you have
to develop the right "ecotactics," and, if necessary, commit
"ecotage"—sabotage in behalf of ecology. They were full of
suggestions for protecting the earth: It might be possible to kidnap factory managers and set them free only after their plants
stopped polluting; members of Congress who voted for freeways
and other "paved paradises" should—as a warning—find their
lawns covered by concrete. For such enterprises "ecorillas" might
be mobilized (ecological guerrillas, of course). And so they went
on. They reported so quickly about their own endeavors that I
asked for some paper to make notes. A girl handed me a sheet
filled with writing on one side. "We now always use both sides to
save paper," she said. "Each sheet is a piece of forest."

America's bookshops were still selling tens of thousands of copies of Alvin Toffler's *Future Shock*, which advises one to get used to living in a throwaway society, and here young Americans agitated for the opposite: "Let's not throw away anything!" In the kitchen I was shown mountains of neatly tied newspapers to be collected on certain days and sold to paper factories. "Recycling" was the big word then. Large cardboard boxes filled with empty cans, those made from aluminum neatly separated from the steel ones—they too could be recycled. The money thus obtained went into "ecofunds" to serve in the battle against pollution.

The girls had this contribution: "Hundreds of millions of dishes and clothes are being washed in America every day by detergents containing chemicals which pollute and poison our waters. We now use only detergents without poisonous chemicals." Above the sink they had tacked a catalogue, printed by some association of ecological centers, which graded detergents on a scale from zero to sixty according to the amount of poison they contained. One of the girls called attention to the cotton kitchen towels. "Before, we were using paper towels which we threw away. That was much simpler. But each paper towel is a piece of a tree; we also use cotton handkerchiefs now rather than tissues."

I was even taken to the bathroom. Did I notice anything? I didn't, and was told: "We only use *white* toilet paper. From the colored paper, poisonous dyes get into the water. This adds up—from more than 200 million Americans." Someone lifted the cover of the toilet tank and asked me to have a look: I saw two half-gallon bottles filled with sand. Thanks to these, the tank each time took one gallon less of water to fill. "At first we used bricks, but they dissolved. Now we have worked out the proper method. If all Americans were to do this, we would save daily almost a billion gallons of water." A notice was tacked above the bathtub: "Save water! Don't shower too long!" Someone had scribbled next to it: "Shower with a friend."

To me all this might seem hysterical, they said, maybe even comical. But I should consider that in the previous year Americans had thrown away packing material to the tune of 50 million tons. They told of the efforts thousands of college and high-school students made some months earlier in cleaning oil-smeared waterfowl after a tanker spill in San Francisco Bay.

Before I left I had to see their garage, filled with bicycles; they had all gotten rid of their polluting cars. They also wanted me to have a look at a tree in the garden. Again I noticed nothing in particular; it was an ordinary fir tree. "This is last year's Christmas tree. We bought it with its roots in a pot and after Christmas moved it into the garden to use again this year. In the past, millions of pines have been cut down in the forests for Christmas trees. Such waste!" All agreed on one thing: the dreadful squandering of nature's treasures could not go on any longer. One even said in all seriousness that the earth would only become truly habitable again when its population was reduced to one million. (*Million*, he said, not billion.)

When I left the house to walk to my hotel (how could I possibly have used a taxi after all this?), they called after me that I should not fail to visit the Ecocenter in Berkeley. There I found some two or three hundred books with titles such as *America the Raped Continent, Not as Rich as You Think!, The Death of the Sweet Waters, Smog, the Killer,* and *Terracide.* There were other books, too—about health food, cooking with roots and herbs, the preservation of wildlife, weaving at your own loom. I received some printed material about "Earth Day," which several thousand schools, colleges, and universities had observed on April 22.

WOMEN'S LIB—REVOLUTION IN THE REVOLUTION

"Women's Lib" is one of those pungent expressions which America has contributed to the languages of the world. To be sure, the women's movement of today has its great-grandmothers, such as the British suffragettes, and even earlier advocates; John Stuart Mill, for example, who at his wedding (1861) formally protested against the existing marriage law for conferring on the husband "legal powers and control over the person, property and freedom of action of the wife," declaring it to be his "will and intention" that his wife, Harriet, should retain "the same absolute freedom of action [. . .] as if no such marriage had taken place."[2] But in scope and intensity Women's Lib goes far beyond earlier experiences. The movement for women's liberation—or rather, movements, since the activity in its behalf is very broad and includes efforts that are organized and others that are loosely held together—received much impetus from the campus. Paradoxically, or maybe not, Women's Lib has flourished mainly (so far) in the United States, where women have long enjoyed more freedom than anywhere else, though evidently not enough.

When the New Left began, women joined it just as young men did, as "soldiers of the revolution," and at the SDS meeting of Christmas 1965 the question of women's rights came up—but only peripherally. A year later, Jane Adams, one of the few women in the SDS leadership, published in the SDS paper an article with clearly feminist undertones, including the new term "male chauvinism." In the summer of 1967, during the annual SDS convention, she pushed through a resolution which said, among other things:

> Women, because of their colonial relationships to men, have to fight for their own independence. [...] People who identify with the movement and feel that their own lives are part of the base to bring about radical social change must recognize the necessity for the liberation of women.[3]

Women were said to be like colored people in the colonies, exploited by men as colonial peoples were exploited by imperial governments, and acknowledgment of this was demanded as a principle of the New Left movement. A year earlier the National Organization for Women (NOW) had been founded, but for female students it was too tame, too much an "organization." They began to look for groups of their own in which they could meet for frank and informal talks—rap groups, as these were called. In America most things come in waves; suddenly there were thousands of campus rap groups in which young women, many for the first time, were discussing their most intimate problems with other women, discovering that others had these problems, too.

A young professor told me of the consequences for his marriage: "My wife soon found herself in her rap group in an orgy of self-incrimination. If one of the girls called her husband a 'male chauvinist,' the others shouted: 'Wait till you hear about mine!' After a few weeks, they had driven each other up the wall to the point where most of the marriages were cracking. Until then, my wife and I had been a normal and harmonious couple; I love her, we have two sweet children—but overnight whatever I said or did confirmed her conviction that I was a male chauvinist, even a male chauvinist pig."

Many leading feminists have come from the New Left—Jo Freeman, for example, author of several books, came from Berkeley.[4] She and many others became feminists because they were deeply disappointed by the treatment accorded them by their male comrades in the New Left. Evelyn Goldfield, Sue Munaker, and Naomi Weisstein—they had been connected with the New Left at Harvard and the University of Chicago—wrote a bitter and sarcastic article against male chauvinists, thus characterizing their own position in the New Left after years of loyal cooperation:

> We were still the movement secretaries and the shit-workers; we served the food, prepared the mailings and made the best posters; we were the earth mothers and the sex-objects for the movement men. We were the free movement "chicks"—free to screw any man who demanded it, or if we chose not to—free to be called hung-up, middle class and up-tight. We were free to keep quiet at meetings—or if we chose not to, we were free to speak in men's terms. If a woman dared conceive an idea that was not in the current limited ideological system, she was ignored and ridiculed.[...] We were free, finally, to marry and raise liberated babies and clean liberated diapers, and prepare liberated dinners for our ass-hunting husbands, or "guys we were living with."[...] What men just can't dig is that we, females, are going to define our movement, that male advice is paternalistic—no less so than when given by a white to a black.[5]

A Columbia psychoanalyst came to the same conclusion in a study about movement women: they complained that male chauvinism was "all too much a part of the movement. [...] The men wished to treat them as revolutionary women in a sexual sense—expecting them to be available sexually without regard for them as people.[6]"

SDS was trying to represent a new and better mankind. But even in SDS women were treated shabbily. During that fateful convention in the Chicago Coliseum, a member of the Black Panthers, Rufus Walls, came to the rostrum as an ally of the old core and started, apropos of nothing, to talk about the women's role. The Panthers, he said, were for the presence of women in the movement, "for love and all that," even for "pussy power." Fierce protests couldn't stop him from continuing in this vein. The shouts grew so loud that he left the rostrum. Now one of his black friends jumped to the mike, declaring solidarity with his Panther brother and reminding the girls of Stokely Carmichael's answer to the question about the position of women in the movement: "the only position for women in the movement is prone."

The anger of the women in SDS was one of the things, though not the most important, that was to lead a few hours later to the disintegration of the group. A young woman who had lived for a number of years with Paul Potter, a onetime president of SDS, hurled an accusation against the movement men that sounded like a raging eruption:

What is most real in my life is my anger and pain at men—all men. Starting with my father, including Paul, and right down to eight-year-old Michael. But mostly, my anger and hurt and humiliation is at my generation, "my people." That is, young men, hip men, revolutionary men. And it is there because it is you men who pose as the bearers of the new liberation, of new life-styles for us all. You claim to have rejected the old order and tell me you are creating a new one—through flowers or bombs or baking bread. But that is a myth, a lie.

She angrily continued: "Here they come. Those strutting roosters, those pathetic male chauvinists, egocentric, pompous and ridiculous bastards."[7]

Jane Alpert turned feminist after years in the underground. An article she wrote in 1973 warned her "sisters" of the pain left-wing men would inflict on them and urged them to break with the male-dominated radical Left. She no longer had any sympathy for her former lover and accomplice in bomb actions, Samuel J. Melville, who meanwhile had been killed in the 1971 Attica prison riot, and even refused to feel sadness over dead Attica inmates: they too had been male supremacists.[8]

Feeling degraded in the new Left, many women redirected their energy to Women's Lib, taking with them all their talents and movement experiences, finding there a new home and new challenges. In the mid-sixties, the blacks had begun to discover their history and to demand "black studies" courses, which were granted to them in many colleges. Now women came with like demands and with the same success. Hundreds of colleges introduced courses on women's questions. In the 1975 catalogue of Barnard College in New York City, I found such courses in eleven different departments—for example, theology offered "Women and Religion"; history, "Women in Antiquity" and "The Image of the Woman in the Intellectual History of America"; Romance Languages, "French Authoresses." In 112 colleges and universities the master's degree, and in one case the doctorate, could be obtained in women's studies.[9] In Berkeley, the University of California opened a Women's Center which offered in 1975/76 courses such as these: "Stereotypes of Female Sex Roles in the Film" and "An Alternative Art Gallery for Women," "Radical Psychiatry for Women," and "Lesbianism—a Lifestyle."

Women who have been out of touch with the campus environment for a while or who are starting college for the first time now have special undergraduate programs to ease their adjustment. A

California junior college district, for example, offers a "Women's Re-entry Program."

It cannot come as a surprise that the often violent rejection of the male sex may lead to lesbianism of various degrees; many women hope to find a community of women in which they can withdraw from the storms of heterosexual eros. This is being accepted more than some years ago. In 1974, Elaine Noble, a thirty-year-old graduate with two master's degrees, campaigning as a lesbian, won election to the Massachusetts State legislature. New in all this is the growing openness in accepting homosexuality in general. Specialists assume that the number of homosexuals has not grown appreciably, but all homosexuals profit from the increased permissiveness of modern society

Understandably, Women's Lib has called forth countercurrents. The business of teaching "womanliness" thrives, and special courses have been attended by hundreds of thousands across the country. By the summer of 1975, a million copies of *Fascinating Womanhood* had been sold, and around 600,000 copies of *Total Woman*. Such books tell a woman how to win influence over her man by becoming again "the girl whom he once thought he married."[10]

But Women's Lib, in contrast to the student movement, is still in its phase of expansion. Every year it finds ardent recruits among almost a million new divorcees. Many of them accept their new status as permanent; some even want it this way. In 1975, I met a young woman whom I had known previously as a newlywed and who now was divorced, with a four-year-old son. She spoke of her divorce almost as if she was referring to a completed examination at a university. For her it was not a catastrophe, just a stage in life which many of her acquaintances were also experiencing at the same time. She even spoke of "Creative Divorces"—referring to a college course of that name. She was preparing herself for a life without a man. Of course, she is a feminist.

Feminism has even reached the race track. In the summer of 1975, at Belmont Park, New York, the women in the crowd of 50,000 cheered as one for the mare who was racing against the favored stallion.

8
TURNING INWARD

ONE morning in the summer of 1975, while crossing the campus of Stanford University, I saw workers cleaning off the bulletin boards to make room for the new quarter's announcements. I gathered the discarded posters—mostly mimeographed or hand drawn—that many different student groups had prepared and put up on the kiosks. A few days later, in San Francisco, I was walking with friends to a restaurant and saw many more such notices tacked or pasted to telephone poles and walls. If there were several of a kind, I took one home—with a somewhat bad conscience. So my collection grew, and I added more in the following weeks.

CULTS AND OCCULTS
Six years earlier, at the height of the youth rebellion, I had also collected posters. In those days they called for demonstrations and sit-ins; they urged young people to fight the "pigs," to help the students of "oppressed universities" through solidarity actions, and to found communes; or they listed left-wing offices for legal and medical aid. And now? Among my roughly 300 posters of 1975, only 20 could be called political (about one dozen advertising black meetings, one each agitating for Peking, for Marxism in general, for the Weathermen, for the liberation of two men from prison). Some solicited customers for karate courses or classes in natural childbirth. All the others dealt with totally nonpolitical problems, largely religious and, even more, occult. The mere enumeration would cover several pages. Here is a selection:

A "Psychic Festival"; a "PEG" (Personal Exploration Group); a

71

"New Dimensions Foundation," which promised to "locate and dissolve energy blockages" with the aid of a lady named India Supera, said to be a pupil of "Sathya Sai Baba from South India"; an "Active Imagination Workshop," which made use of "events in the unconscious psychic hinterland" and promised "archetypal imagery" and "active passivity"; an "Institute for Applied Meditation," specializing in the use of the "alpha level of consciousness"; a "City of Resurrection" (if you looked more closely, it consisted of but a single house), which held a "night of miracles" in store; a "Magical Child Seminar" led by the author of *The Crack of the Cosmic Egg*; a "Humanist Institute," which taught the "Craft of Dying"; an "Association of Humanistic Psychology," teaching "How to Educate Your Dreams"; and a "Center for Utopian Psychology," promising to open "the way to righteous, natural highness."

The "King's New Messengers" promised to "teach the message of perfection"; the "Aquarian Research Foundation" offered, among other attractions, films on witchcraft and voodoo; a "Survival Research Foundation" offered, for only $5, a secret code with the help of which the customer would be able to, after death, transmit messages to his living friends. Then there was a "Center for Feeling Experience"; two "Science of the Mind" centers, with the same name but different addresses; a "Center of Parapsychology and Metaphysics"; a shop named "Big Sur," which had tapes on many topics, including "Choose Your Own Death, an Experimental Experience," and "The Art of Death"; a "Polarity Therapy Workshop"; a "Creative Community Project"; a "Transactional Analysis Institute" (TA); a "Quadrinity Center"; a "Cosmic Joy Fellowship"; "ECKANKAR," teaching the "ancient science of soul travel"; a dream workshop ("we will work on your dream material"); a "Sekai Mahikari Bummei Kyodan" with three-day courses on Mahikari No Waza ("the super power of concentrating the spiritual light into the palm of one's hand and radiating it upon the body of another"); a "cosmic dance" class, with particular emphasis on the five senses, the four elements, the Yin and Yang, and the Tai Chi.

Yoga was taught by thirteen different institutions, with many wonderful additions: Kinesiology, Chakras, Cabala, I Ching, Kriyas-Yoga Hygiene, and Reflexology. Someone with a Ph.D. to his name offered a special kind of yoga ("please bring your own cushion and mats"). Two institutes promised information about Tibetan secrets (about the "Three Yakas," for example), taught by

Lama Chime Rinpoche, and a lecture by Yeshe Dhondon, the "personal physician of the Dalai Lama."

The German word *Gestalt* was much in use, a far cry from the Gestalt psychology which Wolfgang Koehler founded in Berlin during the twenties. I read this term on seven different posters, one of which offered "private lessons employing Gestalt alchemy." One lady (who gave her phone number) taught Tarot "as a tool for psychic and spiritual development" (the medieval Tarot cards have become quite the thing lately, not as a card game but for the purpose of fortune-telling). Three "universities" in and near San Francisco, of which I had never heard —Heliotrope, Orpheus, and Lifeskool—offered their services. Among their courses were Indian temple dances, Chinese vegetarian food, belly dancing, alchemy, chaotic meditation (that's what it said), wicca (a thousand-year-old witchcraft, we are told), and all that with the help of Tarot cards.

One might expect notices of the cult of Krishna, but it is by now so firmly established that it does not have to solicit converts by posters. This is even more true of TM, the transcendental meditation of Maharishi Mahesh Yogi, by now a worldwide enterprise with a turnover of millions of dollars. Equally prosperous is est, the Erhard Seminar Training of the industrious Werner Erhard, who "transforms" his customers in 60 hours of extreme psychological pressure, for $250 a person.

What had happened to the youth of America? In the second half of the sixties it participated in a political explosion of considerable dimensions, and now there was withdrawal from politics, attraction to the problems of one's inner life, one's soul—an amazing jump, to take terms from physics and technology, from explosion to implosion. Young people hurt themselves badly when, in a passionate assault, they tried to conquer the external world, so now they turned inward. The world had not become any better, that was obvious, and Watergate, the young people felt, had proved it anew. Apparently, the world could not be changed. Was it not more important to concentrate on one's own soul (and body)? The true adventures—were they not to be found by grappling with the secrets of life (before and after death) rather than in fights with the "pigs"?

At every step I found evidence of this turning inward: ever more labels such as "occultism" and "parapsychology" on the shelves of the bookshops, new reviews such as *Psychic Times* or *New Age*. Science and technology? Well, yes, they are able to

73

crack or fuse the atom and to annihilate millions of people within fractions of seconds; they can build planes moving faster than sound; can reach the moon and Mars. But they cannot answer a single one of the real problems of man: Is there a God? Whence do we come, whither do we go? How should we live? The established churches have lost much of their attraction because they are too strongly linked with politics and government; ever more people are trying to find the truth by other means. All over America young people have joined religious groups and communes of a new texture. In one of them I spent a few days.

IN NEW AMERICA

This commune (I shall call it New America, because its members believe they are working for a renewal of America) is in the hilly countryside of California—golden-colored slopes and valleys with dark green patches of magnificent oaks all around and a clear sky above. Cows and sheep graze on some 750 acres of land; in the garden apples ripen and vegetables grow. A few barracks stand at the foot of a slope. In the evening, the folding chairs which are used during meetings are put away and sleeping bags are spread out on the floor, but now, Sunday evening, shortly before the departure of some of the participants, we were listening to talks by members of this commune. They spoke more or less on the same topic: How I came to New America. All of them agreed: We have searched far and wide and finally we have found.

All told about their youth, a youth full of confusion and uncertainty. One girl said: "When I was a child, I thought my father knew everything. When we were traveling, we kids were allowed to ask him anything we wanted, and always he knew the answers—about trees, rivers, or mountains. But as we grew older we had other questions. We wanted to know why the Negroes were poor and where all those many poor people came from in our richly endowed land, and why the Vietnam war. But our father evaded our questions and gradually we knew—he didn't have any answers. From then on I was looking for people who would know them. I hoped to find them in the university; I studied psychology. My professors knew an awful lot, but nothing that was relevant to my big questions. They knew the working of the brain, of the nervous system, all its functions, but they did not know man himself. Always they said they were preparing us for life. But none of them said how life on earth was going to continue now that it was threatened on all sides. I joined the SDS; its arguments were presented so effectively that I thought I had finally attained my goal. Here was the answer: The revolution was imminent, and I would participate in it. I marched, I demonstrated. But the longer it lasted, the clearer it became that the SDS had nothing to offer but destructive criticism and analyses of the old political system; no vision of a new and better one. When, after four years, I graduated, I didn't know what to do, so I continued studying. I landed in a lab where they were experimenting with rats. I had come to the university to understand Man—and here I had to dissect rats. I gave up. First, I lived in a commune on the East Coast, but I didn't like it; they were always quarreling with each other. I hitchhiked to California. Here too, I had wanted to try communes; the first one was not my cup of tea. And then finally I found this one; I found what I had been looking for all these years—harmony and openness for the big and true questions of life."

One young man said: "You can't trust the government, you can't trust the universities, and who wants to spend his life working for the Coca-Cola Company? Much better to live in a community with personal friends, to live a simple life."

A young woman with lovely features and a radiant smile, truly a prototype of the all-American girl, was visiting New America for the first time. She described the spiritual and intellectual trials she had experienced before. For two years she tried existentialism, but this philosophy had only made her sadder and lonelier. Perhaps, she said, life in New America was the road to true happiness. She was nineteen years old. Two hours later she applied for admission.

A few days are too short to judge this (or any other) community. But it was obvious that the young people out there (I was the only old one) liked their new life and that quite a few of the visitors were debating seriously whether to enter the commune and to accept its life-style.

New America is not a leftist commune; rather, it is religiously oriented. Most songs which the young people sang over and over again had a religious or semireligious content: the *Battle Hymn of the Republic,* for example, with its combination of God and nature so characteristic of America. Woody Guthrie's *This Land Is Your Land* also was a favorite.

The young people in America have preserved a characteristic that impressed me when I met them for the first time almost fifty years ago, and that distinguishes them from the youth of

75

Europe—a naïve and unprejudiced nonchalance, an easy cama-
raderie. Compared with the Americans, the citizens of my Old
World are sophisticated skeptics, in Hamlet's phrase, "sicklied
o'er with the pale cast of thought," and voice critical reservations
about whatever is being said or done. Compared with us, the
Americans are happy "joiners." If someone in New America
suggested a song, asking "How about this one?" you could hear a
unanimously roared "yeaaaah." Whether games were suggested
or teams selected—always "yeaaaah." For the young Americans
the threshold on which they are willing to communicate freely
and to talk about themselves is much lower than for the North
Europeans. Their informality is a constant surprise to the European on a first visit, and maybe also on a second or third. I still
remember my amazement when a salesman at Roos Brothers in
Berkeley, where I was buying my first corduroys, in 1928, started
calling me by my first name right away.

THE JOY OF RELATING
In contrast to Europe, where you are either a Protestant, a
Catholic, or a Jew, and your passport says so, America possesses
countless religious denominations, many of them minute sects
that defy classification. But there is one thing they all have in
common: They are on their own feet, not only in their dogma and
their inner structure, but also economically. With an ease amazing to most Europeans (particularly to those who pay their church
tax simultaneously with other annual taxes), they all use modern
publicity and business methods. A good deal of showmanship is
employed by those who want to win converts and financial contributions. Some consider it helpful if church members stand up
and speak their testimony—how they were wicked unbelievers,
how God entered their lives, and how they found in precisely this
church a new happiness and purpose in life. The church is not
only their place of worship on Sundays, of baptism and marriage—I know quite a few couples who found each other in the
course of their church's many social activities. Parties, dances,
and holding hands are expected to promote ties with and within
the church community.

To "relate" and to "communicate" are frequently used expressions. Americans, especially the young ones, want to have someone or something to whom or to which they can relate, and it is
the same with "communicating." Anything else is dismissed as if
it did not exist. I'm reminded of the students at a junior high

school in southern California who wanted its name changed from "James Monroe" to "Marilyn Monroe School," since they couldn't relate to James Monroe.

During recent years, the country has been swamped with "encounter groups." The participants often address each other as brother and sister, though they are not relatives, and "family" is what many groups call themselves. The detached observer finds many similarities between the mood of restless young people of our time in general and the mood of those among them who are particularly attracted by the intense religious life in small, often newly emergent sects. Here are some characteristics which the two moods seem to have in common:

The original impulse which starts the drive toward something new often comes from a highly personal experience; it can reach ecstatic dimensions (the word "high" being sometimes used to describe it). The stimulating effect of music, preferably of a driving and powerful type, is made use of, as is the magic of symbols (portraits of Che and Mao, religious scenes), or the invocation of sacred texts (the Bible, as well as Marx and Mao, plus a host of other self-appointed prophets). Our century's technical civilization is viewed as a Moloch which devours our life and God's wonderful creation. In addition, both moods share contempt for the materialistic consumer society and indifference, even hostility, toward the entire Establishment (government, political parties, conventional churches) and its traditions, many of which are discarded as irrelevant to life and happiness, such as wedding ceremonies of the usual type. Both feel the pull of utopian visions and of work for a better world in an exalted crusade far more exciting than day-to-day drudgery.

The existing world is sure to perish—on the day of the Last Judgment (say the Christian believers) or in a violent revolution (according to the young rebels). What Satan is for the one group, "monopoly capitalism" is for the other, the paradise of the faithful being the "classless society" of the revolutionaries. Solidarity with the poor, with the oppressed and exploited, with the losers, the lonely ones, the handicapped, even the imprisoned criminals, is characteristic of both moods, as is the disdain for the rich and the powerful.

This closeness of spirit helps explain the ease and speed with which political activism has been followed by religious involvement. Within a year or two, antiwar demonstrations, political riots, and acid rock gave way to the hymns of "Jesus freaks,"

"Moonies," and "Children of God," as these and countless others took over the enthusiasm and even some of the methods of the sixties.

WOW!

It started with coffeehouses. When the hippie movement in the San Francisco Haight-Ashbury district was on the way out, some church people, touched by the plight of the hippies, opened a place in San Francisco called the Living Room. There they held Bible classes to supply a firm spiritual basis for the completely confused flower children. Similar coffeehouses and centers for the care of hippies emerged at other places. The Salt Company Coffee House in Los Angeles mobilized thousands of young Christians to march along Hollywood Boulevard, on Christmas in 1969, and again some months later, on Easter Sunday, to testify for Christ's resurrection in front of the city hall. Young people who were searching for "true" values and emotions, tested and proved in the trials of life, and who could no longer believe in the New Left, were deeply impressed by these young Christians who stood up so bravely against ridicule and derision.

Soon the wave was rolling, and newspapers began to appear. The *Hollywood Free Paper* was handed out at no charge, and reached or claimed a circulation of a million. In Berkeley, *Right On!* was distributed by the World Christian Liberation Front (the religious groups even took the vocabulary of the preceding political movements). The publisher of *Agape* (the New Testament word for spiritual love) advertised his paper by dropping thousands of copies from an airplane on an open-air concert. In Los Angeles a man forced a reluctant neighborhood of bars and night clubs to tolerate the opening of a Jesus center by chaining himself to a cross.[1]

A special way of greeting was found: the upraised hand with the index finger pointing heavenward (in contrast to the clenched fist of the radicals). Nor does the language of the Jesus people avoid terms used by their more worldly oriented peers. I often heard them use that sound which young Americans love so much because it permits them to express so many different degrees of emotion: "Wow!" If I were to tell such a group, "Last night Christ appeared to me in person," the answer would be: "Wow! He has seen Christ!" Wow covers everything favorable—satisfaction, delighted surprise, admiration, Amen.

78

IN PLACE OF DRUGS

An American journalist who spent some time among the Jesus people distributed a questionnaire to the members of thirty different groups. Among other things, he asked which of seventeen terms meant most to them. By far the largest percentage opted for "Accepting Christ," followed by "Divinity of Christ"; not a single point was given to "Existence of the Church" or "Virgin Birth."[2] A Catholic priest who had been trained as a psychiatrist named "community," "personal experience," and "security" as the three strongest desires on the part of the young.[3]

We have known for a long time that desires such as these have not been satisfied by the modern consumer society, and that this explains the passionate fervor of young people's involvement in political and nonpolitical movements, together with many of their forms of behavior, incomprehensible to the outside observer—the rapt features, the frenzied joy, applauding, stamping, and climbing onto chairs, the sobbing, the indiscriminate embraces.

The soliciting methods of some sects are highly aggressive. Suddenly their members appear on a street corner. First they burst into their lively songs, catchy in melody and rhythm, accompanied by guitars; when enough passersby have been attracted, they abruptly stop their performance and swarm into the crowd, distributing leaflets and forcing discussions. They are so well trained for these discussions that the surprised addressee is soon left speechless. In San Francisco, one group hit upon something special: the young members, usually girls, came with bunches of roses, handing a rose to each person they confronted, and they did this with such charming smiles that hearts simply melted.

Many young people within these groups had gone through dangerous tribulations before finding their anchor of salvation in a sect or community which gave them religious ecstasy in place of drugs. I met an eighteen-year-old girl who had run away three years before from a well-to-do middle-class home, taken up drugs, and lived with a bisexual drug addict, and now was one of the most determined and aggressive members of a religious group.

Doomsday mentality is particularly widespread in California because of the frequent threats of a catastrophic earthquake. Toward the end of the sixties, in Los Angeles, Reverend David Berg told his small Children of God community that he had received a revelation in Los Angeles announcing the imminent destruction of the state. For eight months he and his people moved through various parts of the United States mostly in great poverty. In their lore this migration has turned into a big thing, like the march of the children of Israel from Egypt, or Mao's Long March in 1934–1935. Returning to a still undestroyed California, they have kept their faith in the leader and formed more Children of God groups, even some overseas. Their long march is not over yet.

An American columnist wrote that many Jesus people whom she had questioned had been acquainted with drugs before joining the movement—62 percent of those over eighteen years, and 44 percent of those below that age. She emphasized the similarities between drug experience and "Jesus trips," both being outside of the normal American life-style, both anti-Establishment and in search of alternatives to middle-class conformism. She voiced alarm that Jesus trips and drug trips were so similar and said she had heard young people compare their meeting with Jesus to a "rush" from LSD.[4]

Johnny Cash, one of the most popular country-western singers, is supposed to have said that he had tried all kinds of drugs but never found anything as satisfactory as the experience of the Kingdom of God growing within him.[5] One of the main arguments in favor of transcendental meditation is the decrease in drug consumption among those who practice it. A Harvard study of 2,000 TM adherents claims that 80 percent had smoked marijuana before and that meditating had freed them from the drug.[6]

Whenever people are moved by religious desires and exaltations, they experience a growing interest in "last things." I have met students who firmly believed that the world was coming to an end and who, in their general confusion, hoped that the end would come speedily. One of them told me late one evening: "I sure would be disappointed if the world would not come to an end during my lifetime."

This apocalyptic mood explains what happened on the West Coast in the fall of 1975. Two people appeared, calling themselves simply "The Two," and said that they had come from the outer world, having adopted human form only temporarily. Soon they would be taken home by a spaceship. Those willing to give away their worldly possessions could join them, thus escaping the end of the doomed world. Dozens of people responded to their call, mainly young men and women.[7]

SPIRITS AND DEMONS

The often hectic mood of the new religious movements did not affect all their young adherents favorably. There are desperate

80

parents who are trying to tear their children away from the clutches of one sect or another, and a black social worker named Ted Patrick has made a profession of winning back young people for their families. (He has since been sentenced to a prison term for his practices, which involved abductions and violent sessions of counter-brainwashing.) Some parents formed an organization against the Children of God, called FREECOG (meaning "Free Our Children from the Children of Gold"). The methods used by them and Ted Patrick were not too unlike exorcism.[8] (Some youths were happy about being saved from their obsessions; others ran away from home at the earliest opportunity, back to their sect.)

Devil cults and necromancy have grown during recent years with almost explosive force. Some movies—*The Exorcist*, for example, and *Rosemary's Baby*—have contributed to such macabre trends. A publisher specializing in literature on occult subjects has reported a twenty-five-fold increase in turnover. When he organized an "Aquarian Festival of Astrology and Occult Sciences," the interest among young people was strong. One observer explained this by saying that they already had known psychedelic experiences *with* drugs, now they wanted them *without* drugs.[9] The festival's participants interpreted the interest in the occult as a revolt against our scientific and technological age, which promised so much but withheld inner peace. Even the traditional universities began to open their doors to new spiritual topics and currents. The University of Washington offered courses on yoga, numerology, hypnotism, extrasensory perception; the University of Wisconsin offered some on witchcraft and astrology (500 students participated); at San Francisco State there was a seminar on dreams, and at a college in Los Angeles a lecture series entitled "The World of the Supernatural."[10]

America's youth is incomparably more open for changes and new sensations than Europe's. What it has experimented with during the last two decades is truly breathtaking. From the crassly materialistic consumer society to the Beatniks and Ginsberg's *Howl*, Haight-Ashbury, the FSM, Weatherman, and faraway rural communes to Hare Krishna retreats where the sacred words must be repeated 1,728 times a day. The scene is confusing in its wild commotion. But to be moved and moving is normal with young people, and for us that may be a source of hope more than fear.

It may well be that the Jesus people have passed the high point of their influence and attraction. To me, it seems likely that their

81

movement will leave fewer traces in the American mind than the New Left did—because it is more closely linked to the American tradition, which it will strengthen without adding anything fundamentally new to the nation's bloodstream.

The religious and semireligious groups in America have rarely been accused of political designs, except for the Unification Church of Sun Myung Moon, the Korean evangelizer. Moon considers himself a prophet in the service of Christ, called upon to change the spiritual *and* the political world. This is how he begins his biography:

> On Easter morning in 1936, Sun Myung Moon was deep in prayer on a Korean mountainside when Jesus Christ appeared to him and told him that he had an important mission to accomplish in the fulfillment of God's providence. He was then sixteen years old.[11]

I have met a number of his leading disciples and found them persuasive, energetic, well organized. His is one of the fastest-growing sects—I have run into branches even in Germany. But its main strength was for some time in the Bay Area. His people point to the fact that all great movements have begun with a handful of believers and that everything depends on the proper historical setting and the firm will of a determined community. One explained: "Always the Bay Area has been fertile in ideas and movements; it was from here that the Beatniks, the Hippies, the radical students have turned on the whole of America and in effect the entire world."

An old-timer of the Bay Area, a diligent observer of its manifold activities, concurred. After watching the radical social movement of the sixties being replaced by religious and quasi-religious fervor, and considering the undeniable search of young Americans for something to believe in, he could well imagine that the country could come to be ruled by a dynamic religious community, perhaps even by one from Asia.

It is undeniable that some of the Asian gurus have developed a remarkable understanding of the West's ills, even though they may clothe their observations in strange words. Gopi Krishna, for example, diagnoses thus our, and especially our youth's, problems:

> There is a rebellion against the existing order, because the brain has reached a state of development where the riddle of existence looms larger than it did before. This is the reason why millions of

young men and women in Europe and America are eagerly on the search for masters and effective methods of self-awareness. [...] At a certain critical state in the development of the human mind the unanswered "Riddle of Life" attains an urgency which no treasure of the earth can counteract. This is the state of mind of millions of disillusioned young people of the world today. Modern psychology is absolutely dead to a most powerful impulse in the psychic make-up of man that has always been in evidence from the very dawn of civilization to this day. When thwarted in its mission, the impulse can lead to social and political unrest, [...] craving for drugs, promiscuity or other social evils and even violence.[12]

"BUDDHA'S REVENGE"

In 1973, I spent a day in a Hare Krishna House in New York, among some thirty young Americans of both sexes, in yellow robes, with the men's heads shaven. Who am I to decide whether they were living there as real monks and nuns or whether they were just playing a monks' and nuns' game? At any rate, everything looked very Indian. The walls were plastered with cheap Krishna prints, the smell of incense was in the air, Indian food was being served (we ate squatting on the floor, of course), and scenes from a Krishna legend were being performed, with Indian music and gestures. Monks and nuns were looking after each guest, answering questions, praising the glory of Lord Krishna and hoping for the guest's conversion. There is, we know, nothing sweeter for a convert than to convert others to his or her newly found faith.

How are these new movements financed? This question is more easily answered for the religious groups than for the New Left. Many well-to-do people are glad to support groups whose members are clean and orderly in clothing and haircut, and who are trying a lead a life without drugs and crime and with little sex. These benefactors undoubtedly give their contributions in the hope that young people who move from revolution to evangelism will not be a danger to the American social structure. Neither the Hare Krishna devotees nor the Jesus people show much interest in society's reform; very few of the "inward" groups do. When they mention revolution, as they like to do, they mean a spiritual one. And if father and son do speak different languages, then the father will prefer to see his son with a Bible in his hand, rather than Marx's *Capital*.

Some of the quickly developing religious communities have surprisingly large sums of money at their disposal, considering the simple life of their devotees. Some two years ago, the International Society of Krishna Consciousness Inc. (with 2,000 members, according to its own figures) bought property in a quiet section of Berkeley worth almost $350,000. Twenty-four monks, all of them U.S. citizens, moved in. Soon neighbors were complaining to the city council about the noise and the cars at all hours of the day, the crowds arriving for free meals. A Krishna car was demolished, and a protesting neighbor was locked up by the monks for several hours to teach him a lesson. It seems that the self-confidence and the missionary zeal of the sect is growing year by year.

Some Americans speak of "Buddha's revenge" when they watch the increasing influence from Asia. For centuries, they say, Christian missionaries went out to Asia to convert its masses, and now we have the opposite happening. Many of the new cults have indeed a strong admixture of Asian culture, even if they do not specifically propagate an Asian religion. Gurus from India traverse America amid countless thousands of devotees, erecting their own schools and universities; the Korean Moon has a sizable army of followers; Zen Buddhism has found enthusiastic apostles (the late Alan Watts, for example) and won thousands of followers. (Even newly arising Christian sects often use some Asiatic concepts. In one group that I visited, Buddha's name was mentioned almost as often as Christ's, and certainly far more often than that of Moses.)

Fifty years ago, during my first stay in America, I did not notice anything of this kind. At the University of California one or two of my classmates had read D. T. Suzuki's books about Zen Buddhism, but more out of intellectual curiosity than in search of a new life-style. During the long years of the Occupation in Japan, however, tens of thousands of young Americans imbibed Japanese culture and traditions, including Zen. The campus mood of the sixties had certain traits in common with Zen: the feeling of superiority toward the materialistic world, the proud distance from all exterior phenomena, the lightning-like enlightenment which corresponded to the "Now!" desire of the young. ("Wow" could easily be a Zen word.) In Tassajara, California, there has existed since 1967 a much-visited Zen monastery, inhabited exclusively by young Americans. Even the Indian Sikhs have their adherents in America; they call themselves the 3HO—the Healthy Happy Holy Organization. Practically all had been drug addicts before they joined, one of its members said.[13]

Transcendental meditation has so far gained the widest following. The secret of its success seems to lie in the experience of its adherents that in all the drive and stress of our age they gain relaxation by their twice-daily twenty minutes of meditation, which in itself is a concept foreign to the mainstream of Western culture. The turning inward expresses itself also in the large number of books with the word "self" in their title—*Self-Therapy, The Importance of Self-Consciousness, How to Overcome Self-Deceit*. If you cannot change the world, then at least clean up your own self.[14]

Even traditional politics has been invaded by Eastern influences. The popularity of the young governor of California, Jerry Brown, especially among young voters, is due not only to his age (he was born in 1938) but also to some features of his life-style. When he took office, a Hindu choir sang *Om sri ram*, and he is known to have performed some official functions while sitting in the lotus position. Among the aims of his administration he specifically mentioned that he wanted to help his countrymen toward more self-knowledge, for the purpose of developing their potential.[15]

In a Krishna Consciousness Temple in Detroit there lived awhile among the monks and nuns Alfred B. Ford, a great-grandson of the automobile king, and Elizabeth Reuther, the daughter of Walter Reuther, the longtime boss of the United Auto Workers. The most extravagant imagination could hardly have conjured up a more impressive example of America's changed mood.

GERMANY

9
THE GERMAN SDS, ITS ENEMIES AND ALLIES

WHENin 1967 the German students suddenly went wild, everybody else was shocked, angry, and perplexed. Had the students gone crazy? The nation had barely emerged from the ruins of the Second World War (and ruins were still all over the place). It had begun to heal its wounds and restore relations with its neighbors. It had adjusted itself, after twelve years of Hitler and war, to the joys of peace and an unexpected prosperity. And here the students, instead of appreciating what their parents had accomplished through hard work, were turning against them—in fact, against almost everything, calling it "shit." This was unbelievable.

But the nightmare did not go away. It became worse. And gradually people began to understand that the student unrest had not come out of nowhere. It was in the Western sectors of Berlin that the unrest was most evident—and students elsewhere seemed to take their cues from there. The Free University of Berlin had begun its work in 1948 under unusually favorable conditions—not in the material sense, as practically everything was lacking (the first lecture hall was in a subway station), but in the intellectual and political sense. Not since the Napoleonic wars and the emerging of the *Burschenschaft* (a patriotic type of fraternity) had the students and the citizens been as united as in the years when Berlin was the *Frontstadt*, the city at the front line of the West. The students had been acclaimed as an avant-garde of liberty when they left their alma mater in the Eastern part of the divided city, where unbiased research and teaching were no longer possible, to open a new university in West Berlin (to which, incidentally, the Ford Foundation contributed money). In this spirit of a new, determinedly *free* university, the professors and the city administration agreed to an academic constitution which gave the students a voice in running the university. Thus, for its students and for many students outside Berlin, it stood as a model of a new, more democratic university.

This model, to be sure, permitted radical groups to enter student organizations, and here and there even to obtain a majority. Through the generosity of the university administration, moreover, nonacademic organizations obtained lecture halls for their meetings, and some of them were of the Left, some quite radical.[1] Still, in the fifties, the German students in general, like their counterparts in America, just wanted to finish their education as quickly and successfully as possible in order to enter the professional world; they showed little interest in academic politics.

West Berlin had a second peculiarity. Because of the special status of the city, whoever lived there was exempt from military service, at least temporarily. How many West Germans went to the Free University in Berlin to escape the draft nobody can tell, although there is no question that the political motivation of the draft resisters helped the growth of left-wing groups. Still, until the beginning of the sixties, the solidarity of the city was not disturbed. In August 1961 all West Berliners were shocked and outraged by the building of the Wall, a symbol of the East German Communist government's tyranny and fear of Western ideas. Vast numbers of students demonstrated in the streets, and many attempted to help comrades in East Berlin flee to the West by digging tunnels under the wall. But soon estrangement set in; perhaps disappointment over the passive attitude of the three Western powers (and also of Chancellor Adenauer) contributed to it.

The first open conflict came early in 1963. The Free University's student parliament had elected as its president a man from a Burschenschaft, who was considered to be on the Right. Then a number of student political groups, hitherto without significance, organized an election and the student body voted to replace the new president with one considerably to the left of him. The following year the students of West Berlin entered the arena of foreign affairs for the first time when they demonstrated against a guest of the city, Congolese Prime Minister Moïse Tshombe, whom they branded as the "murderer of Lumumba." In the spring of 1965 there was a student strike—new in the history of German universities—as the result of a quarrel over whether to have a certain writer lecture at the Free University.

In the summer of 1966 some departments imposed regulations which limited the time available for the students' political activities, and in protest the students staged the first political sit-in in German academic history. They stressed that they were not just fighting this new regulation, but rather were seeking the destruction of the "power of a small oligarchy" and the realization of democratic freedoms in all German society, of which the university was merely one element.[2]

Into this situation, on December 1, 1966, burst the news of the formation of a new government in Bonn by the two largest parties, the Christian Democrats (Adenauer's party, which had been in power since 1949) and the Social Democrats, who until then had been the Opposition, the political home of most left-leaning intellectuals in the country. Personally, I considered the formation of the Grand Coalition at that time a necessity, but a few days later, in the current-events colloquium I was conducting, I found many of the politically interested students unhappy about it. Obviously, they felt that, as the Social Democrats had entered the government, there no longer would be a powerful Opposition in parliament. The next step was obvious—an Extraparliamentary Opposition. The author Günter Grass prophesied correctly: "The youth of our country will turn its back on the state and will move either to the Left or to the Right as soon as this wretched marriage [of the two great parties] has been agreed upon."

THE DEATH OF BENNO OHNESORG

The first big chance for students to show their anger, to demonstrate before a wide audience, came during the visit of the Shah of Iran and his wife in the early summer of 1967. The demonstration in West Berlin against the imperial visitors was well prepared, with radio and TV on hand to broadcast it. The entire nation tuned in on the fight (first between pro- and anti-Shah Persian students), the arrival of the police with their nightsticks, the fleeing students. What was not shown on television was the death of a student, Benno Ohnesorg, shot on a side street by a policeman.

This event caused an explosion in the German universities, though not immediately—the first reaction was muted by the preparations for Ohnesorg's funeral. In Berlin some 20,000

91

students followed the coffin to the border of the city. In his hometown, Hanover, the funeral turned into the birth of the Extraparliamentary Opposition. It was on this occasion that most Germans first heard about an organization which had been obscure until then, but now quickly became known as the driving force in the Extraparliamentary Opposition—the SDS.

"SDS" stands in German for the Sozialistischer Deutscher Studentenbund (German Socialist Student Union), founded in Hamburg in 1946 by the Social Democratic Party, which wanted to draw socialist students closer to itself. As the party moved to the right (for the formation of the Grand Coalition), the SDS turned further left. A conflict developed, and in July 1960 the students were cut off from the party's finances. A year later, the party presidium declared simultaneous membership in the party and the SDS to be illegal. Some members withdrew and joined another Social Democratic student organization (the SHB), which also was later to move away from the parent party.

The hard core remained in SDS and carried on its work more radically than before, unhampered by regard for the party. The SDS produced several studies, on topics such as "The University in a Democracy" (1961), and participated from 1966 on, at first mainly in Berlin, in general political activities—against the war in Vietnam, against the Emergency Laws, against newspaper and magazine publisher Axel Springer, against the visit by the Shah. After Ohnesorg's death, SDS became the obvious leader in the student rebellion and for the entire Extraparliamentary Opposition, thus establishing a position similar to that of its American namesake.

Rudi Dutschke soon became the dominant figure within SDS (more about him in the following chapter). The most effective speaker in the young Left, he was soon the bogeyman of most Germans, drawing upon himself all their negative feelings about the students. On February 21, 1968, some 100,000 West Berliners staged a counterdemonstration in response to an SDS protest march three days earlier against the war in Vietnam (and thus against the United States). There were shouts of "Dutschke, get out of West Berlin"; signs like "Dutschke, Public Enemy Number One" were carried; and a passerby who looked like Dutschke was beaten up and had to be taken to the hospital.

The West Berlin populace was particularly angry over the rebellious students' lack of understanding as to the precarious situation of the divided city, whose Western portion was but an island within a hostile Communist environment, connected only by fragile lines of communication with the Federal Republic of Germany. A demonstration against Tshombe—that might be all right. But collecting money for the Algerians made the French angry and was not all right. And when students demonstrating against the Vietnam war broke windows in America House, pulled the U.S. flag to half-mast, and hoisted the banner of the Viet Cong, there were indignant headlines in the American press. The security of all West Berliners depended on the three Western powers, most of all on America, and these Berliners *lived* in the city, while the students came and went—they were not affected by the consequences of their actions once they departed. Thus the populace was horrified on learning, in the spring of 1967, that some students, led by one Fritz Teufel, were preparing an assault on U.S. Vice President Hubert H. Humphrey, who was coming to visit the city. It was not considered very funny when it turned out that the attack was only to be made with pudding and yogurt.

On the other hand, West Berliners showed little interest in problems that the left-wing students considered important. As one study found: "The experience of dangerous crises—from the Blockade to the Wall—and life in the front line of the Cold War had produced in the population an anti-Communist solidarity and a political attitude which overshadowed the social and economic problems of the city for many years. The Berliners, whose indomitable courage was admired throughout the Western world, considered internal problems to be of secondary importance."[3]

The Berliners' solidarity against the leftist students was strengthened by the suspicion that they were being infiltrated and even led by the Communists. The local trade-union leaders condemned the Vietnam demonstrations, saying that the students were really not interested in Vietnam, but in "destroying our democratic order,"[4] and even a left-wing group among the Berlin Social Democrats attacked the "small number of mini-revolutionaries and hooligans," saying: "There can be no community between the overwhelming majority of young Berliners and those who show films teaching the construction of Molotov cocktails, who smash windowpanes, disrupt church services, and give aid to the Communists whether they want it or not. [. . .] Those who demonstrate under Ho Chi Minh portraits, under the slogan 'Make two, three, Many Vietnams,' have the opposite of peace and liberty in mind."[5]

Günter Grass, living in Berlin, wrote ironically:

Wherefrom come these all-or-nothing demands, if not from the well-fertilized small gardens of German idealistic philosophy, and has not this German idealism always been a youthful extravaganza, to be followed by exhausted reclining on the conservative plush sofa? How many of the young revolutionaries are going to vote loyally and meekly for the Christian Democrats when their exaggerated expectations remain unfulfilled and they have, after leaving the university, sacrificed more and more [of their youthful idealism] in the interest of their career, which of course will not prevent them later on, in their circle of friends, as well-to-do men in their thirties, from remembering pleasantly their revolutionary past with a glass of Moselle wine. [...] An electrician twenty-four years old is vastly superior to a student of sociology of the same age, in life experience and political insight.[6]

Thus Berlin was the least suitable ground for Dutschke and the SDS. Soon they found themselves surrounded by a fence of hostility. In this atmosphere, on the Thursday before Easter, April 11, 1968, a deranged loner fired the shots that came close to killing Dutschke. The reaction to this was the wild Easter rioting that exploded in many university towns and caused two deaths in Munich.

When order was restored, public interest, especially on the Left, turned to another topic: the events in and around Paris. There was more talk about Cohn-Bendit than about Rudi Dutschke. A few weeks later came the summer vacation, then the invasion of Czechoslovakia by the Soviet Union and its allies. In France, de Gaulle seemed to be firmly back in the saddle. The news from Peking indicated the demise of the Red Guards. In October, when the universities again opened their gates, the New Left in Germany found itself in a new phase.

THE RED KALEIDOSCOPE

The events in Berlin and West Germany, from the riots during the Shah's visit in June 1967 up to the winter of 1968/69, constituted a true revolt—spontaneous, surprising, exploding simultaneously in many places, incalculable, with a leadership that seemed to have emerged overnight. But when the New Left's great effort produced no success, when the Emergency Laws were accepted by a large majority in Parliament, disappointment spread, especially now that the most powerful speaker of the movement, Dutschke, had been eliminated for a long time. The first wave of the assault had been broken, the leading role of SDS was no longer self-evident. Discussions began—What went wrong? Where do we go from here?—and grew sharper from month to month.

The New Left had risen against the society itself and its authorities—the professors, the political parties, the police, the Springer press. Some of these bastions had been breached and brought into disarray, especially the university faculties, but the Establishment was not seriously shaken. There were no more big actions to fill the imagination, and public interest waned. The newly won positions on the academic bodies absorbed the time and energy of the politically active students; the police had learned how to handle young demonstrators, and if there were incidents (occupations of institutions or deans' offices, disturbances of lectures or faculty meetings), the public reacted more calmly than it had two or three years before.

Beginning with the winter of 1968/69, many new radical groups emerged, formed alliances or fought among themselves, sometimes throve, and sometimes split or disappeared. Until that winter SDS had held the leading position among radical students; its competitors were hardly noticed. Today the German SDS no longer exists, having formally dissolved itself in March 1970, while the extreme Left organizations have become too numerous to be counted.

These organizations have several themes in common: they call themselves socialists or Communists; they seek a profound change in society, particularly through the abolition (or at least drastic restriction) of private ownership of the means of production, and they believe in the application of violence for achieving their aims. (A clear definition of what is meant by violence has proved difficult; "violence against things," which is considered necessary, can easily turn into "violence against persons," which many reject—are not policemen persons?) Thus, one of the most heatedly debated questions concerns the special role of the students in the fight against capitalism and imperialism, and thereby their relationship to labor.

Some extreme Left groups depend on Moscow for their ideology and funds; they are the largest and probably the best financed. On the campus they usually go by the name of "Spartakus." Originally Spartakus arose within SDS, as the SDS-Spartakus. When the three letters lost their appeal, Spartakus made itself independent. In the mid-seventies it claimed 110 campus groups and

4,500 members, the largest number of any of the leftist campus organizations.

Student groups calling themselves Maoist no longer possess the attraction they had in the days of the Little Red Book and the Great Proletarian Cultural Revolution. Later cultural revolutions in China did not fire imaginations abroad: who, outside China, can understand a cultural revolution against Confucius? Maoist groups constantly fight among themselves; their relationship to Peking is not clear. Some have remained antiauthoritarian; others have moved—out of disappointment with the foreign policy of Peking, particularly its rapprochement with Washington—closer to Tirana; still others follow a course that is anti-Moscow but pro-Stalin, without entirely recognizing Peking. And all of them have been thrown in disarray by the events following Mao's death—the elimination of the Chinese left wing, now branded "The Gang of Four," and the rise to power of a moderate and pragmatic leadership.

The Trotskyists—the study of them is a science in itself. As in other countries, they consist in Germany of numerous sects (in 1974 there were ten). They recognize Trotsky (as their common ancestor) but not each other.

The anarchists have, as groups, never possessed the strength in Germany they enjoyed in other Western European countries, especially in Spain. But anarchist ideas are widely spread, even though people may not be specifically aware of this. (More about anarchism in Chapter 27.)

The Sozialdemokratischer Hochschulbund (Social Democratic University Union, or SHB) has moved away from the Social Democratic Party, as the SDS once did. In 1972 it struck the term "Democratic" from its name (which still leaves it as SHB). Since then it has been moved still further leftward, cooperating with Spartakus in university politics on many campuses. It claims to have 3,000 members. The Jungsozialisten (Young Socialists) are a youth organization, not just a campus one, standing on the extreme left of the Social Democratic Party.

Finally, there are the rest, those who swear neither by Moscow nor by Peking, neither by Trotsky nor by Bakunin. A center in Offenbach which calls itself the Sozialistisches Büro (Socialist Office) tries to coordinate these and other Left groups.

In popular lingo, *Spontis* denotes any groups or individuals who act spontaneously and are unattached to larger organizations and to ideologies but are relatively closest to anarchism. The *Dogmis* are, of course, those prone to stress dogma. The term *Chaoten* ("chaosites") refers to those employing especially chaotic and erratic tactics, often to the Maoists.

A full list of left-wing groups in Germany would fill several printed pages. It would also serve little purpose, in view of the constant kaleidoscopic changes within the extreme Left.

10
RUDI DUTSCHKE

IN 1960 there appeared a book by the Harvard sociologist Daniel Bell entitled *The End of Ideology*. As a professor in West Germany, I might have formulated my impressions during the early sixties in the same or similar words. In many discussions with students I found only modest interest in questions of ideology—until the events of the early summer of 1967. After Hitler's abuse of ideology, the nation, including its youth, was tired of it. People wanted to move on with practical work, thus following, on the whole, the American pattern, though there was uneasiness over the absence of a convincing idea to give life a purpose beyond purely material achievements.

Then the unrest broke out, and the bookshops were filled with dozens, hundreds, of theoretical books and monographs, and students were buying them. Publishing houses famed primarily for their novels and poetry now offered young political authors a platform, often in the form of paperback series, and new publishers specializing in left-wing literature quickly appeared. In addition to new works, political classics, particularly those by Karl Marx were reissued and avidly read.

Talking with students and young faculty members, I soon realized that this was not just a fad copied from Berlin. It sprang from the earnest desire to find, in an uncertain, less and less comprehensible world, something more than just descriptions of events and ideas—namely, a firm ground from which to look at the world, some theory that would explain all political and social phenomena and banish all anxieties. Only gradually was it understood that there was no such theory and that there never would be one. But as the students with Germanic thoroughness divided each problem into all its possible subissues, to the point of sheer hair-splitting, they were also forming smaller and smaller groups, which became less and less intelligible to others. Soon their vocabulary was so specialized that they were increasingly isolated from the general public, and to some extent even from rival political groups—"sociological Chinese," their lingo was soon to be called. Least of all could their thoughts be followed by the workers, the very people the young rebels hoped to mobilize for the revolution.

If we try to classify the ideas common to all these groups, we think immediately of a negatively formulated expression— antiauthoritarian. It soon became a key word in the field of education, where the books of Benjamin Spock and A. S. Neill were being read and antiauthoritarian kindergartens were being founded, the first ones by students in Berlin. The aim was always the same: the formation of truly free persons. A true democracy, so it was claimed, was only possible if the individual was free of repression from his earliest youth; the child should not be influenced; even toilet training was "repression." Repression damaged not only the personality of the child but also the society of which he was to become a member, since it led to the development of an urge which was supposedly the archenemy of any kind of community—the urge for aggression.

For its philosophical and sociological foundation, the antiauthoritarian movement was indebted to the "Frankfurt School," especially to Herbert Marcuse, a professor and author with a powerful and suggestive literary style, the "apostle of rebellious youth," as he has been called. (More about him and the Frankfurt School in Chapter 26.) Some of the terms used by Marcuse were quickly accepted in the new language, such as "one-dimensional man" and "repressive tolerance" (the titles of a book and an essay) or "Great Refusal."[1] This last expression, however, was coined by a greater writer, Dante, more than six centuries ago in his *Inferno*, as *il gran rifiúto*. Marcuse proclaimed the right of oppressed minorities to use extralegal methods, once the legal ones had proved insufficient: "If they use violence, they do not start a new chain of violence, but try to break an established one."[2] For him, tolerance as we had understood it until then was "repressive," an instrument of the Establishment for manipulating the ordinary people.

The very term "manipulation" spread far beyond the circle of sociologists. It meant those methods of power which, employing the subtle means of persuasion and publicity, were said to be just as dangerous for the free development of the personality as was violence. The aim was a society without hierarchy.

In Germany during the sixties, Rudi Dutschke was not only the best-known but also the most consistent leader of the antiauthoritarian movement. The youngest of four children of a Lutheran family in Luckenwalde, East Germany (the father, a peasant's son, had a job in the postal service), Dutschke moved in 1961 to West Berlin after hearing rumors that the G.D.R. (German Democratic Republic, i.e., East Germany) might be closed off. He reached West Berlin shortly before the building of the Wall and enrolled at the Free University, with sociology as his major and theology as one of his minors.

Dutschke found friends mainly in the circles of the *Abhauer* (a slang expression for people who had escaped from the G.D.R.). In those years the *Abhauer* constituted a considerable portion of the Free University student body, and most of them were anti-Stalinists.

ANTIAUTHORITARIAN IN ALL DIRECTIONS
Dutschke and his friends considered themselves antiauthoritarian socialists. They were against the type of socialism practiced in the Soviet Union and the G.D.R., where the economy was not in the hands of society, of the people, but in those of a bureaucratic state. They advocated transfer of the property and administration of all enterprises to the workers concerned. Not finding any inclination for such changes within the Social Democratic Party, they abandoned their original plan of joining it. Some fifteen of them founded a group which they called Direct Action; they had contacts with some "situationists" in Munich who were connected with a movement which at that time was quite influential in France.[3] Soon the Berlin group was attracted to Marcuse's criticism of the Soviet system. They studied his *Soviet Marxism* in English (it was not published in German until 1964). At about that time, Dutschke's group made contact with the Berlin SDS, whose leaders were graduating from the university, and was able to gain control of this most important branch of SDS in Germany.

Dutschke's "antiauthoritarian" attack on the university, the administration, and the Berlin Establishment annoyed many people; he became, as we have seen, a much hated man. However, unlike many antiauthoritarians in the West, Dutschke was consistent in fighting not only what he called the authoritarian structure of West Berlin and of the Federal Republic but authoritarianism of any kind, at any place, including the East, whether in Moscow, East Berlin, or Prague. Even after the attempt on his life there was no problem to which he paid so much attention as that of authoritarianism in the states that called themselves socialist. He came early to the conclusion that Lenin himself had believed the laboring class to be unable to make a revolution, and had decided, therefore, that the workers had to be "organized and revolutionized by someone else, namely, Lenin's party."[4]

This was also the central theme of Dutschke's doctoral dissertation (eventually published in book form in 1974), which he characteristically entitled *Attempt to Put Lenin on His Feet: Concerning the Half-Asian and the Western European Road to Socialism.* How did it happen, Dutschke asked, that Lenin did not prevent his country from moving toward bureaucratization, that he did not know "how to handle the bureaucracy problem," that he "fought bureaucratism only abstractly and in general," that he permitted the machinery of the government and the Party to end up in a swamp which "stinks to high heaven"?

Dutschke's answer: "It was crucial [for Russia] that the democratic aspects in the structure of party, state, and production, and in the relationship with national minorities, were continually and lastingly undermined." This all happened because Lenin had no confidence in the workers, nor even in the majority of the Party members: "Not for a moment can Lenin be absolved [. . .] of this fundamental mistake."

And this was not all—Marx himself had turned in the wrong direction. From Marx, Dutschke thinks, came Lenin's overemphasis on leadership and direction from above. Further:

> Marx, in spite of his criticism of the political economy of capitalism, remained a captive of the categories of capitalism. [. . .] The Socialist movement thus repeats important aspects of the capitalist division of labor. [. . .] This much is certain: the true history of the Soviet Union (and later of the countries of the Warsaw Pact) is more a "socialist development of capitalism" than the realization of the new quality of liberty.

For this Dutschke blames the existence of the state, which enhances the power of men over men. "A person who lives in a state

101

of our day is on the road to becoming a half-person." The only choice facing mankind is "socialism with concrete freedom, or modernized barbarism—this is again the issue."[5]

Nor can Dutschke get away from this problem in his latest publication, an anthology called *The Soviet Union, Solzhenitsyn and the Western Left,* which he coedited and to which he contributed an essay with the rather convoluted title: "Communism, Its Despotic Alienation in the U.S.S.R. and the Road to the Workers' Rebellion in the G.D.R. on June 17, 1953." He and his coeditor are trying to "return a human face to socialism"; they are determined to "support in the Eastern bloc [i.e., in the Communist countries] the 'tendency toward democratization' which appears weakly from time to time, and to do this in spite of all hindrances and difficulties." He calls Communism in the bloc "despotic," and he demands no longer "two, three Vietnams," but rather "two, three Prague Springs."[6]

All this is being said and written by Dutschke and his friends not because he is against communism per se but because he is, on the contrary, a convinced communist who suffers deeply because the despotic Soviet state has discredited communist ideals throughout the world, depriving them of all attraction. Incidentally, Dutschke does not think Chinese Communism is a useful alternative; he searches for communism in its pure form.

In West Germany the majority of the antiauthoritarians are still inclined to prefer the Soviet Union to the United States because, they say, the U.S.S.R. made a big step on the road to socialism when it abolished private property in the means of production; they let it go at that. Dutschke, on the other hand, feels profoundly disappointed because Lenin and his successors have handed over this property not to the workers but to the most gigantic bureaucracy in the world, which shows no signs of yielding its power.

Although the antiauthoritarian drive of the sixties has evaporated, and many former antiauthoritarians are seeking shelter under the wings of the authoritarian Spartakus or in the Communist Party, Dutschke persists in his ideal, which he defends against all authoritarians in East and West, on the Right and on the Left.

Dutschke knows, of course, that it is much easier to unmask Brezhnev and Franco as authoritarians than to offer to the world the blueprint of a nonauthoritarian, repression-free future. What he hopes for is a communism of liberated people who freely decide about their own lives and about society, who are, in other words, not pushed around as they are in the Eastern bloc; only with such people would it be possible to build a humanistic communism. In his earliest publication he put this thought into these words: "Politics without the inner change of those involved is [nothing but] manipulation [of the people] by elites."[7] At that time, he still had hopes for the soviets ("councils") which had sprung up spontaneously as labor representations in many Russian factories in 1905 and 1917, only to be emasculated by Lenin and turned into a mere facade, called the Soviet state, behind which the Party (and not the soviets) exercised dictatorship. Today he is more skeptical. In our conversation he said that the soviets were "fascinating, but not a program." I asked about the labor councils in Yugoslavia. His voice sounded doubtful; they were an interesting experiment, but hardly a model.

That conversation showed Dutschke's full awareness of the dilemma of all political movements: If they remain spontaneous, they disintegrate; if they build up a disciplined organization, they lose the character of a movement, become inflexible and bureaucratic. The German SDS collapsed late in 1968, and the American SDS less than a year later; neither had been able, he found, to resolve this dilemma.

What then did he want—a New Left organization? Perhaps someday, he answered; the time had not come yet; we were still in a phase of stagnation which had to be replaced by a phase of movement, in the Federal Republic as well as in the G.D.R. (Dutschke still thinks in terms of Germany's reunification— under socialist banners, of course.) He showed much interest in China, hoping that, after Mao, it would not follow the authoritarian example of the Soviet Union.

Dutschke is not identical with the German Left. But his name has not lost its attraction during his years of recovery and silence. Within the Red kaleidoscope he is still the most important figure. That he has remained antiauthoritarian, many may dislike; that he is consistent about it, toward West and East, must be recognized.

11
STUDENT AND WORKER

EVER since Karl Marx declared the working class to be the vanguard of humanity on the march into a brighter future, political parties that call themselves Communist or Socialist have sought to include—and show off—workers in their ranks, especially if they claim to speak for the mass of the working people. They may be followers of Marx, Bakunin, Lenin, Mao, or—for that matter—Mussolini and Hitler; they want to have, or anyway to claim, the support of the workers.

Yet their leaders have rarely been workers themselves. Marx, the son of a lawyer, was a journalist and writer; his friend Engels was both the son of and himself a factory owner. Bakunin came from the Russian landed nobility, Lenin from a family ennobled on account of the father's position in the official hierarchy. Mussolini and Hitler were of the petty bourgeoisie. Mao, the son of a peasant, was a teacher by profession. None of them ever worked in a factory. (Castro, a lawyer, and Guevara, a physician, started cutting sugarcane after they came to power, but only in order to give prestige, by their occasional example, to the workers in the fields.)

Lenin, Mao, and Castro, at their advent to power, had fewer workers in the ranks of their parties than Hitler had among his National Socialists, and, in any case, many party members who were called workers in the official statistics (because perhaps in youth they were employed in a factory) had long been party functionaries, apparatchiks.

Of the New Left it can be said: the more radically a "workers party" behaves, the fewer will be the workers who join it. This fact, which at first sight seems paradoxical, has been explained convincingly by Herbert Marcuse. He describes the Western world of today as a society without opposition, "capable of containing social change." This, "perhaps the most singular achievement of advanced industrial society," appears "to reconcile the forces opposing the system," partly with the help of a "collusion of business and labor within the strong state." Marcuse continues: "Under the conditions of a rising standard of living, nonconformity with the system itself appears to be socially useless, and the more so when it entails tangible economic and political disadvantages and threatens the smooth operation of the whole." This means that the consumer society, by offering the worker every year more and more, is pulling him away from the revolution which could not be accomplished without such "disadvantages." Marcuse finds "an overriding interest in the preservation and improvement of the institutional status quo [which] unites the former antagonists in the most advanced areas of contemporary society," business and labor, and prevents any radical change.[1]

When Marcuse wrote these words early in the sixties, the American campus was still quiet. He therefore put his revolutionary hope—in an oft-quoted passage of his *One-Dimensional Man*—on the "outcasts and outsiders," since these were not integrated beneficiaries of the consumer society. They—and they alone—might perhaps someday turn to revolutionary action by "refusing to play the game."[2] Later, when the rebellious Berlin students in their fight against a vastly superior state machine were looking for a suitable ideology, they discovered, largely through Marcuse, the necessity of mobilizing the "outcasts and outsiders" and withdrawing from society themselves—thus making the Great Refusal. It was mainly because the students claimed a special role for themselves as bearers of the revolution that Moscow's ideologists jumped on Marcuse and his "werewolves"—the radical students.

These students, of course, were by no means "without hope" (as Marcuse had declared in one of the book's last sentences); they did hope to awaken the consciousness of a proletariat corrupted by consumer society, to unmask the delusion of the "common interests" of capital and labor, and thus to help a correct consciousness to emerge, built on the true interests of the workers. But this hope was unrealistic, even though not many were quite as caught up in the myth of the worker as that Japanese student who exclaimed: "I was looking for a lover. And, then I found him. The worker is my lover."[3]

Disappointment was inevitable. The workers did not show any interest in the alliance offered to them—not even during the struggle against the Emergency Laws in 1968, which the students had expected would lead to common actions with the workers in a powerful attack against the government of the Grand Coalition. During those days, a meeting was held at my school in Aachen, to which the SDS invited the local trade-union leaders. These did come, did attack the Emergency Laws, and did praise the students' courageous zeal—but they kept their distance. A request that the trade-union leaders admit SDS speakers and leaflet distributors into the factories was coolly declined. And that was that. It was not only the trade-union leaders who steered clear of the New Left. There was practically no fraternization between students and workers. When leftist agitators in the autumn of 1973 arrived in buses at the gates of the Ford factory in Cologne to promote an ongoing strike, one of the labor representatives sarcastically said, "These *Chaoten* are like eunuchs; they know what they want, but they don't know how to do it."[4]

The New Left met with similar disappointments in other countries—in France during the "Paris May" of 1968, and in the United States the following year, when SDS students went to the aid of striking Standard Oil workers in California, only to find themselves treated as expendable as soon as higher wages were achieved.[5]

There had been true fraternization between students and workers, even sealed by blood—but that was in Communist countries, Hungary in 1956, Czechoslovakia in 1968, and not in a left-wing movement. In the West the workers distrusted the radical students. To quote Marcuse: "The prevalence of a non-revolutionary—nay, *antirevolutionary*—*consciousness among the majority of the working class* [was] conspicuous."[6] [Emphasis supplied.]

Small wonder that no other topic has agitated the rebelling students, and still continues to do so, more than the relationship between themselves (and intellectuals in general) and the workers. Many attempts have been made to determine the sociological position of the students. Are they a social stratum of their own? Yes, say some; others, no; and still others, "an intermediate stratum." What is their relationship toward production? Science being a productive force, all those connected with it are productive and thus related to the workers, say some. Others declare students simply to be workers like all the rest who are exploited. Still others distinguish between productive and ideological sciences, bracketing only the productive ones with the workers and begging the question as to why the ideologically minded (thus, less productive) and frequently most privileged students are more revolutionary than the proletarians upon whom Marx bestowed a monopoly of the revolutionary potential.

In view of such varied definitions of who the students are (sociologically speaking), it does not come as a surprise that there are many suggestions for correct behavior in the student Left. The students should get jobs in the factories in order to form action groups with the workers. They should not go into the factories, but rather radicalize the university and the content of courses, so as to be able, in their professions (as teachers, lawyers, journalists), to revolutionize others. They should influence the workers on the basis of their superior knowledge of Marxism, as specialists in ideology. No, they should not do this, for it would mean that the workers were being manipulated by petty bourgeois youth.

Students were, some claimed, bearers of the revolution on a basis of equality with the workers. No, they were not, since only the proletariat could play this role; the students were simply a recruitment depot out of which the large labor organizations might draw their cadres. They should prepare themselves for their future professions in order later to help demolish the existing system from within. No, they should do this under no circumstances, because they would—like the mass of the workers—thereby be absorbed and integrated by the system. They should work politically in small and independent groups. No, no, on the contrary, only "in the service and under the leadership of the party."[7]

The lack of certainty on the part of the New Left in understanding and judging the workers and its relationship to them stems from the contradictory notions of its most influential mentors. Marx assumed that the proletariat, growing in numbers, determination, and insight, would someday take power; Lenin believed in the power but not in the insight of the proletariat, for which reason he built a party of professional—largely intellectual—revolutionaries to lead it; Marcuse finally completely wrote off the proletariat as a revolutionary power because he believed it to be totally integrated in the consumer society, and put his hope on the Third World as well as on the intellectuals, especially the young ones, the students; and Mao came to power with the help of the peasants, not the workers.

In this jungle it is difficult to find a simple path, and so the discussion continues. One leftist author in Germany states that workers "rarely join organizations dominated by intellectuals," that they "feel themselves to be strangers there and soon drop out."[8]

WORKERS DON'T WANT EVERYTHING "KAPUT"

One young author, Michael Schneider, born in 1943, has described the problem most graphically and from his own experience. After graduating in philosophy and sociology, he worked as journalist, editorial assistant, and theatrical producer, and later went into a Berlin factory as a worker in order to "nurture workers' avant-garde groups and build a Communist Party organization tied to the [workers'] base." It is worthwhile listening to him:

> I considered it my duty to work for "true political consciousness." As a result, I constantly admonished the young workers, who, from the standpoint of the "pure doctrine" [i.e., Leninism] committed one political sin after the other. . . . They soon ceased asking me any political questions at all. They were simply annoyed that a student and fair-weather worker "always knew everything better than they."

Quite a few students who went into the factories behaved as if they were martyrs for the entire working class. According to Schneider, "This masochism of the Left petty-bourgeois intellectuals, which banishes all humor from political work, is but the reaction to their suppressed class arrogance." He deplores the "often unproductive, sectarian struggle against the many, many contradictions among the comrades, which was usually carried out with such doggedness as if it was a question of the life and death of millions." He is convinced that the constant "destroy" slogans (destroy the state, destroy the hierarchies) create among the workers "nothing but anxiety and instinctive resistance," because most of them fear becoming themselves victims of such destruction. One young worker told him: "Shut up, all you want is to make everything kaput!"

Schneider became especially skeptical about the methods em-

ployed by him and other students for the purpose of schooling the
workers:

> After they had been disciplined and "organized" by the manage-
> ment in the factory day after day for eight hours, only to be disci-
> plined and organized after work by some Left intellectuals—this
> necessarily gave them the feeling that they had gone from the
> frying pan into the fire. . . . In both cases they had the feeling that
> they had to accomplish something: in the factory, a material ac-
> complishment in pieces of work produced; in the study sessions, an
> intellectual accomplishment in the number of chapters read in
> leftist texts. In neither did they ever get the pleasant feeling of
> having really accomplished something. In the factories, the en-
> gineers, foremen, and technicians knew everything better. In the
> evenings there were the Marxist-Leninist masters, the *polit*-
> specialists, and the party engineers who demanded of them ad-
> justment to the compulsory thinking and brooding of the Left intel-
> ligentsia.

In the Federal Republic, Schneider continues, there were "half a
dozen Communist organizations which all claimed they had the
'correct proletarian line,' while no proletarian masses who
showed the least interest in these 'lines' were anywhere to be
seen."

He does not think that the Soviet Union could be a model. The
time when solidarity with the U.S.S.R. was demanded at any
price has, he finds, "passed forever." There was no longer any
necessity to side with the Soviet Union unconditionally, the "less
so as the Communist Party of the U.S.S.R. had for decades sacrificed the revolutionary interests of the European proletariat to
the interests of the U.S.S.R.," and had hindered the left-wing
movements instead of aiding them. Leninism was an "old-age
disease."[9]

This criticism of the political work of students among workers
is expressed also by other authors. A professor at Frankfurt University: "If students tell the workers they should take this or that
consciousness as being in their true interest, then this continues
the old class division in new guise."[10] Finally, a judgment from
the other end of the world. Héctor Béjar, once the leader of the
extreme-left National Liberation Army in Peru, wrote in 1965:
"Discipline, warm affection, and modesty are not always characteristics of young students and politicians; the self-centeredness
of intellectuals repulses simple people."[11]

12
ENTER THE THIRD WORLD

"ON December 18, 1964, the Third World came alive for the first time in West Berlin," Rudi Dutschke stated a few years later. On that day the then prime minister of the Democratic Republic of the Congo, Moise Tshombe, visited Berlin. Shortly before, a student group, including some students from the Third World, had heard a lecture about Frantz Fanon, the revolutionary black author. Now a crowd of them shouted slogans against the "murderer of Lumumba" and plastered Tshombe's automobile with tomatoes. Compared with later events, this one was rather harmless, but it was the beginning. It was, Dutschke said, "the start of our cultural revolution." Thus the German student revolt was linked early to the Third World.

Once the Third World had captured their attention, the SDS and its supporters saw the Vietnam war through different eyes, and some began to study it more thoroughly. The winter of 1965/66 was declared by the SDS of West Berlin "a semester of enlightenment on Vietnam." During the night preceding February 4, 1966, posters were pasted up, ending with the words: "How much longer will we allow murder to be committed in our name? Amis out of Vietnam!" ("Ami" is the—not unfriendly—colloquial German abbreviation for "American.") The following day, eggs were thrown at America House and its flag was lowered. When the Free University's president apologized to the U.S. city commandant, SDS was outraged: the president was behaving as if West Berlin were being defended in Vietnam, while in reality "by their excessive zeal in Vietnam the Americans had lost any moral justification for speaking of defending liberties anywhere in the world." From then on, according to Dutschke, "an increasing erosion of the authority of the official and established institutions of our society" became noticeable among the students. On February 13 he declared: "The fight of the Viet Cong or of the MIR in Peru is our fight."[1]

At about that time, Che Guevara's writings and actions captured the interest of the Berlin students. Was his thesis correct, they asked, that the revolution did not have to wait for "objective conditions," that it could be unleashed by the individual actions of determined revolutionaries? The excitement grew. It led to the demonstrations against Hubert H. Humphrey on April 6, 1967, and culminated during the Shah's visit a few weeks later.

The Persian Bahman Nirumand contributed to the hostile attitude toward the Shah by publishing a paperback book about his country in March (40,000 copies were sold by June) and by his speech at the Free University on the eve of the Shah's arrival. The death of Benno Ohnesorg on June 2, 1967, linked the student revolt still more with the problems of the Third World.

In June, an article very critical of the Left intellectuals in Germany was published in the left-leaning *Kursbuch*, signed "A. A." This was, the editors said in the following issue, a pseudonym for Nirumand. The Persian author found fault with the Federal Republic because "the revolutionary utopia was drowned out by social care" (meaning that social services had developed to the point that people no longer were interested in making revolution—the old Marcuse idea) and the intellectuals had become "accomplices of oppression." He urged them to use "the only adequate method: violence."[2]

In June a year later, *Kursbuch* again published an article by Nirumand. Looking back with satisfaction on a year of violent student unrest in the Federal Republic, he expressed his conviction that, without the shock of Ohnesorg's death, the ideas of the New Left would have been "absorbed by the pluralism of opinions." Now he demanded that the German students form guerrilla groups which would "turn their struggle into a general people's war."[3]

In 1967–1968 Nirumand was considered an authority among the radical German students; he traveled, lectured, published. This was—quite irrespective of the content of his statements—an interesting symptom of the international character of student unrest at that time. Had not the Paris students in May 1968 accepted a German citizen, Daniel Cohn-Bendit, as their spokesman? And had they not answered his French enemies, who attacked him as a German Jew, with "We are all German Jews," thus showing that for them nationality and race had become irrelevant? Had not Nirumand said "we" when speaking of himself and the left-wing German students? (Demonstrations against the Shah and his regime took place later on in other countries, always triggered by Persian students; in 1975 I witnessed them on the Columbia campus in New York and at the Iranian consulate-general in San Francisco; but they were less violent and did not have the serious consequences of those in West Berlin.)

By far the strongest influence on the many young people who were criticizing their own and Western society in general was the Vietnam war. In April 1968 there was a "World Day" against it. In Copenhagen 18,000 demonstrated, and even 800 in Prague. In Rome, 3,000 students fought the police; in Tokyo, 1,800 attacked—without success—the U.S. embassy, and even in Tel Aviv the police had to defend the embassy.

As a result of the Shah's visit and the Vietnam war, the Third World had become part of the German student unrest and, at times, a main preoccupation, while in the fifties and early sixties those countries had been seen by the idealists among the young only as objects of Western economic aid or of Peace Corps activities.

Lenin, at the Congress of the Toilers of the East (Baku, September 1920), had urged the colonies to fight for their liberation in order thus to weaken the capitalist colonial powers, and Marcuse had declared the Third World to be an ersatz proletariat, and hence the bearer of the revolution. In addition, a colored son of the Third World had stirred a passionate interest in its problems among the New Left. Frantz Fanon, born in Martinique in 1925, was in Algeria after 1953, first as chief physician of a psychiatric clinic, then as supporter of the anti-French National Liberation Front, and died in 1961 (of leukemia) on the same day that his most important book, *The Wretched of the Earth,* was published in Paris. (In 1964, Fanon's stirring theories triggered the Berlin demonstrations against Tshombe, as we have seen; at that time the book had not yet appeared in German, but ideas were traveling fast.)

Fanon's book, which urges the colored people to rise against the white race, is best known for its preface, written by Jean-Paul Sartre. It was largely to the great name of the French writer and

112

philosopher, and to the dramatic concentration of the book's contents in his preface, that Fanon owed his initial success in the Western world. Fanon's three messages: Europe has committed immeasurable crimes against the colored nations; Europe is finished; the colored world can find itself only through violence against the white.

> Leave this Europe where they are never done talking of Man, yet murder men everywhere they find them, at the corner of every one of their own streets, in all the corners of the globe. For centuries they have stifled almost the whole of humanity in the name of a so-called spiritual experience. Look at them today swaying between atomic and spiritual disintegration.[4]

It was this book that brought France's Algerian war (already ended in 1962) to the attention of young Germans; there many of them read for the first time about the atrocities, the tortures, committed by white Frenchmen in Algeria. And this knowledge made them look at Vietnam too with the eyes of Fanon. What they learned about Vietnam increased, according to Dutschke, "the existential loathing against a society which babbles about liberty and yet suppresses subtly and brutally the immediate interests and desires of individuals, and of entire nations fighting for their social and economic emancipation."[5]

ICONS FROM OVERSEAS

The longer the war lasted in Southeast Asia, and the more brutal it became, the higher rose the leader of North Vietnam in the estimation of the New Left as the symbol of anti-imperialism. Ho Chi Minh's portraits floated like icons above the heads of the demonstrators; his name furnished a battle cry, which one could chant impressively: "Ho-Ho-Ho Chi Minh." Che Guevara's features, to be sure, were much more romantic, and he is to this day the object of idol worship; his death in Bolivia in 1967, although the conclusion of a fiasco, added the halo of the martyr. But he was now a legend, while the war in the jungles of Indochina was real and the man from Hanoi was in the daily headlines.

Mao, however, was and remained "the greatest"; hundreds of thousands bought, and thousands waved, the Little Red Book. Yet there was (and still is) one great difficulty: All the left-wing radicals, whatever their sect, could more or less agree on Marx and Lenin, on Guevara, Fanon, and even Ho Chi Minh, but not on

Mao. Since the early sixties, whoever praised Mao made Moscow, and all the pro-Moscow parties, mad and thus contributed to the infighting among the world's leftists.

To the older generation, of course, it remained strange that young Germans marched in the name of men (that of a woman, Angela Davis, was added) who did not belong to the European cultural tradition in the proper sense of the word. Especially strange that they marched under alien flags. Many of the young reached the point where, strictly antinationalist at home, they behaved as if they were burning nationalists of Cuba or Vietnam. And not only did they display the flags of North Vietnam and the Viet Cong; they ended their speeches with Castro's battle cry in Spanish: "Venceremos." One of the German SDS leaders said frankly that many young radicals identified themselves with Third World revolutionaries because they expected from them "the impulse for the overthrow of their own society," and felt themselves to be "the agents of the wars of liberation in the metropole" (i.e., in Europe and the United States).[6] In Marcuse fashion, a young American leftist called the international proletariat of the Third World the true proletariat of American capitalism.[7] Thus, the Third World gave to the New Left not only an ersatz proletariat but also an ersatz nationalism.[8]

Even when, with the departure of American troops, the issue of Vietnam began to lose its explosive power, foreign issues were taken up surprisingly often—Portuguese colonial rule, Rhodesia, South Africa, the death of Allende and the military dictatorship in Chile, the executions in Franco's Spain. At the large meeting in Offenbach (October 1975) to protest Franco's rule, the language of some of the slogans displayed was ... Basque! The Basques under Franco had, in a way, become part of the Third World.

Once I asked Dutschke why the SDS had jumped on problems that were far away from West Berlin and the Federal Republic, instead of fighting for issues closer to home. He explained that this was due to his and his *Abhauer* friends' disgust over the contradiction between America's claim as "guarantor of Berlin's freedom" and it role as the enemy of freedom in the Third World. They were attacking American imperialism as the stronghold of reaction throughout the world. Here one student activist could hope to have some effect. In the Eastern bloc such chances did not exist; but as time went on, he explained, SDS was thinking of moving its emphasis from the Third World to concrete German

114

problems. Before this could be accomplished, however, SDS collapsed.

It says a lot about the relatively high degree of social justice in West Germany that the rebelling students felt it necessary to challenge their government by means of issues imported largely from abroad.

13
THE GERMAN TERRORISTS

TERRORISM in its present form came to Germany relatively late, for a good reason: there was no tradition of it. The Germans killed—mostly—on orders; those who gave the order, they felt, ought to know why. They had learned from Clausewitz that war was a possible continuation of politics by other means, but—with few exceptions—they did not look at murder and assassination in that way, unlike the Western European anarchists and Russian social revolutionaries, who did. The assassinations of two leading politicians of the Weimar period were considered isolated and atypical, and the vast majority of Germans would then have believed impossible the murders which Hitler was to order later in millions of cases.

Now Hitlerism was dead, the dreadful specter was gone and almost forgotten; thus the people were completely surprised and profoundly disturbed when, in the midst of order and prosperity, some young Germans turned to violence and their leaders openly confessed to it. A pastor's daughter, Gudrun Ensslin, helped start a fire in a department store, coolly accepting the possibility that people might get hurt. "A burning department store with burning people," she wrote in her notebook, "would furnish the true Vietnam feeling."[1] One leftist, brought to trial, exclaimed in the courtroom to the judges: "With hirelings of the capitalists one does not speak, one shoots them." And the pacifist Ulrike Meinhof, a mother of two children, affirmed: "Of course, one may shoot."

It all began with that arson in the Frankfurt department store on April 2, 1968. Many other acts of terrorism have been committed since then. To mention but a few: In May 1972 there was the bombing of an American military installation at Heidelberg, in which four U.S. soldiers were killed. There was the kidnapping of the leader of the Opposition in West Berlin's assembly in 1975, and shortly afterward, the terrorist attack on the German Embassy in Stockholm (see below). Apart from Ulrike Meinhof, who was in her forties, almost all those involved were young and, except for Andreas Baader, students and intellectuals. Among the Stockholm terrorists, two were students, a third was the son of a millionaire, and another the son of a writer. In court, the terrorists carried out their defense offensively, supported by their lawyers; they considered it a continuation of their underground struggle. They spoke about political motives and aims only, treating their criminal methods as irrelevant.

We know most about Ulrike Meinhof, largely because of the indiscretions of her divorced husband, Klaus Rainer Röhl, who in his autobiography and in a novel has told all he knows about her; we also have the columns she published for more than ten years in the Hamburg review *konkret*. Ulrike Meinhof was born in 1934 in Jena, in what is now East Germany. Her ancestors included several pastors. Her parents were art historians and also were religious; during the Hitler period they belonged to an oppositional branch of the Protestant church. The mother died after a brief but stormy extramarital love affair which was harshly condemned by all her relatives and which she deeply regretted; then the father died of cancer. At fourteen, Ulrike was taken in by a friend of her mother, Mrs. Renate Riemeck. The influence of this woman—a professor of education, cofounder of a short-lived pacifist party, and a deeply religious Protestant—strengthened the moral and religious impulses already instilled during Ulrike's childhood.

While studying German literature and language at the universities of Marburg and Münster, Ulrike was drawn into a first (and relatively mild) experience of political excitement. This was the campaign against atomic weapons in the years 1958 and 1959, more or less patterned after the British Easter marches. (Germany neither had nor has atomic weapons.) There she met Klaus Rainer Röhl, the editor of the left-wing, sex-oriented student paper *konkret*, for which she began to write a widely read column. By the end of 1961 they were married. Röhl had been a member of the illegal Communist Party since 1956 (he left it in 1964); soon

117

she also joined—a religiously inclined left-wing intellectual much concerned with social problems.

Two events proved crucial for Ulrike Meinhof, as for so many others. The formation of the Grand Coalition government toward the end of 1966 caused her to have doubts about the Social Democratic Party, which previously she had supported. Then the death of Benno Ohnesorg in June 1967 "blew out some fuses also with Ulrike."[2]

She moves further to the Left. The word "revolution" begins to appear in her vocabulary. She wants to "cut off the road that might lead from a bad conscience to resignation."[3] When she hears about the department store arson, she travels to Frankfurt and attends the trial of the two accused, Andreas Baader and Gudrun Ensslin, whom she meets for the first time. Her feelings are still ambivalent: she finds an element of progress in their lawbreaking, but she does not want to "recommend" it as a model.[4] And the example of the two arsonists makes her question her secure middle-class existence, her social life in Hamburg. All along she had felt a discrepancy between this kind of life and the topics of her columns, such as neglected children or the squalid housing of Turks working in German factories. This discrepancy begins to "tear her to pieces."[5]

The following year she separates from her husband, who she feels, had edited *konkret* with too much regard for commercial considerations (peppering it with pornography), and she now lives "as if without a compass."[6] After their divorce she moves with her two children to Berlin and witnesses there the decline of the student movement. She is shaken by the attempt on Dutschke's life and deeply disappointed by the failure of the Paris students and of the fight against the Emergency Laws in Germany. When the Soviet armies overrun Czechoslovakia in August 1968, she loses her last possible political alternative, belief in Soviet Communism.

IN THE UNDERGROUND

In her "defiant hopelessness" (a term used by Mrs. Riemeck), Ulrike Meinhof decides to act on her own, rather than to debate and write. She is one of those people who believe that the world must be as they want it to be—or must not be at all. Again she meets Gudrun Ensslin and Andreas Baader, along with other people who are awaiting a signal for violence. When Baader is caught after violating parole, she visits him in jail and declares herself ready to help him escape. In May 1970, Baader receives permission to spend a day, accompanied by a guard, at an institute for social problems in Berlin—supposedly to collect material for a book that he and Ulrike Meinhof are to write together. There the two of them engineer his escape; during the shoot-out an employee of the institute is seriously wounded.

Ulrike Meinhof goes underground with Baader and joins the Red Army Fraction, a group that considers itself an urban guerrilla band of the Latin American type. She even publishes a small textbook on guerrilla warfare—of course, anonymously (Berlin 1971). For quite a while the search for her goes on without success; time and again she is hidden by left-liberal friends from former days, usually of the intelligentsia.

When she tries to find a place for the night with a young teacher, Fritz Rodewald, he reports her to the police. He belongs to the Left (he too is one of those who were radicalized by the death of Benno Ohnesorg), but he does not want to have anything to do with those who accept murder and terrorism, for he is convinced that "these people have furnished the Right wing with the arguments to defame the entire Left."[7] On June 15, 1972, Ulrike Meinhof is arrested and jailed. In her luggage, still in the teacher's apartment, the police find bombs, pistols, homemade hand grenades.

The road traveled by Ulrike Meinhof from a religious pacifist who fought German rearmament to a most-wanted terrorist deserves our interest beyond her personal fate. We will never know exactly what it was that caused her to change. But the strongest factor might be the moral rigidity which she was taught at home and by Mrs. Riemeck. Measured against such notions, the Federal Republic with its burgeoning prosperity and its materialistic values did not appeal to her. She did not want to come to terms with it. All the political forces on which she placed her hopes for the breakthrough into a better future had disappointed her—the Social Democratic Party, the New Left, the Soviet Union. Because she refused to resign herself to the status quo, she felt obliged to do her part in order that Andreas Baader, the leader, could do his work. After Baader's escape, accomplished in terrorist fashion, it seemed necessary to continue to "hit in exemplary fashion" and thus to "give signals." Otherwise, all their actions would be "like robbing banks without any political background."[8]

But there was no response. The "masses" did not rise. The terrorists suffered losses: some were killed in shoot-outs, while others made their peace with the powers that be, and even gave evidence against their confederates. One, still underground, issued a statement saying: "Friends, throw away your shooting-irons!"

But for Ulrike Meinhof the point of no return had been passed. She remained with the hard core of the Red Army Fraction, which came to be known as the Baader-Meinhof gang.

Neither was there any turning back for Gudrun Ensslin. Born in 1940, the daughter of a Black Forest pastor, she too had been a good student, and like Ulrike Meinhof had held a prestigious scholarship—even from the same foundation. She too had been radicalized in the conflict between her religious idealism and the surrounding reality. She too wanted, in the words of a Frankfurt psychiatrist after the department store arson, "to put into reality what she had learned in a parson's house."[9] She too looked for a man of action and thought she had found him in Andreas Baader; she attached her life to his. It was probably she who persuaded Ulrike Meinhof to participate in the freeing of Baader. She too went to prison: two weeks after Baader's arrest in June 1972, she was recognized while shopping in a Hamburg boutique; one of the shop girls saw a pistol in her coat, laid down during a fitting.

The number of women among the terrorists is remarkable. It reminds one of the Russian terrorists of the nineteenth century. Of the twenty-two activists in the hard core of the Red Army Fraction, twelve were women. One of them, "Red Ilse," had a man of the group, who supposedly had turned traitor, shot by her friends. These cases, and many others, seemed to be symptoms of the political mobilization of the younger generation of women.

We know about Jan-Carl Raspe mainly from his self-analysis in the book written by members of the Berlin Commune 2. His father, who had owned a factory, died in 1944 just before the birth of his son, who then grew up in an East Berlin household full of women (mother, two sisters, two aunts). In 1961, while attending a school in West Berlin, he was separated from his mother by the Wall; an uncle in West Berlin took him in, and he studied at the Free University. In 1967 he was galvanized by the dramatic events during the Shah's visit. In the same year, the lonely boy joined the SDS and Commune 2, which was like a "tender cave," some kind of "mother's womb." He loved children and participated in the formation of the first antiauthoritarian kindergarten, but left the commune after two years. He was not the only one to be disappointed by its failure. In the commune book, we read that "practically nothing was left to do but flee—separate from the commune or *plunge into an anesthetizing actionalism"* [Emphasis supplied].[10] For Raspe these two possibilities were not an either/or. He left the commune *and* plunged into anesthetizing actionalism. The latter he found with Baader, whom he joined in 1970.

Baader himself, though intellectually the least interesting, was the unquestioned leader of the group. He was born in Munich in 1943. His father, a Ph.D. and archivist, is still listed as missing in action on the Eastern Front. The boy grew up in a household where women always looked after him (mother, grandmother, aunt). Later, in Berlin, a painter became his mistress, bearing him a son in 1965. In 1968 he left her, having met Gudrun Ensslin. Together the two took the terrorist road. His energy, not hemmed in by any scruples, seems to have fascinated people. One girl who later left the group explained: "One stumbles around as a student idiot without any knowledge of practical life, has never done anything with one's hands, then a man like this sweeps you away—as it happened to Ulrike. . . . To her you have only to say that acting is more important than scribbling—that's enough for her."[11]

Baader had gradually become the commander in the fight against the Establishment. Among the actions that have been charged to him and his group, the last ones, in May 1972, were the bloodiest: the bombing of the U.S. military installation in Heidelberg (four dead), an attempt on the life of a federal judge (whose wife was severely wounded), and an attack on the Springer publishing house in Hamburg (seventeen employees wounded). In court, Baader was able to quote a line from Marcuse, but otherwise he left ideology to others; his best-known contribution to political thought is this: "A criminal action is per se a political action."[12]

We know least about Holger Klaus Meins. Son of a well-to-do Hamburg merchant, he studied at the Film and TV Academy in Berlin, dropped out, and joined Baader. Arrested with Baader and Raspe in a shoot-out in Frankfurt on June 1, 1972, he would have been a fifth defendant in the Baader-Meinhof trial at Stammheim/Stuttgart, but he died in jail on November 9, 1974, from the effects of a hunger strike.

TERRORISM, MURDER, HOSTAGES

Another group that got into the limelight named itself the "Movement of June 2" (the date of Benno Ohnesorg's death). It committed several terrorist actions (one of which, an explosion,

121

killed a person) and succeeded in kidnapping the Berlin politician Peter Lorenz in 1975, setting him free in exchange for five comrades, who had to be flown to Africa.

Nor did the Baader-Meinhof gang become extinct, as had been expected after the arrests of the leaders. It was an offshoot of this group, calling itself the "Commando Holger Meins," which organized the occupation of the German Embassy in Stockholm with the purpose of freeing several members of the Red Army Fraction, including Baader, Meinhof, Ensslin, and Raspe. The Bonn government did not budge. Two hostages, members of the embassy, were murdered; the ambassador and the others, some of them wounded, escaped when one of the terrorists lit a big explosive charge by mistake. Of the six terrorists, two were killed and four arrested.

In addition to the domestic links among the terrorists, international links have appeared during the past few years. Time and again, terrorists of various nationalities have participated in the same action—mainly Arabs, Japanese, and Germans, but also some Englishmen, French, and Latin Americans. The notorious "Carlos" (probably Ilich Ramírez Sánchez, named by his father, a left-wing lawyer, for Vladimir Ilich Lenin) is considered to be a key figure in international terrorism. He comes from Venezuela and seems to have been involved in the hijacking of the French plane which led to the Israeli raid on the airport at Entebbe, Uganda, in the summer of 1976. The international intertwining of terrorists is, of course, not entirely new; one need only remember the international contacts, even congresses, of the bomb-happy anarchists in the last century. A symptomatic case of international terrorism was the Lod massacre in May 1972: the terrorists were Japanese, recruited through agents in North Korea, supported by funds from German terrorists, given final training in Syria and Lebanon, armed in Italy, and sent to a destination, unknown to them in advance, by the Popular Front for the Liberation of Palestine.

What is it that the terrorists have accomplished by their actions? That they have made a mess of their own lives is something they may count as little, so long as they believe in a higher purpose for their actions. To be sure, aside from themselves and a few dreamers, few people have discerned the nature of this higher purpose. Instead of encouraging the revolution, they have succeeded in two unintended directions. First, their violent actions have damaged all Left revolutionary plans and added to the already existing skepticism, if not hostility, of the general population toward extreme Left movements. In the Federal Republic of today, illegal activities assuredly lead "to the destruction of all socialist endeavors."[13] This is the judgment of a left-wing sociologist at the University of Hanover, Oskar Negt. Second, they have done more for the improvement of the police in West Germany than all recent police lobbyists combined. The budget of the governmental crime-fighting organization grew sixfold from 1971 to 1975.

Not even in their own circles have they won new friends. A publication in West Berlin which is not in principle against the use of violence wrote that one could feel "nausea, to put it mildly," after the killing of the supposed traitor at Red Ilse's instigation, and added: "In their tragic loneliness this group seems to be subjected to a process which in the end cannot be seen as anything but pathological."[14] The Left writer Erich Fried called the terrorists "the saddest and most degenerate product of the Left's decay in the sixties."[15] The East also has reacted negatively. The G.D.R. refused to grant asylum to Ulrike Meinhof, and an East German newspaper called the terrorists "muddleheaded anarchists, déclassé petty bourgeois," accusing them of cooperating with the "prison mob."[16]

Terrorism of this type will die out only when all those who feel drawn to it have understood its hopelessness. The most impressive symptom of such despair came in May 1976, when Ulrike Meinhof hanged herself in her cell.

UPRISINGS
EAST AND WEST

14
WITH HELMET AND GEBABO

THEmoment we passed the red gates, we entered a new world. That bright morning, a Japanese journalist and I had driven through the typically narrow Japanese streets, honking loudly at the swarming masses, inching past tiny stores and little bars, shopping and jabbering housewives, employees hurrying to work, freshly combed children on their way to school. Now we went along an almost empty street on the campus of the most prestigious university in Japan, Todai (from the first syllables of "Tokyo University"), between buildings plastered with handwritten posters and spray-painted with characters.

We left the car in an almost empty parking area. As we walked toward the center of the campus, I heard a strange noise. Suddenly, around the corner of one of the buildings, a howling mob surged toward us, brandishing sticks and poles, faces distorted by frenzy—at least, as far as I could see, for all wore blue-painted helmets and most had a piece of cloth tied over mouth and nose, against tear gas and also in order to be less recognizable. Just as I was about to run for shelter, the wild army stopped, came to order in rows of four, those in the first row holding poles to their chests; in front was a man carrying a banner (it was blue and full of characters); another man next to him, facing the column, had a whistle. As the whistle sounded a one-two, one-two beat, the army commenced a slow jog, holding high their poles (mainly of wood, but some of lead) and shouting again, still a little out of breath, a four syllable slogan.

My companion ran alongside the column to make sure that he properly understood the yell:

FU-san KAN-tets
FU-san KAN-tets

In English, it meant:

BArri-CAdes
BArri-CAdes

A new column appeared, this one with a red flag, red helmets, and bamboo poles about three yards long; from afar it looked like an Army of medieval warriors. It too jogged along, had a man with a whistle who gave the rhythm, and similarly shouted a slogan of four syllables, except that the words were different:

AM-po HAN-tai
AM-po HAN-tai

Deciphered, *Ampo* meant the Security Treaty with America, and *Hantai* meant "anti."

The group came to a halt, laid the poles down neatly on the street, threw itself on the ground, and practiced push-ups to the rhythmic sound of the whistle. Then they got up, grabbed their poles, and resumed their jogging and yelling.

We met with more such scenes as we came to the square in front of the library. It was filled with helmeted, stick-carrying students, all standing in columns and looking toward the wide steps leading up to the building, where their leaders were speaking, each addressing his own column. Speaking is not quite the word; trying to make themselves heard above their equally loud neighbors, they shouted into bullhorns held by assistants. The noise was hellish, for while some in the columns appeared to be listening, others were yelling slogans or singing the *Internationale.* Here too there were banner carriers—swingers of banners, rather, as in medieval times. Some of the young leaders had Plexiglas visors and looked like knights before a jousting tournament. The girls in the columns were hard to distinguish; they too had helmets and sticks. Only when they lifted the cloth from their mouths and noses, to rub away sweat, could one see the more delicate features.

At the edge of the square stood a group of women of middle

age—housewives, to judge from their clothing. Horrified, barely able to control their tears, they were watching the spectacle, giving everyone who passed a handbill. It read (I attempt to suggest the clumsy phrasing): "We mothers of the students have hurting hearts when thinking of the conditions at Todai. When we hear in the news about Todai—VIOLENT CONFRONTATIONS, VIOLENT CONFRONTATIONS!—Oh, the anxieties your parents at home suffer every day! Are there no other ways to protest? Please, remember the feelings of your mothers!" The signature on the sheet, which the women had mimeographed at their own cost, read: "Association of Concerned Mothers of Todai Students." Nobody paid any attention to them. The candy they brought to calm the students had been distributed long before.

We asked some students to explain what this was all about. Some just mumbled, others answered willingly but not clearly. First I asked them to tell us what they had in mind when they were yelling about barricades; did they want to build barricades against the police? No, said the students, obviously surprised about my lack of knowledge, not against the police, but against the *Yoyogi*. They gestured outwardly in all directions. But, why barricades against the Yoyogi? "Student power," they answered, using the English words.

The German language also, I should mention, has enriched the vocabulary of Japanese students. The word *Gewalt* (violence), pronounced *gebaruto*, has become important for the Japanese revolutionaries, who use it so much that they have abbreviated it to *geba*, applying it in many combinations: *gebasuru* (make violent revolution), *uchigeba* (inside violence, or violence between different student groups), *sotogeba* (outside violence, or street-fighting with police), and *gebabo*. With *bo* meaning stick or pole, *gebabo* is the "violence stick" used by students in their battles.

But back to our group at the library square: I wanted to know what they meant by student power. There was an issue, they explained, over which students—themselves or the Yoyogi—were to hold the power on the campus. Now I was curious to find out the difference between the columns all around and the Yoyogi outside. This appeared to be a difficult question. They debated and then said that the Yoyogi were Communists. "I thought *you* were the Communists," I exclaimed. Yes, of course, they themselves were Communists, in fact the only true Communists, while the Yoyogi were false ones. With this they excused themselves.

Just as I was about to ask other students for explanations,

several gentlemen in dark suits appeared on the square, carrying white banners inscribed with slogans such as "No strangers on campus!" and "We must solve the problems of our university ourselves!" They came to a halt and stood silently. As I soon found out, they were professors; some of them knew German, and one I had met in Germany. Now I received more helpful information, and in my own language to boot. They took me around the campus. Todai, formerly the Imperial University of Tokyo, had at that time (1968) about 14,000 students. Nearby, the main lecture building, Yasuda Hall, was heavily barricaded; nobody was allowed to enter, a red flag was hoisted on its roof, and a female voice was shouting slogans through an unseen loudspeaker.

A hundred yards away was the student-union building. The professors did not want to enter it, so I went there by myself. Inside it looked as if a tornado had blown through: dozens of mattresses scattered on the floor, the walls covered with slogans, everywhere dirt, piles of *gebabo*, empty bottles. A few bleary-eyed and tired students stood or lay around.

Meanwhile, in front of Yasuda Hall, an army of several thousand students had taken up positions. Now a male voice shouted from the rooftop, interrupted by enthusiastic yells from the columns. From time to time students came rushing up, shouting something through bullhorns and causing howls of indignation. These were scouts, I was told, reporting what the Yoyogi were doing. High above, a police helicopter circled about because the campus was closed to the police.

STUDENT ARMIES

There were two armies facing each other on the Todai campus, the Yoyogi and the anti-Yoyogi. Yoyogi is the name of that part of Tokyo in which the Japan Communist Party (JCP) has its headquarters. Thus, Yoyogi has become a colloquial abbreviation for the JCP, and also for the students associated with it. The anti-Yoyogi are the students in those many groups and organizations which, while frequently quarreling among themselves, band together to fight the hated Yoyogi, who in their view are not sufficiently revolutionary-minded. Whenever the JCP takes a cautious course in order to win support among the nonradical parts of the population (as was the case in 1968 and during the following years), the Yoyogi on the campus also demand reform rather than revolution. The anti-Yoyogi, on the other hand, desire revolution *now*. They were therefore trying to make the campus a police-free bastion from which to carry out their attacks against the Diet Building, the Foreign Ministry, and the U.S. embassy. For them, the Yoyogi were cowardly tacticians blocking their road to victory.

The Yoyogi had not made prisoners of professors, as the anti-Yoyogi had done with, among others, the highly respected Kentaro Hayashi, then dean of the literary department at Todai. One professor, who was held for a week, told me that he had been interrogated up to fifteen hours a day by about a hundred students shouting in megaphones (a method taken over from the Red Guards in China) and demanding "confessions." Professor Hayashi was so exhausted that he finally had to be carried out on a stretcher and taken to the hospital.

There was an especially wild group, so I was told, known as Kakumaru—its name formed by the first syllables of *kakumeiteki* (revolutionary) and *Marukusu-shugiha* (Marxist group). Kakumaru, which is Trotskyist, calls for a struggle against the imperialist Soviet Union (hence also against the Yoyogi students) as well as the imperialist United States. The history of Kakumaru, which stems from an organization founded in 1968, seems as complicated as the genealogy of a noble family which for centuries has married and fought everybody around. A brief summary requires twelve printed pages to lead the reader through the labyrinth of conflicts and alliances.[1]

A week before my visit to Todai, both Yoyogi and anti-Yoyogi had still been on the campus. The Yoyogi had occupied the library, while the anti-Yoyogi had entrenched themselves in Yasuda Hall. Then the Yoyogi were pushed out of the library and off the campus. It was against the danger of the Yoyogi trying to come back and take over the university that the anti-Yoyogi were yelling for the erection of barricades.

As we left the campus, at dusk, I noticed about a hundred normally clad students and some professors near the gate. They displayed slogans appealing to both armies not to let things come to a battle. Next we passed through the armies of the Yoyogi, who looked just as warlike as the defenders of the campus.

Over the next several days I witnessed student unrest on many a campus. The Catholic University, Jochi Daigaku, was barricaded, with passageways guarded by students. Work there had been paralyzed for months, and this sad state of affairs was repeated elsewhere.

At the State University of Kyushu the situation was somewhat different. Here the radical groups had a common enemy—the Americans. A few months earlier, in June 1968, an American military plane, coming in to land, had crashed into an eight-story building under construction which was to be a computer center for the university and the island of Kyushu. Fortunately, no one was hurt. But the indignation against the nearby military airport and the American presence was revived. The plane wreckage should have been removed and the building completed, but the radical students would not permit this. They wanted to preserve the wreckage in order to stimulate support for their protest against the Americans. It didn't bother them that by keeping the construction workers away they also prevented completion of the computer center, which they said would only serve Japanese monopoly capitalism.

During the following months a number of Japanese universities were taken over by the police—even the main campus of Todai, where a force of more than 8,000 was used. But the struggle continued, now not so much against the universities as against the government and Prime Minister Sato, especially his pro-American foreign policy. In April 1969 students briefly occupied a half mile of the Ginza, one of the main thoroughfares of the capital, and declared it "liberated territory."

In sum, the battles of the students among themselves and with the police lasted longer and were wilder in Japan than elsewhere during the sixties.

STUDENT UNREST—FOR DECADES
For Japan this was nothing new. In no other country have the universities so reflected the break in the continuity of civilization and the tensions resulting from it. In their radicalism, Japanese students were in advance of their peers in the West for a long time.

After centuries of total self-isolation, the island nation had suddenly been pushed into the vortex of modern development. Within a brief span of time, a few decades, it became a modern industrial state, a great power, a victor over the empires of China (1894–1895) and Russia (1904–1905), and a member of the exclusive circle of Allied powers after a brief campaign against the imperial German forces stationed in the Far East (1914). Even in the first phase of this breathless rise there had been student unrest in Japan, often for very modern reasons. In 1901 thousands of students marched to the copper mines north of Tokyo in protest

132

against—as we would say today—the pollution of the environment, and in 1904 against the war with Russia.

But the age of chronic student unrest did not begin until after the end of the First World War. Revolutionary winds were blowing into the country: from America, the high-minded message of Woodrow Wilson about a victory for democracy in the whole world; from Russia, Lenin's call for a socialist revolution of all nations. There was much excitement in Japan, the workers struck, and in 1918 students founded the "Society of the New Man" (Shinjinkai), which had a publication of its own and even a commune. Hardly a campus was free of disturbances, not even the Women's College of Dentistry or the College for the Blind. The slightest occasion triggered riots, such as the "unfair distribution of tickets" for a baseball game between two universities. The students learned early the skillful use of the press in gaining publicity for their demands.[2]

When I visited Japan for the first time, in the summer of 1929, at the age of twenty-two, I met a number of Japanese students at Todai, then still the Imperial University, and in Kyoto. To be sure, I had experienced some excitement at universities in Germany and the United States, but nothing that could be compared to the tense atmosphere among my Japanese comrades. Most of the time they were battling against something; enemy number one was the 1925 "Law for the Preservation of Public Peace" (the basis for strong security measures, it was also applied against the students). One thing surprised me above all: Among my friends in California very few had ever heard of Karl Marx, and at the German universities his teachings had been adopted only by a minority, while in Japan almost every student I met believed in Marx and Lenin.

Seven years later, when I came to Japan again, the country had greatly changed. Since the occupation of Manchuria in 1931, Japan had been swept by steadily growing waves of nationalism. The cult of the emperor was now the big thing. Liberal politicians were being assassinated (among them a prime minister in 1932). The Left was on the defensive, if not underground; almost all the well-known Communists were in prison, and many students too. An officers' coup d'état, in which a number of cabinet members were killed, had barely been overcome a few weeks earlier, in February 1936. Like Germany, the country was on the road to war. At Pearl Harbor and later, the Japanese divisions and warships went into battle as if to a religious service. When the emperor announced the surrender after Hiroshima and Nagasaki, the world seemed to collapse for the Japanese, especially the young people.

The American Occupation forces started the reeducation of the people with m''·h zest and surprising success. This might not have been the c..se if, under the uniforms which almost the entire nation was still wearing, there had not remained alive the memory of the twenties, of the ideals of democracy and socialism. As a counteraction against the extreme right-wing course of the preceding years, the Americans aided everything that was not right-wing; and many of the American educators were left-liberals themselves. The Japan Communist Party and other leftist parties came to life, the liberal or left-liberal professors and journalists who had been fired during the thirties were returned to their jobs. Many university chairs were held during the first two postwar decades by men who had been familiar with, if not members of, the prewar Left student movement.[3] Left-wing parties and left-wing campus people cooperated closely. Soon the students were leaning toward the Left as much as those of the twenties, but there were many more of them (135,000 in 1925; 610,000 in 1955; 1.6 million in 1970) and therefore many more leftists.[4]

On one point, however, the Japanese campus had changed. In the twenties, "Left," "Marxist-Leninist," and "Communist Party" were almost identical in meaning. Now a gap had opened between the majority of the left-wing students and the JCP. There were two reasons for this. One was the JCP's dependence on the unloved Soviet Union and its zigzag course from political conformism to revolutionary fervor and back to conformism. The other was that the Soviet Union, once considered the bastion of peace and justice for the people of the world, had lost much of its prestige. The Japanese have never forgotten that the U.S.S.R. attacked Japan in 1945 just a few hours before the end of the war, that it took land away from them (the Kuril Islands, about which a quarrel still goes on), and that it sent hundreds of thousands of Japanese soldiers, captured at the war's last moment, into Siberian prisons from which tens of thousands did not return. The unmasking of Stalin by Khrushchev in 1956, the invasion of Hungary in the same year, and soon the criticism from Peking— these too cost Moscow many followers in Japan.

The consequences for the students is typified in the fate of Zengakuren, the Japanese student union. When it was formed in 1948, as an umbrella over all the student unions of the individual universities, Zengakuren was almost exclusively in the hands of people close to the JCP. Gradually the picture changed. Groups which called themselves Communist but were hostile to the JCP, to the Yoyogi, now moved to the front. Some splintered off, saying that *they* were the true Zengakuren, so that at times there existed four or five groups bearing the name. Often they worked more against than with each other. Yet the battle against the state (Japan's own government, as well as the Occupation) continued, most of all against the U.S.-Japan Security Treaty, which supposedly was turning the country into an American colony. There was always some new reason for protests.

In the mid-fifties, a decade before Rudi Dutschke proclaimed the revolt against any authority, there emerged in Japan a kind of SDS, the Bundo (from the German word *Bund*, "union"). One of its founders described Bundo as a revolutionary student group which refused any authority, including that of the JCP and the Moscow-led international Communist organizations.[5]

In 1955, in Japan for the first time since the war, I witnessed the fight against the enlargement of the U.S. military airport in Tachikawa (near Tokyo). Changing shifts of thousands of students were staying in the village of Sunagawa, whose fields were to be used for the airport, sometimes struggling with a thousand or more policemen. Eventually the government had its way, and many students were arrested, later to be acquitted by the courts. The affair contributed considerably to the growth of anti-American feeling among the young.

Five years later, students in Tokyo were fighting fiercely among themselves. Zengakuren (no longer in JCP hands) had become the spearhead of the attack against the renewal of the Security Treaty. It organized protest strikes (in one, 300,000 students participated), assaulted the Diet Building, and tried to prevent the departure of Prime Minister Kishi for Washington to sign the new treaty (he barely got through to his plane). The climax came in the summer of 1960, when President Eisenhower wanted to visit Japan to plead for ratification of the treaty. I saw tens of thousands of frenzied students trying to storm the Diet. One student, Michiko Kamba, was killed in the process, and tens of thousands of students demonstrated at her funeral. The car of Eisenhower's press secretary, who had come to make arrangements for the visit, was surrounded, and the secretary himself was threatened, vilified, and jeered by students. Finally came their greatest triumph, the calling off of Eisenhower's visit. While three quarters of a million people, with Bundo students at the head, were besieging Parliament, the treaty was ratified—but at the price of Kishi's resignation.

The following years were a little calmer, but 1967 brought further signs of storm. Trips abroad by the new prime minister Eisaku Sato, were disrupted; before his departure for the United States, about 500 people were injured. Early in 1968 there were big protest actions against the U.S. carrier *Enterprise* and against a U.S. military hospital which treated Americans wounded in Vietnam.

The battles of 1968 and 1969 not only crippled Japan's universities but also exhausted the students. The renewal of the Security Treaty in 1970 took place amid protests but without the violence of the previous decade. The law for the control of the universities, effective August 10, 1969, gave the government considerable power over campus affairs. As everywhere else, the police had become stronger in numbers, armaments, legal powers, and skill; terrorism had frightened the general public even more than the university revolt. Whenever something happens now, the police arrive immediately and with overwhelming strength.

From time to time there have been dramatic conflicts. By far the most expensive one occurred at Tokyo's new airport, Narita, built because Haneda was no longer able to accommodate all the traffic. Completed by 1973, it was designed to handle 16 million passengers a year. But the farmers of the neighborhood fought the airport tooth and nail because it was built partly on their former property. They vowed not to allow a single plane to use it, and with the support of students who immediately flocked to their side, they raised steel towers at the ends of the runways, one of them almost 200 feet high. In the summer of 1977 the airport was still idle.

Despite such protests, there were signs of declining interest in political and social problems among the students. Life in the universities became more normal. True enough, there were still militant gangs, but they were now more of the Hell's Angels variety (except that they were devoted to automobiles). Tokyo alone had more than 200 such groups. In 1973 police arrested almost 10,000 members for speeding. A Tokyo psychologist said: "Automobiles are the only possibility for them to get over their rage and frustration."[6]

The stress of examinations in schools and universities has increased, and with it the intense competition. People speak of "examination hell." Many more young people are trying to enter the universities than can be admitted. Those fearful of not being accepted are desperate and sometimes prone to suicide.

A German instructor whom I visited in 1972 at a provincial Japanese university told me of an incident during one of his lectures. A radical student stood up and began a rousing antigovernment speech. The instructor explained that as a guest of Japan he could not allow political agitation against his host country, but added that he was willing to discuss political subjects in German, since this could be considered part of the classwork. The other students approved. "I now expected," he said, "an explosion of anger on the part of that student. Instead he quietly sat down, buried his head in his arms, and began to sob until two friends quietly led him out of the room."

There have been many such symptoms of nervous overexertion—that result of the merciless pressure for achievement, of disappointment over the far-too-slow evolution of society, and perhaps also of despair over the splintering of the once powerful student movement into a few large organizations and hundreds of tiny groups of not more than five to ten members.[7]

Unable to accomplish anything except by individualized shock tactics, some students in Japan, as in America and Germany, turned toward terrorism.

In the years since March 1970, when nine young men, armed with bombs and samurai swords, hijacked a Japanese plane to North Korea, there have been many terrorist actions by Japanese—the most notorious on May 30, 1972, when three Japanese fired submachine guns into a crowd at the Lod Airport terminal near Tel Aviv, killing twenty-eight persons and wounding seventy-five. (There is a good study on the surviving terrorist, Kozo Okamoto.[8])

I shall not try to unravel the confused story of the "Red Army" (Sekigun), which was believed to be behind most of these plots. This group hit the front page when it turned its terrorism against its own members. The murder which Dostoevski so powerfully describes in *The Possessed* (the novel in which some members of a terrorist group kill one of their own) is far surpassed by the atrocities committed by the Red Army in the spring of 1972 in a lonely villa at the resort of Karuizawa. With unspeakable cruelty some of the gang—under the leadership of a twenty-seven-year-old woman—killed thirteen of their comrades, among them four girls (one in the eighth month of her pregnancy), supposedly because they had committed treason.

The Japanese terrorists are in close contact with the international terrorist underground, especially the Palestinian one. This internationalization may be partly the result of successful police action. The terrorists, complaining that the Japanese people have not yet matured to the point of revolution, have shifted their field of action to the Middle East, to the Third World. In this we can see, as elsewhere, a search for revolutionary situations outside one's own frontiers.

IN JAPAN TOO—A CHANGED YOUTH

The biggest contrast with the traditional image of Japan can be found in the attitude of young people toward the established representatives and institutions of the state. The question of whether one should leave politics to the leaders of the existing parties has long been answered negatively by the majority in the group aged 21–24: in 1953 by 54 percent; in 1958 by 60 percent; and in 1973 by 67 percent.

Along with the authority of government and political parties, that of the trade unions has declined. In 1972, workers aged 20–24 were much less likely to express "high" confidence in the trade unions than were those 40–49 years of age: among workers in electrical factories, 46 against 79 percent; steel workers, 14 against 30 percent; railway workers, 55 against 60 percent. As for civic consciousness, in 1956 about 54 percent of those 20–24 years old declared their readiness to vote in national elections; in 1968, only 34 percent. Even industriousness is no longer what it used to be. In 1971, among those 16–24 years old, 54 percent considered work "important," compared with 73 percent among those 40–49 years of age. Loyalty toward one's own firm, traditionally very strong among employees and workers in Japan, has declined too. The statement "I owe thanks to the firm and am happy about its success" was considered acceptable only by 50 percent of the group aged 20–24, against 72 percent of those 40–49 years old. On the other hand, "Live as you like, without bothering about fame and fortune" was approved in 1953 by 43 percent of the group aged 20–24, and fifteen years later by 67 percent.

In a modern comedy, the generation gap is set forth in a conversation between two Japanese, an adult and a young man of the hippie type:

> **Adult:** You're a perfectly healthy young fellow.
> Why don't you get up and go to work?
> **Young Man:** What will happen if I go to work?
> **Adult:** You'll make money.

138

Young Man: And what happens if I make money?
Adult: You'll get rich.
Young Man: And what happens if I get rich?
Adult: Then you can lie around and take it easy.
Young Man: Well, that's what I'm doing right now.

There is increasing doubt about the value of progress. Among those 20–24 years old, the belief that life has become more comfortable as a result of science and technology, but also less humane, was held by 27 percent in 1953 and by 54 percent in 1973.[9]

OLD AND NEW—SIDE BY SIDE

And yet, behind all the trends shared with modern Western countries, there is much left of the traditional Japan. In the autumn of 1968, during the climax of student unrest, I lived in the old imperial and university city of Kyoto, in a Japanese home which still cultivated the tea ceremony. That ancient rite, with its extraordinary forms of courtesy, was an important element in family and social life. One Saturday afternoon, twenty-two young people, friends of the family, took part in it, the girls—like flowers in their many-colored kimonos—performing the ritual gestures which can be mastered only after years of practice, the young men seriously concentrating upon the movements assigned to them, all kneeling and bowing, their foreheads almost touching the floor.

Two weeks later, in highly modern and Americanized Tokyo, two anti-Yoyogi took me to a teahouse; one of them, his hair like Che Guevara's, a beret on his head, ordered the foamy green ceremonial tea. When I asked whether he participated in tea ceremonies, he answered evasively, "Sometimes."

A friend of mine learned where the sympathies of the population were when he happened to be in a district where students were assembling for a demonstration. They were hemmed in by a swarm of men who had come armed with sticks. By talking with the grim-looking men he learned that they were the owners and employees of neighboring shops, angry at the students and ready to defend their livelihood. He heard the multitude applaud when the students were attacked by the police and their leaders were taken away in vans.

15
GUERRILLAS

THE Spanish word *guerrilla,* so prominent for the past few years, has a long history. For the Spaniards it awakens memories of their war against Napoleon, in which they were the first to cast doubt on the myth of the invincibility of the Corsican and his armies, thereby encouraging liberation movements against his power in other parts of Europe, too. Goya, the great Spanish painter, has immortalized the execution of Madrid rebels on May 3, 1808, in a huge canvas, the pride of the Prado, which he is said to have completed (in 1814) with the help of sketches made on the spot the morning after the executions.

In the Second World War, the people who fought the Germans behind the front were called "Maquis" by the French, "partisans" by the Russians—the latter a word of Italian-French origin which the Russians themselves were using as early as their war against Napoleon.

The fact that the whole world is now using the ancient Spanish word and speaking of "guerrilla warfare" is easily explained: Since Castro's victory and Guevara's lonely death, the Spanish-speaking guerrilla fighters have won worldwide attention. Although *guerrilla* is the diminutive of the word for war, *guerra,* it is frequently used for the individual who is fighting a guerrilla war (more properly, a *guerrillero*). Che Guevara speaks in his most often quoted book of *la guerra de guerrillas.*

At first, to be sure, the events in Cuba which had brought young guerrilla leaders to power seemed far away. Who would have thought that, a few years later, "urban" guerrilla warfare would afflict many countries in Latin Ameria and even spread to Germany? People who looked into the history of guerrilla warfare soon discovered that guerrillas had existed in Latin America for a long time. So had a strong student movement, starting at Córdoba, Argentina, fifty years before 1968—the stormiest year of our rebellious students. In countless rebellions, *pronunciamentos* of ambitious generals or politicians, and revolutions the guerrillas were almost always present. They served Juárez, the Indian president of Mexico, as a weapon against the invading troops of Napoleon III and his pawn Maximilian (1863–1867), and contributed largely to making that country's great revolution (1910–1917) the longest and bloodiest in Latin America. Guerrilla operations in Brazil (1925–1927) and Nicaragua (1927–1933) possessed modern features and foreshadowed the fighting of Fidel Castro, whose triumph over the demoralized army of Batista has affected the whole world.

Fascination with this latter event produced, far beyond the confines of Cuba, movements known as "Castroism" or "Fidelism" which Castro himself promoted assiduously; guerrilla warfare became an article of export. His first and most influential lieutenant was Ernesto "Che" Guevara, the leader of one of the three columns that attacked the fortress of Havana (whose garrison was executed on Castro's orders). Guevara later became minister of industries and spokesman for Cuba on many trips and conferences abroad until his unexpected (and never totally explained) separation from Castro and departure for a new front, his last one—Bolivia. The Andes, Castro had declared on July 26, 1960, were to be for the whole of Latin America what the Sierra Maestra had been for Cuba, the starting place of a continental war of liberation.

Guevara, the first chronicler of the war in Cuba, was also the first theoretician of modern guerrilla warfare. His works have circulated widely, in many languages. Much the same can be said of the French journalist Jules-Régis Debray, Guevara's friend and admirer, and for a while his companion in Bolivia, who escaped death there by getting caught (sentenced to thirty years in prison, he served three). Having published some articles about his experiences in other parts of Latin America, Debray was commissioned by Castro (and given much material) to produce, on the basis of Castro's ideas and his own observation of guerrilla warfare, a textbook combining theory and practice. Published in 200,000 copies in January 1967, it was made compulsory reading for all political cadres in Cuba. Guevara had a copy with him on his last expedition.[1] It is not likely that his recent melodramatic novel, *L'Indésirable,* about urban guerrillas in Latin America has pleased his erstwhile fans; it draws a desolate picture and shows the hero (Debray himself) an undesirable agitator from outside.

It was not the ideology of guerrilla warfare that inspired young people the world over. Rather, it was the personality of Guevara. For many, he was a youthful yet melancholic hero with whom they could identify in their dreams; who had found at the age of fifteen an ideal which he thought worth sacrificing one's life for; and who actually did sacrifice his in faraway Bolivia after a brief, dramatic career during which he withstood the temptations of prosperity, comfort, and even power.

One thing must be stressed, because it has decisively influenced the New Left. Although Castro, Guevara, and Debray officially professed their allegiance to Marxism-Leninism and the principle of the dictatorship of the proletariat, they claimed the right to get there by their own route, the Cuban one, and they did so at first to an extent which could hardly be reconciled with some of the fundamental dogmas of Marxism. This was true especially of the thesis, developed by Guevara by 1960, that the guerrillero does not have to wait for the "revolutionary situation," that he can, in fact, bring about this situation from his *foco*—his stronghold. In the words of another guerrillero in 1968, "revolutionary actions create revolutionary situations."[2]

Guevara had gone even further by warning against imitating models from outside, whether their creators were Lenin or Mao, Trotsky or Ho Chi Minh. At that time Castro was about to create in Havana a "Latin American Solidarity Organization." To clinch this, a new spectacular guerrilla action would be the most effective help. Guevara was called back from the Congo (where he was working without success) to be dispatched in October 1966, after lengthy preparation, to lead a new operation in Bolivia. Apparently something had to be done, at whatever cost, although the conditions were not exactly favorable. The prerequisite which Guevara himself had declared indispensable for the success of guerrilla warfare was lacking—the support of the population, which according to Mao is the "water" in which the revolutionary must be able to swim like a fish, while the unsupported enemy eventually must drown. Guevara declined the help of the Bolivian Communist Party because he did not want to submit to its leader, Mario Monje. Then, after the first five months, no more aid came from Cuba, nor any communication. To avoid being linked with a Bolivian failure, Castro had written off Guevara. The end came barely a year after the beginning: Guevara was wounded, captured, and, on orders from the capital, La Paz, shot on October 9, 1967.

FROM THE COUNTRY TO THE CITY

After the death of Guevara, his type of guerrilla warfare was practically abandoned. The hour had come for a new strategy, that of the "urban" guerrilla, a concept which Guevara and his friends had rejected because they felt the city would corrupt the guerrilleros. Its most important theoreticians were Abraham Guillén and Carlos Marighella.

Abraham Guillén was born in 1913 into a Spanish peasant family. Sentenced to a long prison term for his participation in the Civil War, he escaped in 1945 to France and afterward moved to Argentina, where he studied economic problems and did editorial work for a review published by the Ministry of Economy. Research on the influence of U.S. capital in Latin America caused him to write books about American imperialism[3] and furthered his political radicalization. In 1962 he asked for and obtained asylum in Uruguay, where he devoted himself to the revolutionizing of that country. Because the mainly flat terrain was unsuitable for Cuban-type guerrilla exploits, Guillén formulated the thesis that revolutions were determined by men, not by geography; the cities, he explained, were jungles of concrete in which the guerrillas could be even better hidden and supplied than in the mountains.

Guillén and Guevara reportedly had a secret meeting in 1962, during which Guillén vainly argued the advantages of urban guerrilla warfare.[4] A literary product of the next few years was a book by Guillén (1966) which soon became the most important manual of the urban revolutionaries.[5] In Argentina Guillén's ideas influenced the (Trotskyist) Revolutionary People's Army (ERP), the Revolutionary Armed Forces (FAR), and the Argentinian Liberation Forces (FAL); in Brazil, the National Liberation Action (ALN)—directly and also through Marighella—and the Revolutionary People's Vanguard (VPR); in Uruguay, the Tupamaros. For his own part, he acknowledged having had many teachers—Marx, Bakunin, Castro, and Guevara. This is a rather mixed bag, particularly since Marx and Bakunin had unremittingly fought each other. Guillén's American translator and editor, D. C. Hodges, considers his linking of them into a common theory of anarcho-Marxism to be his particular achievement. The joining of such contrary minds and temperaments is, however, more than an intellectual game. Guillén probably hoped that his strategy would halt the splintering of the extreme Left.[6]

Among the Latin American guerrilla theoreticians, only Guillén takes into account the Paris events of May 1968. In a new edition of his manual (1969) he claims that with only fifty more urban guerrillas there would have been a great revolution in Paris.[7] I do not find any indication that the most successful—and bloodiest—guerrilla war of our time, in South Vietnam, has particularly affected their thinking (apart from Debray's criticism of Viet Cong tactics as being unsuitable for Latin America).

Carlos Marighella is much better known outside Latin America. Born in Brazil in 1911, the son of a white man and a black woman, he was for a long time a loyal member of the Communist Party of Brazil, representing it in parliament for several years. At the age of fifty-six he was excluded from the Party because of irreconcilable differences of opinion. A year later he founded his own organization, the National Liberation Action (ALN). In 1969 he completed, not uninfluenced by Guillén, his *Small Handbook of the Urban Guerrilla*.[8]

Originally Marighella had taken over for Brazil Guevara's and Debray's theses, according to which the guerrillas had to operate in the countryside. But his doubts grew, and the total failure of Guevara in Bolivia caused him to revise his own theory. He then declared that the guerrilla war had to be moved to the cities, the aim being the destruction of the state's power from the urban centers rather than from the rural periphery. The methods— assassination of leading opponents, bank raids, bomb attacks, kidnappings. The most prominent hostage taken in Brazil was U.S. Ambassador Burke Elbrick, freed only after the government allowed fifteen political prisoners to leave the country.

Soon Marighella was dead; the police had lured him into a trap and shot him. Carlos Lamarca became his successor, a former army officer trained in antiguerrilla warfare. In December 1970 the German ambassador to Brazil, Ehrenfried von Holleben, was taken hostage and not released until the gates had been opened for forty prisoners. (The German ambassador to Guatemala, Count Karl von Spreti, was less fortunate; he was murdered by his kidnappers.) The Brazilian government now turned all its attention, including specially trained "death commandos" and a wide use of torture, against the urban guerrillas. Within a year they were either destroyed or pushed into a hopelessly defensive situation.

Guerrilla warfare, as we have seen, is very difficult to wage. But its principle is simple. Long before Mao and the Latin American theoreticians, the poet John Milton in his *Paradise Lost* put these words in the mouth of Moloch, a leader among the angels who rebelled against the Lord:

> ... and by proof we feel
> Our power sufficient to disturb his Heaven,
> And with perpetual inroads to alarm,
> Though inaccessible, his fatal throne:
> Which if not victory is yet revenge.

THE TUPAMAROS

The urban guerrillas of Uruguay took their name from an ancient Inca king, Tupac Amaru. Beginning large-scale activities in 1968, for several years the Tupamaros made sport of the country's police. Then, almost at the same time as in Brazil, the army moved against them. Within a few months it demolished the best-led and most successful urban guerrilla organization of Latin America, went on to stage a coup d'état (June 1973), and organized a military government. The Tupamaros' best-known hostage was the British ambassador, Geoffrey Jackson, who in 1971 was kept for eight months in a secret "people's prison." From Jackson's moving book about his experiences we learn little of his captors, except that they were very secretive and that the majority were students, male and female.[9]

For decades, university students had formed the core of political opposition in Latin America; in their eyes all the existing governments were corrupt and were either brutal dictatorships, which they hated, or weak democracies, which they held in contempt. High school students also joined their ranks, frequently supported by left-leaning teachers who were dissatisfied with their working and living conditions. The history of the Latin American universities records far more student rebellions than have occurred on the campuses of the United States or Europe.

Strong sympathy, often even aid, has been accorded the Latin American guerrilleros by some members of the Catholic priesthood. Camilo Torres, a student chaplain and sociologist, joined a Colombian guerrilla group at the age of thirty-six, in 1965. A few weeks later he was killed in a fight with soldiers. Soon he became the idol of many young left-wing Catholics who called themselves Camilistas. Among the older clerics, Dom Helder Camara, archbishop of Olinda and Recife in Brazil, advocated "peaceful violence," meaning moral and political pressure. On the other hand, Pope Paul VI, during the Eucharistic Congress at Bogotá in 1968, condemned all kinds of violence. One should not, he said, "fight evil at the price of a still greater evil," since violence "produces new injustices, new disturbance of the equilibrium, and new ruins."[10]

Varying attitudes are found also among the officer corps. From its ranks have come dictators at one extreme and guerrilla leaders—like Carlos Lamarca—at the other. Lamarca went AWOL early in 1969 together with some coconspirators, taking plenty of weapons and ammunition, and joined a guerrilla unit of the VPR. In the beginning he was quite successful (he was also famed for his extraordinary marksmanship), but then the new military dictatorship in Brazil turned its energies against the guerrillas. Their fortunes waned. Lamarca was able to hide for a while, having undergone plastic surgery to change his appearance. In September 1971 he was captured and killed.

The guerrillas in Latin America, having found support mainly among the intelligentsia (including the students) and in the ranks of the clergy and the officer corps, were disappointed by the small numbers of peasants or workers who joined them. They tried time and again to raise the percentage of the proletariat in their units, with little success. At the end of 1970, among more than 200 Tupamaros either captured or on the wanted list, there were "almost no workers and not a single peasant." Most were "male and female students, academics, teachers, etc."—intellectuals belonging largely to "the upper layer of society and the middle class."[11] Guevara had found among the Bolivian peasants more traitors than supporters, and it was a peasant who set the police on the trail of Carlos Lamarca, one of those poor Sertão peasants whom Lamarca had believed to be the soldiers of the future revolution.

In an esteemed study, the German writer Fritz René Allemann analyzes the guerrilla movements in Latin America country by country and comes to this conclusion: "the guerrillas of the last decade [i.e., after the Cuban revolution] have not reached their goal; rather they have led the revolution into a whole series of catastophes." His book is one long chronicle of failures and shattered hopes. In the countryside and in the city, the guerrilla experiment had led to "what practically amounts to liquidation of the underground organizations." Even worse for the guerrillas, by weakening the first beginnings of a democratic order, or even destroying it, as in Uruguay, they opened the road to regimes far to the right and even for military dictatorships.[12]

Allemann explains that many guerrillas acted according to the infamous motto "The worse, the better." They believed that only through a radical worsening of the situation in their countries could the ruling classes be forced to drop their democratic masks and show their true brutal features; then the underprivileged people would finally recognize their own real interest and cooperate with their liberators. He quotes a Guatemalan urban guerrilla who explained that his friends had abducted the country's foreign minister in order to prevent him from running for president, thereby (they hoped) bringing victory instead to a right-wing candidate whom they hated and called "the butcher." Why? "Because the repression which he would unleash would force many people to come to us." They wanted to sharpen the crisis in the country in order to create proper conditions for the revolution.[13]

Chalmers Johnson, Asia specialist and professor at the University of California at Berkeley, defines the tactics of the guerrillas as being designed to elicit one of three kinds of intervention:

> Intervention by foreign imperialist forces, whose depredations may bring about the mobilization of the masses (e.g., the Japanese in China, or the Americans in Vietnam); intervention by international socialist forces in order to support a struggling revolutionary party and to prevent reactionaries from gaining power by defeating the guerrillas (e.g., the Soviets in Cuba, or the Indians in Bangladesh); and intervention by the masses of a country themselves as their aspirations for dignity and social change are mobilized by the examples of heroism that the guerrillas provide.[14]

In all three cases, especially the first two, everything would depend on the creation of a serious, perhaps even desperate, crisis.

But these tactics so far have not brought success. U.S. troops have not intervened in Latin America, except in the Caribbean Dominican Republic (the memory of the catastrophic Bay of Pigs operation still being vivid). Nationalism has been, since the days of Napoleon, the mightiest ally of all guerrillas, and the presence of U.S. advisers—supposedly some 40,000 for the training of local troops in counterinsurgency warfare—and the unearthing of the CIA's role in Latin America, especially in Chile, have indeed strengthened existing anti-Americanism—but not to the point that guerrillas have been hailed by the people as national heroes fighting the national enemy. Other appeals, such as Marxism, Leninism, antifascism, or socialism, have as a rule fired only parts of the population. Only religious fanaticism can be compared to the explosive power of nationalism; more often than not, each has served the other for justification.

The guerrillas so far have not obtained sufficient help from abroad. Castro did send help—but to Angola; perhaps the lack of such aid for Guevara in Bolivia may be explained by Castro's fear of a rival. The Kremlin has supported only the Communist parties that are tied to the U.S.S.R. and, like itself, hostile to "petty-bourgeois guerrilla adventurism."

Nowhere did the guerrillas succeed in elevating their operations to the level of a civil war. Here and there they were able to disturb the regime and alarm the population, but the masses of peasants or workers did not rally to their cause. "Fish in water" they were not.

Finally, the Latin American guerrillas foundered because of their constant splitting. Debray had prophesied that the guerrillas would close their ranks as the struggle developed against the common enemy. But this did not happen. By creating their own guerrilla units, the many hostile left-wing groups transferred their quarrels to the guerrilla movement as a whole. (Uruguay's Tupamaros succeeded in staying together for a long time partly because they had made up their minds to refrain from ideological discussions among themselves, as well as with other groups.) The guerrillas were also harmed by underestimating the strength of the state machine, of the army, and of the Americans, who despite their engagement in Vietnam persevered in training thousands of Latin American officers in counterinsurgency fighting.

The guerrillas also underestimated the terrible effects of torture, which is still being used in several countries and with such rigor that few prisoners are able to withstand it. Many of the counterinsurgency successes have been based on information torn from prisoners by torture. And in Brazil the extraordinary economic upswing destroyed all hopes for economic crisis.

Yet the guerrilla movement, although reduced, has not died. Everything now depends on the way in which the governments use the time won by its decline. The governments will not win until they have eliminated not only the guerrillas but also the conditions in which they grow—misery and despotism. In the words of John F. Kennedy, "One cannot save the rich who have money, unless one helps the poor who lack the money."

At the same time, the dilemma of the guerrillas has become quite obvious. They want to cause by their actions so much confusion and disturbance that the government capitulates and flees the country, as Batista fled from Cuba. But the upheaval must not be so strong that the population will turn against the guerrillas, calling for law and order and a strong government, which then is likely to be a government of the Right. Castro succeeded in overcoming this dilemma because to Cubans the corrupt and dictatorial Batista regime and the hated American imperialism were one and the same enemy; national as well as liberal emotions favored Castro. Nothing of this kind has happened since. There was a time when young revolutionaries in Latin America, in Guevara's words, cheerfully prophesied and demanded "two, three, many Vietnams." Not a single one has occurred there.

As of now, by far the greatest success of the Latin American guerrillas can be found in the worldwide propagation of their methods and their spirit. The wave caused by Castro and Guevara has, on the whole, ebbed since it became clear that Guevara's— and any other—rural guerrilla action was likely to fail, and that Castro himself had become Moscow's satellite. But the *urban* guerrillas have served as a model outside Latin America.

It was the guerrillas who started taking hostages (in Havana they kidnapped the famous Argentinian racing-car driver Fangio; in Caracas, the professional football player di Stefano). At first they sought only to call attention to their demands. But gradually, kidnapping came to be used for political blackmail, which we have witnessed in recent years in many cases outside Latin America. The hitherto unsuccessful attempts of arousing the masses against their governments by public disturbances of law and order (e.g., arson in department stores) was employed in Latin America earlier than elsewhere in the West. Allemann has recently said in a lecture that the term "guerrilla" is no longer appropriate for actions such as these. They are not steps in a "small war." They are pure terrorism.[15]

Guevara is no longer a model, he is a myth. The fact that he lost and that he even caused his failure by his own carelessness made him the more beloved by the rebellious young people, as they began to sense, in the months and years following his death, that they too would fail. In Guevara's diary, later published by Castro, they could read that he had to struggle during the last months of his life with this presentiment.[16] Thus Guevara came to be the idol of a generation which had plunged into the battle against the existing order and after early euphoria began to doubt, as he had, the chance of victory.

I have asked young people at demonstrations in various countries why they carried around the portrait of Che Guevara, a man who had failed, as if it were an icon. In Berkeley, a girl answered: "Out of defiance. We know that we will be crushed as he was. That's why we feel as one with him."

A block away the police were waiting for the order to enter the campus.

16
THE YEAR OF THE STUDENTS

THE campus unrest climaxed in 1968. This chapter will describe briefly the events of that year in some countries not yet treated: Belgium, Spain, Italy, the Scandinavian nations, Great Britain, France, Senegal, Austria, Switzerland, and Mexico. A premature "1968" occurred in South Korea, delayed ones erupted in Portugal and Greece.

BELGIUM

The 1968 events began very conveniently for me in the Belgian university city of Louvain, an hour's drive from Aachen, West Germany, where I was teaching at that time. I went with a Flemish student to Leuven, as he and other Belgian Flemings call it—the usual "Louvain" is their French-speaking Walloon compatriots' version. Louvain is one of the loveliest university cities in Europe, truly a Belgian Oxford. Its great school, founded in 1425, has gone through many storms (from the uprising against the Spanish in 1570 to the destruction of the First World War), but none like that of 1968. Before, there were foreign enemies against whom all stood united; this time the enemy was within the walls.

The central problem of Belgium, the conflict between its Flemish and Walloon populations, had seriously disrupted the peace at the university. The Flemings wanted a purely Flemish-speaking university. Hence they demanded the removal of the French-speaking departments, fearing that the growing numbers of Walloon students and professors would dangerously strengthen the Walloons' political power in Belgium. Shortly after New Year's Day 1968, a plan for extension of these departments was published, and the storm broke. Within three weeks it led to the fall of the government, and soon after that to the dissolution of Parliament. Passions were aroused to a point where four months were to pass before a new government could be formed.

The day we came to Louvain, the university buildings were covered with spray-painted slogans: "Walloons, Get Out!" and "Leuven Flemish." An ancient lecture hall had been damaged by Molotov cocktails, and windows were broken. At the headquarters of the Flemish students, there was a constant coming and going of messengers, leaflet distributors, poster painters. Police patrolled the streets. In short, Louvain looked the way hundreds of universities looked later in the course of that year.

I heard bitter threats by the students: If the Walloons did not get out, Leuven would burn as Watts did. Some young leaders used the SDS vocabulary and spoke of oppression of the under-privileged Flemings by the economically and politically more powerful Walloons, of a class war. Portraits of Mao and Che Guevara were displayed.

As the months went on, excitement grew. During the "Paris May," the nervous government in Brussels unanimously denied entry to Cohn-Bendit when students invited him to lecture. Other Belgian universities were soon aroused. In Brussels, students oc-cupied the main lecture hall of their university, formed a "council of the forty" which demanded a purge of the university's adminis-tration and entry for Cohn-Bendit. Even after the decision to move Louvain's French-speaking departments to Walloon terri-tory, unrest continued to simmer.

SPAIN
Almost at the same time, the universities at Madrid and Bar-celona exploded. For several years Spanish students had been somewhat restless, usually after the Christmas vacation. The "free elections of student representatives" were not considered free. In January 1968 there were violent disturbances; many stu-dents demanded not just truly free elections but total political freedom. Some university departments were closed down for weeks, and in Madrid the government formed a brigade of "uni-versity police" to supervise the students. In Barcelona—where political distaste for the Franco government was increased by local Catalonian distaste for the central government in

Madrid—students attempted to storm a conference of university presidents. Rebellions followed at other universities as a matter of course.

Among the leaflets I got from Spain that year was one declaring that students engaged in a sit-in would not leave their university until a dean was fired and their freely elected representatives were recognized. The leaflet closed: "For a Democratic University! Down with the Fascist Press!" Confrontations with the police became more bitter and violent. During police interrogation a student jumped out of a window and died of his injuries. But Franco was not willing to grant to the students rights which he withheld from everybody else. The government kept the upper hand—not least because the population, with the smell of smoke and powder from the Civil War of the thirties still in their noses, had little sympathy with rebellious youth.

ITALY

In February 1968, in the words of a German correspondent, "Hell broke loose" on Italian campuses. The universities of Turin, Milan, Pavia, Padua, Florence, Pisa, Bologna, Rome, Naples, and Messina were occupied by students. The Italian news read like bulletins of mobilization for war. Some 450,000 students were ready for battle. "The Universities Must Become a Vietnam," a poster said. In Italy too, 1968 was the year of the students.

They had remained quiet well into the sixties. Three of the universities, however, had produced intellectual ammunition for the revolt: Trent, Turin, and Venice. Trent was the first in Italy to offer a major course of study in the social sciences. Catholic groups close to the ruling Christian Democratic Party founded the Social Science Institute at Trent in 1962, wishing to develop a modern Catholic sociology. But many of its students came in order to learn critical, not Catholic, sociology. First they turned their eyes on the institute itself—they demanded far-reaching administrative powers and the abolition of examinations—then on social and political conditions in the country. They went on to propagate a *contestazione globale,* urging that society as a whole should be questioned and improved. They were strongly influenced by the ideology developed in Berlin which they called "Dutschkismo." From Berlin they also took the idea of a "critical university" (which was never seriously tried out, in Berlin or any other place).

Turin, one of the great industrial cities of Europe, has long had a particularly lively university. Here the students found their chief inspiration not in Marx and Engels but in Freud and Marcuse. The memory of Mussolini's authoritarian rule was still fresh, and notions developed by Marcuse about the detested "authoritarian personality," seemed relevant. In January 1968 the Turin student movement issued a manifesto. The students had come to the university, it said, to study history, law, physics, or medicine. But what did they learn? "To obey and to command." The professor was master, the student was subject, and the power difference between them must be abolished. After thus disavowing the academic establishment, the students attacked the entire Italian social system.[1]

Students of Venice added the "permanent occupation" of university buildings. Suggesting that others do the same, they recommended that students hold out all by themselves and not enter into confrontations or discussions with outsiders, in order to escape bourgeois contamination.

If to ideas such as these one adds the extreme differences between poor and rich in Italy, the not-very-inspiring behavior of the politicians, and the leftward trend within considerable sections of the Catholic clergy, it cannot come as a surprise that disorders followed at many universities. Students and police clashed violently in Rome on March 1, as a wave of "collective enthusiasm" spread, although Italy had neither a theoretician comparable to Rudi Dutschke nor a showman on the order of Cohn-Bendit.[2]

Italy has a large Communist Party with considerable influence on the campus and, in addition, many extremist groups to the left of it, all of them frequently fighting among each other and with the Communists. The most serious clash within the Italian Left occurred at the University of Rome in February 1977. Damage: 500 million lire.

SCANDINAVIA

The northern countries remained relatively quiet. These welfare states, which met most of the wishes of university youth halfway, were not a suitable soil for violent eruptions. In Sweden, the problem was not political unrest; rather it was drugs and acts of vandalism, evident at Stockholm late in the summer of 1965.[3] Student demonstrations were usually concerned with situations outside Sweden, and these, in the course of the Vietnam war, took an increasingly anti-American direction. In Stockholm I witnessed one of the wilder actions in March 1968 when, during an international conference on currency problems, many young people protested against the presence of the American Secretary of the Treasury.

In Denmark, 10,000 young people demonstrated at Copenhagen in April to protest the Vietnam war, and students occupied some laboratories in order to underline their demand for participation on an equal footing in decisions concerning the curriculum.

On lecture tours to Norwegian universities I found the students much opposed to capitalistic development of their country. "Progress" had no allure for them. More than on campuses elsewhere, I found in Norway the antimodern attitude which had been so dramatically expressed by the American hippies. They were against Norway's participation in the European Economic Community, and they surprised me by being unhappy about the recent discovery of Norway's vast offshore oil resources. They did not want the country to become a leading oil producer, because this would mean entanglement in the affairs of international capitalism and the destruction of the peace and quiet which they wished to preserve.

Helsinki witnessed turbulent scenes later in the year when demonstrating students stormed a student union building and staged a sit-in as a sign of their general discontent. The immediate object was to halt an academic function celebrating the hundredth anniversary of student representation in Finland. The country's president, Urho Kekkonen, had to give his speech in another building. In spite of the disturbance, it was one of the friendliest speeches which the New Left was to hear from a head of state.

GREAT BRITAIN

At about the time of the anti-American riots in Stockholm's Gustav Adolf Square, London's Grosvenor Square witnessed a violent street fight between the police and the participants in a large demonstration against the Vietnam war. While this was not entirely a student affair, it had many characteristics of student marches and it was (as in many other countries) directed against the U.S. Embassy. In October a new confrontation took place on the same square and for the same reasons; a by-product of one of the bigger demonstrations against the Vietnam war, a march had been organized, from the Embankment to Hyde Park Corner, for which the London School of Economics served as organizational headquarters.

Here we must briefly consider the background of the British students' unrest. When I came to England for the first time, in 1926, there were two things which especially impressed the young student from Germany: the amount of idealistic pacifism in British universities (which, I soon learned, had a long tradition in the country), and the large number of militant Asian and African students in positions of authority among their British comrades.

After the Second World War both these phenomena became more pronounced, the one due to the threat of the atom bomb, the other because of the increased influx into Britain of people from the crumbling colonial empire—among them many students desirous for a speedy liberation from their colonial rulers and from the capitalist order established by them. While these trends did not entirely overlap, they reinforced each other and produced—more on campuses than in the country as a whole—a socialist-pacifist-anticolonialist atmosphere. Some students joined the Communist Party, some the Labour Party (or the Labour clubs on the campuses), some the Trotskyists, while some, of course, also turned to the Liberals or the Conservatives. In addition there was a considerable reservoir of students who, while under the influence of that general climate, did not join any such organizations but were staying in contact and carrying on discussions with all of them. A young colored Jamaican Rhodes scholar at Oxford, Stuart Hall, was fairly representative of these nonjoiners. He and his friends, as he told me years later, fit in none of the existing categories and were thus able to discuss everything with anybody without observing any particular orthodoxy.

Then came the autumn of 1956. The risings in Eastern Europe, Poland's "Spring in October" and the assault of Soviet tanks on the young freedom fighters in Hungary, were all terrible blows to countless young Communists (who already had been profoundly affected by the de-Stalinization begun by Khrushchev). Many left the Party forever. The Suez intervention in turn proved to many Labour adherents that British imperialism was still very much alive, and the inglorious end of the Egyptian adventure caused dismay and disappointment in the nation as a whole. It swept aside the various veils with which the liberal intellectuals had sought to cover Britain's decline in power; "the real position was revealed in all its nakedness," and this "spiritual crisis in English life" produced much criticism of society.[4] By November 1956 there were many spiritually homeless Communists, Labour Party members, and socialists in general looking for a new intellectual home.

It was just about this time that the nonjoiners came up with a new publication. Originally they had thought of producing a periodical for the universities. But now they decided to set their aims higher, wishing to reach all those who, disillusioned with the various old Lefts, wanted a new Left; thus, in 1957, the *Universities and Left Review* was born at Oxford. (In 1960, by merging with the *New Reasoner,* it became the *New Left Review* with Stuart Hall its first editor.) From the start, the new review was a great success. It had appeared at the right moment. Soon it had a circulation of 8,000. When its staff called a first public meeting in London, in an old hotel in Bloomsbury, instead of the fifty or sixty people expected many hundreds came. "New Left" groups sprang up all over the country; soon there were about forty of them. A move from Oxford to London became imperative. Money was collected and a small house acquired in Soho, at 7 Carlisle Street, with a much frequented café, the Partisan (no longer in existence), on the ground floor and the editorial as well as the sales offices of *New Left Review* (and later New Left Books) on the upper floors. Many authors became widely known through the pieces they published in the review: Ralph Milliband, Ralph Samuel, Clancy Sigal, E. P. Thompson, Raymond Williams, and C. Wright Mills. Gradually, the new review's horizon was extended; while its predecessor had focused primarily on English issues, the wider world began to enter into its pages, starting with Cuba (in numbers 8 and 9, 1961), which Stuart Hall and some of his friends soon visited.

For the new review and its editorial staff all subjects were treated and discussed politically. Although their movement never became a formal organization, it participated in many events promoted by others, notably in the marches of the Campaign for Nuclear Disarmament, which had been formed in 1958 to demand unilateral nuclear disarmament by Britain. As time went on, the review became more esoteric, turning primarily into a theoretical organ after Stuart Hall's resignation.

The elections of 1964 and the formation of a Labour government gave a new impetus to the British Left in general and the New Left in particular. But soon it was found that the government, in order to govern, had to be far more pragmatic than the party's ringing declarations in the previous years had indicated. Disillusionment set in and with it the search for a new approach. It was the time when the idea of an extraparliamentary opposition was tried out, not only, as we have seen, in West Germany, but also in Britain. The *May Day Manifesto* (published as a Penguin Special in 1968) attacked Labour for its participation in the "managed politics" of a technocratized capitalism. It went on: "We are faced with something alien and thwarting: a manipulative politics, often openly aggressive and cynical, which has taken our meanings and changed them, taken our causes and used them; which seems our creation, but now stands against us, as the agent of the priorities of money and power."[5]

The *New Left Review* in the meantime had lost its political force. This was due, David Widgery explained (himself a man from the Left), to the review's "extraordinarily arrogant belief that it is the role of the intellectuals to make the theory, the job of the workers to make the revolution and that what is wrong in Britain is that the latter are too backward to understand the former's instructions."[6] Those on the left who were dissatisfied with the performance of Labour moved into various groups, all of them radical, but with countless quarrels among each other. There were so many varieties of the Trotskyists alone that a chronicler of the New Left, Peter Sedgwick, once a Trotskyist himself, found them "very difficult to describe." The Maoists too fought among themselves. As for the Solidarists (named after the left-wing monthly *Solidarity*), Sedgwick again confessed: "It is rather difficult for the outsider to keep up with what the group is saying."[7] Personally I am inclined to believe that anarchism was a very strong undercurrent in the British student movement (as it was on the Continent); there is not much, after all, that a true anti-authoritarian can be except an anarchist, even if he has never heard the word and never subscribed to the monthly *Anarchy* (started in 1961) or the weekly *Freedom* (founded by the famous Russian anarchist Prince Piotr Kropotkin in 1886).

As the Third World entered into the young people's field of vision, they became interested not only in the countries whose governments were leftist, like Cuba, but also in most of the "struggles for national liberation." The Congo affair, it is true, had not yet aroused the concern of the young generation, except perhaps for the deaths of the UN's Secretary-General Dag Hammerskjöld, one of the few glamorous personalities of that period, and of Patrice Lumumba. National liberation struggles were then still less a matter for excitable youngsters than for tough journalists, such as the BBC television reporter (real or invented) described by columnist Bernard Levin—the one who, having stepped off the airplane at a Congo airport, amid refugees milling desperately about "went briskly down the line of ashen, numbed, and silent women crying: Anybody here been raped and speaks English?"[8]

The civil war in Nigeria, which brought "Biafra" into the world's vocabulary, made a deeper impression. But Nigeria had become independent and was on its own. Rhodesia on the other hand was still very much a British problem, the government in London considering as illegal Rhodesia's Unilateral Declaration of Independence (November 11, 1965). The London School of Economics (LSE) took up the Rhodesian question in meetings of its Socialist Society. In October 1966, there were attacks against the newly appointed director of the LSE, Walter Adams, who previously had been the director of Rhodesia's University College at Salisbury. The quarrel between a growing number of protesting students and the LSE's administration led to the suspension of two students, which brought about the first occupation of a university building in Britain; it lasted six days and involved more than 2,000 students. This event aroused emotions in the country not only because it was something many Britons had thought could "never happen here," but also because one of the school's employees collapsed and died when the students forced a bolted door leading into the administration building. (Similarly, a few weeks later the death of a young German student, Benno Ohnesorg, during the demonstration against the Shah's visit to Berlin, was to aggravate seriously, as we have seen, the situation in that country. Death escalates any conflict.)

Why, one might ask, was the LSE—one of the most prestigious institutions of higher education in England—the scene of the country's first big student incident? Probably because the LSE had exclusively students of the social sciences (about 4,000 at the time), many of whom had been attracted by the school's leftist reputation, including some who came over from the United States in order to avoid the draft for the war in Vietnam. It was the Vietnam war which soon overshadowed all other political concerns of the students. It led, as we know, to the confrontations in Grosvenor Square in 1968.

After LSE, it was the University of Essex's turn. The issue that sparked off the disturbances there was similar to the one that caused unrest at several American universities—protest against outside lecturers who were working in government military research. At Essex the students, in the summer of 1968, disapproved of a guest lecturer because he was a specialist in biological warfare (which, however, was not the subject of his talk). He came nevertheless, and the meeting at which he expected to speak was disrupted. When the vice-chancellor of the university, Dr. Albert Sloman, suspended three students whom he believed to be responsible for the affair, the reaction on the campus went far beyond a request for their being reinstated. The entire question of the relationship between students and university administration was raised, joint committees consisting of staff and students were requested, and the abolition of examinations was demanded. Even a "free university" was created, which at first attracted about a thousand staff members and students.

The news of the Paris events poured across the Channel, inspiring the British students, who now realized that the entire Continent was rebelling—as far east as Czechoslovakia and Poland. (Kuroń and Modzelewski's "Open Letter to the Communist Party Members," mentioned in the following chapter, was quickly translated into English and published by "International Socialism," an organization to which the leading LSE leftists belonged.)

But on the whole not much happened in Britain during the hot summer of 1968. When Daniel Cohn-Bendit, the French student leader, came to London at the invitation of the BBC, his visit was turbulent (he spoke at the LSE and had himself photographed at Karl Marx's grave), but it did not cause any serious incidents.

Altogether, in 1967 and 1968, in the whole of Great Britain, only twenty-three universities and colleges were the scene of direct student actions. At five of these, the demand was for student representation on college governing bodies. At eight, the demands were "concerned with a variety of essentially campus issues, ranging from the suitability of the Director [of the LSE . . .] to inadequate transport facilities between annexes." At the other ten (Oxford and Cambridge among them), visiting speakers were subjected to violence or stimulated violent demonstrations.[9] In May 1968, disturbances at the Hornsey Art College caught the attention of the country's intellectuals when students staged a seven-week sit-in and demanded a new curriculum and an approach different from that of ordinary colleges of higher education, including the abolition of examinations.

The last year of the decade witnessed some disturbances at Cambridge, one of the country's two grand old universities. During a Greek Week, which was to promote holidays in and trade with Greece, Garden House, the town's most expensive hotel, organized a Greek food banquet. Students, demonstrating against the military regime in Greece, broke into the hotel, damaging windows and spoiling the food. The trial, held for security reasons in another town, ended with sentences of up to eighteen months in jail.

Northern Ireland did not belong to the Third World, and the civil war there did not at first arouse the same passions as Biafra had. But the rise and brief prominence of Bernadette Devlin, soon turned into an Irish Joan of Arc, captured the imagination of students; she was young and she was fiery. Her book, *The Price of My Soul* (1969), sold 140,000 copies in England and was published in more than a dozen languages, including German, French, Italian, Spanish, Polish, and Japanese.

By the end of the sixties the various left-wing flames had burned down. To be sure, the *New Left Review* had returned to the political field in the narrower sense of the word; in issue number 43 (May/June 1967), entitled *Student Power,* it showed its interest in the radical student movement by publishing a report by Ben Brewster and Alexander Cockburn, "Revolt at the LSE." But it never recaptured the commanding position it had held ten years earlier; too many other left-wing organizations had been formed, pursuing their own lines, producing their own publications.

The seventies did not see a comparable wave of student uprisings. But three academic institutions were affected by disturbances: the Polytechnic of North London, and, once again, the University of Essex and the LSE.

The Polytechnic of North London (PNL) was created in 1971 by the merger of two existing institutions, Northern Polytechnic and North Western Polytechnic. The school has had a history of conflict from the very start. It had hardly been opened when sit-ins began, in February 1971; there were disruptions of meetings of the court of governors and of the academic board, and disturbances at ceremonies. In the beginning, the attacks centered mainly on the PNL's director, Terence Miller. He, like the LSE director, Walter Adams, had been in Rhodesia (as principal of University College), he too was fought as an alleged racist (although he had been critical of the Ian Smith government).

Another prolonged fight was caused by the "Jenkins affair." Director Miller had suspended Professor Wycliffe Jenkins in July 1972 from his position as head of the department of business studies, mainly for failure to conduct examinations in the proper way, but he found himself unable to enforce his decision in the face of a prolonged occupation of Ladbroke House. (Among the occupiers' slogans: "Today Ladbroke—Tomorrow the World.")

Events at the PNL are of particular interest because, on the whole, technical institutions in Britain (as everywhere else) are less likely to be centers of unrest than other universities. One of the reasons for the PNL's troubles is that although a polytechnic, the PNL includes very active departments of sociology and applied social studies. Also it has, among its students, a most virulent and determined left wing, which, although a minority on the campus, has succeeded in capturing decisive positions in the Student Union and among the student members of the board of governors, as well as a large proportion of the members of the PNL's supreme academic body, the Academic Board, in which the PNL students have 36 percent of the seats—more than in any other comparable college of the country, the average for all polytechnics being 11.5 percent. Of late, the situation at PNL has quieted down, but one professor whom I questioned called it "a lost institution."

The University of Essex made the headlines in 1973. The Student Union decided to hold a "Day of Action" on November 15, in order to support its demand for higher maintenance grants. That day, a Thursday, passed relatively peacefully. But after the weekend the tempo quickened: The administrative offices were invaded, the vice-chancellor's files forced, and confidential documents copied in the dean of students' office. The next morning, three "nonnegotiable demands" were presented by the students: an immediate reduction of cafeteria prices by 15 percent; a guarantee that, as student numbers increased, new restaurants, bars, and accommodations would be opened; a 55 percent reduction in rents in four properties where students were housed off-campus. The same morning the occupiers were warned to vacate the premises by midday or a high court order for possession of the buildings would be obtained. They did not leave and the order was obtained, putting all students who remained in the area in contempt of court. A general meeting of the Student Union, attended by 800 students, voted in favor of the occupation and delegated the union's power of decision making to a "Committee of Occupation," a clear breach of its constitution, as it transferred authority from the Student Union to a small group not responsible to it. But the court order was never enforced. The occupation lasted until shortly before Christmas. The damage caused by it and by other disturbances amounted to about £10,000; more than half of this sum had to be spent on replacing locks as the keys of the entire university had been stolen during the occupation. Of the further events, here is a summary given in the very detailed Annan Report, put out by the university in 1974 and named after its author, Lord Annan:[10]

In February 1974 disciplinary hearings against individual students began. When the first student to be found guilty was expelled from the university for one year, pickets were mounted and barricades erected to close the main entrance of the university. All delivery traffic was disrupted. In March students broke windows and stole equipment, causing £6,000 worth of damage. Picketing became more serious. On March 18, the police arrested fifteen persons for blocking the entrance to the university, and a few days later ninety more were arrested. Then 200 students, mostly from other universities, forced their way into the office of the vice-chancellor and held him under duress for two hours. In April, once more the vice-chancellor's office was invaded. In May, the Appeal Committee changed the penalties imposed by the Disciplinary Court: the two students to be expelled had their sentence amended to suspended expulsion, a fine of £50 was changed to £25 and a fine of £25 to a suspended fine. After that the university became more peaceful. The Annan Report concludes dryly: "The university had acquired an unconventional blessing by saving £11,000 on oil which would have been consumed for heating the premises, but the total damage from the sit-in, the general repairs and the blockade of the pickets was over £32,000."

Three years later, in February 1977, Essex came once more into the news. Sir Keith Joseph, a Conservative front-bench M.P. responsible for policy and research, was pelted with eggs and flour bombs and taunted with shouts including "Fascist" and "racist" (Sir Keith is Jewish) while addressing the students. The *Sunday Times* headlined its editorial on February 13, 1977: "Shut Down Essex," to which Dr. Sloman vigorously objected one week later.

Finally—once again the LSE. When it became known that, by autumn 1977, university fees would be considerably increased all over Britain, LSE students demanded a reversal of the govern-

163

ment decision. The new director, Professor Ralf Dahrendorf, from West Germany, while in full sympathy with the students' desire, declared that he was not in a position to rescind a decision that was the government's, not his. Thereupon the students occupied four floors of the administration building.

Fees for British undergraduates were raised from £182 a year to £500 and for postgraduates from £182 to £750; for non-British undergraduates, from £416 to £650, and for postgraduates, from £416 to £850. This fee increase hardly hit the British undergraduates, whose fees are paid for them by the local authorities in the areas from which they come, but it was serious for the postgraduates (about 50 percent of the LSE students), most of whom have to pay their own fees and, for the same reason, for the students from abroad (36 percent of the student body, four-fifths of them from the Third World).

At a lively meeting in the school's old theater on February 14, 1977, which I attended, the students passed a resolution demanding that the director make a public statement denouncing the increases, while the director insisted that the occupation be ended, threatening otherwise to invoke a high court order. I found opinions divided among the students. Many British students were for solidarity with the foreigners; others felt: Why should the British taxpayer support foreign students? There was more unanimity in combating the fee increase for British postgraduates, because most of the LSE students were (or soon would be) in that category.

Clearly the leadership in the conflict lay with the left wing. In the debate, some speakers deplored the fact that a small minority (mostly Trotskyists and Maoists) were using the fee issue to disrupt the school's work. This argument was strengthened when Tariq Ali—the Trotskyist founder of the International Marxist Group, one of the leading radicals of the late sixties, a Pakistani with British passport—arrived at the scene to support the sit-in. Four students resigned from the twelve-member executive body of the Students Union, claiming that the sit-in was being used by the school's ultra-Left to create a conflict in which they could take over the union. The conflict at the LSE ended after two weeks in a rather well-mannered British way. With the High Court Order in his hand, the Under Sheriff of the County of London told the students that he hoped to enter the occupied building as peacefully as he had twenty-five years ago while himself a student at LSE. In fact, his 300 policemen had to smash a few locked doors and to remove a barricade, but the students left without a fight. A

164

few days later some 100,000 students from about a hundred colleges took action in protest against the government's proposed tuition increases. But the climate of the conflict was markedly different from that of the sixties. Director Dahrendorf told the *Daily Telegraph* correspondent (February 15, 1977):

> In 1968, students thought they were a rising social group and should demand a place in the sun. In 1977, students are behaving as though they were a declining industry. They are asking for more money and Government support, just like the textile industry.

The public reaction was mostly negative and supported the statement in the already mentioned Annan Report of 1974. While previously during university troubles the press treated the university authorities with skepticism and the student body with sympathy, there was now "an almost total absence of support for the militants in editorial comment" and "a total condemnation of the Essex students in the Press." The trade unions told Lord Annan "bluntly that the Essex students were living off the backs of the workers who paid taxes for them to study not to agitate."[11]

In one more respect, England showed a similarity with America and the Continent: England too had its terrorists. I am not speaking of those in Northern Ireland—they are of a different brand and need not be dealt with here. But a group similar to America's Weathermen and Germany's Baader-Meinhof gang appeared in the early seventies—the Angry Brigade, described in detail in Gordon Carr's *The Angry Brigade* (1975). It operated under the slogan: "The War will be won by the organized working class. With bombs." After committing two dozen bombings, including one in Biba's boutique and one at the home of the secretary of state for employment, four members were sentenced in 1972 to ten years in prison. The two girls were dropouts of Essex University, the two boys, of Cambridge. The release of one of the girls on parole caused some public excitement early in 1977 and brought the group's actions back into discussion. The *Guardian,* in an editorial (February 15, 1977) described the four as "naïve" and as "revolutionary Pollyannas." Reminding its readers of some of their earlier do-good activities (an attempt, for example, to set up a free legal-aid center), which never amounted to anything, the editorial concluded: "What they lacked was the self-discipline and application that is needed to be successful in non-violent community politics. Instead, they turned to gelignite which required far less effort."

Thus, in England too, the drama had run its course—from the

writings of the Angry Young Men to the bombings of the Angry Brigade.

FRANCE

In May the storm broke over Paris. There is no phase of the youth revolution about which we know as much as the "Paris May." More has been written about the events in the United States, but these were scattered across a continent, while in France everything happened in a single city. The dramatic unities of place and time were Paris, May 1968. (The universities in the provinces offered only sideshows.)

Five years after the revolt, more than 300 books had been published about it, and thousands of articles.[12] There were illustrious names among the authors—from the sociologist Raymond Aron, who expressed in caustic words his revulsion against the "collective delirium," to the historian Alain Touraine, who praised the "holy wrath" of the young rebels—and also those of some of the activists, with Daniel "Dany the Red," Cohn-Bendit in the front rank.

On Saturday, May 11, radio and TV reported the dramatic events of the preceding "night of the barricades." Two days later, on the train to Paris, I read the newspapers and tried to reconstruct the course of events. It had all began at France's newest university, a modernistic affair of concrete and glass which a shortsighted government had built in Nanterre, close to Paris, amid slums where Algerian workers dwelt. The event that started the trouble was more worthy of a comedy than of a serious drama: Fired by the books of Wilhelm Reich (*The Function of Orgasm* and others), the students of Nanterre had been carrying out a "campaign for sexual enlightenment" when, on January 8, 1968, the head of the Ministry for Youth and Sports happened to visit the university in order to open its new swimming pool. A student, Daniel Cohn-Bendit, totally unknown until then, heckled him for omitting any mention of sexual problems in the ministry's recently published white paper on student affairs. Sarcastically, the minister suggested that if the student could not cope with his sexual needs, he should cool off by jumping into the new swimming pool, whereupon Cohn-Bendit called him a fascist.

The police arrested Cohn-Bendit and wanted to deport him as a foreigner (his Jewish parents had left Germany under Hitler and had later gone back). Students demonstrating in his favor clashed with the police, and after March 22, when they occupied the university's administrative offices, called themselves the "March 22 Movement." They wanted to change not just their university but the whole of France. When Nanterre's department of philosophy was shut down, the spark of rebellion leaped to the Sorbonne in Paris. On Saturday, May 4, it too was closed. On the following Monday, new fighting began between students and police. Irresistibly, events were moving toward the "night of the barricades."

In Paris, I took a taxi from the station straight to the Latin Quarter, which includes the Sorbonne. The driver unmistakably expressed his dislike for the students, and when I got out at the rue Gay-Lussac, next to a barricade of cobblestones, he said with an undertone of envy: "Monsieur, in Germany this could not have happened—you were clever enough to have asphalt streets." The cobblestones, *les pavés,* have a long revolutionary tradition in France; in May, they even became the subject of student songs:

> Par les pavés des rues
> et par les barricades,
> par les jets de grenades
> et les flics qui se ruent,
> Je vous salue,
> Paris![13]

("Through the streets' cobblestones/and through the barricades,/ through the hand grenades/and the running police,/I greet you,/ Paris!")

Things looked pretty bad in the Latin Quarter. Burned-out cars lay in the streets like corpses, fallen trees obstructed the way, windows and doors were broken in, *les pavés* were stacked in barricades—where they had lain before, one walked through sand. Student-made revolutionary posters covered the walls, together with slogans that quickly became famous during those days: "All Power to Imagination!" "To Prohibit is Prohibited!" "Forget What You Learned, Start Dreaming!"[14]

Few people were to be seen. Even the boulevard Saint-Michel, beloved "boul' Mich' " of the Paris students, was almost empty on this May morning, except for a column of young marchers. Hundreds of them had been injured during the night of the barricades, hundreds arrested; now thousands were on the way to organize the giant demonstration for that afternoon.

It proved to be the largest anywhere that year (except perhaps in China), the 750,000 participants topping even the Vietnam demonstrations in America. Many workers joined in, for a variety of reasons—some wanted to overthrow the capitalist system, some demanded higher wages, and many were just caught up in the general excitement. At times I saw two different currents of demonstrations flowing through Paris, one of students, the other of workers. In both there were red flags, raised fists, and the strains of the *Internationale,* and at times they converged. While the student leaders were exuberant, the Communist trade-union leaders walked with clenched teeth—used to being in charge of demonstrations and calling each signal, the effects of which had been premeditated to the last detail, they were suspicious of the students' spontaneity; in fact, they disliked it, and around 8:00 P.M. they dissolved their columns. The workers went home, but the day had not yet ended for the students; they occupied the university, which they said would be open from now on to everybody except the police.

The following days were hectic: more demonstrations, more activities of exuberant students, more occupations—of factories, schools, and even the Odéon-Théâtre close to the boul' Mich', which was turned into a combination parliament and showplace, much to the horror of its director, the great mime Jean-Louis Barrault. President de Gaulle broke off an official visit to Romania, and upon returning uttered a sentence which soon was to be quoted everywhere: *"La reforme oui, la chien-lit non."* Reform, yes—but what was *chien-lit*? Linguists racked their brains. The rarely used word has various meanings; what de Gaulle probably had in mind was bed-wetting, or worse. The toilet-language of the young had penetrated even into the Elysée Palace.

The wave rolled on. Soon 10 million workers were on strike, more than 200 factories were occupied. A chain reaction was setting off countless explosions. "Doctors, lawyers, accountants, engineers, researchers, statisticians, journalists, museum curators, actors, film directors, athletes, and shopgirls joined in a general revolt against authority."[15] The demand for de Gaulle's resignation became ever louder. Mendès-France announced his readiness to succeed him, and de Gaulle left Paris. Did he go to his private home in the countryside to formulate a letter of resignation? By no means. Unnoticed, he flew to Baden Baden, to the French troops stationed in Germany, secured the support of their commander, General Massu, and on May 30 announced over radio and TV the calling of new elections in which the French nation would have to choose between him and the Communists. That evening, hundreds of thousands again marched through the streets of Paris, only this time they were Gaullists. The enemy now was on the Left, and "Cohn-Bendit to Dachau!" one of the slogans.

Tensions then gradually subsided. The workers were granted higher wages and shorter working hours; they withdrew from the front lines. Police cleared the universities. On two election Sundays, June 23 and 30, thoroughly frightened Frenchmen voted overwhelmingly in favor of de Gaulle, sending 92 more Gaullists to Parliament than before, and giving them an absolute majority; the Communists' strength declined from 71 seats to 33. The *chien-lit* was over. (For the inventor of this slogan, too, time was running out. Fear of revolution rather than confidence in him had caused the majority of the French to vote for de Gaulle. He lost a plebiscite on a minor issue ten months later, resigned, and died the following year.)

It came as a surprise to the students of the March 22 Movement and other radical groups that the workers who participated in such great numbers in the demonstrations of May 13 should withdraw from the struggle after securing higher wages. They considered it nothing less than treason. The leaders of the strongest labor federation, the CGT, had collaborated closely with the French Communist Party and taken part in the revolt only halfheartedly; they as well as the Communists were courting the middle class, and they could easily foresee that student disturbances and the specter of revolution would swing public opinion to the right. The great majority of the students, in turn, because of their antiauthoritarian attitude, had no love for the Moscow-oriented Communists. The well-known writer Louis Aragon, a member of the Party, tried to establish contact with the students and met with jeers: "Long Live the GPU [the Soviet secret police]!" "Long Live Stalin, Our Father!"[16] (I have described Moscow's anger with the Paris May in another context; see Mehnert, *Moscow*, Chapter 3.)

In the end, there were many losers: de Gaulle's prestige was badly—as it turned out, irreparably—hurt; the student rebellion was defeated; the Party was cut down to size. The only winners were the workers, and not in the political or ideological sense. Realistically, they had understood that the upheaval favored their struggle for higher wages; in the general excitement they pushed through a number of demands, and then they went back to work.

The return to normal university life was more difficult. There were recurring troubles. At the Sorbonne in January 1969 about 400 students were arrested. In Nanterre in the spring of 1970 students attacked the dean, throwing the contents of a garbage can on him. And the splintering of the extreme Left continued. In 1970, in Paris alone, six Maoist and seven Trotskyist groups were counted.[17] The Communist Party, however, gradually managed to recover from its low point of the summer of 1968.

Shortly after the Paris May a German journalist wrote that Che Guevara had died a second time on the Paris barricades. Guevara's doctrine that, through permanent action, rebels could by themselves create the conditions for a revolution had been refuted there, as it had been in Bolivia.[18] But, like Guevara, the Paris May also spawned a myth from its failure. The memory of May 13, when students and workers marched through the streets, helped some young rebels forget the sad and now confirmed thesis of Marcuse that the workers in a modern industrial state are useless when it comes to making revolution.

SENEGAL

Events in Senegal were symptomatic of the spreading of the Paris May to former colonies of France. On an African trip in the summer of 1968, I found this spillover effect at the University of Dakar. To be sure, there had been some conflicts in Senegal before (and where not?), such as the one in 1967, when for reasons of economy the government decreed that scholarships were to be paid for only ten months, not twelve. But without the exciting news from France there would hardly have been the riots in Dakar. The connection between France and its former colonial empire is still strong.

Troubles began at Dakar University on May 23 with a strike by students, who were joined by young people from the upper grades of the lycées (high schools). Purely academic demands were soon augmented by others; there was criticism of the high salaries and allowances of cabinet members, and of the political system as a whole. Policemen blocked off the beautiful campus, where the president's office and other administrative buildings were occupied by students. Then some students were arrested and one of them was killed. The trade unions called a general strike (again following the Paris example), pushing demands of their own. Looting began in the city, a state of emergency was declared, and all public assembly was forbidden, even for the Friday prayer at the mosque. But the government came round, agreeing to the workers' demands for increased wages and better health insurance, and the strike ebbed. When the arrested students were set free, I met some of them: their vocabulary was taken from that of the Paris students, with anti-French undertones added. In November the university was reopened on orders from the country's president, L. S. Senghor, one of the foremost intellectuals and poets of Africa. There were further disturbances, but on a smaller scale.

AUSTRIA

My friends on the Danube will not be too angry, I hope, if for the sake of comic relief I mention an incident which, compared with the drama on the Seine, was but a piece of satire, and one lacking the charm for which Vienna is justly known. Still, it was part of the astonishing scope of academic unrest in 1968 and was about the only excitement in Austrian universities during that year.

During the May Day parade there had been a minor clash between the police and some left-wing students who tried to disturb a concert on the City Hall square, carrying posters with slogans such as: "We Want Marx! Or Do You Know Something Better?" But nobody was particularly upset.

It was only on June 7 that something happened which was to get the University of Vienna into the news. A left-wing organization, modeled on the German SDS, invited the public to a discussion evening on "Revolution and Art," and arranged for some young people who called themselves artists to appear as living examples. Before an audience of 450 in a lecture hall of the new university building, a student announced at the outset: "We uncover the covered person. You are about to see something you have never seen before." How right he was.

According to newspaper reports, there followed: the whipping of a naked youngster by two equally naked men; masturbation to the strains of the national anthem; a competition for distance in urination, with a measuring tape to determine the victor; and, at the end, an appearance by "three long-haired naked young men who left their excrements on the stage as a 'contribution to the discussion.'" After that, it was announced that this was meant to be only the beginning: "Go to the Cathedral of Saint Stephen and do the same thing there. That will really be a provocation!"[19] Indignation among students and the general population of Vienna was such that the organization responsible for the evening promptly dissolved itself.

SWITZERLAND

The Swiss, like the Austrians, congratulated themselves on being spared youth revolts on the scale of those in neighboring countries. But by the end of June 1968 the wave had reached Switzerland, too. Even the solid *Neue Zürcher Zeitung,* not easily panicked, wrote that the street fighting on June 29 and 30 was distinguished by a smaller degree of destruction, though not in principle, from the events in Berlin, Rome, and Paris.[20]

Earlier, "Red Rudi" had been invited to lecture at the University of Zurich, and "Dany The Red" at the University of Basel (neither could come, Dutschke because of his wounds). During the May 1 demonstrations, a radical student group demanded close cooperation with the workers, saying "The workers would bring decades of experience—the students, thousands of ideas."[21] Portraits of Dutschke, Ho, Guevara, and Marx were carried by the demonstrators.

The climax which disturbed even the *Neue Zürcher Zeitung*— two nights of violent confrontation close to Zurich's central railroad station—was not provoked by students; rather, it was the result of unsuccessful demands by a youth group that the city fathers allow a large empty building to become a youth center. On the first night 129 were arrested and 41 injured; a child wounded in the melee died because an ambulance could not get through the throng quickly enough. The second night was not quite that bad.

Could such riots have occurred, in this quiet and staid city, if there had not been the examples of Berlin, Rome, and Paris? I doubt it.

MEXICO

Soon the quiet of the summer vacation reigned at the European universities; the defeat of the French students also had a calming effect. The next story about student riots came from the New World.

From the history of the conquest of Mexico by the Spaniards, we know of the *Noche Triste,* the sad night of June 30, 1520, during which Cortés lost half his army in heavy fighting. In 1968 the term was used again, but in the plural. From the end of July to early October 1968 there was hardly a night in Mexico without a confrontation. Official figures for the number of dead were never made public; the *New York Times* mentioned a probable total of 300.[22]

It began harmlessly enough, with scuffling between the students of two high schools in Mexico City, and only acquired some importance when the *grenaderos* (riot police), feared because of their toughness, came on the scene. Demonstrations of sympathy at other schools, even at the universities, followed immediately, involving up to 150,000 marchers, among them many professors, and producing more actions by the *grenaderos,* with army units added toward the end. Meanwhile, with the scheduled opening of the Olympic Games on October 12 coming closer every day and the government most anxious to restore order before guests arrived from all over the world, the violence escalated. For almost two weeks police occupied the National University, where some of the games were to be held, causing students in New York to demand that the United States withdraw from the games.

The saddest of the sad nights came ten days prior to the opening of the Olympics. In the Tlatelolco quarter of the city, on the proudly named "Square of the Three Cultures" (Aztec, Spanish Colonial, and Modern), some 10,000 students held a meeting. Reports differed as to who fired first, but dozens of students were killed, the estimates running from sixty into the hundreds; there were countless injured, while more than a thousand were arrested. The following day, the horror felt by the population was such that students and police agreed upon an unwritten armistice until the end of the games. When the universities opened for the winter semester, there were more demonstrations, but without the previous violence.[23]

For many years, Mexico was regarded as a country whose social revolution had been completed, once and for all, in the second decade of our century. Indeed, the memory of the chaos of that upheaval had built into the consciousness of the people a powerful barrier against new disturbances. But the events in the autumn of 1968 showed that discontent had accumulated against the party which had been in power for almost forty years—the Partido Revolucionario Institucional—and which through close cooperation with the administration, the trade unions, and big business had formed a true *establecimiento.* There was discontent also over the glaring contrast between poor and rich, and the strong position of the U.S. corporations.

The "sad nights" of Mexico were the last grim episode of 1968 on the campuses of the countries treated here. Student unrest had not come to an end, but the "year of the students" had.

In the course of the sixties I witnessed student disturbances or their consequences in a number of other places, including Afghanistan, Canada, Egypt, Hong Kong, India, Indonesia, Iran, Jamaica, Nepal, Pakistan, the Philippines, Puerto Rico, Singapore, South Africa, and Turkey. I shall not enlarge upon my observations there because they did not contribute to any new understanding. In other countries that I visited in connection with lectures, there was no rioting during my stay. In Lebanon I lectured at the American University at a time when no one could have predicted the tragedy that befell the country in the midseventies. Nor did anyone foresee chaos when I was in Uruguay, then an exemplary and orderly democratic country, or in prosperous Argentina.

SOUTH KOREA

When I visited South Korea in 1955, shortly after the end of the Korean war and the Geneva Conference, Syngman Rhee was the leading Korean statesman, time and again reelected the country's president, and still the respected "father of the Fatherland." His iron will had held the people together during the early years of independence and through the war. But during the next five years Rhee had become ever more difficult and stubborn. The elections of March 1960 were generally considered to have been rigged in his favor. On election day there were antigovernment demonstrations in the port city of Masan, with shots and deaths.

A first student demonstration in Seoul began without serious incident. Two thousand University of Korea students surprised the police by jogging quickly from the campus to the center of town, where they held their demonstration. Then, returning to their campus in small groups, they were badly mauled by "police bandits." The next day, 20,000 students marched in protest to the palace of President Rhee, urged on by the sympathizing population. The police opened fire. More than 100 students were killed, more than 700 taken to hospitals. Horror gripped the city. Two hundred professors now demonstrated in front of the palace, demanding Rhee's resignation. Meanwhile, thousands of angry people were milling in the streets, and the house of the vice-president was burned down. On April 27, Rhee resigned at the suggestion of his own generals (and of his American advisers). The rest of the day belonged to the students. Organizing their own effort for restoring order, they cleaned the streets of rubble and barricades.

When I arrived in Korea, shortly after these events, I interviewed a number of the students and professors. They said that a few thousand students, carried along by a wave of popular appreciation, had demonstrated against a regime that had become old and rigid; the students had sacrificed and won, had removed the wreckage, and had returned to school. It was a revolution neither from above nor from below, but rather from the side. Therein lay its problems. Those who had accomplished it—the students—were neither willing nor able to form a new government. This had to be the job of the politicians. But after years of police rule, which had stifled all healthy opposition, they were unfit for this task. The political parties could only squabble with each other amid unstable conditions. One year after the students' victory, the military staged a coup d'etat and established their own regime, which proved to be even harder on the students than that of Rhee.

My talks with students in Seoul, especially with those still in the hospital (some of them crippled for the rest of their lives), and my observations in Tokyo during the wild student demonstrations a few weeks earlier, contributed to my later decision to write this book.

PORTUGAL AND GREECE

The Portuguese and Greek students were behind the times. They had rebelled off and on, but their great hour came after the authoritarian regimes in their countries had already been overthrown by others.

Young Portuguese officers, disgusted with the colonial wars in Africa and the lack of hopeful prospects under an antiquated, inept government in Lisbon, staged a coup d'etat on April 25, 1974. In Greece, the military junta, after the bankruptcy of its Cyprus policy was exposed, committed political suicide on July 23 of the same year, handing the government over to Konstantin Karamanlis, who returned from exile. Only then did the students in both countries have their chance. On visits during the following months I found them in a mood like that of students elsewhere six years earlier.

In Lisbon it was easy to know when one was near the campus, thanks to the many-colored, frequently hand-painted posters. The walls of the university foyer and, even more, the dining hall, were plastered with slogans signed with initials as yet unknown to me, or with symbols such as the hammer and sickle, the hammer or sickle alone, or just a pair of pliers. Leaflets littered the floor. The

175

discussions following my lectures had nothing to do with their
subjects, but were, as I had hoped, focused on the political problems of Portugal. Whether to use violence in the expected domestic quarrels, whether to move on to a social revolution or to seek
reforms, whether to have a dictatorship of the proletariat or a
democracy—these and many other issues of our time were
paraded before me during those hours. Among the students
present were Maoists, Marxist-Leninists, Trotskyists, anarchists,
pro- and anti-Moscow communists, socialists—all quarreling with
each other. Some of this dissent exploded in an unsuccessful rising a few months later.

The universities of Athens offered, as could have been expected,
a more normal picture. The Greek students had proved themselves in fighting the colonels' junta in November 1973, when
Athens experienced its *Noche Triste*—army tanks stormed the
Polytechnical Institute, then occupied by students from various
schools, causing thirty-four deaths. Hence students in Greece had
less need than those in Portugal to exhibit revolutionary enthusiasm. Also the splintering on the extreme Left was less
bizarre. Most important: In contrast to Portugal, where the dis-
graced conservatives had been in power for almost half a century,
in Greece the conservatives had not been discredited. Few of them
had cooperated with the junta, and from their ranks had come,
after the end of the junta, a statesman of high prestige, Karamanlis, who was not a naïve military man but a professional politician
with years of experience in government. Finally, Greece had a
middle-of-the-road party, attractive to many voters, with an
equally respected leader, Georgios Mavros. In the last years
Greek students have moved toward the left, which, however, is
split into several communist groups, only one being pro-Moscow.

In both Portugal and Greece the students were searching. In
the years of the dictatorship it was enough to be against the
regime, ideological nuances being irrelevant. It was afterward
that these nuances began to be discussed. The students in Athens,
on the whole, stood to the left of the general population, but were
calmer than those in Lisbon. In talking about their extremist
political sects, they called them *chaotikí*, reaching back to ancient
Greek cosmology for the term, as we Germans had done for our
Chaoten.

17
UNDER RED FLAGS

DICTATORSHIPS, whether they call themselves
people's democracies or something else, do not permit youth rebellions. But the extent of repression is not always the same. In
the countries with "Socialist" in their names (an adjective which
many socialists in the world deny them, and which some do not
apply to each other—for example, Peking not to Moscow, and vice
versa), the first stirrings of an independent youth movement
came quite late. They were only possible after Stalin's death
(1953), especially after his condemnation by Khrushchev (1956).

The following pages do not tell the whole history of youthful
protest within the Red world; but it, too, has not remained untouched, as we shall see.

MOSCOW
In the spring of 1959, I went several times to the former riding
school, that huge classicist building along the Kremlin wall, to
see the art exhibit of the "Socialist States," especially the Polish
section. While all the other countries, well behaved as they were,
displayed paintings and sculptures of the type approved by Moscow and called "socialist realism," Poland had dared to send very
modern and, in part, even abstract works. Whenever I came to
this exhibition (in all I spent about ten hours there), it was always
the same: relatively few visitors in the other rooms and throngs of
people, many youngsters among them, in front of the Polish
paintings. Quite often I witnessed violent disputes.

A young man who had shown much enthusiasm for these pictures (he was a student of aerodynamics, it turned out later) was asked by some people whether he actually liked the stuff or praised it out of spite. He answered:

> Is this art? Perhaps this question will be answered only in years to come. All I know is that contemporary Soviet art bores me; it always shows the same few things, copies of our reality which we know anyway, illustrations. But art?—No. That is why I think artists should be given the chance to search for themselves. Not only artists, but also the public. We do not want to be treated any longer as if we were children who are told by the grown-ups, "This is beautiful, and this is ugly." We want to develop our own tastes. We are an adult nation.

He had spoken calmly, including the decisive *My vzrosly narod,* "We are an adult nation." These three words stood there like a courageous challenge to all intellectual tyranny.

A scene such as this—and I have witnessed many like it since then—would have been unthinkable a few years earlier. The break with Stalinist rigidity was symbolized by a young man from Siberia, Yevgeny Yevtushenko, born in 1933. His long *Station Sima* (1956), his other poems, and the carefree courage with which he recited them (in front of growing audiences, once even in a stadium because the lecture halls became too small), flung open the nailed-up windows, allowing light and air to enter, dispelling the musty dogmatism in which people had lived for so long. In later years Yevtushenko was occasionally criticized even by his erstwhile fans in the West: He had, so they said, made too many compromises with the powers that be. Let history judge Yevtushenko—for Soviet youth he provided in the years after Stalin's death the most impressive example of independent thinking. From him they learned: You may think again. More: You *must* think. Toward the end of *Station Sima* the poet's friend tells him:

> Today, my friend, all people started thinking . . .
> Think long and hurry not.

Yevtushenko proved that you could even say what you were thinking—this was big news. He was not to remain alone.

What the young man from Siberia said calmly in 1956, and the student of aerodynamics in 1959, was sounded in a shrill outcry when *Phoenix* rose from the ashes. This was an underground publication, typed and mimeographed in 1959, which went clandestinely from hand to hand in the Soviet Union and also reached the West.[1] *Phoenix* was not the only anthology of the literary underground in those years, but it was by far the most exciting one. Its contributors were mostly young people—all of them deeply moved by the post-Stalin surge and its throttling after a few years, full of bitterness against the regime and even against Khrushchev, who had disappointed them by his later antiliberalism. An impressive example of the sentiment in *Phoenix* came from A. Vladimirov. To give an idea of the Russian original, here are the first few lines; the signs indicate where the stress (unmarked in Russian) should be:

> O poslúshai, poslúshai
> Ne tebyá li zovút?
> Po vodé i po súshe
> Razpolsáyetsya zvúk.

The following translations are mine, with apologies to the Russian poets; I have tried to preserve rhythm and meaning to the best of my ability. The whole of Vladimirov's poem goes like this:

> Oh listen, oh listen,
> Is it you whom they call?
> On land and on water
> Rumors come, rumors fall.

> Sounds are echoing, mingling,
> Voices here, voices there,
> Madly torn you see blowing
> In the storms our hair.

> Murmur moves ever closer,
> Trouble near, trouble near,
> A roar is approaching,
> Land and water in fear.

> All is blue and is misty,
> No one knows what is true.
> In the holster the pistol
> Is cold and is blue.

> No, we shall not panic,
> In Christs we don't trust.
> We look into the mist
> From the cross of the mast.

> Closer, closer, the noises,
> Rumors creep everywhere,
> Murmurs, roars, are approaching,
> Call you here, call you there.
>
> We come not empty-handed
> When all values grow old
> In the holster the pistol
> Is blue and is cold.[2]

These verses come very close to the threatening motto of *Phoenix:*

> Write all the truth, the words must be alive.
> Then thought, still veiled, unlit,
> Will tense into a coil
> And kill those touching it.[3]

V. Nilsky finishes his call to Russia to free itself from the strait-jacket:

> Arise!
> Now,
> In this blue night
> I've had it up to here! Enough! Enough![4]

"Arise!" is the repeated cry of Yuri Galanskov in his *Human Manifesto,* and then:

> Go and destroy down to the ground
> The rotting prison of the state![5]

Quite in the spirit of the Russian intelligentsia of the nineteenth century, which took on the role of a parliament that did not exist in the authoritarian tsarist empire, N. Nor writes:

> Not we are shooting with pistols
> Into the green-clad troops,
> Not we are loading the pistols,
> But on days when history swoops
> The epoch creates the poets
> And the poets create the troops.

Still, under Khrushchev repression had returned. The poetess A. Onezhskaya was right with her sad prognosis:

180

> The world shoots the poets,
> Puts them in a common grave.[6]

In the following years many young poets went to their "common grave"—the forced-labor camp, the insane asylum, the forced exile from the homeland. A few names: Andrei Amalrik, historian, born in 1938—to the labor camp; Yosif Brodsky, poet, born in 1940—forced labor, now in the United States; Vladimir Bukovsky, student of biology, born in 1942—since his twenty-first year in "psychiatric clinics," prisons, and especially tough labor camps because of publishing the underground periodical *The Martyr* and similar crimes; Yuri Galanskov, born in 1939, contributed his "Human Manifesto" to *Phoenix 1* and edited *Phoenix 2* (1966)—forced labor. At the end of 1967 and the beginning of 1968, when the American and German SDS were at their height, the trials of young members of a secret movement which called itself the "All-Russian Christian-Social Union for the Liberation of the People" took place in Leningrad. Those arrested, aged twenty to thirty-three, were almost all intellectuals (specialists in literature and Oriental studies, young lawyers and teachers); they were sentenced to prison for periods of one to seven years. Of the seven who dared to demonstrate in Red Square on August 25, 1968, against the invasion of Czechoslovakia (and who deserve to enter Russian history as the "Moscow 7" more than the "Chicago 8" into that of the United States), Vadim Delone, poet, was twenty-one; Vladimir Dremlyuga, laborer, twenty-seven; Pavel Litvinov, physicist, grandson of the former foreign minister, twenty-eight. By early 1977 all persons named in this paragraph were in the West, except Galanskov, who died in a camp in 1972.

Yet the protest movement did not stop. Underground literature, called *samizdat* (self-publishing) in Russian, and letters of protest against repression, often bearing numerous signatures, reached the West. Those who emigrated brought additional information about the widespread unrest.[7]

One way in which the Soviet government shows its profound concern over the absence of enthusiasm for its ideology and policies among young people is by the frequent accusation of *apolitichnost* (apoliticalness). One of the manifestations of such *apolitichnost* is the withdrawal of many young people from public life into small private circles where they pursue their interests. This is particularly true of artists. In May 1976, I found large crowds taking interest in works by young Soviet painters who

181

were regarded with suspicion by the authorities because they did not stay within the canons of socialist realism. Although the exhibit was not mentioned in the press, word about it spread from small circle to small circle, usually by telephone, and people even lined up in the rain outside the cellar where the paintings were shown. Here—and at other exhibits in private homes which served as meeting places for artists—I saw mainly young people.

PRAGUE

I went to Prague in the spring of 1968. The "Golden City" was happy in the enjoyment of its newly won freedom from tyranny. Each day was like a holiday. In the evenings and during the weekends, the streets and parks were crowded with joyful people. Above all, the students were delighted. Ready to talk, they took me to their dormitories in the suburb of Strahov, where in the previous autumn the "Prague Spring" had its origin. Still earlier, during a congress of writers in June 1967, some of the most respected authors had criticized the regime and even the party boss and state president, Antonín Novotný. But it was the serious confrontation between students and police on October 31 that led to the breathtaking developments of the following months: the fall of Novotný, the elimination of many "small Novotnýs" (among them, in March, the chief ideologist Jiří Hendrych, who had been particularly obnoxious to the students), the pilgrimage of students from Prague University's department of philosophy to the grave of Jan Masaryk (on the twentieth anniversary of the death (probably by assassination) of the country's last non-Communist foreign minister), and finally the Prague Spring. There had come to pass what the left-wing students in Berkeley, Berlin, and Tokyo had been dreaming about—students and workers hand-in-hand for democratic socialism.

This solidarity remained alive even after that black day of August 21, 1968, when the tanks of the Soviet Union and its allies crushed the new movement. When the Czech Student Union was dissolved, the workers at the five largest factories in the capital struck to show their sympathy with the students—but they only struck fifteen minutes, and by then even that required courage.

A student, Jan Palach, expressed the desperation of the people when, on January 16, 1969, he turned himself into a human torch in the center of Prague, at Saint Wenceslaus's statue. Hundreds of thousands then marched with flags down, past the monument, which had become doubly sacred. A few months later I found the place where Palach had died still covered with flowers. All other traces of the Spring had disappeared.

WARSAW

The Poles had their Spring too—in September and October 1956, when they replaced their Stalinist leaders with Gomulka, a Communist who had long been in disgrace because of insufficient subservience to the Kremlin. Their hopes for more freedom proved illusory, but were not extinguished by the continued repression. On October 21, 1966, Leszek Kolakowski, professor of philosophy, forty years of age, respected and loved by students, gave a speech in memory of the rising ten years before. As if absentminded, he began by saying, "Why are we here today?" and went on: "Ah, yes, it is the tenth anniversary of our October revolution. . . . But that was ten years ago. What is there to celebrate now? Nothing, absolutely nothing." The roar of applause seemed to "explode the building," one of those present reported.[8]

Early in 1968 the Poles' anger erupted. During the theatrical season of 1967/68 the national drama *Dziady,* by the great poet Adam Mickiewicz (1798–1855), was given a new production in which the passages attacking the Russians (who in his day occupied large parts of Poland, including Warsaw) were clearly stressed:

> The noble Polish blood and our youth are dying,
> Death and destruction to all Muskovites!

Each time these words were spoken, such storms of applause followed that the government demanded the withdrawal of the play. After the last performance, on January 31, 1968, at which the theater was packed to the last inch, 200 students marched in protest to the Mickiewicz Monument. Fifty were arrested, among them the leaders of the march, Adam Michnik and Henryk Schlaifer. This brought on protests by the students of Warsaw University and other schools, especially after the two young men were expelled. Their comrades collected 3,000 signatures in favor of their readmission, but to no avail.

On March 8 students staged a mass demonstration which started a confrontation with the police lasting three days. Many were arrested. Tension remained after the fighting ceased, and spread to the universities of Krakow, Lodz, and Poznan. On March 13 a mass meeting at the Warsaw Institute of Technology

183

(8,000 students are said to have participated) decided upon a thirteen-point resolution. The demands included: strict observance of the civil rights guaranteed in Article 71 of the Constitution, release of the arrested students and an end to all repressive measures against them, punishment and public condemnation of everyone who had behaved brutally toward the students, no more inciting of workers against students, a public recantation in all the media of the stories published hitherto concerning the confrontation, and inviolability of the students on the campus.[9]

One of the points specifically repudiated anti-Semitism because recent articles in the press, beginning with *Trybuna Ludu* of March 11, had hinted that some of the rebellious students were the offspring of Jewish families. Latent anti-Semitism had existed before, partly because a number of Jewish families belonged to the higher-income bracket and enjoyed various privileges which were resented by many less fortunate Poles. Hence the government sought to isolate the young rebels from the mass of the population, both as Jews and as "banana children" (a term used for children of the upper stratum who came to school bringing bananas, a great luxury, for a snack). These tactics worked; in contrast to Czechoslovakia, there was no fraternization on the part of the general population or the workers with the students.

On March 21, ten days after the end of fighting in the streets, students initiated a three-day sit-in, the first in Poland. It was meant to emphasize the thirteen demands of March 13, and again thousands were involved. To make themselves visible, many wore colorful student caps, out of fashion for years; soon signs appeared in the hat shops—"Student Caps Sold Out."

This test of strength too brought no success. When the schools, which had been closed since the sit-in, were reopened in April, the students returned to their classes. In November 1968 the trials of the arrested students began; they lasted well into 1969 and ended with prison terms.

The students paid particular attention to three trials—those of the two ideologists, Kuroń and Modzelewski (of whom more will be said), the leaders of the demonstration near the Mickiewicz monument on January 31, and of Irena Grudzinska, the daughter of a former minister of forestry, who was known as "Miss March" because of her beauty and her participation in the March rebellion.

Jacek Kuroń (born 1936) and Karol Modzelewski (1937), two

young assistants at the Institute of History in Warsaw University, had produced what in my view is the most remarkable theoretical document of the student movement in Eastern Europe, their "Open Letter to the Communist Party Members." These young men were considered by many Warsaw students as spiritual successors to Karl Marx. Employing his methods, the two analyzed Polish society of the early sixties. Instead of accepting the Party's interpretation, they scrutinized Polish conditions in Marxist fashion and summarized their findings in 1964 in a lengthy document.[10]

Kuroń and Modzelewski proved in their "Letter" that Poland was not a socialist country, because power lay not in the hands of the people, nor in the hands of the working class, but exclusively in one single monopolistic and monolithic party which was nothing but a bureaucratic dictatorship. The monopolistic bureaucracy, they wrote, disposes of all important means of production, acts as main purchaser of labor, and deprives labor—by means of economic coercion and political power—of the surplus value, which it uses for purposes that are foreign and objectionable to the workers, namely, for the strengthening of its hold on production and society. The system is based on the exploitation of the workers, hence the power apparatus of the monopolistic bureaucracy is primarily directed against the labor class. Because socialism aims at labor democracy, not at bureaucratic dictatorship, the latter must be overthrown—by means of a revolution. As one can see, this was a document of fundamental importance. After the letter was made known, its authors were imprisoned, then released; for their participation in the March events, they were arrested again and sentenced to three and a half years in prison.

The rise and glory of the student movement in Prague had been watched by the Polish students with sympathy, even enthusiasm; therefore, so much greater was their shock when Czechoslovakia was invaded by the armies of the Moscow-led Warsaw Pact countries, including Poland (but not Romania). After this, there was no more open student unrest in Poland. The next two risings, in December 1970 and June 1976, originated with the workers, not the students.

BELGRADE
The leaders of Yugoslavia believed that their country was immune to the crisis being experienced elsewhere, in East and West,

because they had developed a special kind of socialism of which they were very proud, a socialism with a fair amount of workers' participation and free of influence from both Moscow and the West. Then, suddenly, while the whole world was watching the dramatic events of 1968 on the Seine, student unrest burst forth on the Danube. At first, the reports from Belgrade seemed rather confused. In the following year, *Praxis,* an important review unloved by the Tito regime, published 518 pages of documents with detailed information about the events of those days and weeks.[11]

On June 2, 1968, at eight o'clock in the evening, a variety show for young workers was to be performed under the open sky in New Belgrade, a suburb of the capital, not far from the university and its dormitories. The show was called "Caravan of Friendship," admission was free, and students were also admitted. But rain began to fall, and the performance had to be moved to a hall with only 400 seats.

Soon there was a free-for-all, as the young workers and the students scrambled for seats. By 8:45 P.M., riot proportions were reached and people had been injured. The police, not used to such experiences, appeared at ten o'clock—forty men with helmets, nightsticks, and a fire department truck. More and more students arrived on the scene; they smashed dozens of windows in the workers' settlement, seized the truck, used it (like the students of Berkeley with the police car in 1964) as a platform for their speakers, and decided to deliver student demands to Parliament that very night.

The demonstration march did not get further than an underpass where many policemen had by then assembled. In the ensuing street battle, the police used tear gas. The students set the truck on fire and pushed it down a slope, but then withdrew. Some were arrested, some taken to the university hospital. Later the students maintained that shots had been fired and one student had been wounded; this the police denied.

At 6:30 A.M. on June 3, the university council met, with representatives of the Party present. The council declared the situation at the university to be abnormal, and even considered a one-week protest strike. Less than two hours later, the vice-president of the university, students, professors, and again some Party members held a meeting in the student village. Those responsible for the mismanagement of the "Caravan of Friendship" apologized for their poor organization of the show. The students at the meeting decided to march from the university to Marx-Engels Square in the center of the capital. At 9:40 A.M. the march began. Some of the slogans were neutral ("Tito—Party"). But others were critical: "Do or Don't We Have a Constitution?" "Down with This Socialist Bourgeoisie!" "They Shot at Us," "Down with the Murderer Bugarčić" (the chief of police), "We Are Sons of the Working People." Again the demonstration got stuck at the underpass. Politicians arrived to talk to the students. Shortly after noon the police, in great numbers, attacked the students with nightsticks and tear gas. In the turmoil 134 students, twenty-one policemen, and nine workers were wounded.

After that, the students occupied the university and passed a resolution which the university senate accepted and sent on to the government. Of the four main demands in the resolution, only the last one dealt with student problems—and this was remarkable, because the university was quite old-fashioned. The other demands criticized social inequalities (all special privileges were to be abandoned), the large number of unemployed, and the country's bureaucratism (demanding "democratization of all social and political organizations," especially of the ruling League of Communists of Yugoslavia, together with freedom of assembly and demonstration). The specific student demands called, among other things, for "participation of the students on an equal footing in all university organs in which important social problems are decided" and for the democratization of professional appointments.[12]

The official reaction differed from that in most other countries. It was quick and positive: On the same day, the cabinet of Serbia (the constituent republic of Yugoslavia in which Belgrade is located) assembled and promised to fulfill the greater part of the students' demands; it also voiced regret for the behavior of certain radical student groups. Meetings of workers expressed sympathy with the students, but at the same time urged them not to go outside the channels offered by Yugoslav law in seeking solutions for problems. On June 4 the city parliament of Belgrade met in special session. The students' demands, it declared, were justified—but democratic principles must not be violated. Even the Central Committee of the Party found words of approval.

The next day the Yugoslav Parliament issued a decree to double the workers' pay; it further promised to diminish unjustified wage differences and improve the living standard of students. On June 9, a Sunday, Tito spoke on radio and TV. Although the student movement had been infiltrated by hostile elements from abroad, he said, many of the demands were justified, and students should no longer be treated as schoolchildren. He agreed with the students that the great discrepancies between high and low incomes were objectionable. The events of June 2–3 would be closely investigated, and all officials who had made mistakes would be punished. If he, Tito, were to prove unable to solve these tasks, he declared himself willing to retire.

Thus, Tito, the Party, and the government made the demands of the students their own, taking the wind out of the activists' sails. The students gave up their occupation of the university; at other universities affected by the unrest in Belgrade, the situation also soon returned to normal. To be sure, there were still some confrontations to come, because the realization of the promises given in early June was very slow. The conflict with the *Praxis* group sharpened, and some young professors who had been involved on June 3 were refused permission to lecture. But for the time being, order had been restored.

When I went to Belgrade in September 1968, hardly anyone mentioned the student uprising—other problems completely overshadowed it. On August 21 the Soviet Union had overrun Czechoslovakia. Was it now Yugoslavia's and Romania's turn? Belgrade was full of reservists hurrying to the barracks, and many students were among them. The ranks were closing against the danger from the East.

HAVANA

Many young Leftists the world over had mixed feelings about the U.S.S.R. They respected, even venerated, the revolutionary history and achievements of the Soviet Union, but knew that it had time and again sacrificed foreign Communist comrades to its own interests—from as far back as the Spanish and Chinese civil wars, and in the pact with Hitler. They wanted a country to believe in, and they turned their eyes toward Cuba. Castro had overthrown the dictator Fulgencio Batista without any aid from the pro-Moscow Cuban Communists, who instead had collaborated with Batista and called Castro—prior to his victory—a "petty-bourgeois adventurist." He in turn had attacked them as just another breed of totalitarians and as sectarian and bureaucratic accomplices of the counterrevolution.[13]

To be sure, Castro has since toned down his criticism of Moscow, publicly declared himself a Marxist-Leninist (December 1961), and combined his own followers with the Communist Party

188

of Cuba; but for this he was forgiven because, it was argued, pressure from the United States had forced him to obtain economic and military aid from the U.S.S.R., paying for it with some minor concessions. And had he not made the Communists serve his purposes? As a matter of fact, Castro continued to hold the reins of the combined parties firmly in his hand—the old pro-Moscow Communist Anibal Escalante, who was slated to be the secretary-general of the united party, had been quickly exiled when, in the spring of 1962, he hesitated to follow Castro's orders. Also, for some time, Castro refused to side with Moscow on its conflict with Peking.

But all this was ancient history. When I visited Cuba for the first time, in the summer of 1975, I found the island clearly following Moscow's course. The bookshops displayed shelves upon shelves of Spanish translations of Soviet books, including the works of Brezhnev; in the cinemas, Soviet films were mostly run, even Mark Twain's *Huckleberry Finn*—the Moscow production. Lenin's portraits and words were everywhere; a factory that I visited showed off its Order of Lenin (Cuban version); the largest park was the Lenin Park, the largest school—opened by Brezhnev in 1974—the Lenin School.

Castro did not do all this for nothing. The Soviet Union has helped Cuba's bankrupt economy to survive, poured billions of rubles into the island (there was talk of the equivalent of $6.3 billion), and granted deferment of the repayment of all Soviet credits until 1986. Meanwhile, Havana's dependence on Moscow has continued to grow. The new constitution, accepted in a plebiscite of February 15, 1976, shows Moscow's handwriting in many places, and planning experts from Moscow have helped establish a bureaucratic-centralist economy. In the interest of Moscow's world strategy, Castro dispatched an estimated 10,000 Cuban soldiers to participate in the civil war in Angola. It may be that Castro is unhappy (as I know many Cubans are) that his country, which he detached from U.S. domination, has now become a Moscow satellite, and that almost nothing remains of the "Cuban Road to Socialism" which he had dreamt about as a model for the whole of Latin America. But there is no use in trying to guess his feelings. He is in Moscow's camp, and he will remain there as long as one can now foresee. In the literal financial sense of the word, he has pawned Cuba's future to the Kremlin.

Of course, Castro makes frequent appeals to the youth of Cuba, and many may feel some enthusiasm for his leadership, but the

Soviet Union's ambassador has his say in the country's affairs. Hence, Cuba's attraction for the rebellious students abroad is fading.

PEKING

Shortly after the Communists came to power in China (1949), they began to move away from Moscow. But even though China tried to travel on a road all its own, it too experienced during the sixties a youth revolution, which in size and vehemence was to overshadow everything that happened at the same time in other countries. This was the Great Proletarian Cultural Revolution. But—one might ask—was not this Chinese revolution of 1966–1968 totally different? Was it not triggered from above, from very high above, by Mao himself? Was it not manipulated, while the youth rebellion in other parts of the world came spontaneously and from below?

The Cultural Revolution in China was, in reality, both a power struggle at the top and a movement of the young generation. Two things had come together; Mao, who had been pushed into the background for several years (after the failure of the Great Leap Forward in the summer of 1958), wanted again to determine the policy of the country. This he could do only against the leadership of the Chinese Communist Party, which in his opinion was moving in a totally false, namely Soviet, direction. And he needed a weapon that was not at the command of the Party—the youth. Many of the young generation, in turn, were ready to rebel because they were disappointed and embittered by the bureaucratic petrification which China, under the "new class" (the Party functionaries), had undergone. By itself, their dissatisfaction could have started nothing but small ripples. It was only when Mao's will for a comeback and the mood of the young generation coalesced that the Cultural Revolution was born.

In its first phase (1966–1967) the Red Guards, as the rebellious young people soon were to be called, and Mao (together with his closest collaborators, one of whom was his wife, Chiang Ching) were in agreement. In the second phase (1967–1968), however, Mao, after overthrowing his opponents in the Party leadership with the aid of the Red Guards, wanted law and order restored. So the Red Guards were demobilized and millions of their members were sent to the countryside—"down to the village and up to the mountains," as the slogan said. According to official information, 12 million young people were thus affected from the beginning of the Cultural Revolution until early 1976.[14]

Some of the Red Guards, disappointed again, later left China. One of them, Yeung Cheng, told about his dissatisfaction with the boring routine of life before the Cultural Revolution, his opposition to the Party establishment, his enthusiasm for the Cultural Revolution and wholehearted participation in it, his leadership position in Canton, and his dismay when, in September 1967, things began to go back to the way they were prior to 1966. He joined a group of leftists who wanted to continue the revolution, and fled the country when the group was uncovered by the police.[15]

The name of this rebel group, which had its main strength in Hunan Province, was Sheng-wu-lien. Some of its documents have reached the West; I published the most significant of them in a small book, *Peking and the New Left,* and in them we find to an amazing extent the sentiments and even the vocabulary of the New Left in the rest of the world; their authors attack repression, bureaucracy, capitalism, authoritarianism, and the existence of a privileged class—all the things they had fought against with the Little Red Book in their hands during the Cultural Revolution and now saw reemerging.

These documents were written in the winter of 1967/68, when the wind was blowing into the faces of the Red Guards. The most interesting—"Whither China?"—is dated January 12, 1968. That was just about the time when the student rebellion was climaxing in the West, and even in some countries of Eastern Europe. The decline of the Sheng-wu-lien and similar leftist groups in China in the year 1968 coincided with that of the New Left in the West.

YOUTH UNREST—WEST AND EAST

The parallel developments in the Communist and non-Communist worlds, which, for the sake of simplicity, I shall call the East and the West, raise the question: What were the similarities and the differences? Of course, the differences are more obvious, because of the contrasting situations in the two worlds at the outbreak of the unrest. In one, there was a liberal consumer society with high prosperity; in the other, a totalitarian dictatorship with its constant scarcity of goods, which had barely begun, with Khrushchev's "goulash Communism," to improve the modest standard of living. What was still a vision of the future in the U.S.S.R.—more consumer goods and more freedom—was possessed in the West in abundance, causing among the young generation the dismal feeling of satiety. However, it would be unrealistic and even unjust to overestimate the difference. During

191

our quick survey of the countries under the Red flag we did not find the demand for more consumer goods to be an important motivating force behind the student rebellion. What the young generation in the East lacks, what the students there need as much as their daily bread, what above all they demand passionately for themselves, as well as for the masses, is a nonmaterial value which we in the West are inclined to take for granted and therefore undervalue—liberty.

This is the reason why the key word of the radicals in the West, especially in Germany, also fits the students in the Communist countries—*antiauthoritarianism*. In saying this, however, I must emphasize what is sometimes overlooked, that the authorities opposed by the students in the East are infinitely more powerful than those in the West; in the Soviet world the means of production have been nationalized and turned into a mighty instrument of the bureaucracy and the party. It is much more difficult to fight against this concentrated, truly total, power than against "capital"; this we must remember when the demands—and successes—of the young rebels in these countries appear to us to be rather modest. When seven persons protested in 1968 on Red Square in Moscow against their government's invasion of Czechoslovakia, this action was comparable to a march of 7,000 in New York, Paris, or West Berlin.

Hostility against the power of the state necessarily is expressed differently in East and West because of the differing circumstances, but in both worlds the rebels are young people (almost without exception) and they share certain attitudes. What Marcuse calls the "Great Refusal" is one of these—the turning away from public life to one's own small circle. The "implosion" that we have noticed in America is one of its forms. We even find religious searching, and in East and West alike it benefits the small sects more than the established churches.

Anticapitalism is another attitude which the rebels in East and West have in common. Of course, to many young Russians it sounds silly and ridiculous when the government attacks the private sale in Moscow of a few pounds of tomatoes from Tbilisi as "capitalism." Still, in my observation, young Russians, despite the failure of socialism, are not yearning for the return of a capitalism that they never knew; rather, they feel some vague anticapitalism, and in part this is directed against the system of state capitalism under which they live. They also feel that socialism is, in principle, superior to capitalism, although they may grant that in practice it is far less efficient. Re-privatization of the economy is certainly not one of the desires of restless students in Russia. Many are, like Kuroń and Modzelewski in Poland, dissatisfied with the economic system in their country without, however, having a plausible alternative to suggest.

In the West, the anticapitalism among the youthful rebels is much more obvious. For them, capital—especially "monopoly capital" and now the multinational companies—is the big enemy. The question is only whether to destroy private property completely or to control it by laws. Yet I have found among Western leftists a growing number of those who are aware of the fact that socialism, as practiced in the Soviet Union and the countries ruled by it, does not lead automatically to freedom and human dignity. The desperate cry for a "socialism with a human face," especially in Hungary, Poland, and Czechoslovakia, has proved that there is also a socialism with an inhuman face, which no longer merits its name.

The third "anti-" grows out of the second. Lenin, in a famous book written during the First World War, described imperialism as the "highest stage of capitalism." Now *anti-imperialism* is upheld by many young people in both worlds—with the difference that in the West the rebels are anti-imperialist toward the governments of their own countries and allies, while in the East the governments themselves use anti-imperialism as a weapon in the ideological war with the West. The Chinese Communists are telling the world all the time that there is also a Soviet imperialism—and among the young people in the areas inhabited by national minorities in the U.S.S.R., or in the Moscow-ruled states of Eastern Europe, quite a few would agree in this regard with Peking.

In the West, including Japan, the New Left thinks almost exclusively of the United States when it attacks imperialism. The same can be said of the Third World, especially because of the Vietnam war. Many in the Third World are prone to forget the imperialism of the Soviet Union, thanks to weapons and propagandistic support they get from Moscow in their struggle against the remnants of Western colonialism.

In some other respects, the differences in attitudes are more visible. Western young people are inclined to be critical of technical and material *progress* because they are familiar with its disadvantages, while Eastern youth in this respect is still optimistic. In the East, terms such as "limits of growth," "population explosion," and "environmental pollution" have as yet touched and moved relatively few. In the West, governments and youth concur in the demands for a cleaner environment (even though the big corporations responsible for pollution are in many ways connected with the government). In the East, on the other hand, the governments are more cautious in talking about the fight against pollution: They own the entire economy and thus are themselves the polluters.

There is also a different attitude toward *achievement.* The slogan which could be heard in the German New Left, "From the Achievement Society to the Enjoyment Society," could only grow in the Western world, which indeed can exist comfortably without extreme exertion on the part of each individual. The United States, during the prosperous sixties, could afford long weekends and vacations for those who worked, and in addition, support millions of unemployed. In West Germany the steady shortening of the workweek—without decrease in pay—has become almost routine. The young generation in the East still lives far from abundance, and the necessity for hard work and achievement is taken for granted, as it always has been: Those who want to rise are ready for hard work; those on the top can, if they so wish, take it easy.

The same holds for the students in their place of work, the *university.* In the free world—from Berkeley to Nanterre and Tokyo—the traditional university has been attacked. Nor have the professors been spared—despite all their sympathy for the students, most of them did not want to have their lives and work disturbed, and so were in favor of law and order. For the Eastern student, the traditional university is still the institution he loves, to which he considers it a privilege to belong; he venerates his teachers and senses that they are just as doubtful about the virtues of a totalitarian state as he is.

In the next decade or two it will become easier to tell whether the development of youth in the East, compared with that in the West, is merely delayed or is moving in a *different* direction. I have discussed this question in those chapters of my *Moscow and the New Left* where I describe the struggle of the Soviet leaders against Western influences on their young people, a struggle that has become more pronounced since then (even on the trivial level of attempts to enforce haircuts by withholding wages).[16] In spite of decades of fighting it, alcoholism is not decreasing; it affects, as in the West, ever younger age groups (you can hear of alcohol consumption among sixth graders). The newspapers now refer openly to the problem of drug use.[17] A recent German study of suicides (in which the secretive U.S.S.R. was not included) has found that "among the countries of the world with the highest present rate of suicides are five socialist countries, with Hungary, the G.D.R. (East Germany), and Czechoslovakia heading the entire list."[18] The difference between facade and reality is much smaller in the open society of the West than in the authoritarian one of the East, where the hard facts of reality are constantly whitewashed (lacquered, as the Russians say) to the point where the picture produced finally has little in common with the reality it is supposed to portray.

From time to time this layer of lacquer is broken through. Vladimir Tendryakov, one of the most gifted contemporary writers, tells in his story "The Night After Graduation" of how masks drop, true faces become visible, friendships that lasted for years turn into hatred, all because of the shock felt when Yulya, the valedictorian, says in her speech: "The school forced me to learn and to know what the school wanted. One thing it has not taught me: to judge independently, to know what I like, what I love, what I want." [19]

The complaints of a Polish high school youngster, printed in a Warsaw paper, indicate that the alienation known in the West can also be found in the East, expressed in almost identical words. The teachers, the lad said, were shying away from the exchange of ideas, from discussions, and forming a common front with one purpose, "to treat us like children.[...] I want to have more freedom. Studies are better advanced by freedom than by constricting regulations."[20]

II

THE STYLE

Despite the differences in its development, the unrest among the young during the 1960s shows many common characteristics: It happens within the framework of a worldwide *scene*, mainly on the *campus*, consisting of thousands of universities and colleges and 30 million students; the young are searching for new forms of life in *communes*, experimenting with *sex* and *drugs*, finding their own "esperanto" in rock music and employing—in confrontations with authorities and society—similar, partly new *methods*, not the least being physical *violence*.

The youth unrest is affecting all fields of life, leaving not a single taboo untouched. All possible reactions of the individual to our civilization are being acted out, from mild withdrawal to bloody terrorism. Methods and aims are inseparable; the methods employed affect the aims.

18
THE SCENE

DOZENS of such scenes come to my mind:

Tokyo. A small café, two blocks from the university. The young men have long hair, pale and tense faces, threadbare black student uniforms. Incessantly, they smoke cigarettes and order Coca-Cola. One of them walks to the jukebox, we hear American rock. The girls are more reserved, neater, but by no means elegantly dressed, some wearing faddishly large glasses with black frames. The students speak quickly, in English, careless of their many grammatical errors. They use with ease the words they have taken from the New Left's international jargon: *Karu Marukusu* (Karl Marx), *tellolu* (terror), *gelillas* (guerrillas). I try to order something substantial for them to eat, but they hurriedly decline: No need. Still much to do. A meeting coming up. Tomorrow *demo* (demonstration).

Berkeley. A student cafeteria on Telegraph Avenue, not far from the campus. These young people too have long hair, pale and languid yet peaceful and beautiful faces. They are dressed as if they were going to a costume party—one as an American Indian with a bright headband holding back his hair, one as leatherstocking with a fringed suede jacket and high boots, one as a soldier from the days of the American Revolution, his greasy three-cornered hat lying on the table. Another has a wild-looking sheepskin coat over his shoulders: he brought it back from a hash-smoking expedition to Afghanistan. There is one who has his head shaved and is clothed in a Buddhist robe. A girl wears an undefinable costume—wide-brimmed black hat, leather jacket, floor-length Mexican skirt. A boy and a girl in relatively normal clothes wear heavy pendants on chains around their necks, he a cross, she something of Indian design set with rough turquoise. The jukebox emits conversation-drowning rock music. On the way back to the campus, along the avenue, a number of young people are sitting on the ground like Indians (some actually *are* Indians), their backs against a wall. Meanwhile, dozens of street vendors, all of them young, offer their wares on simple tables, sometimes just on a piece of cloth on the ground—handmade leather belts with primitive buckles, macramé plant hangers; there are young girls among them, some with children tied on their backs. It might have been a native market in Nepal or in the Andes.

Katmandu. In the almost dark tavern only the proprietors are Nepalese; their guests are young people from the West, usually couples, their long hair disheveled, begging or bumming spare change. Two young women have babies, one carried on the back, the other bundled up and lying on a chair. A hashish joint passes from hand to hand. The air is sweet with the drug. Not many words are spoken—what the price of hash was today (very cheap), where one can cross the border easily, whether Goa is actually as beautiful as those who went there claim. Here and there one grows silent and sinks into sleep, his head cradled in his arms.

A Small German Town. A "party cellar" in the house of friends. The light draped with red cloth, the walls and ceiling painted purple. On the walls: three posters, two psychedelic, the other showing a Model T Ford, also photos of many rock stars— the Beatles among them of course, as a group and individuals. A stereo speaker, placed above the door, blasts a deafening rock song; it is controlled by some people in the adjoining room. On the floor a mattress and many pillows, on them eight young people, high-school students; three of them are girls. They all get up to greet me, somewhat awkwardly and unsure of themselves, although my visit is not unexpected. We sit down. Most of them smoke (ordinary cigarettes) and all drink Coca-Cola, of which there are two cases in the corner. The mother, who remains invisible, has fixed a big plate of sandwiches ("How was it down

there?" she is going to ask me anxiously when I surface). All wear
jeans purposely ragged and faded, and their hair is long ("We
don't even look at boys with short hair," a fourteen-year-old told
me then—the young girls nowadays are no longer quite so particular). The conversation isn't exactly flowing. What I have to
tell from the wide world of politics does not interest them particularly, and the latest items about the Beatles and the Stones,
which I read up on in preparation for this visit, are not quite
enough for a bubbling discussion. The whole atmosphere in the
"party cellar" doesn't seem so very bubbling anyway. Even prior
to my coming, the conversation—I was told by my only acquaintance in this group—had been gluey, even somewhat affected:
everyone did this or that thing because everyone else was doing
it. The main thing was to do it.

San Francisco. A psychedelic shop. You can find it with your
eyes closed, smelling from afar the incense sold and burned there.
In no other place the world over are there such shops: Thousand
and One Nights, bazaar, witches' coven, Indian temple, Chinese
magician's den, all in one. Outfits from all longitudes and periods
are for sale, saris and ponchos, even Buddhist monks' robes, the
shelves full of Eastern mystical literature, sex objects, including
giant candles in phallus form, tables with hundreds of posters.
Many knickknacks, mostly produced by hippies in their pads, all
kinds of bells and candleholders, exotic footwear, "Jesus sandals"
and moccasins, Indian headbands, records of psychedelic music,
knapsacks for child carrying, mystical signs made of wood, metal,
or clay, handwoven rugs, preferably with American Indian designs, piles of holy books from the Bible and the *I Ching* to the
Tibetan Book of the Dead, not to mention the *Kamasutra,*
fortune-telling equipment, including Tarot cards, handbooks on
astrology and chiromancy, Buddha and Christ statues. . . .
    Behind the shop, a psychedelic temple had been closed by the
police after large quantities of drugs had been found there. On the
walls, hung with red and yellow cloth, were many posters with
religious meanings—scenes from the life of Christ, pictures of
Hindu gods and bodhisattvas, African ceremonies, ritual dances
among South Sea tribes or American Indians. Young people were
sitting in front of a many-armed golden idol, some in the lotus
position, some putting flowers on silver platters. The light came
from oil lamps. Endlessly, a man with a shaved head mumbled a
mantra, as did the others. They seemed to be almost in a trance.

Stockholm. An antidrug discotheque managed by the city administration, a place for young people to entertain themselves without drugs. Coca-Cola is served inexpensively. The rock music is thunderous, the lighting minimal, though beams of many colors play on those who dance—it can hardly be called dancing. The two rooms are overcrowded, and people are waiting outside to get in. I had barely squeezed in through a back door. Girls and boys alike wear long hair and undefinable clothes; the sex of those holding each other closely on the dance floor is hard to figure out.

Copenhagen. A German student took me to a group of buildings that looked like barracks; they had been turned over by the city to the young people. The taxi driver didn't want to get near them, so we stumbled on in the dark, through the puddles, led by dim lights and loud rock. The student opened a half-shut door. Up a dirty and barely lit staircase, the second floor was nothing but a large unfurnished room. By the light of bare bulbs dangling from the ceiling, we saw some forty or fifty young people, squatting or lying on the floor, some with sleeping bags, all with bundles. The air was heavy with marijuana. One boy played a guitar. A small circle had formed around him, and we joined it, inspected by curious eyes. When it was understood (to the general disappointment) that I had nothing interesting in the way of smoking to offer, the features became dull and apathetic again. We sat down with one or two other groups, with young people of many nationalities—mostly Americans and Germans. The conversations were minimal and as empty as the eyes that gazed at us.

New York. An eight-room apartment shared by nine students and an ex-student. They were of both sexes. (Who lived with whom I didn't ask; had I inquired, I might have been considered "square.") Five guests were present also. After I sat down in a kind of deck chair, I noticed that all the others were squatting on the floor. In the whole communal room not another chair was in sight. Some sat on pillows, others just on the floor; some leaned against the wall, some were in the middle of the room.

"Why do you always sit on the floor?" The answers to my question differed—it was more comfortable, it was good for meditation, and of course it was cheaper. Ann, who had invited me, brought two thick books, *Nomadic Furniture*, Volumes I and II, whose simple drawings showed how to make one's own furniture —my deck chair, for instance, and mattress beds. To make the pillows scattered around the room, she and her friends had bought sacks and filled them with shredded foam (in a corner of the room there was still a whole mountain of the stuff).

One of the young people said: "We couldn't live with our parents' furniture, it has no style and costs an outrageous amount of money, also it ties you down with all its weight—how can you move with it? We like nomadic furniture. If we want to move, we simply leave it behind. The next tenant may use it, or throw it away." Two others explained to me their interest in building a Mongolian yurt, somewhere far from the city; one even knew how to do it from a book, *Build a Yurt,* which he bought just before it was sold out.

I inquired about the professional work of those who had finished college. This subject did not attract them much. But they all had big plans for the improvement of New York and later of the world. In their immediate life, to be sure, these plans did not figure very prominently. "My girl friend and I will fly to Mexico for two or three weeks"—this from a young man who had just expounded on an urban renewal project for a New York slum. "After weeks of fighting with the bureaucrats I must get some fresh air." Another had discovered the shortcomings of a hospital where he had been a patient. He explained how he intended to reform it, but for now he was quite fed up: "Next week I'm going to Trinidad for the carnival; I have found an inexpensive excursion rate."

"You want to change America," I said, "and you have declared war on the political and economic Establishment. But the strength of the Establishment lies in its machinery, its constancy, its bureaucracy. You have neither machinery nor bureaucracy, and not much constancy either, and at the moment when you might really come to grips with something, you fly to Mexico or Trinidad."

No one objected. One even admitted that, on the basis of his own experience, a firm could indeed work infinitely more efficiently than a bunch of well-meaning but erratic enthusiasts. Taking up this thought, a student elaborated on it, painting a picture of the future: "Someday all progressive idealists in America, and later in the whole world, will join together and take matters in their own hands"—the New Left had, in a way, shown the right direction. "Why not through the existing political parties?" I inquired. "No, no, not through the parties," the student exclaimed. "They are much too ossified. This is true of the Communist Party, too; it has not produced a new idea for years. And it's the same with the outdated trade unions."

His train of thought found approval. There existed quite a few connections among people and groups of similar attitudes, I was told. When I asked where all these people came from, the unanimous answer was: "From the university, from the campus." Many of them knew each other from their student days, they explained, had been moved by the same intellectual winds, had participated in the same political actions, a community of millions of students and graduates, their number growing every year.

Then we talked about other things. When I tried to telephone Ann ten days later, I learned that she was surfing in Hawaii.

A WORLD OF ITS OWN

I could draw many more pictures of this kind. But enough. All together, the young people who figure in them form a world of their own, which suddenly emerged about a decade and a half ago, and exists to this day; if we don't notice it quite as much now, this is the consequence of our getting used to it. People have tried to find a common name for this world, have advertised it in book titles. "Underground"[1] sounds too much like a furtive criminal world. "Subculture," or "counterculture"—too much like culture in the narrower sense of the word.[2] "Bohemia"—makes one think of artists and writers.[3] "Hippies"—but they were only a passing phase.[4] I prefer "scene," mainly because the young themselves use it in manifold variations—drug scene, beat scene, campus scene, commune scene, or simply the Scene. A scene, therefore, played on many stages, some of which merit their own chapters later on.

First should be mentioned a few characteristics that can be found in most of the scenes that we will deal with later—for example, the supreme neglect of (or is it contempt for?) orderliness. Whenever I visit pads or communal living quarters I find clothes, books, dishes, leftover food in picturesque confusion on the floor. The wall space is not used for cupboards but for posters: bright dreams, often in the style of the turn of the century, if not actually reproductions from that time (printed by the millions, they have become big business), and also handmade ones—symphonies of color within flowing lines, usually in gentle, sometimes in garish tones. You can find everything on these posters: occult signs, explicit sex, abstracts, lyrical landscapes, portraits of popular rock stars or of the Kennedy brothers.

The rooms smell of incense from the faintly glowing sticks, put in Asian vases or empty tin cans, or of marijuana. A private life can rarely be found. Young people come and go, cook, eat, kiss, put records on, pass a joint around, drink a lot of coffee, talk (with plenty of four-letter words), or sleep curled up on the floor. At home they would have a room and bath, they could use their parents' entire home for their parties. But they prefer living quarters in the style of a poorhouse. Even while they were still at their parents' home, their social life did not take place in the living room, but rather, out of protest, in a musty basement.

If I ask young people, from Tokyo to Kabul, from Copenhagen to San Francisco, why they like to go barefoot, their answers vary: It is beautiful to touch Mother Earth (more often than not, it is asphalt) with one's bare soles, it is cheaper, it is like a club badge and a symbol to recognize each other by, it clearly separates you from the older generation, which is unable to take even a single step without footwear. For the beards, too, I found various motivations: protest, of course, but also contempt for the daily shaving routine, considered to be a form of repression, or just the desire for "something new and different." One student mentioned that he wore his beard for the sake of camouflage from the police.

There is a certain cohesiveness among the various scenes, as the participants all live at the periphery of society. They help each other; they all consider themselves abused prisoners of society as much as the men behind bars. Many no longer distinguish between political and criminal violence. Hence the remarkable interest in prisons—they visit inmates, send them packages, establish connections for them with the world outside, and sometimes help them escape. I knew a white student who felt closer to a black in prison, condemned for murder or rape, than to the members of his own family.

Crimes against property are not considered serious, because property itself is not valued highly. For some, naturally, this is just a pose: they go secretly to the bank with their father's check. For many, however, the contempt for property is not faked. Seen historically, this attitude is not new; it is characteristic of most religions. (As a child, I often heard from my mother that "property is a burden.") But as a mass phenomenon among the sons and daughters of well-to-do families, the concept of freedom from property as a precondition for freedom in general is unusual, at least in our time.

For many young people on the Scene, only *one* property seems important—a dog (or perhaps a cat). I have seen students bring their dogs to class, not in order to disrupt the lecture but because they could not part even for a moment from their "one and only." At times I have read almost tearful advertisements for lost dogs, posted on campus trees and bulletin boards. Apart from its other aspects, this love of dogs is a symptom of loneliness. One has had disappointments concerning the loyalties of people, yet one does not want to live all by oneself, and only a dog will give you absolute loyalty and unconditional love.

Belgian veterinarians at a convention in the autumn of 1975 reported that, together with psychologists, they had come to this conclusion: Caring for dogs (of which there are a million in Belgium) was good for the psyche, especially of the city population, which was suffering most from loneliness and the indifference of those around them.[5]

EVERYTHING IS PSYCHEDELIC

Along with "scene," another new term has made its appearance: *psychedelic*. The Greek words *psyche* (soul) and *deloun* (make apparent, show) combine to mean, approximately, "consciousness-making." It means raising something from the unconscious to the conscious mind, enlarging one's consciousness, particularly with the aid of drugs, meditation, or religious ecstasy. However, the meaning was quickly enlarged, and "psychedelic" became the adjective for the entire Scene. Drugs, music, love, posters and incense, clothes shops, dance, poetry, songs—everything characteristic of the Scene was psychedelic. The German poet and novelist Hermann Hesse—one of my favorites in the twenties—is now considered psychedelic; since the sixties his works have had a remarkable renaissance, especially in the United States, where he was practically unknown before. His *Steppenwolf* has become a key novel. Cafés and bars are named after it, a well-known rock group adopted the name, and cinemas show the *Steppenwolf* film. His *Siddhartha* is popular, too.

Much that is called psychedelic one may like or dislike. About one of its aspects it is impossible to feel anything but sadness: the countless victims of the Scene, through drugs, venereal diseases, psychoses, suicide. During the first years, young dropouts and runaways, often still children, were the most endangered; they were migrating by the tens of thousands from one center of the Scene to another, to the Bay Area in particular, living by begging, prostitution, or dealing in drugs, often using drugs themselves and having, apart from pleasant hallucinations, dreadfully bad "trips," eventually going to pieces and down the drain. The newspapers, especially those close to the Scene, were full of "Please Come Home" ads, and the streets of San Francisco saw desperate parents tacking the names and photographs of their missing children to bulletin boards and telephone poles.

The Scene looked happy enough, from afar, and the flower children were smiling sweetly, but melancholy cast its shadow on them. The Scene did, however, include some people who tried to pep it up with humor and jokes, the clowns of the movement, types such as Teufel and Langhans in Germany, Jerry Rubin and Abbie Hoffman in America.

The humor of Berlin's "Commune 1," to which the two Germans belonged, was intended to make fun of the state, the courts, and the police. The great hour of Teufel and Langhans came when they were on trial, accused of instigating arson. When the court informed them that they were going to be psychiatrically tested, Teufel declared himself willing, "provided the members of the court and the public prosecutor will also be examined." With simulated eagerness, he inquired of the court: "Is psychiatry familiar with a disease which one might define as the pathological imposing of penalties, and with a therapy that could be recommended?" Once, when there was laughter in the courtroom, Langhans said with a fake threat in his voice, "Quiet in those back rows! Otherwise I'll have you kicked out by the prosecutor." Teufel's reaction when he was asked to rise has become famous: "Gladly, if it helps in finding the truth."

The two Americans amused their contemporaries with what formerly would have been considered just "college humor" but which now was seen to have political connotations. Jerry Rubin appeared in 1966 before a congressional committee in the uniform of a soldier of the Revolutionary War. Two years later, he founded a political stunt organization, the Yippies (the name was a mixture of "Hippies" and the exclamation "Yippee!" but was declared to represent the initials of the Youth International Party). At the head of a small group of Yippies, Rubin went to Chicago that summer during the Democratic National Convention. The Yippies, he declared, also wanted to nominate a candidate for president. A pig, which they brought along and named "Pigasus," thereby transforming the mythological poet's horse Pegasus into a swine, was solemnly nominated as their candidate. In a confrontation with the police they pretended fear for the pig's life. How could America bear, Rubin said, after the assassinations of the

Kennedy brothers and Martin Luther King, Jr., the death of a fourth outstanding personality? In Rubin's book, which includes this bad-taste remark, there are these often-quoted mottoes: "Don't buy, steal." "Shit on the floor." "When in doubt, burn." "Fire is the revolutionary's god." "Fire is instant theater." "Burn the flag." "Burn churches." "Burn, burn, burn." "We've got America on the run." "We've combined youth, music, sex, drugs and rebellion with treason—and that's a combination hard to beat."

After the Yippies worldwide victory, Rubin promised, all watches and clocks would be destroyed, and also: "Barbers will go to rehabilitation camps where they will grow their hair long.[. . .] The Pentagon will be replaced by an LSD experimental farm. [. . .] People will work in the morning, make music in the afternoon, and fuck wherever and whenever they want to."[6]

On the jacket of a book by Abbie Hoffman, the young were asked to leave their families, burn the schools. It was recommended that the book be read when one was high on drugs.[7] From Hoffman comes the not-wholly-unjustified sentence "Confusion is mightier than the sword" (in a book with a jaunty title, *Revolution for the Hell of It).*[8] Since March 1974, when he jumped bail, Hoffman has lived in the underground. Three times he has had plastic surgery to disguise himself. According to late reports, he is trying just about every self-improvement fad and is even leaning toward the Communist Party[9]—proof of despair in the case of any good *Chaote.*

The picture of the Scene would not be complete without reference to its grotesque equivalent in high society. There were times when everyone who was anyone wanted to participate in some way in the life of the Scene. One of the most amusing American authors, Tom Wolfe, a true enfant terrible, has made fun of the "radical chic" in these circles.[10]

INFLUENCES ON FASHIONS AND LANGUAGE

A scene of many colors, indeed, the Scene includes aspects that are sad and happy, grotesque and revolting, ingenious and banal. Unquestionably it has influenced millions of people everywhere. The revolt against middle-class respectability, against the style of our time in general, explains the trend away from normal attire toward unusual dress and simple clothing. Blue jeans are *the* dress of the Scene. The triumphal march of these pants (later also jackets of the same denim) had its origin in the invention of a twenty-year-old gold prospector from Bavaria, Levi Strauss, who came to California in 1850 and responded to the miners' need for durable pants to work in (with riveted pockets to hold heavy ore samples). A century later they were the smash hit of the Scene and a billion-dollar business for all jeans producers, with the Levi Strauss firm, which still exists in San Francisco, as the leader. (It is now manufacturing, so I am told, jeans with a fuller cut— necessary as the youth of the 60s cross the Rubicon into the over-thirty world.) Even in Communist countries, jeans are hotly sought after, for the time being on the black market. There have been rumors that the Red governments—which very much dislike this truly proletarian attire because it comes from the capitalist West and might turn out to be a Trojan pair of trousers—are considering producing blue jeans themselves. I mentioned this rumor to a Moscow teenager who, by hook or by crook, wanted to get his own pair of jeans. His eyes began to sparkle, but then he added, in an unbelieving voice: "They would never do it." Only in China are blue pants unlikely to become a fad.

Soon it was not enough just to wear jeans; they had to be old and worn, or at least made to look so. There were many clever methods for accomplishing this—for example, by patching. Much ingenuity was employed in making patches. I saw one girl student who had a patch reading "No Parking" beside her front zipper. Jeans were good for showing disdain for the consumer society, for proving solidarity with the workers, and for plain fun.

The surprising thing was that even "high fashion" took over the forms of "low fashion." Style-minded ladies and gentlemen appeared in new tailor-made jeans, already patched, the cloth prefaded. The United States has a president who favors blue jeans, and his vice president is following suit, so to speak. Thus the generation of the sixties has led to a jeans era in fashions, to what might be called a marriage between the spirit of the time— the *Zeitgeist*—and a pair of trousers. The hippie's dream of world-encompassing love and community found its realization in the most democratic apparel item since the fig leaf.

Discarded army jackets, cheaply purchased, were another favored item. I have always wondered how students who had never been in the army, much less in Vietnam, could wear such jackets at demonstrations against the Vietnam war; many did not even bother to cut off the insignia. This fad has also reached Europe, where "high fashion" did not adopt it but did appropriate elements of Western "cowboy" wear, such as ponchos, fringed leather jackets, shirts with pearl snaps, and cowboy boots.

From the linguistic point of view, the Scene can be divided into two groups: those who speak very little, and those who speak "socio-nese," or whatever one may wish to call their vocabulary, which is based on jargon from sociology, psychoanalysis, and political science, with plenty of four-letter words thrown in. The inarticulateness of the first group has many causes, from the isolation of people in impersonal modern society to the long speechless evenings in front of the TV, occasionally interrupted by a grunt or a groan. In some countries, instruction in speech and writing, especially in grammar, has been so neglected that the universities are appalled by the inability of young students to express themselves. At the University of Wisconsin, in 1975, half the students who wanted to take a beginner's course in journalism were unable to fulfill the minimum writing requirement. At the University of Nevada, three-quarters of the students in journalism had first to be taught grammar. One of the big publishing houses in New York has decided to have its university textbooks rewritten in high school English. A professor of English, formerly acting chairman of the Modern Language Association, raised the question of whether teaching all students the correct use of English was really worth the trouble; he seriously suggested that efforts be concentrated on only 10 percent of them.[11] I have observed indications of a similar development in my own country.

The shorter a word, the more likely its wide use. "Into" owes its popularity no doubt partly to its brevity. (Sample: "I'm into something that's the biggest into since I was into Shinto.") The most famous of all four-letter words is practically unlimited in its use, being employed in the most senseless connection ("Fuck the flag"). Abroad it has sometimes been taken over like any other swear word, quite removed from its meaning. At the entrance to the main lecture hall of my school in Aachen I once saw the spray-painted words "Fuck den Rektor" (*Rektor* is the equivalent of "university president"). With "wow," "into," and a few four-letter words you can carry on quite a conversation, especially if you add a number of words like "like," "you know," and "man," the last even used by girls speaking to girls.

Perhaps this aversion to speech has something to do with the inclination toward taciturn cults (Zen, meditation) and with the willingness to repeat endlessly the magic syllable *Om*, the *Hare* of the Krishna cult, or one's secret mantra. But there is also, to an extent unknown in the West since the Dark Ages, a distrust of speech, logic, and rationality. On the Scene, if you are honest, genuine, and real, you must stammer, you must intersperse your words with frequent *umms,* and must sound confused—as confused as the world is. The Scene's language, according to one of its critics, suggests that of "parrots awakened from anesthesia."[12]

The proliferation of new words, or new uses of old ones, in the language of the Scene proceeds at such a quick pace that many books about the young generation include a glossary. An "underground" dictionary with 3,000 key words has been published by a psychologist who compiled it especially to help parents, teachers, and judges understand better the young people who only speak the slang of the Scene.[13]

In most countries that I know, the language of the Scene has a tendency to employ, figuratively, the gutter words denoting sexual intercourse, certain bodily parts and functions, and the products of those parts. After all these years I still wince when I hear American or German girls who belong or pretend to belong to the Scene enrich their language with the words for feces. Ulrike Meinhof's former husband, the onetime editor of the left-wing review *konkret,* has filled a whole page with selections of toilet and genital language, giving ten examples alone for word combinations with "shit," including "shit orgasm."[14] In his book *Kent State,* James Michener devotes an entire subchapter to this phenomenon. After quoting from a grand jury statement that "the language of the gutter has become the common vernacular of many persons posing as students in search of a higher education," he tries to find the reasons for this shift in the use of language. One explanation given to him by a Kent State left-winger was this: The young people of the Scene felt that the old generation had stolen so much of their life-style (fashions, for example) that they wanted to possess something of their own which their seniors certainly would not touch:

We used to say "Cool it, man" and now you'll see this in advertisements everywhere. [...] We said things like "blow your mind" and *Harper's Bazaar* is advising women whose husbands earn $50,000 a year to blow their minds with pink blouses.[...] I'll bet that within two years Buick will come out with full-page ads claiming that the 1972 Buick is a real motherfucker. [Therefore] young people are devising a language which older people cannot steal from them. We seek to outrage those who have been outraging us.

To this Michener adds his own thought that the debasement of language is one of the most powerful agencies for the destruction of society. "The assault on language became the spearhead of an assault on all authority, and students who felt free to shout previously forbidden words also felt free to attach other restrictions. [...] The shock value of having a pretty coed shout obscenities [...] was quickly recognized." To put it into one sentence: "If you destroy the word, you can destroy the system."[15]

A second linguistic group on the Scene uses mainly sociological jargon. The vocabulary of these young people stems from Marxism (in its many varieties), from psychoanalysis, from the Frankfurt School of Social Research, and from constantly emerging new disciplines. This language is international, using many words with Greek and Latin roots (image, repression, frustration, transparency, and so on); with such words one can cross the language frontiers. Marx's *Entfremdung,* translated into English as "alienation," has been adopted by the Russians as *alienatsia.* A recent book in Switzerland is devoted to the "sufferings of the new words."[16]

The Scene has not been described here historically, for good reason; it presents not a process that has had a beginning and an end (as, for example, the American and the German SDS had), but rather a state of affairs, a style, or, well, a scene. The hippies had a clearly definable climax, the mass love-in in Golden Gate Park, January 1967, and even an official end, the celebrated mock funeral in the same park, "on the sixth of October 1967, after sunrise." And yet, the worldwide spreading of hippie-ism took place after that—it has now even reached the Soviet Union. I found traces of hippies in Moscow in 1976, and an American magazine has described one group, whose members boasted such assumed names as Nixon, Kennedy, Jagger, Chicago, and Ophelia and displayed English-language slogans: "Not War" and "Make Hair Everywhere."[17] Even though the word "Hippie" is now rarely heard, the Scene and its styles are still alive. What died was the first intoxication, that mixture of flowers, drugs, and hopes; it died, however, not on that October morning in Golden Gate Park but two years later, on two occasions in 1969.

The first time was during the night of August 8–9 when the "family" of Charles Manson entered a house in the Los Angeles area and killed five people there, partly under the hypnotizing influence of their prophet, Manson, and partly for the hell of it. The girls who committed these murders were, as a type, not much different from the flower children of the Scene.[18]

The second time the innocence of the Scene died was at Altamont in California on December 6, when a young man was killed while three quarters of a million young people were listening to the Rolling Stones, as Mick Jagger sang *Sympathy for the Devil.* The nation awoke as from a trance and shuddered. One of the participants said: "In 24 hours, we created all the problems of our society in one place: congestion, violence, dehumanization." Another wrote of that evening when a decade and a great hope had come to an end: "Paradise Lost."[19]

19
THE CAMPUS

THE end of the Second World War ushered in the American Age. The American way of life has spread throughout the world: Coca-Cola, the musical, and . . . the campus. In Europe, to be sure, there are still many universities whose buildings are all over town, but when new universities are built, the American campus is the model—for instance, in Germany at the Free University of West Berlin and in France at Nanterre. Outside Europe, wherever I have lectured, in nine out of ten cases it has been on a campus—in Dakar or Cape Town, in Cairo or Tehran, in Bangkok or Singapore, in Jamaica or Puerto Rico, even in Japan and China.

A campus is not only a conglomeration of buildings in a lovely landscape; it is a world in itself, with its own rules and customs. For the professors a campus is—or was until recently—a very pleasant world, and also for the great majority of the students, in spite of examinations and occasional gripes. ("College education is wonderful, it feels so good when it stops," I remember one of my friends sighing in Berkeley back in 1928.) The campus is by far the most agreeable of worlds and compares more than favorably with factory, farm, office, or hospital. Contrary to the notion of radical students (and professors), in my own experience as student and professor well into the sixties, the campus has provided a life of privilege and intellectual comfort. Nowhere else were there so few burdens and duties and so many possibilities of living according to one's inclinations. The student had to fulfill certain tasks if he wanted to obtain a degree, but apart from that he had all the intellectual and spiritual treasures of humanity at his disposal in libraries, lecture halls, and seminars. The professor, for his part, carried a certain number of hours of lectures and seminars, had term papers to correct and dissertations to read, and some administative work to handle. But then he could do research in the fields of his interest, and it was usually up to him to decide what these were. He was generally well paid, and in addition to the salary there were grants for research and for travel, extra fees for consultations, and from time to time, sabbaticals.

Thus, professors again formed a world by themselves, especially in the universities of the campus type. This world has often been described; Edward Albee's *Who's Afraid of Virginia Woolf?* (1962) has been staged everywhere. A recent novel, *The War Between the Tates,* offers the opinion of its author, herself a professor at Cornell, that professors develop an occupational disease "the way workers in asbestos plants get fibrous lungs."[1] The "occupational disease" of professors is their intellectual-liberal attitude; they feel obliged to see things from all sides, and thus to consider the possibility that the rebellious students might also have good reasons for their opinions and demands. Especially historians, sociologists, and political scientists do not want to deny students the right to put into practice what they have taught them about democracy and human rights, about Socrates and Abraham Lincoln; some may even have a guilty feeling that they themselves have not gone beyond theories.

In America, many professors found it difficult to quarrel with the students for taking to the streets in their opposition to the Vietnam war. To a large extent, the professors themselves considered the war a sad mistake, if not a political crime. In a way, no professional group was less prepared to handle the student revolt than were the professors; it just had never occurred to them that such a thing might happen. Their perplexity contributed to the quick rise of temperature on the campus. University presidents and their staffs were wavering between capitulation and calling the police, losing one confrontation after another in the process.

To my knowledge, only one campus president put himself physically on the line. This was the Canadian-born, Japanese, and internationally known linguist S. I. Hayakawa, the president of San Francisco State College—then in his sixties. Climbing onto the roof of the students' loudspeaker truck and surrounded by the amazed students, Hayakawa dismantled the sound equipment.

Even this action, which instantly propelled him into national prominence and later led to his election to the U.S. Senate, did not prevent his college from teetering for several months on the edge of chaos.

But here we are mainly concerned with the students. How did they live, think, feel during that time? How was it possible that the campus, to use the language of their critics, should suddenly turn into a refuge, a hotbed, a launching pad, a bastion of the revolution?

Student unrest, by no means new, had in former days mainly the character of humorous play or frivolous mischief. The students gave vent to their exuberance, often fired by a goodly quantity of alcohol. The inhabitants of university towns took this with equanimity, with a "boys will be boys" shrug; sometimes they were angry, sometimes they laughed; and just in case (at least, in the good old days), they kept their daughters under lock and key. University administrations were usually able to handle such eruptions without great difficulty. Some people, and especially the concerned parents, might be appalled by panty raids and similar foolishness, but one thing was true of all these extracurricular activities: they did not aim at the overthrow of society. If they had a target at all, it was the philistines, the narrow-minded middle class, often ridiculed in student songs. However, the most popular of German student songs also included the lines *Vivat nostra civitas* (Long Live Our Community) and *Vivat academia, Vivant professores!*

All this more or less held true (Japan excepted) down into the sixties. In many German university towns, including Aachen where I taught, there existed a friendly and jocular relationship among students, professors, and townspeople. At times, long tables were set up on the market square, with all the people mingling, steins in their hands and songs on their lips.

In the second half of the sixties, all this changed, and not only in Germany and America. Confrontation took the place of the frequently (and justly) quoted "community of those who taught and those who learned." Anyone who had not visited his alma mater for some years was likely to be startled, if not shocked, by the mass of people now crowding the university buildings, sometimes sitting on the steps of the lecture halls, and even standing outside to hear the loudspeaker voice of a professor whom they could not see. Personal contact between professor and student, previously the rule, had become an exception. When I was a student in Germany and in the United States during the twenties, most of us knew personally one or several professors. They called us by our names, sometimes inviting us to their homes. Today the professor teaching large classes sees a nameless and faceless mass in front of him.

The change from elite institution to mass-production factory was less noticeable in America, where for decades the percentage of undergraduates among the student age-group has been very large. In contrast, the European university was not meant to prepare one just for life in general, was not in effect a continuation of high school for a few more years, but was a place where one acquired knowledge and skill for truly academic professions, as is the case with graduate schools in America. Because their numbers were small compared with those in American universities, European students were given a great deal of academic freedom; in many fields they could choose their courses and seminars as they saw fit, without being told which professors to hear and which books to read.

Thus, the unprecedented growth in the numbers of students in all European countries has created problems that never existed before. The student is no longer a member of an elite corps but rather feels as if he were drowning in the mass of his fellow students. He feels lost and disappointed and has difficulties in finding his way through the now anonymous campus. As the quality of high-school instruction declines, the university receives new students who are less well prepared. Having to provide some instruction formerly given in high school, it tends toward a more rigid curriculum. So perhaps there may emerge in the European universities a student body similar to that of the American undergraduates.

A NEW STUDENT TYPE

Social life on the campus has changed, too. The student organizations that formerly dominated the image and life of the university —fraternities and sororities in America, Germany's dueling *Burschenschaften* and *Korps* with their colored caps—were relegated to the background in the sixties, and politically oriented groups such as SDS took their place. The unions of foreign students, largely from the Third World, became powerful organizations, where formerly they had been barely noticed small clubs. In Germany the Iranian students played, as we saw in the case of West Berlin, a considerable role in the radicalization of the stu-

217

dent body. Students from Arab countries have banded into Arab unions, cooperating closely among themselves, even though the countries from which they come might be at political odds with each other. These foreign student unions do not just gather to sing folk songs—they are politically active in the interest of their countries or of certain political groups at home, usually quite far to the left.

Studying abroad has become a mass phenomenon, changing the image of many universities. In 1972 more than a half million young people were studying outside the frontiers of their homeland. Relatively few countries attract the bulk of this migration: The United States had almost 150,000 foreign students in 1972 (only 36,000 in 1955), the Federal Republic of Germany, 34,000 (7,500 in 1955). For curiosity's sake, we might add that in 1972, according to Soviet figures, only 249 young Soviet citizens were studying outside the Communist bloc.[2]

When the universities were politicized in the sixties, their whole character was affected. One aspect of academic freedom which had been previously of minor significance was suddenly found to offer extraordinary opportunities to radical students: The campus was a sanctuary to which, as a rule, the state and its forces would have no access. It was not by chance that the student revolution in America was triggered on that strip of university territory in Berkeley, 26 feet wide, which the students claimed as their own.

As the gap between the campus and the outside world increased, the campus became the true world for millions of students, even a counterworld opposed to the existing one beyond. The more the radical students condemned that other world, the less willing they were to condone capitalism and imperialism, to work for the Establishment, the military-industrial complex, the consumer society, and the oppressive legal system which they perceived outside the campus.

On the campus, political actions were invented and prepared, day-and night-long discussions were carried on—often in "liberated" (that is, occupied) lecture halls. The desire to remain aloof from the outside world as long as possible caused tens of thousands to take up a new project or field of study after barely (or not) finishing the preceding one. A student told Herbert Marcuse in Berlin (July 1967): "It is no secret that many of us postpone our examinations time and again, not because we are stupid or lazy, but because we believe that only from the sanctuary of the university can we push the concrete practical work which, instead of confirming our [social] system, will fundamentally change it."[3]

A sense of humor has become rarer, although it has not left the campus completely. During a solemn commencement at the University of Hamburg, some students unfurled over the heads of the faculty a big placard:

> *Unter den Talaren*
> *Muff von tausend Jahren.*

Perhaps one could translate it thus:

> Under the gowns,
> Stale old clowns.

They rhymed also against those medical professors who spend more time collecting fees from their patients than teaching their students:

> *An jedem zehnten Klinikbett*
> *Wird ein Ordinarius fett.*

Translated:

> For every tenth clinic bed,
> A doctor on his fees grows fat.

The Marxists had expected for a long time that the battalions of the revolution would arise within the factories (in revolutionary Russia this was actually the case), but in the sixties it happened on the campus. To be sure, not all students participated. There was a small core (or several small cores, frequently cooperating) whose members became what one might call professionals of activism; around them coalesced sympathizers who felt similarly but did not want to disrupt their schoolwork; and finally there was by far the largest group, the silent majority, called in Germany the "gray mice." That majority could be mobilized only on certain occasions—in Japan against the prolongation of the security treaty with America, in Germany to march in honor of the deceased Benno Ohnesorg, in the United States after the deadly shots at Kent State and in Jackson. This was not enough for the activists. They wanted the solidarity of all students on all political questions. To achieve it, nothing was more effective than to provoke conflicts between the students, whether politically interested or not, and the police. This worked very well in many places. The police (sometimes even the army) became part of the campus scene. The trick was to escalate the conflict through four stages: assembly—street demonstration—scuffling with the police—arrest.

In many a country I have seen student meetings, especially if thousands attended, quickly produce an atmosphere favorable for solidarity. Whatever the occasion, the development was usually the same. First the activists arrived; next, those with an interest in the cause that was being pushed; finally, those motivated by curiosity. The activists, who often furnished the chairman and always a considerable number of speakers, kept close to the loudspeaker and had a say in the choice and sequence of speakers; they then introduced questions intended to excite a large proportion of those present.

Usually such meetings begin in orderly fashion, concentrating on the issues for which they are called. Then come the first heckling interruptions and the reaction of the audience: laughter, protests, counterprotests. Next: the raising of hands to get the chairman's attention (fists clenched to show one's political allegiance), the unfolding of banners, the distribution of leaflets. Then: a rush to the stage, some scuffling for the microphone, the chanting of slogans, fisticuffs which cease after a while or are continued outside. Storms of applause for aggressive speakers, howls of disapproval for those who plead for prudence. After two or three hours, people begin to leave—some of them tired and bored, others making a show of their disagreement—while the temper of the remaining ones becomes ever hotter. At the end, majorities for radical decisions are obtained by acclamation, and committees of extremists nominated in order to circumvent the constitutionally elected organs, such as the student parliament.

It is a time-tested observation that radicals receive more applause at mass meetings than do moderates, and the extremists more than the radicals. The resolution passed at the end is almost always more radical than the average mood of those present; many students feel, because they have come, that they ought not to vote against the resolution, and vote for it from a vague feeling of solidarity. Sometimes they vote in favor for fear of being abused if they don't. Perhaps not one in a thousand would be discourteous to a professor; but if a professor is pushed against the wall, jeered at, humiliated by an entire mass meeting, students may feel a tense satisfaction, as if they were watching a cruel film. The spectacle offered by the victim is embarrassing and exciting at the same time, almost a striptease, if only an intellectual one.

If the call "Into the streets!" is sounded, the second level has been reached. The students pour out and form marching columns, often holding onto each other. They shout, they sing, they are pleased when they see the people in the street nervously running for cover and cars escaping into side streets. Policemen appear, then disappear to call for assistance; the shutters of the shops clank down, while people watch the excitement from the higher floors of buildings. The marching columns meet the first rank of policemen, who try to stop them and dissolve the columns. Angry words of derision are heard, and obscenities. The column holds, but wavers. The decision is imminent.

When the first rock has been thrown, the third level is reached. (In the presence of TV cameras, it is sure to be thrown.) The fighting that follows may be the baptism of a radical, the first blow from a nightstick his confirmation. The arrests—level number four—unleash a development which, for the time being, leads deeper and deeper into confrontation.

But among the activities of change-minded students confrontation is only one. There is also the search for a less noisy move toward a new and better life—communal life.

20
THE COMMUNE

IN the years 1930–1933 I visited a number of communes in the Soviet Union, and even lived in one. Then they disappeared; those in the countryside were integrated with the newly established kolkhozes, and Stalin dissolved the urban ones. Some of their egalitarian and truly communist principles (e.g., no member should possess more than the others) did not fit into the "achievement society" Stalin was fashioning. In a diary of one of the Moscow youth communes, which I published at that time,[1] the problems that arise in living closely together were quite apparent. Similar experiments were being made by German youth communes; under Hitler, they disappeared at almost the same time as those in Russia. After that, the word "commune" was rarely used until we began to hear about the "people's communes" in Maoist China in 1958. It was soon clear that these were not experiments in communal living, but rather organizations of collectivized peasants.

I use the term "commune" here for any organizational form adopted by people living together (under one roof or, at any rate, in a limited area), dividing the daily chores among themselves, and contributing whatever they earn through individual or collective work to a common fund which takes care of their needs on a basis of equality or near equality.

Within the field of my own observations, it is rather surprising that the best, most successful, and most enduring communes have not served as a model in the West—perhaps in part because they are not named communes. These are the kibbutzim in Israel. The kibbutz comes closest to the communist ideal: The members live without private property (leaving aside the goods of daily use, such as furniture, books or a radio); they work hard, without the stimulus of piecework wages; they get along without a bureaucracy or an Establishment, because the members themselves handle the communal functions by turns; and they do not grant parents a monopoly on early education—the children grow up, from infancy on, in separate children's houses. Kibbutz members are, however, only a small elite within the population of Israel, about 100,000 out of more than 3 million. It may be largely owing to the pro-Arab and therefore anti-Israel attitude of the New Left that the kibbutz, as far as I can see, has not served as a model for experiments in the United States and Europe; for their restless young people the kibbutz is also probably too well organized and patriotic. Only in Japan have I found lively interest; there a "Kibbutz Society" has organized trips to Israel and propagated the ideal of communal living, especially among students tired of the violent infighting on the campus.

In the West, the word "commune" came into vogue in the late sixties. On the following pages, I report only on communes in the United States and Germany, partly because these countries have produced the richest material, but also because the strong contrasts produce a clearer picture of what communes can be.

A member of a commune does not have to be communist. Communal living has its advantages for people from any walk of life, particularly for students, with its communal shopping and babysitting and sharing of rents. However, I wish to discuss mainly communes that are based on more than material advantages, namely, on common convictions and beliefs, and are meant to last a long time—ideally, forever. To exclude any misunderstanding, I call their members not communists (which could suggest Communist Party membership or sympathies), but communards.

In America it was the hippies who—after the withering of the flowers of San Francisco—founded communes in large numbers. When life there and in other cities became unpleasant for the flower children, thousands of them fled to the countryside, to live as the "lilies of the field" (many, anyway, not expecting to toil or spin) with congenial young people in small communities called tribes, families, nests—and communes. Thus began the newest among the countless migrations which make up American history, with the difference that this time the movement was not toward any still open western frontier but away from the cities into the countryside, into the mountains—upriver to where the waters are clean, as they say.

Vivid information can be found in books by Robert Houriet and by Richard Fairfield, who visited 50 and 34 communes, respectively, and analyzed their observations (Fairfield's bibliography lists more than 200 titles). Richard Atcheson, a journalist, and the couple John Rothchild and Susan Wolf give more personal accounts of their experiences. A New York sociologist, Keith Melville, presents an analysis that uses historical and sociological methods and data. Additional books based on personal experiences, some by communards, are mentioned at the end of the notes to this chapter.

American communes, very many of them youth communes, were estimated in 1970 to number between 2,000[2] and 3,000.[3] Their members one might call refugees—refugees from the stress of the city, from oppressive authorities, and, more often than not, from themselves. Their notion: The commune was to look after everything that needed looking after, including the children, and would guarantee a simple life—in freedom and community, in play, pleasure and meditation—without the burden of responsibility. Some looked for an extension of their adolescence before the real struggle of adult life began, and some hoped, with the help of the commune, to avoid this struggle once and for all.

Modern civilization, so they said, had overdeveloped the intellectual faculties of man; it was high time to return to the forces of emotion and to go far back in the history of humanity—to that fork in the road where the West turned in the wrong direction—and now finally to take the right road, the road of harmony between man and nature. Where could one realize this ideal better than in a commune far away from coercion and stress? There everybody would find his true "identity" and discover the purpose of life, in communion with the universe, between the soil and the stars. One communard said:

People [in the cities] go running back and forth and up and down like wild rabbits and crazy deer, what for? Just stop and open up, be receptive to the good earth, tune in to natural vibrations, no one has to work for anything. God provides all if you don't get uptight about it. That Old Man knew what he was doing when He made all of this. A lot of us used to live in the Haight-Ashbury. You had to shoot speed just to survive in a scene like that. It was nowhere. God meant men to be close to the land, not on concrete. Cities—wow! Freeways, cars going zoom zoom, here, there—lights blinking— rush, rush. Man, that ain't natural, that's insanity. The city is doomed. Those who get it together on the land will be the survivors.[4]

Hopes of this kind were nourished by a number of publications. B. F. Skinner's *Walden Two,* which takes up the tradition of Thoreau's famous book about life in the woods became one of the bibles of the commune. "Most of our institutions we have taken from *Walden Two,*" said one girl communard. Some young people were attracted by notions of group sex: they had read books by Rimmer, where such practices were described pleasantly, and by Wilhelm Reich, who based his teaching of sexual permissiveness on psychoanalysis. Some acclaimed the anarchistic life-forms depicted by Paul Goodman and Murray Bookchin, or found their imagination fired by Robert A. Heinlein's utopian novel about the creation of ideal humans by a visitor from Mars.[5]

Almost all who moved into a commune expected an instant solution to their cares and problems; the step into the commune, they hoped, would be a step into paradise. To cut themselves loose from their past, they adopted new, funky names for themselves—Odessa, Vesta, George the Bodiless. In the commune everything would belong to everybody, even the clothes. There was another way, of course, to solve the clothing problem; in some communes nakedness was considered an important element of the communal life. A commune functions less well than a modern factory, you say? "That doesn't matter. We've got plenty of time. It's people that count."[6]

Many communards had participated in cults before they joined—they had been Hare Krishna followers in yellow robes, "Jesus freaks," or Zen Buddhists. Some communes consulted the ancient Chinese oracle, the *I Ching.* "They spent more time throwing I Ching sticks than working in the fields," it was said of one commune. Another decided on the basis of an I Ching oracle to move from Vermont to New Mexico.[7] Drugs were more or less the rule, though usually in small doses.

SEARCHING FOR NEW LIFE-STYLES
All kinds of prophets made their appearance, such as Allen Noonan, the "cosmic messenger" of the "One World Family." I met him once in Berkeley, where, surrounded by disciples, he was

preaching a "crusade for the Messiah." A commune called "Here and Now" had been founded by him near Berkeley.

Many a folly was taken up in the communes under the rubric of "science" (or "scientific"), which means so much nowadays; for example, the "science of proxemics" (from Latin *proximus,* "the nearest"), which pursued experiments on the influence of body touching. Another one propagated the "Anthropodeic Church," the name taken from the Greeks (*anthropos,* "human being") and from the Romans (*deus,* "God"). Still another science offered to pregnant women the slogan "Open land, open cervix." Out in the open country and under the open sky, it was easier to bear children; the mother and her friends were advised to eat the placenta together "as if it were a sacrament."[8]

Such peculiar behavior becomes understandable if one knows its origins. One commune reported about its members:

> At fourteen, Deja had been raped. Kathy had experienced recurring episodes of schizophrenia. Morgan, known as Count Morgan, had escaped the mental institution to which his parents had committed him. Taking too much speed had impaired his neural pathways, causing him to stumble as he walked mooselike through the woods. Wanda was a violent Virgo who took morphine, talked of assassinating George Wallace, and read books on witchcraft. Ross had grown up in a tough section of the Bronx, a war zone for rival street gangs.[9]

In his account of a commune which bore the inspiring name of Sunrise Hill, Houriet remarks: "Happy people it is said do not go voluntarily to war, neither, I add, into communes."[10]

In one commune, all the members met to discuss the meaning of their dreams. In the evening they went into the forest to look for the monkey demon; some swore they had seen his green eyes in the dark. One girl communard danced nude on the house roof, supposedly to chase away curious tourists. The result was that even more came. Eventually, some fellows from the neighborhood raped her.

The communards often aroused the hostility of the nearby farmers and the local authorities, who considered them to be disturbers of the peace, thieves, drug addicts, and carriers of loose morals and venereal diseases. Some communes were closed by the police and even destroyed by bulldozers; here and there the communards—like the Indians of yore—fought with the sheriffs; they considered society to be their enemy and used the term "Amerika" (with k instead of c) to brand their country as fascist.

Despite their indifference toward material goods, the communards could not dispense with them entirely. The chronicles of communes agree on this point: Not one of them was able to survive on its own.

The communards accepted aid from their otherwise rejected parents and even from the government, saying that society should have an interest in paying for experiments in new life-styles. Some communes found private sponsors: one man, for example, invested his whole fortune, about a half million dollars, in communes, only to end up having a nervous breakdown. Another man gave land to a commune, even fed the communards to give them a start, but was abused by them when he demanded a minimal amount of work; finally he couldn't stand the chaos and threw everyone out.

Many communes tried to improve their finances through the sale of handmade articles: they turned out necklaces, hammocks, or moccasins—sometimes going to the nearest Indian reservation for instruction. (One would like to know what the Indians thought about these curious palefaces.) They experimented with various wage forms. Some communes finally decided to give work points for labor performed, coming to the same conclusion that I had seen emerge in the Russian kolkhozes forty-five years before.[11] Quite an original method was developed by a commune in Virginia: chores for which more than one person applied were valued less; people who did unpopular work received more work points, and thus could work shorter hours than those who chose more pleasant duties.

What came of all this, of the great, all-too-great hopes, efforts, and sacrifices? Feeling sympathy for idealistic young people who renounced the comforts of modern civilization and experimented with new life-styles, I would be glad to find favorable reports on the outcome. What I have found is rather muted. An ideal commune, says Fairfield, would be one whose members developed and matured while at the same time helping their comrades, one in which firm regulations would be unnecessary because everyone would do of his own accord whatever was needed. Such a commune, he adds, exists only in the imagination; here on earth a commune which consists of nothing but ideals is sure to be a failure.[12]

Houriet found

everywhere, a screaming need for privacy, to be alone in a place called your own, one that was sacred and uncommunal.

227

Everywhere, hassles and marathon encounter meetings that couldn't resolve questions like whether to leave the dogs in or out. Everywhere, cars that wouldn't run and pumps that wouldn't pump because everybody knew all about the occult history of tarot and nobody knew anything about mechanics. Everywhere, people who strove for self-sufficiency and freedom from the capitalist system but accepted food stamps and handouts from Daddy, a corporate sales VP. Sinks filled with dishes, cows wandering through gates left open, and no one to blame. Everywhere, instability, transiency. Somebody was always splitting, rolling up his bags, packing his guitar and kissing good-bye—off again in search of the truly free, unhung-up community.[13]

Atcheson reports that in most communes he quickly became claustrophobic and was unable to stay more than a short time, feeling as if he were in a foreign country where he knew neither language nor customs. Melville felt often that the communes he visited were inhabited by the wrong people trying to do the right thing. He gave most of the communes only a small chance for survival.[14]

How are these harsh judgments to be explained, judgments from chroniclers who started out as friends of the commune movement, not as enemies?

STONES ON THE WAY

Practically all young people who joined communes underestimated the difficulty of the tasks ahead; many probably had not given any thought to them. To get a communal farm going was an "incredibly difficult thing," said one communard. In principle, all agreed that each member should do some useful work in the commune, but always it turned out that the chores had to be taken care of by a few, by the core of the commune, and they gradually grew tired of working while the rest of the group loafed. One of them, who was told by a novice that God, after all, would know how to take care of them, replied that the novice should look for another god: "Our God here is not going to feed you if you don't work." Young people who had joined the commune because they wanted to live in a community that was truly alive soon afterward did not show the bare minimum of community spirit. "The communal garden was a monstrous failure," one said. As soon as the first enthusiasm of planting had vanished, there was hardly anyone left who showed any interest in weeding, and there hadn't been much enthusiasm for the planting. "Look into the garden. How many people do you see working? One. It's planting time and

228

you see only one who is working in the garden." One commune did not even own a clock. "I believe it is Monday," somebody said. Not only the quality of labor suffered, but also hygiene. Of a relatively well-functioning commune Fairfield reports that the two toilets were "flooded by a river of shit."

A communard who had been a longtime supporter of the commune movement finally came up with this simple conclusion: "Communes don't work, 'cause people don't work." And he continued: "Too many people with a pile of high-sounding ideas on utopia. But there is no utopia, only a few guys who are looking for chicks for their bed, and who expect of the commune that it look out for them."

A central problem of all communes was how to combine the members' urge toward liberty with the minimum of order necessary for the commune's functioning. New communes often began without any kind of administration; in their enthusiasm, the communards thought they could survive on sheer improvisation. As enthusiasm waned, they experimented with all kinds of administrative forms: They elected steering committees, allotted responsibility for the various chores in turns, and tried to tie certain members to certain jobs. But the membership was in constant flux, and they soon had to experiment anew. In the background, to be sure, there was the ideal of total democracy, of plenary meetings in which all members would discuss all matters and all decisions would be reached by voting. Yet it is precisely this administrative form that costs most in time and nerves, all observers agreed.

If no necessity exists for a speedy decision, debate can go on endlessly about anything. In one of the communes someone suggested that chickens be kept in order to save money otherwise spent for eggs. Immediately a chicken crisis arose, causing long discussions:

Did we eat the eggs (wasn't wheat germ good enough)? Was it morally right to take eggs from chickens; wasn't it cruel to keep chickens caged—but if we didn't cage them how could we keep them out of the garden? Were we really saving money on eggs, if we had to spend money on the chickens, chicken wire, and all kinds of feed? Who was going to plant an acre of millet and an acre of corn to feed them? Who would build the chicken coop? This was the first time I remember hearing anyone say, "Well, *I* won't give any money for chickens"—using money as a weapon, a personal source of power. And it wasn't long before money again became a personal possession.

229

Music being the most important source of entertainment, particularly among the young ones, there were frequent quarrels about the choice of records. In a number of communes the record player was finally abolished entirely as the only way of avoiding such conflicts. One communard in his first enthusiasm donated his entire collection of records to the commune and soon found to his dismay that dozens were missing.

Max Ernst, a German painter who left his country, once said about German intellectuals that they couldn't even piss without ideology. Well, American communards were not much better. In some communes, everything turned into an ideological problem. Which was ideologically correct, outhouse or bathroom? Toilet paper in rolls, or cut-up newspaper? Should the rooms be cleaned up or everything left in a mess? And so it went.

Fairfield came to the following conclusion:

> People who are new to each other and who refuse to develop any sort of structure, group consensus or methods of dealing with problems inevitably become enemies rather than friends. The larger the size of the group, the worse the problem, and the greater the need for structure. If they are reasonably compatible, two people may be able to live together well without structure, but five or ten or more people will need some sort of framework for dealing with the inevitable variety of problems that will arise.[15]

The tendencey to turn every decision into a matter of principle had a destructive effect on community spirit, and especially on the stability of marriages (whether legalized or not). The relationship between the sexes and the education of the children were among the most ardently discussed topics at the commune meetings.

The best information that I have found about the commune children is in a book published in 1976, *The Children of the Counter Culture,* by John Rothchild and Susan Wolf. The authors—a couple with two young children—stayed in many communes across America for the very purpose of finding out what became of the children born during the years of the rebellion, who might now "outnumber many of the larger Indian tribes in America." The little family started out with a friendly kind of curiosity, but what they found disappointed them. Their lowest marks go to the urban communes of various types, full of freakish people: the woman who taught her six-year-old son to make love with her so he would solve his Oedipal problem and "would never

230

have to be an atomic scientist and make bombs," or the boy of ten who informed visitors that his mother had "the hottest pants in the commune." One mother who took acid every day and lived in a mess explained: "You want to have a straight kid, then be a freaky mother." True enough, out of opposition, her ten-year-old daughter lived in a self-made little girl's bedroom "from the Sears showcase"; she had "teddy bears and lace curtains and a gingham bedspread," creating a "little American refuge for herself." Commune mothers who gave in to their offspring's every whim produced whiny brats, "incessantly demanding and rarely satisfied." These children's "incredible sense of displeasure with the world" provoked the authors to say "The cradle of American radicalism is rocked by the fearful, overgiving permissive mothers of the land."

The one major exception in a long gallery of failures was "The Farm," in western Tennessee; it had existed since 1968 and was populated by about 600 adults, mostly people who had given up professional careers to live in voluntary poverty, "eat soybeans and get up at 4:30 A.M. at the sound of primitive shell horns to go to work. [... They were] strict believers in marriage; single people were isolated by sex, premarital sex was discouraged, extramarital sex was anathema." The authors are enthusiastic about the "totally socialized" children of The Farm, who grew up almost entirely on their own—"the best behaved, most responsible children we had ever seen." Assuming that this impression (from a four-day visit) was correct, it is not too encouraging when compared with the large number of other communes where the authors made very negative observations. But even at The Farm the authors confessed that they "couldn't have taken another day of it." As they left, they "both let out a simultaneous shriek" that had been "hiding out" in them "for four long days."

The commune movement as a whole is a bold step away from the mainstream of Western civilization, and one might well admire its spirit. But even if all favorable comment about The Farm were true and there were a few more communes like it, they are (and want to be, in order not to be contaminated) tiny islands in the vast ocean of American (and Western) life. The successful communes produced the most likable children but did this "at the cost of the self-centered drive that leads to great personal achievement," say these authors, who admit: "We couldn't see famous writers or scientists coming out of that generation of ragamuffins."[16] A question that must be considered seriously is whether the—let us suppose—truly happy ragamuffins of the communes can become models in a world as overcrowded and complicated as ours.

Leaving aside The Farm and its children, the general verdict of those who studied the American commune scene is rather discouraging. The main reason for the failure can be put into one sentence: "Somehow people aren't big enough to do what they said they were going to do." In the days of the pioneers, people had to stick together out of sheer necessity, against hostile nature and against Indians—but today? Nobody is used to overcoming difficulties anymore. Far too many people go to the communes not in search for a new world, but on a highly personal "trip."

In "Why Communes Fail," a report with the subtitle "For Those Who Hadn't Known They Did," three main reasons are given:

> Members of the commune fail to clarify what they expect out of the experience before they decide to come together. Or they fail to develop mechanisms to hold the group accountable to collective aims. Or they are incapable of changing the goals of the commune in response to the new situations and insights.[17]

Every communard knows that "If the going gets tough, I can move on." Fairfield notes that during the summer things do work out somehow, but with winter comes boredom, and "the little private problems take over." In the long run, many young people find it difficult to do without the amenities of American bourgeois civilization. Fairfield, who started out with the hope of finding new freedom in the communes, in the end discovered that

> anyone not adrift in a dream world recognizes that people don't really want complete freedom. Freedom is a difficult thing to handle. [. . .] No structure, no rules, no compulsion to work from nine to five, no one telling us when to do this, to do that—it sounds great until we try it."[18]

Many communards therefore returned to the despised world of Middle America.

In recent years the number of rural communes has declined. The business recession has had its effect; lucrative jobs in which one can earn within a few weeks enough money for living in a commune during the rest of the year have become rare, and parents' bank accounts thinner. Chiefly there remain urban communes, especially on the fringes of universities. These offer fewer problems. There is no agricultural work to be done, and it is easy to keep out of the others' way by going to the library or a nearby bar. You start by renting a house or a large apartment. (Whether there are two or ten of you, the neighbors nowadays hardly pay attention.) The less rigid the rules, the more durable the community. It seems to function best if each person (or each couple) has a separate bedroom, while the group as a whole has one or two community rooms. *The* problem is the cleaning of the common areas, particularly the kitchen and bathrooms. "Until Dishes Do Us Part," was the title of an article describing life in a commune.[19] Promiscuity of the "every man with every woman" type is not the rule; usually couples live together, at least for a certain period of time. In this respect many communes are not quite so exciting as some outsiders imagine.

COMMUNE 2, WEST BERLIN

Much less material is available about the German communes. The most interesting document so far is a report on the "West Berlin Commune 2" (also called "K2").[20] It gives a picture very different from what we have seen in America.

Early in 1967, Communes 1 and 2 emerged in West Berlin. The latter, K2, became well known because young Jan-Carl Raspe of the Baader-Meinhof group once belonged to it, and is of particular interest because of the report its members compiled. K2 weathered its first serious crisis in June 1967 and disintegrated in June 1968, after an existence of less than a year and a half. As far as I can see, these two communes did not try to imitate American examples, but were a homegrown product.

The K2 report was compiled from records kept while the commune lasted, partly from taped discussions. The difficulties encountered by the commune are described in much detail and with much use of terms like disintegration, apathy, frustration, collapse, disappointment, resignation, "feeling of void," confusion, "depressive stickiness," and—time and again—failure. "We had failed definitely," one reads toward the end of the book, "in our attempt to overcome, by living together, the isolation of the individual; a lot of hopes went down the drain; the energies and feelings that we invested were frustrated and their purpose was lost."

K2 had to struggle, as did the communes in the United States, with the problems of keeping house. ("Periodically, there reigned a totally unproductive chaos. Dirt everywhere. One didn't like to take a bath because the bathroom stank from a thousand dirty

towels lying around.") On the other hand, the commune children
fared relatively well because some of the members, Raspe especially, were fond of children. Nor did the finances of the communal household pose any problem; the members had little desire
for expensive goods and pastimes.

On both sides of the Atlantic we find psychological difficulties
as the reason for joining communes. In Germany, as in America,
the young people hope to be better able to handle their personal
problems when they are among their commune friends than when
alone or with their own families, whose closeness has deterio-
rated. The young Germans, however, are less playful; they take
things more seriously and use psychoanalysis for solving their
problems, though in a rather amateurish way which brings them
more confusion than clarification. Their seriousness and honesty
can hardly be doubted, but it is sad that in the end they do not
experience an increase in happiness, in maturity, or in understanding, and that on the grave of their hopes there is but a stone
inscribed "Frustration."

Personal problems prevail. One of the communards, for example, refused to participate in the political discussions of K2 as long
as its members did not help him in "solving the problems he was
experiencing after separating from his former girl friend." This
was one of his reasons for leaving K2. Some of the members were
sexually inhibited, saying they were extremely repulsed by the
sexual act or had "orgasm problems." There was a remarkable
desire for the "separation of sexuality and tenderness," which I
have encountered repeatedly among young people of our time. To
quote Raspe: "I have at present no desire to sleep with a girl. For
me the commune is a 'tender cave,' some kind of 'mother's womb,'
which offers a substitute for the relationship with a girl." One girl
confessed to being afraid of sexual intercourse, "of male bodies in
general," but having a "strong need for tenderness." Sexuality in
the widest sense of the word was problem number one for the
commune members.

For months the group was busy dissecting the psyches of its
members. The amount of time used for these discussions was
enormous, yet the report shows no evidence of progress; there was
mainly a repetitious moving in circles. The members had hoped
that they would succeed in breaking through the spiritual armor
surrounding everybody in the world outside, and they expected
that among their commune friends they could say everything that
was on their minds, as if on a psychoanalyst's couch (some would

lie down on the floor during these intimate discussions), and this, they thought, would bring about an internal liberation they had not known before. It may sound plausible that one will feel better if he communicates than if he closes up. The K2 members, however, did not feel better; their existing problems were not removed by the endless talking, and instead tended to become still more subtle and complicated. The story of the red candle could have served Dostoevski for one of his psychological studies.

Marion and Eberhard had shoplifted a red candle together. Their love relationship went to pieces when, during a group discussion, Marion lit the candle to lessen the amount of cigarette smoke in the air. To Eberhard this was an indication that Marion had renounced him. (Previously they had lit the candle only when they were making love.) Eberhard said, according to the tape: "The experience with the candle confirms my feeling that Marion didn't pay any attention to my despair. [...] When the other participants in the discussion said that they could not follow my reasoning, my feeling of insecurity grew immensely because I had expected the exact opposite from this discussion." Shrinking violets, these revolutionaries!

Actually, they did consider themselves revolutionaries. The entire purpose of the commune was summed up in the subtitle given the K2 report, "Revolutionization of the Bourgeois Individual." Its young members, all daughters and sons of the bourgeoisie, desired to become, through their life in the commune, true revolutionaries. That they did not succeed in this and were not even able to handle their candle problems was the real reason for the commune's failure. The "privilege of not having to have a job for two years, and of devoting ourselves exclusively to the revolutionization of the bourgeois individual," did not lead to success. They recognized this, and therefore had a bad conscience. "All we did was amuse ourselves with the ordering of our private lives," the report soberly confesses. And what came of it? "A total paralysis, an apathy which produced tremendous frustrations in all of us."

A reason had to be found for this failure. It was found: The intellectuals needed the proletariat for their own revolutionization, but the proletariat refused to play along. For the future, it was planned that groups which would closely cooperate with the working class should be formed. Nothing came of this, either. The result was apathy, or desperation. It led Raspe to Baader and to the Stammhein prison.

The publication of the K2 report, telling of the group's disappointment, and the decision of one of its members to join a terrorist band had a negative influence on the commune idea in Germany. People who decide to move as a group into a house or an apartment are now more modest in their expectations. They do not, as a rule, envisage the emerging of a "New Man," or of a "family" of people with similar convictions that will replace the traditional family based on blood relationship. More often than not, these people are now small nuclear families themselves, and they move in with others for purely practical reasons and check out again without much fuss.

Such urban communes, of which there may be some 10,000 in Germany alone, are something new. In a way they are taking the place of the old family clan, which no longer exists. As a child, I still experienced its last manifestations. In addition to parents, brothers, and grandparents, I had countless uncles, aunts, and cousins, all of them forming a strong and reliable community; the sixteen brothers and sisters of my parents produced in turn numerous children and grandchildren. It may well be that modern communes, as a kind of substitute for the clan, are a form of protest against the reduction of the family to husband, wife and perhaps one or two children. Communes of this kind may have a place in our society. The far more ambitious communes which aimed at a "New Man" or a family based on convictions have—so far—failed. They have lacked stability and continuity. Human communities can survive for decades and even centuries only if they are, as many religious orders were, places of service to others and not just excuses for concentrating on one's own problems.

21
SEX AND DRUGS

IN the spring of 1969, I gave a few lectures on one of the modern campuses in California. As usual, I asked the students what issues were being debated most among them; after all, this was a time of particularly violent confrontations between students and police all over America. One answer, given frequently and without hesitation, was nonpolitical and had a rather academic-sounding name—intervisitation. It had to do with this: Could male and female students living in segregated dormitories visit each other? The students said that anyone old enough to be sent to Vietnam surely was old enough to look out for himself in private life. Before the summer was over, the intervisitation discussion ended with walls being broken through and doors put in.

Would that have been possible twenty or even ten years before? Since time immemorial, students have praised love and also practiced it. Even way back in my youth, in German university towns, when most students were boarders in family homes, rooms with a private entrance were much in demand. But whatever happened, vis-à-vis the outside world, at least had to happen within the limits of decorum. On the American campus, students were under the moral supervision of the university administration and the campus police. (I well remember how terrified I was, one evening in 1929, when the glaring light of a campus cop's flashlight suddenly was thrust in my face while I sat on a university bench with a Berkeley coed.) *In loco parentis,* in place of the students' parents—that was how the American university saw its role. Years later, as a young professor in the States, my wife and I, together with colleagues and their wives, had to serve as chaperons at student dances, to make sure that everything was proper. Well into the sixties, not much had changed in principle, but supervision was becoming less strict. Then the unrest of the mid-sixties blew a new wind onto the campus.

In Europe, where student mores had always been freer and *in loco parentis* supervision was impossible because students did not live on university grounds (campuses did not exist), there was less cause for such confrontations. Yet there, too, the rebellion of the young generation brought a certain merging of sex and politics. Having declared war on the "achievement society" because it was held to be oppressing human freedom, students coined the slogan "From the Achievement Society to the Enjoyment Society." (I heard it for the first time in 1965, in a discussion with Berlin high-school students.)

From that slogan it was but a short step to the proclamation of enjoyment and pleasure as a weapon against any oppression. During a lecture tour in Sweden, I attended one of the first showings of Vilgot Sjöman's film *I Am Curious (Yellow)*, in which the young heroine alternately waves the Viet Cong flag and makes love with her boyfriend—once, even, as an extreme provocation against the Establishment, on the wall surrounding the royal palace at Stockholm, in full view of a dumbfounded guard. In America, the best-known slogan combining sex and politics, which spread all over the world, was "Make Love, Not War"—a modern version of the ancient Greek stratagem of Lysistrata.

The sex and politics mixture soon found expression in the American and German student and underground press. In Germany, words such as *sex-pol, politsex,* and even *politporno* made their appearance. The editor of the Hamburg student paper *auditorium* claimed that it was perfectly in order to pepper his paper with sex material in order to gain more readers and thus win support for his left-wing political views. Much the same thing might have been said by the editors of similar papers in America. In Germany the best-known example of sex-pol was for many years *konkret,* founded in 1955 by the liberal-arts student Klaus Rainer Röhl. Two things were responsible for its success. One was the secret subsidy from East Berlin (which Röhl later revealed in his autobiography).[1] The other was the startling and new combination of revolutionary articles (among them the columns of Röhl's wife, Ulrike Meinhof) with sexually explicit pictures and texts. In January 1969, Ulrike Meinhof complained about the review's sensationalism, its "sex appeal, horror appeal, crime appeal," and left it shortly afterward. The ensuing decline of *konkret*'s influence was due not only to her departure—by then one could see dozens of bare bosoms in other magazines on the newsstands.

The advocates of sex-pol took strong arguments for their position from Wilhelm Reich and Herbert Marcuse. Reich, one of the most talented pupils of Sigmund Freud, very early developed theories which led away from those of his teacher. While Freud considered sublimation, the mastering of one's desires, to be the absolutely necessary precondition for human civilization, Reich preached the total fulfillment of the sexual drive; he did this not only as a psychoanalyst but also as a Communist revolutionary (at that time he was a member of the Party). In a book written while he was still in his twenties—*The Function of the Orgasm* (German edition, 1926), a title which became firmly linked to his name—Reich still proceeded with some caution. The book was, in fact, dedicated to Freud "in profound reverence." By the time of *The Invasion of Compulsory Sex Morality* (German edition, 1932), Reich was expressing his ideas quite openly. His main thesis: Capitalist society, like other societies before it, denies sexual gratification to the people, the better to hold them in subjugation. Marriage and the family, like church and school, serve only one purpose—to destroy the independence of the person. Through sexual oppression, Reich wrote, there emerges the unfree, subjected person who is both slave and rebel. Thus, sexual revolution was for him one aspect of the socialist revolution.

Early in 1932, Reich finished a pamphlet, *The Sexual Struggle of Youth,* which was written for the young generation.[2] It was published after some delay—in 1933, just before Hitler came to power—because of considerable opposition to it within the Communist Party of Germany. (The quarrel over the pamphlet eventually led to the author's expulsion from the Party.) While condemning the bourgeois notion of permissiveness, Reich stated in this pamphlet that he did not object to promiscuity among young Communists as long as it served the revolution. The main thing, he explained, was to channel the sexual rebellion of the young generation into the revolutionary struggle against the capitalist order. Here Reich also sketched his picture of the new sexuality: After the victory of the revolution, sexuality and labor would no longer contradict each other; they would blossom forth together, each enhancing the other.

239

Reich's prophecy was dead wrong as far as the Soviet Union (which he visited in 1929) is concerned. There "sexual liberation" existed but for a very short time—if one wants to apply this term at all to the chaotic conditions during the time of revolution and civil war. For the Bolsheviks, "free love" was all right then, if for no other reason than that it helped to undermine the stability of the bourgeoisie. But after the full victory of the revolution, the days of free love were numbered. Stalin enforced extremely puritanical rules and decreed very conservative moral laws. Both divorce and free love were systematically impeded. To some extent, his attitude is felt to this day.

Not long ago, the Soviet press reported the case of a girl, sent with many other young people to do temporary work in the countryside, who was suspected of having had improper relations there with another "volunteer." For this she was publicly chastised and harassed to a point where, after overcoming much bureaucratic resistance, she finally succeeded in getting a medical examination and a certificate of virginity.[3] I might remind the reader that today in China early marriages are discouraged (for women under twenty-five and for men under twenty-eight years of age) and sexual relations before marriage are frowned upon. Reich, incidentally, was sufficiently honest to confess later that he had been wrong about the Soviet Union. In the preface to a new edition (1945) of his *Sexual Revolution* he wrote: "The Soviet Union, the product of a proletarian revolution, has become reactionary in its sex politics. I am profoundly sorry to have to admit this."[4]

Reich's later life ended, as we shall see, in loneliness; for a while he was forgotten. But his thesis of the inseparable connection between sexual and political revolutions surfaced suddenly in the New Left. Bertell Ollman, a political scientist, in his preface to a new edition of one of Reich's works, gives his impressions of the university of Nanterre in the spring of 1967. He found *The Sexual Struggle of Youth* being sold in the student dormitories "from door to door," contributing to the occupation of girls' dormitories by male students, actions which, as we know, triggered the "Paris May."[5]

In Berlin, Röhl found that "Reich's *Function of the Orgasm* travels as an illegal reprint from hand to hand and, together with Marcuse, pushes aside [...] Marx and Engels. By bringing sex into play, the Movement acquires wide, previously untapped reserves of followers, breaking into the masses of high-school stu-

240

dents. [...] Information about Vietnam and information about the pill were no longer unrelated, rather they were two aspects of the Movement which supplemented each other."[6]

"TOGETHER WITH MARCUSE"

Röhl mentions Reich and Marcuse in one breath, and indeed there is some similarity in their views, but Marcuse himself does not think much of Reich, whom he sharply attacks in his book *Eros and Civilization,* calling him a Left deviationist from the teachings of Freud. One American author has placed Marcuse's book on a par with Marx's *Capital.*[7] It is hardly that, but it was the first literary breakthrough for Marcuse.

The philosophical and political significance of *Eros and Civilization* lies in the author's attempt to join Freud with Marx (who is not mentioned but always present). His strong influence on the restless generation is due primarily to the fact that he condemns the achievement principle and praises the enjoyment principle. Marcuse maintains that a society ruled by achievement thinking tries everywhere, in the name of achievement, to inhibit the trend toward enjoyment.

This book, so it seems to me, suffers from a lack of empirical data, as does his *Soviet Marxism.* Unlike Freud, Marcuse had not spent many years in clinical work and observation; nor did he have personal experience of the Soviet Union. But these deficiencies do not diminish the political import of his *Eros and Civilization.* However, in my observation, historical theories and political criticisms as offered by Reich or Marcuse had little to do with the "sexual revolution" of the sixties; rather, it grew from primarily personal (i.e., not revolutionary) motivations. By the time the campus exploded, not much was left of the parental role of university presidents.

The relaxation of traditional mores, especially in the Western world, was also promoted by one object that weighs only a fraction of an ounce and yet has proved to be not less explosive than a ton of TNT—the Pill, bought furtively at first with a doctor's prescription, but soon without inhibition. As unwanted pregnancy became easily avoidable, the sex manuals became ever more explicit—and cheaper. In the old days, one had to pay a lot of money to get a voluminous book about the love life of animals: now illustrated human manuals are to be had for one or two dollars at the corner drugstore.

Novels claiming to be literature contributed their share to the change in morals. In one of them, an international best-seller, the author hopes to solve her problems by what she calls the zipless fuck, meaning intercourse without any personal involvement, without so much as taking cognizance of the partner.[8] Sex to pass the time. Some go to group sex "as if it were a game of tennis."[9]

In Western society today it is being widely accepted that unmarried people of different sex live together; according to a press release of the U.S. Statistics Administration (February 9, 1977), their number in the United States is 1.32 million, as compared to 654,000 in 1970. Even the parents are adjusting. I know more than one father who was just about ready to kick his daughter out of the house because she had disappeared with her boyfriend for a week or two, but who, after some months, could be seen sitting peacefully next to the young man, in front of the TV set, with a glass of beer.

AND YET—NOT SO REVOLUTIONARY

It may well be that the intellectual attitude toward sex has changed in connection with the youth revolt, influenced by Women's Lib about which we have spoken, and also by some teachings of Reich and Marcuse. Yet it seems to me that the fundamental reason for the alterations in the sexual *behavior* of the new generation lies not in political *ideology* (nor in a sudden outburst of sexual energy), but rather in the desire of many young people of both sexes for emotional security, a desire which is especially strong in our age of rapid change and profound skepticism. This security, seemingly lacking in their families and communities, they hope to find in a firm and exclusive one-to-one relationship (which they often do, at least for a time), and in the inimitable, profoundly personal, primordial experience of closeness, which by its overwhelming power extinguishes all doubts for a brief eternity—in the embrace. The urge for emotional security seems, for many young people, to be even stronger than the purely physical desire. Perhaps the sexual act per se, so much more easily available now than a generation or two ago, has lost some of its magnetic attraction, while the importance attached to tenderness has gone up.

There are indications that this assumption may not be totally unfounded. There are reports about a growing inclination toward sexual abstinence. A 1975 report tells of people who desire intimacy without the complications of sexuality, and of others who are taking upon themselves voluntary celibacy while they are

242

relatively young, at the height of their sexual strength, and often with considerable sexual experience behind them. A therapist for sexual problems at the University of California speaks of people who have had so much sex in the last ten or fifteen years that the thrill has declined. Because everything that one might wish to do is permitted and even declared to be "good for one's health," some people, after doing whatever they wanted, have turned conservative, mere sex having lost its charm for them. Some of these people, having acted under the pressure for high sexual performance, began to think that they may have overdone it, and that this has not been good for them.[10] Perhaps the pressure to perform has also caused "shorts," as in an overloaded electrical circuit. Ann Landers, who receives hundreds of problem letters every day, has declared impotence to be complaint number one in the campus clinics of America.[11] Thus, to use a European expression, it seems that even in the country which claims to have the tallest trees (and these, of course, in California), the trees do not grow to heaven.

Anyone who looks at the newsstands in the big cities, scans the endless number of explicit sex magazines and books in the "adult" shops (850, it is assumed across America), or spends a few minutes before the rows of manuals on the shelves marked "sex" in many bookstores must assume that we are undergoing not just a sexual revolution but a sexual *explosion*. This is, however, not the case, as we learn from a detailed analysis by Morton Hunt, based on his own research and, especially, on data collected by the Research Guild, Inc., of Chicago.[12] The guild obtained its material in the first half of 1972 by asking about 2,000 Americans of both sexes more than 1,000 questions each. The special value of Hunt's book lies in his comparing these 1972 figures with those found a generation earlier in Alfred C. Kinsey's research on the sexual behavior of American men (1948) and women (1953).

By far the greatest change has occurred in the field of premarital relations. While Kinsey reported 18 percent of single white women under 20 years of age as having had sexual intercourse, Hunt found that 81 percent of women under 25, married at the time of the questioning, had experienced it before marriage. According to his research, "the change was beginning by 1965"—that is, simultaneously with the student rebellion. But—and this "but" seems very important—among the young women with premarital coital experience, more than half had it with one partner only, usually the man they intended to marry (or had married in the meantime). To be exact, Hunt's figure is 54 percent; the corresponding finding in Kinsey's study was 53 percent. (In absolute figures, premarital sex had, of course, risen very much.) Hunt found that the percentage of young women having had premarital coital relationships only with their future husbands was even greater in the group aged 18–25 years than in that aged 26–35. Among women below the age of 25 years, 64 percent thought that premarital sex relations with the man they later married were good for the quality and durability of the marriage; only 18 percent of those above the age of 55 thought so.

Promiscuousness among the young has not reached the proportions frequently supposed by the general public. Partner swapping, for example, had been tried in the under-25 age-group by 15 percent of the men, by 4 percent of the women and by most men and all women "only once"—that is, on an experimental basis and not as a habit. To my knowledge, research on a similarly great scale has not been undertaken in other countries. In Western Europe, which has been less puritanical than America, the recent changes in premarital relations are probably less spectacular.

There has been an impressive rise in the frequency of premarital intercourse. In the case of unmarried young women it has climbed about threefold, from once every three weeks to once weekly, and thereby—a statistical miracle—surpassed that of the corresponding male group, which increased from 23 per year in Kinsey's day (not counting sex with prostitutes, who at that time were still relatively frequent partners for young men) to 37 in the early seventies (when prostitution had practically vanished from their lives).

The tendency toward open discussion of sex problems has led, among other things, to greater attentiveness on the part of men toward women and, probably in connection with this, to an increase in the number of women experiencing orgasm. In Kinsey's generation about 50 percent of young sexually active single females had experienced orgasm; in our day it is around 75 percent. But sexual explicitness in print and film has, unfortunately, also increased the tendency toward deviant sexual behavior. Hunt reports that about 10 percent of the men and also of the women had "obtained sexual pleasure" by means of pain—the men more from inflicting pain, the women more from receiving it. Kinsey found almost no indication of such behavior.

This *quantitative* information, interesting as it may seem, is less important than information about the *quality* of young people's attitudes toward sex and love. Such qualitative information, is of course, far harder to come by. But Hunt has the courage to offer it. While noting that "permissive attitudes about sex were more common among the young," he found also a "strong tendency for the sexually permissive to become more conservative as their own children approach puberty."

Most important (and, I think, reassuring) are Hunt's general observations, which I quote not from his book but from his article published earlier, summarizing his conclusions from the data he obtained. He writes:

> Premarital sex in a loving relationship still has marriage as its implied goal—and the quality of sex within marriage still seems to be integrally connected to the strength and security of the emotional security. Most sexually emancipated unmarried young women still feel liberated only within the context of affectionate or loving relationships.

Here I excerpt at some length his remarkable conclusions about the sex life of the young people in our decade:

> They continue to attach deep emotional significance to their sexual acts rather than regarding them as sources of uncomplicated sexual gratification. [...] The inhibitions of the *demivierge* of the forties have been replaced by sexual freedom within the confines of emotional involvement, not by free-and-easy swinging. [...] Liberation has not cut sex loose from significant personal relationships or from the institution of marriage, [and] has not really sundered sex from emotion. [...] Sexual liberation has not replaced the liberal-romantic concepts of sex with the recreational one. [...] For the great majority sex remains intimately allied to their deepest emotions and inextricably interwoven with their conceptions of loyalty, love and marriage. [...] Sexual liberalism is the emergent ideal that the great majority of young Americans are trying to live up to. [...] It combines the spontaneous and guilt-free enjoyment of a wide range of sexual acts with a guiding belief in the emotional significance of sexual expression, [...] the concomitant or the precursor of monogamous heterosexual love, whether within or without marriage. [...] There has been no chaotic and anarchic dissolution of standards but, rather, a major shift toward somewhat different, highly organized standards that remain integrated with existing social values and with the institutions of love, marriage and the family.

245

The changes in sexual attitudes, Hunt ends, have not destroyed "emotional values that we rightly prize" and have not demolished "institutions necessary to the stability of society itself."[13]

This statement is the more weighty for having been published in *Playboy*.

DRUGS

This is one subject about which I have no personal experience to offer; as a son of the old German Youth Movement, I don't even know how to inhale the smoke of an ordinary cigarette, let alone a joint.

Use of drugs, an age-old experience of mankind, reached a new level when the English writer Aldous Huxley published *The Doors of Perception* in 1954, describing in poetic language the delights he felt in using an ancient American Indian drug, mescaline. To present-day Americans this drug was easily available in their neighbor's garden, in Mexico. Soon science—more specifically psychology, always eager to experiment—began its research. In 1960 two Harvard professors, Timothy Leary and Richard Alpert, began large-scale tests using prison-inmate and student volunteers, tests which immediately were given wide publicity. These experiments with various drugs met with criticism, causing the university to dismiss Leary and Alpert in 1963, whereupon they went to Mexico and, with the help of private donations, founded the "International Federation for Internal Freedom." This institution evoked wide interest, not least because it defined its activity as an attempt at "transcendental community life." Expelled from Mexico, Leary moved his organization to New York State, calling it the "Castalia Foundation" after the holy spring of Delphi. Eventually Leary was put on trial and jailed for transporting marijuana in his luggage.

With unexpected rapidity the use of drugs spread through the campuses. I remember well how I felt in the winter of 1968/69 when I first heard about and then witnessed drug parties in Berkeley; I was dismayed and only slightly reassured by the thought that this was just a fad that would pass and surely would not affect young people in my own country. By the time I got back, in late summer, I heard of drug use not only in German universities but even in high schools. New habits which traveled slowly in the past now race from one continent to another.

Just as in the case of sex, so the use of drugs acquired an aggressive, political character. In smoking pot one defied society, parents, police, school authorities—the whole damned Establishment. One proved that one was different from the old generation, that one was bold and hip and could do things the old fogies never dreamed about. In Washington, an official in the government medical service considered drug use to be the "clinical version of the Vietnam protest." A German author, reversing Marx's famous dictum about religion, wrote "Opium is religion for the [young] people."[14] To get high on alcohol was not interesting because it did not sufficiently shock the old people, many of whom, to the disgust of their children, were drinking far more than they could hold.

Drugs were not only a sure method of protest, they were also expected to fulfill many functions: "combatting fear; exploring one's self; achieving religious experience; satisfying cravings; relieving boredom; combatting depression, sexual impulses, tension, anger, dullness, panic, and psychosis; elaborating moods; facilitating friendliness, learning, and sex; preparing for stress; changing or reducing appetite; shutting out the world."[15] Leary and his followers elevated drug consumption into a cult, frequently with outlandish rituals—poetry, chants, strange musical instruments, weird apparel, incense. Some claimed that collective drug use was an essential element of communal life; at a commune in Oregon, it was said, when a novice swallowed his first LSD the others were jubilant: "He has taken it! He has taken it."[16]

As more and more social scientists sought the causes of drug use, it was found that the typical college users came from families of the middle or upper middle class, that they were likely to be students of social sciences or liberal arts in a college not far from a city, that they were politically to the left of their parents (with whom they had differences of opinion), that their families had moved repeatedly, and that the users were indifferent to traditional churches, uninterested in sports, and critical of their schools and of society in general. They considered themselves to be revolutionary innovators and were pessimistic with regard to their personal future.

Richard A. Blum of Stanford University, one of the leading researchers in the field, attaches great importance to family backgrounds. He finds "high-risk youngsters" to a large extent "in the troubled and pathological families" where "pain and chaos may take a variety of forms, all of which visibly reflect disharmony, discontent and a search for elusive meanings and gratifications."[17]

There are indications that drug use peaked in the first half of the seventies, but the figures are still frightening. In 1973 close to 400,000 young people (under 25 years of age) were arrested in America for offenses against narcotic drug laws, and in 1975 almost 200 deaths of young people in the Federal Republic of Germany were caused by drugs. At the height of the drug epidemic, a representative poll of some 5,000 high-school students of both sexes, carried out in Hamburg by order of the city government, produced these results: 13.3 percent used drugs regularly (all kinds of drugs, not counting tobacco and alcohol); another 9.6 percent had "tried" them; and 13.5 percent were trafficking in drugs. About three-quarters of those who were acquainted with drugs had undergone their experience at the age of sixteen years or younger and had taken hashish as their "first drug."[18]

Two years later, Bavaria's Ministry of the Interior polled 2,700 young people and 650 of the parents. On the basis of that sample it was projected that, in a total population of 12 million, 80,000 young people between the ages of 12 and 24 (mainly between 18 and 20) had been using drugs around the time of the poll, although not necessarily on a regular basis. As has been the case in various other countries, the poll showed that drug use increases with the duration of education. Among the motives, curiosity was mentioned most often ("I did it because I heard so much about it").[19] The Communist press, of course, knew better: an East German review declared drugs to be a "whip" with which West German capitalists were trying to make young people into obedient slaves.[20]

But the imputed ardor of the capitalists seems to have slackened, while the efficiency of the police has increased. It is true, to cure addicts has proved exceedingly difficult, the relatively highest quota of success being achieved by ecstatic religious groups. But some people, after experimenting during the sixties with various hard drugs, settled for a moderate use of marijuana, while others shifted to alcohol to which no social stigma is attached.

Some of the drug prophets have changed their minds: Timothy Leary has recanted. Richard Alpert has turned into a Hindu guru. Klaus Rainer Röhl, whose konkret had published articles in defense of drugs, confessed himself guilty of having underplayed the dangers of drugs "to a truly criminal extent." During 1970 and 1971, he published two articles on the subject. In one, he said:

"Hash doesn't solve any political problems. Hash doesn't solve even private problems. Hash makes you stupid." The other he entitled "Comrades, We've been Shitty [about drugs]!" He had, like many others. The epidemic had gotten into the bloodstream of the young generation, affecting their health. Politically, however, with the return of order to the campus, it had lost its significance.

22
ESPERANTO OF THE ROCK GENERATION

THE youth of the sixties possessed an international language of its own, which is still in use. From California to West (and East) Berlin, from Poland (skipping over China) to Japan, there are countless millions of young people, not only students, who live with the rhythms and lyrics of the Beatles and many other groups, who exchange records and make tape recordings of songs, who know everything about the private lives of their heroes, who dance to the music and, preferably sitting on the floor, listen to it. Even in Tashkent and Irkutsk, Soviet young people are staying up at night in order to tape rock music from Western radio stations. For all of them, this music is an exciting experience that spellbinds them and makes them high, a magic language the knowledge of which is in their blood—while the older generation pleads with them: "Please turn it down!" (A good reason to turn it still louder.)

When I arrived in New York in 1975 for a half-year's stay in the States, I asked all my friends to find me a teacher for this Esperanto. The way things go—in the end I had three. But I owe most to Marc. He is a composer himself, living entirely in the rock and beat scene, in an old farmhouse by the Delaware River. He took his job very seriously, lecturing to me hour after hour, using as illustration many records, his own or borrowed ones. He started with the First World War, when Storeyville was closed down for sanitary and moral reasons, and Negro music began its triumphal march, first to the North, then to the whole world; and he came all the way up to the present time. For homework he gave me piles of books.

My second teacher was a young professor of music. He lived a few minutes from the Columbia campus in an almost empty apartment, where the floor was covered with mountains of records and books. He took me to the rock clubs.

The third, a young political scientist, became my teacher by mere chance. Once as we drove on the freeway he said, "How about a little music?" and pointed to the tape deck. When I nodded, he pushed a button; we listened to a song. The performer sang very rapidly, and I couldn't understand the lyrics, yet the young American seemed quite satisfied. "Wonderful," he finally said. "I play this song often when I'm driving. It expresses exactly my own feelings."

What we heard was, he explained, a song by Bob Dylan, from 1965, with a curious title: "It's Alright Ma (I'm Only Bleeding")). It was played again, and I listened more carefully and became electrified. The music and the way it was sung now fit together. The following day I obtained the words.

There are moments in history when groups of people are so much in unison that they understand every word spoken by one of them, be it ever so vague. My young friend with the tape deck had never seen the lyrics of this particular song and could not identify every word in it. But he had understood the meaning when he heard the song for the first time. He had felt that it corresponded exactly to his own emotions. When I showed him the text a few days later, he had to admit that even he could not comprehend every one of the obscurities. It almost seemed to me that the song had affected him more strongly before he had seen the printed words in black and white.

There were many other singers in those years, but Bob Dylan, more than the others, was the interpreter of an entire generation. Here is just the first of the song's five parts; it shows Dylan's style, as well as the problem of decoding his meaning:

It's Alright Ma (I'm Only Bleeding)

Darkness at the break of noon
Shadows even the silver spoon
The hand made blade
The child's balloon
Eclipses both the sun and moon
To understand you know too soon
There is no sense in trying.

Pointed threats they bluff with scorn
Suicide remarks are torn

From the fool's gold mouth-piece
The hollow horn plays wasted words
Proved to warn
That he not busy being born
Is busy dying.

Temptation page flies out the door
You follow find yourself at war
Watch waterfalls of pity roar
You feel to moan, but unlike before
You discover that you just be one more person crying
So don't fear if you hear
A foreign sound to your ear
It's alright Ma, I'm only sighing.

The two lines I italicized were quoted by Jimmy Carter in his acceptance speech at the Democratic Convention in July 1976.

It was only when translating these lines into German that I fully realized the difficulty. There, even my American friends could not help me, and Bob Dylan's New York office was unable to furnish an authentic explanation of the meanings of the *silver spoon* (wealth?), the *hand made blade* (own doom?), the *fool's gold mouth-piece* (phony voice?), the *temptation page*. Dylan does not write his lyrics as an intellectual; he is known to have joked about people who have racked their brain in an attempt to interpret him word by word.

A few years later, when the poet-singer no longer stood quite so much in the center of interest, a well-known American musical authority wrote:

> The most serious assault on the structure of the Great Society and its predecessor, the New Frontier, comes not from the armed might of a foreign power, but from a frail, slender elusive lad, whose weapons are words and music, a burning imagination and an apocalyptic vision of the world.[1]

And in 1976 a writer in *TV Guide* called him "the single biggest cultural influence on millions in his own generation."[2]

Robert Zimmerman was born in Duluth, Minnesota, on May 24, 1941, the son of a Jewish couple, Abraham and Beatty Zimmerman.[3] The father had an electrical appliance shop. More than once the boy ran away from home. After finishing high school he moved to Minneapolis, but he didn't spend much time at the university. He now called himself Bob Dylan, and he performed his folk songs in bars for a few dollars an evening. In 1961, Dylan came to New York. He lived and sang in Greenwich Village. Suze Rotalo, his first great love, whom he met when she was 17, acquainted him with the poems of Rimbaud and Yevtushenko, as well as the works of Bertolt Brecht; she also interested him in social issues, especially the civil rights movement, in which she was active. Thus began the first phase in the creative life of Dylan, the period of protest songs—protest against social and racial injustice.

There is no way of measuring which was the strongest in its effect on youth—Dylan's words, his music, or his voice and personality. In the following pages I must deal with the words exclusively. Together with the music, which cannot be reproduced here, they accompanied the youth movement of the sixties, always a few beats ahead.

In April 1962, Dylan wrote his first great protest song, "Blowin' in the Wind." Within a few weeks 300,000 records were sold. The movement now had a new battle hymn, in addition to "We Shall Overcome."

Another Dylan song, "Masters of War" soon became the song of the war resisters. It begins by addressing the masters of war who make the guns and ends with his hope that they will die soon, so that he can follow their caskets and see them lowered into their graves to make sure they are dead.

"A Hard Rain's A-Gonna Fall" was written during the Cuban missile crisis, when for most of Dylan's age-group the world—with Kennedy at the helm—was still in fine shape. Not so for Dylan. In this song a young boy is being asked to tell what he has seen. His answer consists of many disjointed fragments of horrible impressions, truly a surrealistic apocalypse.

There were also songs with different themes, love songs among them. The finest one, "Girl from the North Country," he wrote for Suze, who left him at that time temporarily (and soon after for good), but the emphasis clearly lay with the protest songs. Among them was the bitter-ironic "With God on our Side," which enumerates America's wars since those against the Indians. The First World War, he says, came and went, without him ever understanding why. But, he learned to accept it, even with pride, because one should not count the dead when God is on one's side.

Among the most popular songs of the sixties was Dylan's "The Times They Are A-Changin'," which he wrote in the autumn of 1963. Here he prophesies the rising of the waters and speaks about the danger of the changing times. But the language is milder. Dylan also appeals to the parents to get along with the younger generation.

In the "Ballad of the Thin Man" he jeers at Mr. Jones of Middle America. Jones does whatever is expected of him; he reads many books, has many contacts, keeps a close watch on his pocket and on everybody else, and yet he feels lost because he does not understand what is going on.

But there were also melodies to be heard that announced Dylan's second phase. For example, in "Lay Down Your Weary Tune," a new sunrise is about to come, it is time to prepare for a new tune, a tune that is not being created consciously for the purpose of protest, but one that will flow by itself from the singer. This one, incidentally, was not a new tune at all, but the old white gospel tune "I Came to Jesus," which Dylan used.

Toward the end of the first phase there occurred the romance between Dylan and Joan Baez. In 1960 she had become almost overnight the most popular female folksinger, years before Dylan's rise to fame. Her first album (Joan Baez, October 1960) was, for years to come, the most sold record by a female folksinger. The two met for the first time, at Gerde's Folk City in New York. During the Monterey Festival in May 1965 they became, for young America, queen and king of folk music. Often they were together, even on concert tours, to England and elsewhere. But the rumored marriage never came to pass. Joan Baez remained true to the protest song and to the youth movement, while Dylan moved on.

For Dylan, as for many of his generation, the first phase of creative life ended at about the time of the assassination of John F. Kennedy on November 22, 1963. This event, watched by the whole of America on TV for days on end, left a profound impression on the young people. It confirmed Dylan in his convictions: The political world is hopelessly wicked. There is no point in involving yourself, in trying to change it through protest.

The discussion about Dylan's withdrawal from the protest movement has never come to a stop. Bitter voices have accused him of treason, and some of his remarks contributed to this opinion. To Joan Baez he once explained that his earlier participation in the movement was for purely commercial reasons. The next three quotations I take from Scaduto's biography of Dylan, which is considered the best but was not specifically endorsed by Dylan (and some of the strong words used are not characteristic of him, I am told). He reportedly said: "News can sell, right? You know me. I knew people would buy that kind of shit. Right? I never was into that stuff."

But there may have been other reasons behind this amazing statement. Dylan is a difficult character, full of contradictions, very sensitive to the mood of the time. "The Times They Are A-Changin'"—these words hold good for him, too. He sensed that something new was in the air. He put it into words, and these words in turn sped its coming. What he indicated in a coded way in his songs was said frankly to his friends. To one of them: "Politics is bullshit. It's all unreal. The only thing that's real is inside you. Your feelings. Just look at the world you're writing about and you'll see you're wasting your time. The world is, well, . . . absurd." And to another one: "I stopped thinking in terms of society. [. . .] I'm not gonna make a dent or anything, so why be a part of it, by even trying to criticize it? That's a waste of time. [. . .] There is no yesterday, tomorrow never seems to come, so what's left is today, or nothing."

Dylan did not want his creative career disturbed by political involvement. In identifying with him, many young people found a purpose in life, and at times it was hard for him to escape their enthusiasm. Once a girl almost injured his eye when she jumped on him with a pair of scissors, intending to cut a lock of his hair. When Joan Baez appeared on the Berkeley campus at the height of the FSM, he was apprehensive. The frenzy of these young people scared him. "I'm not responsible for these kids," he said to her. Perhaps it would have been more correct for him to say: "I *don't want to be* responsible for them." Responsible he was. I am inclined to think he knew that his friends, like Joan Baez, felt sad and betrayed when he withdrew from the movement, no longer responding to requests for songs like "Masters of War" and "With God on Our Side."

Thus, the protest singer became the singer of self-encountering, of alienation, and as Marcuse called it, of the Great Refusal. The most important song of this stage was "Mr. Tambourine Man," about a man who appears to be some kind of Pied Piper, a black-marketeer in drugs, perhaps the drug itself. The "trip" in the first verse and the "smoke rings" in the last one point in this direction. In "Subterranean Homesick Blues" Dylan renounced political prophets and made fun of the constantly harping adults.

At about the same time Dylan wrote "Maggie's Farm." In it he sings repeatedly that he is not going to work anymore on Mag-

255

gie's farm, which, of course, was taken by the young as referring to government or society, factory or office. By this time, Dylan's influence reached far beyond the frontiers of America. Naturally, he was best understood in English-speaking countries. A report from Australia concluded that he had "become as important to young people [there] as he had in the United States."[4]

Most Dylan songs of those years had many meanings, sometimes hardly comprehensible, and yet countless young people thought they knew exactly what was meant. "Like a Rolling Stone" taught the vanity of material possessions: Those who possess nothing cannot lose anything. "It's All Over Now, Baby Blue" could mean a farewell to a girl or to a period of one's life. "Gates of Eden" shows the world to be an evil place. Only in Eden, in Paradise (or is it the community of the new generation, or the embrace of a woman?), is everything good. Anything outside of Eden was no longer important for many young people who withdrew from the world into the Eden of their Scene. Joan Baez defined, quite correctly, the difference between herself and Dylan. Although both were convinced that the world was in a mess, she said to him, "I think there's something we can do about it, but you don't."

In 1965, Dylan married Sara Lowndes. The young couple lived in the countryside in New York State, later in the city, and had four children of their own. His third phase was pastoral. In "Sign on the Window" he praised the good life with wife, children, and trout fishing.

Again he had swum ahead of the stream of his time. His songs now spoke of the joy of living, of love, of the Bible. His album *John Wesley Harding* contained some biblical themes. Israel, which he had visited on his thirtieth birthday (1971), caused ambivalent feelings. But the Old Testament became increasingly meaningful for him. Sometimes, prompted by his friends of the protest years, he wrote songs about those in prison, about the death of George Jackson in San Quentin, or about a boxer named Rubin "Hurricane" Carter who claimed to have been unjustly imprisoned—a long ballad clearly directed against the injustice of the legal process (1975). But for him a new morning had dawned (*New Morning* was the name of one of his albums). In "Three Angels" he marveled about the stupidity of men who in their busy activities were unable to hear the three angels' music, and in "Father of Night" he sang of God. Dylan had become a mystic, a man not concerned with mere knowledge that was not connected to the questions of life. In "Tombstone Blues" he consoled a "dear lady" by promising to write a melody for her so simple that it would keep her from going insane and would relieve her from the pain caused by knowing useless things. Even in an earlier song ("My Back Pages") he had expressed some skepticism about his own early wisdom, addressing himself to all those who in youthful precociousness thought they knew exactly what was good and what was bad.

Protest, Great Refusal, pastoral—the three phases in Bob Dylan's creative life. During the first two he was the acknowledged singer of restless youth. And in the third? The contours became unclear, the Great Refusal merges with the search for one's self, for nature and God.

While I was reading Dylan's lyrics and books about him in the subway to Columbia University, I was more than once accosted by young people sitting next to me: "Are you a Dylan fan?" Those who asked were Dylan fans themselves. They owned his albums; some had seen him on stage. For them he was just Dylan, not a singer who went through various phases; he was, they said, "far out." A young construction worker, who intended later to go to the university, especially praised a new album. "There are things in it that really matter—love and nature. Far out. Honest!" With this he repeated almost exactly what Dylan had once said:

> My thing has to do with feelings, not politics, organized religion, or social activity. My thing is a *feeling* thing. [. . .] Those other things will blow away. They'll not stand the test of time."[5]

Dylan was probably right.

THE BEATLES

American rock 'n' roll had stimulated the emergence of numerous groups in England, especially in the middle and lower social strata. One group called itself—after changing the name several times—the Beatles. Their first success came in 1960 in Hamburg. By 1961 they were number one in their home town, Liverpool, soon afterward in the whole of England. Their fame reached America's shores. Their records moved to first place on the "Top 40" lists, and their triumphal march throughout the world was beginning. In February 1964 they came for the first time to America.

With them came a new, bright, and refreshing timbre. They were four young men who had funny haircuts and faces that showed aliveness, who had developed a style that was inimitably their own, no shouted ecstasies, but rather melodically performed everyday thoughts. ("Girl," for example, does not go overboard in the exuberance of first love, or in the desperate agony of parting, but rather treats the long life between the beginning and the end of love.) Neither did they wade in obscenities, and this was appreciated by adults.

The young people listened. They bought records by the millions, sat down on the floor and played them. Whatever the grown-ups might have thought, the Beatles were appropriated by the young people, they were entirely part of the Scene, and thus they contributed (although not politically, in the proper sense of the word) to the emerging of a young world of its own. This was particularly true of perhaps the best-known Beatles album, *Sergeant Pepper's Lonely Hearts Club Band*. When I asked an American friend how many hundreds of times he had heard that album, he exclaimed: "Hundreds, Maybe ten thousand times." More than earlier records, *Sergeant Pepper* treated two problems of the time, the runaways and the drug users.

"She's Leaving Home" tells about a frequent event in the days of the flower children, and about the parents' reactions. The parents are not drawn as caricatures in their helpless mumbling, and the runaway girl is not promised that her fun with "the man from the motor trade" will last very long; the song simply tells a sad story of alienation between parents and child. More questionable were the many hints at the joys of drug use: "A Little Help from My Friends" indicates—but never explicitly—that the little help consists of drugs. In "Lucy in the Sky with Diamonds," the three capitals of the title form "LSD" (which the Beatles later denied intending). But in the same album, as if to console the old people, there was a lovable, if somewhat melancholy, song of a lonely man who tries to imagine how it will be when, one day, he is sixty-four years old and without work.

The weirdest effect the Beatles had was on Charles Manson, who interpreted many of their lyrics as supporting his mania. He linked the Beatles particularly with the Book of Revelation, believing them to be deadly locusts (i.e., beetles) who had "the faces of men" and "the hair of women." They also represented the four angels who came to destroy one-third of mankind with horses who issued "fire, smoke, and brimstone" (the Beatles' songs). All this was to happen, with Manson as the fifth angel, the ruler of the bottomless pit. The Beatles' *White Album,* which included the song "Helter Skelter," especially affected Manson; this is told in detail by Vincent Bugliosi, deputy district attorney in Los Angeles at the time of the murder trial. He even assumes that the many knife and fork wounds in the bodies of the victims in the Sharon Tate home were inspired by the Beatles' song "Piggies," also from the *White Album*.[6]

The Beatles themselves, at any rate, did not want to change the world through violence. Their song "Revolution," despite the dramatic title, recommends rather the opposite; it is a dialogue between some revolutionaries and a few others, perhaps the Beatles, who are hesitating to join them because they do not want to change the world by destruction. Anyhow, everything will somehow be all right.

The Beatles were humorous, which could not have been said about many of the radical youths of Europe. Their words of wisdom sounded quite different from those of the great chairman in Peking. John Lennon was especially good at that: "I want to have money, in order to be rich." This pearl he produced when the Beatles performed before the queen: "The gentlemen in the cheaper seats kindly applaud. The others simply jingle your jewels."[7]

JANIS JOPLIN

Janis Joplin wrote neither lyrics nor music herself; she had a raw whiskey voice, was anything but beautiful, her sloppy clothing grotesquely in vogue. But she sang with the impact of a tornado. She tore people's souls from their bodies by her vitality, her temperament, her twisting torso, her rhythm-pounding feet. I have only seen her indirectly, in an hour-and-a-half film which showed the high points of her career. When I left the theater I was exhausted—from merely watching.

One day she was dead, after shooting heroin—an "overdose," said the medical report. We will never know what she desired that evening alone in her room, to dream or to die. Everyone agreed that she was burned out. Yet her death still stirs people, even today. One young man told me, "When I heard about it, it was a shock to me like the death of Kennedy."

Her most popular song, "Me and Bobby McGee," written by Kris Kristofferson, expressed defiance and, still more, resignation, which was spreading at that time throughout the youth scene. They had all been pushing the limits of their strength. People such as Janis Joplin, who had reached the pinnacle of stardom at the age of twenty-four, could only choose between self-murderous efforts to stay on top—and decline. This grim dilemma was temporarily drowned out for Janis by wild, in the end unfulfilling, orgies; by heavy consumption of alcohol and drugs; and by excessive and indiscriminate sex, with men and women. The last two songs on which she worked compress into a few words her whole life: "I Just Made Love to 25,000 People, But I'm Going Home Alone" and "Buried Alive." The latter title is also the title of the best Joplin biography I have read, a book which catches the mood of the late sixties in America.[8]

Almost simultaneously, Jimi Hendrix, the "king of the electric guitar," died in a similar way, and he too was burned out; he died on September 18, 1970, after only three years as a star, she on October 4.

A year later, the rock culture had reached its culmination and then died within a few months. Woodstock in the summer of 1969 was still a festival of love. About 400,000 young people from all over the United States had assembled on the pastures of an upstate New York farm, defying rain and mud to listen to their favorite groups for three days. They had celebrated a pagan pentecost with drugs for sacrament, the openings of an unheard-of new age of total anarchistic freedom, as the "Woodstock Nation" and as pioneers of the future America—yes, even of a new world. But four months later, in December, a rock festival at Altamont ended in violence and manslaughter. In order to prevent incidents the organizers had entrusted the Hell's Angels, of all people, with preserving law and order. "A nightmare, carnal, gross, uncontrolled, devastating" summed up what I heard of it.

Altamont—the demise of Joplin and Hendrix—the fading of the Beatles and also, for some time, of Bob Dylan—the replacement of the student rebels by the bomb-throwing terrorists in America, in Germany, in Japan: all this was not coincidental. It was the end of an epoch.

JOAN BAEZ

Not for Joan Baez. Her voice, clear as a bell, can still be heard wherever violence is being protested. Even at wild moments during the sixties, her words were respected, although she always condemned violent revolution. During the night of the big sit-in in Berkeley in 1964, the students called her. She came all the way from Carmel and sang. Just before the police started their final assault, she appealed once more to the students not to use violence: "Muster all the love of which you are capable!" There was a lot of forceful resistance, but eventually most of the 800 students who were arrested let themselves be carried like sacks to the police vans.

In the summer of 1975, I spent an afternoon and evening with Joan Baez and her five-year-old son, Gabriel. Around her house, situated in the mountains which shelter the Bay Area against the wind and fog of the Pacific, there is nothing but forest. It is an old, comfortable, lived-in house. Only rarely did she let Gabriel out of her sight. She had detested violence from childhood; it repelled her even more so now when she thought of her boy. Would he see the end of mankind? "Sometimes I have only to look at Gabriel and my tears flow," she said. Her Resource Center for Nonviolence (in Santa Cruz, California) collects information on nonviolence from all over the world. She has experienced violence herself. On Christmas, in 1972, she was in Hanoi among ruins and corpses during one of the heaviest bombardments in history.

Joan's dedication to the ideal of nonviolence is unconditional. To defend a piece of land (i.e., a country), she says, is wrong because thus the chain of violence will become longer still. The population? Yes, one must defend it, but by nonviolent resistance. Patriotism? In an interview she was once asked whether there was anything in America which to her was worth preserving. Undaunted, she answered, "All I can think of is peanut butter and the Grand Canyon."[9] Reminded of this, she told me: "More seriously, I am deeply concerned about preserving one thing, in America and elsewhere, and that is the human race." The sanctity of life is above everything. "Defending ideologies and borders," she said to me, "has not done much for humanity." In the published interview just mentioned, she was asked whether she would have followed her principle with regard to Nazi murderers. Her answer: "Killing is killing, whether it's killing a Nazi or anyone else. And, killing leads to more killing. . . . When you do violence to another, you're also doing violence to yourself, you're diminishing your own humanity." But she is frank in saying that she does not know for certain how she would act if her son were to be attacked in her presence.

The fear that mankind might destroy itself is always with her. On the cover of her album *Farewell Angelina* (1965) she passionately appeals to her audience:

> Here we are, waiting on the eve of destruction with all the odds against any of us living to see the sun rise one day soon. [. . .] Only

you and I can help the sun rise each coming morning. If we don't it
may drench itself out in sorrow. You—special, miraculous, unre-
peatable, fragile, fearful, tender, lost, sparkling ruby emerald
jewel, rainbow splendor person. It's up to you.

I did not ask her about Dylan. Whatever there might have been,
she is sad that he was lost to the movement, but delighted that he
has chosen to come back onstage. When I left, she gave me some of
her albums. *Diamonds and Rust* is very personal and admittedly
about Dylan. *Come from the Shadows* includes the song "To
Bobby":

> You left us marching on the road,
> And said how heavy was the load—
> The years were young,
> the struggle barely at its start.
> Do you hear the voices in the night,
> Bobby
> They're crying for you. [...]
> Time is short and there is work to do.
> And we're still marching on the streets
> With little victories and big defeats,
> But, there is joy and there is hope,
> and there's a place for you.

In 1975 and 1976 the two were on the road together again, for the
first time in years. In an interview Dylan said about her: "Joan
Baez means more to me than 100 of these singers around today.
She's more powerful. That's what we are looking for. That's what
we respond to. She always had it and always will—power for the
species, not just for a select group."[10]

MUSIC AND POLITICS
At the height of youth unrest, in 1967–1968, John F. Scott, an
American educator, studied for a year the music of the youth
programs of a radio station in Massachusetts in order to determine which songs were most popular and to analyze the content of
their lyrics. He found ten main topics, the handling of which
differed considerably from that of the fifties:

(1) Much more direct treatment of sexual matters. Problems
appeared which formerly were not found in hits, such as the il-
legitimate child.

(2) The great new discovery: drugs.

(3) Rejection of the hypocritical Establishment. In one song,

ESPERANTO OF THE ROCK GENERATION

"Mr. Businessman" was described as going on Tuesday to the prostitute, on Wednesday to the shrink, the rest of the week cheating the customers.

(4) Adultery in the older generation as a particularly loathsome form of hypocrisy, although the young people demanded complete freedom for themselves.

(5) The crass description of what is negative in society. In Simon and Garfunkel's "7 O'Clock News/Silent Night," the beloved Christmas song was gradually drowned out by the voice of the news commentator speaking of nothing but aggression, hatred, violence.

(6) Inability to communicate with the adults, expressed in songs such as "Sounds of Silence," where people are talking past each other.

(7) Loneliness and sadness—perpetual topics of youth and the theme of the Beatles' "Eleanor Rigby" and "Sergeant Pepper's Lonely Hearts Club Band."

(8) Love relations across racial lines.

(9) Opposition to war and violence.

(10) Desire for freedom after the end of school. This was linked with subconscious uncertainty about what to do with this freedom and a feeling of apprehension before a world for which young people soon would·be responsible.

Scott found a new morality in these songs:

In contrast to the politeness and social restraints of their elders, the rock generation advocates a direct confrontation with life, whether it be birth or death, deprivation or leisure, survival or destruction. They have put down Organization Man and his materialistic quest and concerned themselves with the issues of life, poverty, sexuality, or any aspect of societal living. Musically, they have faced the incongruities of the society of the 1960's. The Tuned-in Generation's parents, when they were young, handled their rebellion discreetly and in fear, if not of God, then of their parents. This generation bluntly sounds its rebellion in song, and its music, so intertwined with the rapid value changes influencing it, becomes a badge of identity.[11]

Others called the music of the sixties the "common language of the generation"[12] and the "universal language without national frontiers."[13] Music was, and is, the medium through which youth can act out, even unleash, its unrest. But—had this music also a political significance?

Some observers claim that rock—in spite of occasionally demolished concert halls—is fundamentally a support for law and order, because it channels the dynamics of youth into an apolitical area. Nirumand, the Persian whom we met during the Berlin events, in his revolutionary zeal denounced the guitar as an antirevolutionary instrument.[14] Others are inclined to believe that, on the contrary, rock releases aggressions against society. The truth depends on time and place, and, of course, on the singer.

That the protest songs of the sixties contributed to the youth revolt can be assumed because of the content of their lyrics. Since then, as the campus has calmed down, rock has become primarily a vehicle for entertainment. In 1972 and 1973, 2,500 young Germans, most of them between the ages of fourteen and twenty-four, were questioned about their attitude toward rock. Among the reasons given for attending rock concerts, politics was never mentioned. The two most frequent answers: "Because in a live concert I can judge better the quality of the group" and "Because to judge a group the total impression of show, appearance, and musical performance is important." Rock has turned into a hobby that is taken seriously by many of its young fans.[15]

One thing seems certain: Rock is an important element and almost the heart of the Scene. Inasmuch as the Scene turns its back on the world of adults, it is, including the music, a sign of protest and thus of political importance.

The black poet-singer Chuck Berry, who in the fifties helped bring the new music to white middle-class youth, expressed this protest in his song "Roll Over, Beethoven." In the sixties rock was a form of life which belonged primarily to the young generation and was listened to by the adults with discomfort, if not outrage. "Roll over, Beethoven!" Only a cultural revolution?

264

23
THE ROAD TO VIOLENCE

AS the drive of the first rebellious years waned and the hopes for a radical change of society evaporated, the rebels could choose among five roads: returning to normalcy, to regular college work that would lead to professional careers; working for political and social change within the system—as teachers, politicians, urban planners, counselors, and so forth; dropping out, as hippies or drug users; dedicating themselves to nonpolitical and nonmaterial aims, such as religion or occultism; or finally, violence. The last road proved to be the most spectacular; fortunately, only very few chose it.

In countries which publish crime statistics, the curves are steadily climbing (probably also in those which keep the figures secret). And within criminal categories, those of violence are rising particularly fast, and among them, those committed by young people. Many reasons have been given for this development (including violence as vengeance against a negligent mother or as a substitute for the sex act).[1] I am inclined to see the primary reason for the climbing crime rate in the disappearance of moral inhibitions, in the breakdown of ethical attitudes ("God is dead, anything goes"), and in the anonymity of life in the "jungles" of our cities and apartment fortresses.

Keys to the political violence which so many young people accept as a matter of course can be found in the writings of Frantz Fanon and in the history of the Russian terrorists of the nineteenth century. Fanon told the "wretched of the earth," the peoples of the Third World, that they should use violence against

265

their oppressors not only for the sake of liberation, but also because by doing so they could transform themselves into new, proud, and truly independent human beings. Fanon's thesis (which he meant primarily for the Algerians in their war of liberation against the French) found an echo outside Africa, among the blacks of America and among the young people on the campus.

In Dostoevski's *The Possessed,* the antihero Verkhovensky attempts to fasten his little band to himself and his cause forever by committing a crime with them, the murder of one of their group. Unquestionably, joint participation in acts of violence can weld people together; Hegel, Engels, and Lenin have commented on that fact.[2] Let psychologists and psychiatrists check the truth of Fanon's thesis that violence helps in the liberation and discovery of the self. For us, it is sufficient to know that this thesis is being accepted by many, and sometimes even mentioned as their justification for violent action. Some specialists on juvenile delinquency also agree. They report that youngsters who have committed crimes in the slums of great cities rationalize them by saying: "We did it to prove ourselves," to do the proving, that is, in front of themselves and their friends. Even though they may, during a trial, defend their actions primarily by attacking society, their actual motivation is frequently found in the desire to show off their toughness, courage, and strength.

The need to prove one's courage by an act of violence in order to be accepted into the community is common in many societies. In some American Indian tribes the young brave had to bring home a scalp to qualify for full membership; German students were eager to acquire dueling scars to prove their manliness. In a Philippine Stone Age tribe which a German missionary and I visited (with the help of a small plane), young men had no hope of finding brides unless they first killed an enemy. The missionary tried to dissuade them from this violent custom, though an understandable one in the context of a primitive hunter civilization. Many acts of violence committed in our modern civilization are far more repugnant. While in New York I read of a crime committed against a woman: The youthful murderers had been so eager to show off their toughness that they took photographs of each other assaulting the victim (which, incidentally, later led to their identification and arrest).

Curiously enough, proving oneself can also be accomplished by diametrically opposite means. Mahatma Gandhi and Martin

Luther King, Jr., made history with the weapon of nonviolence: Gandhi thereby contributed decisively to the end of British rule in India, King to the acceptance of American blacks into white society. Both have helped their followers no less (and perhaps more) to find their identity than has Fanon, who urged his followers to commit acts of violence. In India the people who followed Gandhi through his nonviolent campaigns and into British prisons are still considered the nation's heroes and for a long time have been its political leaders; and in America, I have met young people who, at the opening of the sixties, went to the South as apostles of nonviolence and whose lives have been determined by their experiences during the Freedom Rides and other actions they undertook at the risk of life and limb.

It is, I believe, possible to find one's identity and to meet the challenges of the day, without having gone through experiments in violence. The notion that one must commit violence in order to master one's own problems and complexes is hardly compatible with human dignity. Nor ought we to accept such arguments from those who, by such reasoning, try to explain away their big or small crimes.

I need not discuss the dispute as to whether man's aggression is produced by heredity or by environment; it has not been settled one way or the other. But one point should be kept clearly in mind. Violence, even bloody violence, including murder, is not by itself to be equated with terror (or terrorism); violence becomes terror only if it is used to accomplish what is expressed in the Latin word *terror*—i.e., to spread terror and thus to frighten the enemy (including the potential enemy) so that he does not dare to resist. Defenders and practitioners of terror have never shied away from calling their deeds humane on the grounds that their victory would justify all previous slaughter. The atomic bombs dropped on Hiroshima and Nagasaki were, in this sense of the word, acts of terror meant to force Japan to capitulation and democracy.

Because of its psychological influence on the population, mass murder is usually mass terrorism, but not necessarily so; when Hitler gassed millions of Jews, his aim was not to frighten but to destroy them. Classical examples of mass terrorism were those pyramids of skulls erected along the victory road of Tamerlane's armies, or the public executions in that phase of the French Revolution known as "The Terror." The Bolsheviks' *terror* was meant both to frighten and to destroy (the number of its victims rivaled those of Hitler); this was proved by the course of the revolution, the civil war, the collectivization, and Solzhenitsyn's Gulag volumes.

THE RUSSIAN TERRORISTS

The terror against individuals with which we have to deal today was rejected by Marx and has been rejected by Marxists of all hues time and again (though some have practiced it under different names). This kind of terror found its most typical manifestation in tsarist Russia during the last four decades of the nineteenth century, when it attained spectacular successes, though without accomplishing its aim—the abolition of the tsar's regime. The idea was to kill some prominent people—cabinet members, police chiefs, members of the imperial family—and thus to "punish" the victims, but mainly to frighten their colleagues or heirs; in the long run, terror was supposed to drive the government and its supporters into a frenzied and blind reaction which would consume its forces and destroy its prestige in the eyes of the population.

This idea was developed systemically in a book, first published in Milan and later in Bern (1884), by a Russian terrorist who in August 1878 had killed General Mesentsev, the chief of the secret police:

> In a struggle against an invisible, impalpable, omnipresent enemy, the strong is vanquished [by] the continuous extension of his own strength [...]. The Terrorists cannot overthrow the government, cannot drive it from St. Petersburg and Russia; but having compelled it, for so many years running, to neglect everything to do nothing but struggle with them, by forcing it to do so still for years and years, they will render its position untenable. Already the prestige of the Imperial Government has received a wound which will be very difficult to heal. An Emperor who shuts himself up in prison from fear of the Terrorism is certainly not a figure to inspire admiration.[3]

The transition of the young Russian revolutionaries, mostly students, from an opposition group to fanatical terrorists was described by the British historian Bernard Pares prior to the First World War:

> The passportless wanderers, desperate and nerve-shaken, rapidly passed into the mood of terrorism. They passed without plan and

almost unconsciously to armed resistance against arrest, and to murders of traitors, spies, and lower officials. From this it was an easy step to the murder of a governor, or even to plots against the life of the Emperor.

The above sentences and also the following by Pares could have been written equally well about the Weathermen or the Baader-Meinhof gang:

> Becoming more compact and businesslike, [they] adjourned the realization of their vague social theories, resolved to dispense with any active popular support, and organized themselves on a basis of conspiracy pure and simple.

Well-meaning patriots, such as the local representatives *(zemstvo)* from Tchernigov believed at that time that the terrorist danger could be banished without the use of police. In a petition to the tsar, they wrote: "The struggle with destructive ideas would be possible only if the public possessed its own weapons—freedom of speech and of the press, of opinion and of instruction."[4] Today, unfortunately, we know better. But at that time even the terrorists thought as did the representatives from Tchernigov. After the assassination of Tsar Alexander II in 1881, the executive committee of the "People's Will" organization, which had carried out the assassination, sent on open letter to his successor addressing him as "Your Majesty." They defended themselves by claiming that Russia's best sons and daughters stood in their ranks. Then they asked him to let the people enjoy human rights and freely elect a national assembly which they, the terrorists, would then acknowledge and obey unconditionally! They urged the tsar to act as the happiness of Russia, his own dignity, and his duty toward the country demanded.[5]

The Russian terrorists generally tried to stick to a policy of killing only enemies whom they had "condemned to death," without hurting other persons. They did not always succeed in this; during an abortive attempt to assassinate the tsar in St. Petersburg's Winter Palace early in 1880, ten people were killed—but this was an exception. Albert Camus built his drama *The Just Ones* on a case from the Russia of 1905: The terrorist Ivan Kalyayev, who had been assigned the task of murdering Grand Duke Sergei, refrained because in the carriage with the grand duke were his wife and two children; the murder was committed two days later, when the victim was not accompanied by his family. Such delicacy has become rare in our time. If we count the victims of terrorism—from Ireland to Lebanon—terrorists have killed far more innocents than enemies.

Russian radicalism, which spawned Russian terrorism, was—like many radicalisms—an expression of the tension between deals and reality. In the Russia of the last century this meant tension between the motivating forces of the Russian intelligentsia (French liberalism and German idealism) on the one hand and the barbarism and poverty of Old Russia on the other. More often than not, in our day as in the past, young persons from sheltered homes with idealistic traditions (like Ulrike Meinhof and Gudrun Ensslin), shocked by the reality of life, have been the ones most likely to decide to make it fit in with their ideals, by violence, if need be and thus to turn toward revolution.

The young Russian revolutionaries of yesteryear also hoped to win the masses to their cause. Therefore they "went to the people," and that meant to the peasants, among whom they found as little response as did the New Left a century later in its attempt to capture the workers. Thus the decision to turn to terror—Russians then, Weathermen or Meinhofs now—is largely due to desperation.

The last great act of terror in that Russian series, which had begun in the 1870s, was the assassination of Prime Minister Stolypin in September 1911. But by then terror had spread abroad. The Serbian terrorists of the Black Hand had learned a lesson from the great Slavic brother: As at the scene of the assassination of the tsar in 1881, more than one assassin waited along the Hapsburg crown prince's route through Sarajevo on June 28, 1914. The first missed, the second succeeded. Gavrila Princip, age nineteen years, high-school student, fired the shots that started the First World War.

Other assassinations or attempts followed, but they touch our problem only marginally, since they were meant to kill, not frighten: the attempt on Lenin in 1918, which served the young Bolshevik regime as additional justification for increased violence; the assassination of the German communists Karl Liebknecht and Rosa Luxemburg in Berlin in 1919, which in the end helped the Bolsheviks more than those right-wing groups that sanctioned the murders; the assassination of two leading German statesmen of the Weimar period in 1921 and 1922, alarming signals of the sharpening domestic conflict; and finally, the failure of the attempts on Hitler's life. We know that Hitler's opponents, men of religious conviction, who tried to kill him on July 20, 1944, had reached their decision only after long and serious soul-searching. I am one of those who considered the action correct and who were deeply shaken when it failed; had it succeeded, millions of people and many cities might have been saved. The decision in favor of assassination in an extraordinary historical situation does not mean agreement to political murder.

THE WORSE—THE BETTER
In the new terror, as it developed after the Second World War, we find cruelty and inhumanity to an extent that did not exist in tsarist Russia. Now terrorists not only want the regime in power to be frightened, confused, and driven into a violent reaction against the terrorists; they also hope that this anti-terror will help in arousing the population against the regime. Therefore: "The worse, the better." The weakening of the enemy by deaths (of dangerous counterinsurgency specialists, but also of as many soldiers and policemen as possible), is, of course, desired, as is the acquisition of money for a war fund through bank robberies or blackmail. But the grand strategic aim is far wider: nothing less than a total psychological effect on the masses.

The Algerian anti-French terrorists were masters of this strategy: They allowed buses full of Algerians, women and children included, to be destroyed by bombs, not simply because they wanted to terrorize the wavering majority of the population, but also because they wished to push the French colonial administration into a specific reaction, namely, the conviction that it could not trust a single Algerian and thus would have to fight each one of them. The total confrontation of all French against all Algerians would, so the terrorists hoped, bring forth a feeling of patriotic unity and thus create an Algerian nation.[6]

It is well known that the Palestinian radical wing uses the same method. The killing of Israeli civilians, schoolchildren among them, is a sure device to provoke the Israelis. The Israelis counter with assaults on terrorists. The results: increased solidarity of the Palestinians against Israel, the discrediting of the policy of conciliation of Washington and Cairo, the undermining (and eventual destruction) of the authority of the Lebanese government.

Other examples: Airplanes are hijacked and destroyed because there happen to be some Israelis aboard; passengers are shot in Athens or Tel Aviv to hurt Israel; the Olympic Games at Munich are brutally disrupted by the kidnapping and shooting of Israeli athletes. The world's reaction: If only the Israelis would agree to a compromise with the Arabs, then we could finally take airplane trips without fear. Result: damage to Israel's position (which was later repaired by the brilliant liberation of the Jewish hostages in Uganda). Always the aim is provocation and escalation, often at the expense of innocent bystanders.

The young German terrorists had the same strategy in mind. They were hoping that the Bonn government would overreact, would resort to emergency measures, and thus "prove" to the population that it was a "police state," a "fascist state." This did not happen. During the worst provocation so far, the occupation of its embassy in Stockholm by German terrorists, the Bonn government kept its nerve. This it was able to do because the terrorists had the overwhelming majority of the nation against them and were thus completely isolated. After twelve years of Hitler and his secret police, aversion to violence is widespread among Germans. Many of them would agree with Joan Baez, who said in an interview in 1971 that anyone committing violence against another person commits violence against himself and thus lowers his own humanity.[7] The late Hannah Arendt, an immigrant from Germany to the United States who made a name for herself by her studies on aggression, came to the conclusion that the use of violence does change the world—but only by making it still more violent.[8]

It is the aim of the guerrillas, Debray has explained, to act as a "small motor" which will push the "big motor," the masses, into a revolutionary movement.[9] So far the terrorists have proved to be too weak a force even to start their own "small motor," let alone move the "big motor" of the masses which is incomparably more powerful. The masses, about whom the terrorists dream, desire reforms and stability, not revolutionary violence.

American political scientists have developed a plausible thesis: The greater the gap that people perceive between their actual situation and the situation which they believe they deserve, and between the influence they believe should be theirs and the influence they find at their disposal, the greater is their readiness to commit acts of violence.[10] This gap is relatively small in the Western industrial nations under existing economic and social conditions, and the chances to influence events through a functioning democracy are relatively great. Hence the rejection of violence by the people and the isolation of the terrorists. Terror is a weapon of the weak; it makes sense only if there is a chance for fighting the enemy on a territory where the weak can be strong, like fish in water. Otherwise, terror is but a mosquito bite that irritates the strong without moving him from his place.

Kozo Okamoto was one of the terrorists at Lod Airport. What is known about him is in many ways characteristic of those young people who take to violence as a way of life.[11] Okamoto was one of six children, his father an elementary-school principal; this means that he came from that same liberal middle class which has lately produced young radicals the world over. Unlike his two older brothers, he did not pass the entrance examination to prestigious Kyoto University; after twice failing, he went to a lesser-known school. There he joined the local branch of "Beheiren," which he soon found too mild, since it was mainly a peace movement. Like so many others, Okamoto was looking for an ideology that would explain everything and set clear goals for action.

Early in 1970 he came in contact with the terrorist Red Army group mentioned earlier in the chapter on Japan, which finally satisfied his needs. An older brother's participation in the hijacking of a Japan Air Lines jet to North Korea strengthened Okamoto's ties with the group, which by then was sending some of its young people to the Middle East for guerrilla training. Early in 1972, Okamoto too went there and, with other Japanese, received military training near Beirut. After a few weeks he was assigned to the terrorist attack on Lod. With two accomplices he flew by way of Europe to Israel. What happened inside the Lod terminal, we have seen in Chapter 14. Okamoto's friends were killed instantly; he was captured, tried, and sentenced to life imprisonment. At the trial he expressed pride in his deed. The massacres must continue, he declared; they would rouse the peoples of the world to make revolution. As for him, he hoped to become "a star in the sky" after his death, along with his comrades and their victims, all of whom died for a noble end.

In March 1976, the U.S. Department of State sponsored a conference of some 200 American and foreign specialists on the problems of terrorism. In his unpublished report, the conference rapporteur, Professor Chalmers Johnson of Berkeley, summarized the discussion and also the prevailing Western attitude on terrorism, which was defined as:

> political, goal-oriented action, involving the use or threat of extraordinary violence, performed for psychological rather than ma-

terial effect, and the victims of which are symbolic rather than instrumental. [It is] explicitly rationalized and justified by some philosophy, theory, or ideology, however crude.

Terrorist actions in the 1961-1970 decade (according to this report) cost approximately 4,600 lives in 63 countries. Between the beginning of 1968 and end of 1975 there occurred 913 terrorist incidents of an international and transnational nature, including 123 kidnappings, 137 hijackings, and 375 cases of the use of explosive devices, killing altogether some 800 people and injuring some 1,700. Thus, we are dealing here with a phenomenon of considerable proportions. But its total political result has been minimal. In the past fifteen years "one cannot identify even one unambiguous instance of a campaign of political terrorism which led directly or indirectly to revolutionary change of the kind championed by the Left." Rather, the opposite would be true; terrorism has usually strengthened the forces of law and order.

The conference distinguished, I believe rightly, four types of terrorism: ideological (including that by anarchist, radical leftist, Trotskyist, Maoist, orthodox Communist, and extreme rightist elements); nationalistic (anticolonial and irredentist, employed by such groups as the Irish Republican Army, the Basque ETA, the Palestinian Al Fatah, the Quebec FLQ); ethnic (in behalf of religious, linguistic, regional, and other particularistic movements which may, of course, overlap with those fired by nationalism); and pathological (against public targets for apparently private, biographical reasons, as in the case of the Manson gang).

The particular movement into which young people desperate in their search for a cause are finally drawn seems often to be determined by chance. Okamoto admitted a feeling of kinship with the right-wing Japanese writer Yukio Mishima (who committed public hara-kiri in 1970 as a sign of protest against Japanese society). Indeed, Okamoto might just as easily have become a devoted soldier in Mishima's private army. There are, certainly, causes which can inspire young people, but there are far more young people in search of a cause because they feel lost and useless without one. Cohn-Bendit is quite right when, in his *Le Grand Bazar,* he flippantly remarks that the Paris May proved costly to the local psychoanalysts because many of their patients were students who got busy building barricades and no longer needed them.

274

FILM AND TV VIOLENCE

In addition to causes and cause seekers there must exist, for violence to erupt, some kind of circumstance (or "water," to use
Mao's simile), that is especially conducive to violence and terror.
One such "water" is the violence-promoting environment in
which our society lives and allows its youth to grow up. Here it
may suffice to say a few words about America, the leader and
example of the free world in things good and bad.

American history has been peculiar for being, from the arrival
of the first Europeans on the Atlantic Coast to the settlement of
the Far West, a history of the conquest of land not so much by
regular troops as by armed pioneers. The glorification of this often
violent westward drive and its hard-hitting, fast-shooting men
has led to, among other things, an extremely widespread possession of firearms which—all warnings notwithstanding—legis-
lators have time and again upheld.

There has been in America for decades now, in addition to the
violent Western, the still more violent gangster film. Americans
themselves take this fare with surprising equanimity. But the
European is staggered by what he sees on his film and TV screens.
I remember seeing once on a transatlantic flight from Europe to
America, in an American jumbo jet, *The French Connection,* an
almost uninterrupted shoot-out between police and gangsters in
New York City. When the lights came on, the Scandinavian immigrant couple next to me sighed. After seeing this, they felt that
they would like to return home without going beyond Kennedy
Airport.

According to American statistics, in children's programs on TV
there is on the average an act of violence every sixteen minutes,
and a typical child watches between his or her fifth and fifteenth
year the annihilation of approximately 13,400 people. In his book
on aggression, Hacker attacks the mass media in a chapter which
opens with this story: A woman has just missed the shooting of
Lee Harvey Oswald by Jack Ruby on TV. Her husband consoles
her. "Don't worry," he says, "there will be a replay in a few
minutes."[12] As indeed there was, over and over and over.

American movie and TV producers have been trying hard for
many years to convince the public that the steeply rising curve of
acts of violence has nothing to do with violence on the screen, and
they always find someone with a celebrated name willing to write
a confirming assessment. I am not convinced. Can it be possible
that watching violence hour after hour, evening after evening,

275

does not help to break down the human soul's inhibitions against violence? I am more in agreement with those who believe that among the children who grow up with such entertainment quite a few will consider violence a part of normal life and will join vicious street gangs by the time they are ten or eleven years old.[13] Nor should the brutalizing effet of the Vietnam war on hundreds of thousands of young Americans be forgotten.

When is violence permitted or even required? The problem remains unsolved. Neither the lawyers nor the philosophers, not even the theologians, know a formula that fits every case and convinces everybody. The clearest commandment is still that of the great religions—refrain from *all* violence. But humanity is very far from following it. The New Left has held long discussions about the use of violence; it, too, has found only opinions convincing for some, not binding for all. The distinction between violence against things and violence against persons, as was pointed out, has proved unusable; in Ireland, Christian enemies are bombing pubs and homes *with people inside* almost nightly. Another example of the close interrrelationship of violence toward things and violence against persons was given in a study made public by Senator Birch Bayh in 1975. In U.S. schools, equipment worth a half billion (not million) dollars is destroyed every year out of sheer vandalism, *and* at the same time 70,000 teachers and hundreds of thousands of students are beaten, robbed, and threatened.[14] Such figures stagger the mind.

Let us end this sad recital with an individual case. The reader knows that at the climax of the rock "festival" at Altamont a young man was stabbed to death. The faces of the people around showed neither rage nor horror, only curiosity. One observer reported: "I was only two feet away, the people said 'wow, far out.' Nobody did anything about it."[15]

A comparative study of violence all over the world, made by an American political scientist, has found that in this respect the United States is number one on a list of seventeen Western countries.[16] But the non-American cannot let it go at that. Violent American films are filling many European movie theaters, and German TV lives on detective series from across the Atlantic.

I realize that the lowering of the violence threshold did not begin with TV. We live at a time of profound change. If someone is completely frightened and confounded by the wild developments of our time, then he seeks (as the great Spanish philosopher Ortega y Gasset understood forty years ago) "the liberating effect of violence," that is, insurrection, and "every insurrection at first means savagery."[17]

We return to our starting point. The urban guerrillas of today cannot count the Marxists of all hues as their ancestors. Marxist ideology demands the revolutionization of the masses; only after that has been accomplished may terror—individual and mass terror—be employed, though under other names; until then, individual terrorist actions are not considered desirable. Nor did the non-Communists among the New Left contemplate terror, kidnapping, and murder so long as they were carried along by the hope of success. But when the wave of rebellion ebbed, when the campus quieted down, and when, finally, the game was up, then some of them turned to terror.

The taking of hostages, this extremely vicious weapon so prominent in the news of today, goes beyond the framework of what might be called classical terror. Its purpose is not to spread fear but to exact what the kidnappers think they can obtain only from those who are anxious to save the life of the kidnapped person or persons. The world has never before seen the taking of hostages for political purposes on the present scale. Even more than "ordinary" terror, the taking of hostages is a weapon of the weak and the few; one man with a hand grenade in a plane full of passengers can blackmail a government. A handful of Palestinian terrorists turned the Olympic Games of 1972 into a nightmare for hundreds of millions who were watching the drama on their TV screens.

Small wonder many are trembling at the thought that terrorists with atom bombs instead of Molotov cocktails could make entire cities their hostages. There is only one way of deterring terrorists and kidnappers from further violence: to show them that their actions will gain nothing but the boundless anger, hatred, and contempt of all people.

METHODS

The American New Left introduced methods of fighting, and also new names for its methods, both of which quickly came into use throughout the world, sometimes with their purpose or meaning changed. The first famous sit-in, on February 1, 1960, was aimed at putting an end to the segregation of races in the South. In other parts of the United States where this kind of separation had not been practiced, sit-ins were used to achieve other aims, such as the right of free speech on the Berkeley campus. Later on, in the

States and abroad, the temporary sit-in was transformed into the long-lasting occupation of campus lecture rooms or administration offices. The sit-in at Yasuda Hall, Tokyo University, lasted for several months. The sit-in was developed into a sit-on at Cologne, in October 1966, when students sat for hours on streetcar tracks to protest increased fares.

Meanwhile, the syllable "-in" had moved on. America's teach-ins against the Vietnam war, first practiced in March 1965 at the University of Michigan, were imitated on many a campus. In the beginning, the students actually wanted to be taught at their teach-ins; they were seeking information from political leaders and other specialists. In London, for example, they were addressed (in June 1965) by the U.S. ambassador to South Vietnam, Henry Cabot Lodge, and in Oxford a few days later by the British foreign secretary, Michael Stewart. But soon the style was altered, the teach-in turned from a place of teaching and learning into a battleground on which only the Left or Far Left had a chance to be heard; in reality it had become a talk-in. The German universities witnessed a wave of such teach-ins during the campaign—it was unsuccessful—against the Emergency Laws (early summer 1968). Strikes, the principal weapon of labor, did not make much sense on the campus, where nobody but the striking students would be hurt in the process; hence "active strikes" were proclaimed, in which all kinds of damage was done on the campus.

Soon everybody was inventing his own "-in." Some were meant purely for protest: from the go-in (which upset the routine work of the building into which one went) to the shit-in, practiced in 1968 in a German university institute. But even if the -ins were not specifically directed against somebody or against something (as the love-in was not in 1967 at Golden Gate Park), they were manifestations of the young generation's urge for independence. For many others the -in was nothing but a fashion; they arranged chant-ins, kiss-ins, and so on.

Demonstrations in the streets, another old method of protest, also acquired new forms. Korean students in 1960 made their famous jogging demonstration, and at about the same time the Japanese came up with the so-called snake dance demonstration. In Tokyo in the summer of 1960, I saw columns of many thousands of students "snake dancing" in rows of ten or twelve from the hill where the Diet Building stands down to the Foreign Ministry—a few running stomps toward the left, a few toward the right, again and again, fired by rhythmic yells. This kind of demonstration was seen in many countries without the stomping, but also in long arm-linked rows, with those in the first row often holding a pole across their chests in order to move as a closed phalanx. In West Berlin during the winter of 1966/67, students invented two further varieties: the "promenade demonstration," where small groups of students drew passersby into discussions, thus blocking traffic on the street, and the "blitz demonstration," where columns with flags and slogans quickly assembled and quickly disappeared when the police arrived, only to do the whole thing all over again a few blocks away.

The carrying of pictures in demonstrations is familiar from religious processions; I saw them in Moscow—in Old Russia the icon paintings of saints, later the pictures of Stalin and the "collective leadership." By now, large-scale portraits have acquired a firm place in most demonstrations, as they have on the walls of student dormitories and campaign headquarters. There are no statistics, but I would say that during the sixties I saw mostly the portraits of Mao, Che Guevara, and Karl Marx, in that order. One particular poster of Guevara could be found in almost every country, some copies even in Russia. This picture one might easily call an icon without using quotation marks; it is stylized like a head of Christ. Demonstrators frequently also carry long pieces of red cloth that are held aloft between poles and lettered with quotations from their ideological masters, or with slogans and witticisms of their own.

Great rhetorical performances are but rarely to be observed. There must have been some brilliant speeches now and then, but usually it is only a matter of repeating those words which provoke thought associations with fanaticizing impact, such as "fascist" or "fascistoid." The academic administration, the university as a whole, the entire country—everything can be called by these terms, which by now mean everything and nothing. For many a follower of the New Left, anything—except him and his group, of course—must be suspected of fascism. In America, statesmen unpopular with the radical young, such as Lyndon B. Johnson in the last years of his presidency, may be greeted with a raised hand and mocking *Sieg Heil* shouts. Another term sure to provoke the desired reaction is "late capitalism," which suggests the approaching death of the existing economic order.

The "happening" was something totally new among the instruments of revolution. I am using this word with hesitation

279

because in its literal sense it does not quite correspond to what it is applied to. By definition, a happening is something that happens spontaneously or unintentionally. Among early happenings were performances that had not been prearranged, comparable in a way to the meetings of certain sects where people unexpectedly start speaking in tongues. But soon it was found that happenings could exert powerful shock effects upon the audience. It was this shock effect, not the event in itself, that made happenings useful for the revolution. Soon, happenings were premeditated and prearranged in great detail, often with the one aim of provoking the police into rash actions.

The arsenal, as such, was in the beginning mainly defensive: face cloths against tear gas, thick pullovers against nightsticks, sometimes shields, soon also helmets. Later on, offensive weapons came into use: sticks, poles, rocks, Molotov cocktails, pipe bombs, mines, and firearms. Automobiles were frequently demolished to be used as barricades. The firearms and bombs seriously disturbed the population once they became weapons in the hands of small and determined terror groups.

One technical achievement, whose inventor hardly anticipated its political significance, has become a most effective weapon: the spray can of paint. Slogans, symbols, abbreviations of the names of organizations, obscenities, and just plain doodles without any recognizable sense to them were sprayed on many campus walls, covering in the end dozens of miles of wall space and requiring tens of thousands of working hours for their removal. The smart Swedes set aside a huge wall at a much-used thoroughfare in Stockholm exclusively for spray-can artists; early every morning it was whitewashed. Still more important for the political struggle was another item of technical progress: the loudspeaker, invaluable for the inciting and leading of crowds. And, of course, who could imagine today any kind of political opposition without the use of mimeograph and Xerox machines?

On the other hand, the significance of battle songs has declined—surprisingly for those who, like myself, remember the techniques of earlier decades of this century. In Germany, during the Weimar period, political warfare was waged as much with songs as with fists; during political campaigns people were hoarse most of the time. Today, some have been replaced by rhythmic yells, such as "Ho, Ho, Ho Chi Minh" or "Che, Che, Che Guevara" (the last word, better to fit into the rhythm, pronounced in German as GwaRAH).

280

A popular way to ridicule the enemy—the state and its representatives, especially the police—is to put them in the role of an elephant gun which shoots at flies. This can easily be achieved by the "provocation" (from which the Dutch "Provos" have taken their name). It has been employed thousands of times by students all around the globe. First, you provoke the police—most often by using obscene language. Michener in his *Kent State* (p. 241) gives many examples, although he found it "embarrassing when reporting what girls said [to the National Guardsmen]" and refrained from going into detail because he "did not want parents to see such words attributed to their daughters." A master of such provocation was Abbie Hoffman; witness his *Woodstock Nation* with its crude attacks on the "pigs" and its vicious illustrations, including a gashed-open dead pig in its own blood.[18] The very word "pig" had an insulting and thereby provocative content for policemen, although it was the mildest of the epithets used. If words are not enough, stones, bottles, and tin cans can be thrown. Then, when the police charge with nightsticks, water cannons, and riot cars, this can be considered an act of violence which justifies the demonstrators in employing "counterviolence."

The cause which triggers a provocation does not need to be important in itself; this has been said frankly more than once. Mark Rudd, first a member of SDS and later a Weatherman, did not hide the fact that he and his friends had manufactured the reasons for the Columbia riots, namely, the protest against the university's cooperation with the Washington-based Institute for Defense Analysis (which was working for the Vietnam war) and against the construction of a gymnasium which would have cut into Morningside Park, mainly used by blacks. He said:

Let me tell you. We manufactured the issues. The Institute for Defense Analysis is nothing at Columbia. Just three professors. And the gym issue is bull. It doesn't mean anything to anybody. I had never been to the gym site before the demonstration began. I didn't even know how to get there.

The young black leader Stokely Carmichael told his followers to provoke the enemy until it would hit back, adding: "If your enemy does not hit back, you have no revolution."[19]

One stratagem was initially to use slogans that could be counted upon to have broad support in the population, such as a demand for cheaper streetcar fares (Cologne and Heidelberg, 1969) or a protest against the demolition of apartment houses to make way for new buildings. Condemned apartment houses are often evacuated long before they are actually demolished, and meanwhile may be reoccupied, often by students who are looking both for quarters and for a chance to provoke the authorities. If the police arrive to eject them by force, they stage demonstrations, which may win the sympathy of people who do not understand why buildings should have to be cleared of their inhabitants weeks or months before they are actually destroyed. Frankfurt witnessed street battles for this very reason, with many otherwise disinterested people siding with the students. In the San Basilio suburb of Rome a young man was shot to death in the autumn of 1974 during riots which occurred over the same issue.

Nothing can quite so effectively solidarize people as the policeman's nightstick. In Berkeley, I remember thirty or forty minority students picketing the university at the Bancroft entrance, demanding an autonomous college within the university for minority students. Nobody paid much attention to them until they decided to form a living chain that would prevent others from entering the university grounds. The moment the police arrived to break open the chain by force, more than a thousand students were motivated to join the picketers out of solidarity against the "pigs."

Knowledge of the methods employed by students in their struggles with the authorities was quickly transmitted from country to country, and imitation came almost as quickly—the teach-in, for example, within a matter of days. At the height of the revolt, I could more or less predict what would happen the next day at my own school when I watched on TV what the students had just done in Berkeley or Berlin.

III

WHENCE?

"Whence comes this unrest, this rebellious spirit?" This question has been asked since the mid-sixties by parents, educators, and politicians. "Why are they so different, and why precisely now?" Many explanations are being offered; among them, even sunspots—which supposedly derange the young—and the effects of modern nutrition. Some console themselves by seeing this unrest as nothing but a modern version of the age-old generation problem which has, in spite of ups and downs, remained fundamentally the same through the millennia, thus proving the ancient biblical wisdom: "There is no new thing under the sun."

We shall look for answers first in external factors (changes in the colleges, the political environment, the personal background of the rebels), then in the intellectual influences (of teachers and teachings, the latter including what they teach as well as how), and finally by looking into the internal, psychological forces that are felt with unusual intensity in a time of crisis, especially by young people.

24
NOTHING NEW UNDER THE SUN?

RADICALISM, anarchism, and nihilism; utopianism, arrogance, and intolerance; vagabondism, libertinism, and amoralism; vandalism, delinquency, and laziness—these are some of the terms that crop up when judgments are passed on the youth of today. In standard texts on youth psychology we find characterizations such as these:

The young generation wants everything at once; its motto is "Now—today, and not tomorrow!" The young people have no sense of history; the past, as far as they are concerned, is bad. The long road of learning, which the parents demand of them, they refute by claiming that the schools are no good and their curriculum has nothing in common with the problems that really interest them. What their ancestors created, they take casually and without a word of appreciation, and they are inclined to see their elders' vices rather than their virtues. A plan, in their view, is almost as good as an achievement, which would require exertion; they have not yet learned that a plan is just the very first step, and that its realization ultimately depends on work, knowledge, and perseverance.

They live in conflict with their parents and transfer this conflict onto society as a whole. With regard to both, they feel like martyrs in a world which does not try to understand them. They provoke the authorities by purposely appearing unkempt and behaving rudely, like nihilists. If quick influence at home and in society is denied them, they try to compensate by living like vagabonds and adventurists, relishing the pungent feeling of power that people have who say no, and they enjoy the lure of danger and of participating in the destruction of society, even by arson or TNT. They often try to find their models among the enemies of society. When they come into collision with authority, they justify themselves by claiming that they are avenging the oppressed. They do not want to obey the penal law, considering it but an instrument employed by the older generation for oppressing the young.

By denying the value system of their parents they claim to be above criticism and moral judgment, and they refuse to be tied to the despised moral code of society. Absolute values exist for them only in fairy tales. They themselves, however, judge society very much from the point of view of moralistic perfectionism and in an orgy of self-righteousness, as fighters for truth and virtue against a hopelessly corrupted world. Their elders are always bad and responsible for all failures, while the young represent a progressive and highly interesting new type of human being.

Unable to put their desires into effect, they are afflicted by psychological diseases, by neuroses. They seek escape from the world's confusion in aimless vagabondism and drug consumption. The latter destroys their ability for self-criticism; they are pleased with themselves, although they do not accomplish anything. Often the roads of escape lead to schizophrenia and sometimes to suicide. In matters of sex they follow their own inclinations and collect their experiences earlier than preceding generations. Many run away from home at a young age, girls as well as boys, and get into sexual conflicts and even crimes, or into relations considered perverted by society.

They are susceptible to sudden revivals of a religious or pseudo-religious nature, usually connected not with the established churches but with small sects, their aversion for their parents often leading to aversion for the parents' church. They love endless discussions, many of which are a pain in the neck for adults, since they usually amount to nothing. They are in an all-or-nothing mood—hence they detest compromise. The world, they feel, must be forced to become good, if necessary by violence.

Wishing to keep the blissful state of unlimited options, they dislike being organized—hence the strong attraction of anarchism. Yet they are in need of support and seek it in the congenial company of their peers; within the group they are eager to adjust both in behavior and thinking. New communities of young people are constantly arising, united by almost eschatological anticipations.

Even politics they judge from the moral point of view, and they are easily fired by big ideals encompassing humanity as a whole. Political ideologies, as long as they remain pure and uncontaminated by reality, can easily travel from nation to nation, and they are readily embraced by young people who, not responsible for day-to-day work decisions, love utopias and are often fanatical in their pursuit.

Looking at this younger generation, adults are deeply apprehensive about the future that someday will be in its hands. Is not a "decline of the West" in the offing, they ask. And often they add, with fear in their hearts, that the world has never before seen young people like these.

Really? Not one of the above characterizations was written during the past decade and a half. They have all been taken from two books published earlier (and thirty years apart), one in 1924 by the late and widely respected Edward Spranger; the other in 1954, by David P. Ausubel, a professor at the University of Illinois.

EVEN CRONUS DID IT

We have now seen that many characteristics of our present youth, considered to be exceedingly dangerous new symptoms of mankind's decline, have preoccupied observers since the first part of our century. More than that: the restlessness of youth and the conflict of generations may be as old as humanity itself. Greek mythology opens with three father-son conflicts. Uranus, ancestor of the gods, was castrated by Cronus, his son, with the help of a sharp sickle, and was thus deprived of his world power. Cronus, in turn, was defeated and banished by his son Zeus. Against Zeus rose his son Prometheus, the ancestor of every rebel, whose defiance of his father's tyranny has inspired generations of adolescents, especially Germans—thanks to Goethe's magnificent verses in the poem *Prometheus* ("I should honor you? Why?").

There is no need to enumerate Prometheus's spiritual descendants. We are familiar with them from the sagas, the history, the literature of all epochs, down to the young rebels of our days1 Until recently, tension between the generations was taken for granted, like the change of the seasons; it is only during the past few decades that psychologists, sociologists, and many others have turned their attention to it, analyzing it in many learned books. (Ausubel's, which we just mentioned, lists 622 titles in its bibliography.)

There is one voice in classical antiquity which is sometimes

287

quoted by the pessimists to show what we are heading for, and by the optimists to prove that the restlessness of youth has not led the world into catastrophe. Plato, in a passage of the *Republic* about the outbreak of anarchy, sketches the following sinister picture in order to warn his contemporaries:

> The father is afraid of his sons, and the son feels no awe or fear of his parents. The teacher fears and fawns upon the pupils, and the pupils pay no heed to the teacher nor to their superiors, while the old are imitating the young for fear they may be thought disagreeable and authoritative. The people chafe at the slightest suggestion of obedience and will not endure it. They finally pay no heed even to the laws written or unwritten, so that forsooth they may have no master anywhere over them. This is the fine and vigorous root from which tyranny grows. The probable outcome of too much freedom is too much slavery for the individual and the state; from the height of liberty they come to the fiercest extreme of servitude.[1]

It is amazing how unprepared sociologists and psychologists of our day were for the youth revolt. For example, the lectures at a conference of the American Academy of Arts and Sciences, published in 1963, gave no indication of the storm that was brewing. Talcott Parsons, one of the grand old men of modern sociology, declared that American youth was at that time "better integrated" in the general culture of the country than during the twenties or thirties what he considered characteristic of the young people of the early sixties was "not a basic alienation, but an eagerness to learn, to accept higher orders of responsibility, to 'fit,' [... and a] readiness to work within the system." Kenneth Keniston, an outstanding psychologist and a generation younger than Parsons, found some symptoms of change, but in general came to similar conclusions. Youth was "not rebellious," he wrote; it was moving "away from public involvement and social responsibilities and toward a world of private and personal satisfaction," and this would "assure a highly stable and social order."[2]

If the ancient belief that there is no new thing under the sun has to be reconciled with the outbreak of the violent and quite peculiar campus rebellion in the mid-sixties of our century, a good deal of explaining would seem to be in order.

Youth has been restless from time immemorial. Yet much is new, very new, in the unrest of our time, in its developments and symptoms. There must be reasons why in the midst of the sixties a special type of unrest emerged, and why this happened so suddenly and all over the world. What external influences (and inner causes, of which later) were responsible? Young people who in the days of Eisenhower and Adenauer had been very serious about their studies and examinations, those doors to wealth and comfort, and who had not been much involved in politics—these same young people had since become rebellious. Who caused this? Or what?

WAS IT THE RED HAND?

Some people blamed Moscow (or Peking—weren't there people around who called themselves Maoists?). Some, bringing it closer to home for Americans, blamed the bearded revolutionary in Cuba who had dared to oppose the United States in its own hemisphere.

The Moscow Communists, as everybody knows, have long had the support of many radical parties and groups throughout the world, and there are many fellow-traveler organizations which the Kremlin supports with money, with training for their cadres, with trips to Moscow. But this book is not concerned with such organizations, which belong to the Old Left. We are dealing with the New Left, which has surprised the Russians and even confused them, as Moscow itself has shown very clearly. At first, the Kremlin refrained from noticing the New Left, or interpreted it mistakenly (as a rebellion of financially underprivileged students). When, during the events in Paris in May 1968, the New Left could no longer be overlooked, the Soviet press was outraged about the "petty-bourgeois adventurers and anarchists" who had only brought harm to the cause of the proletariat. In my book *Moscow and the New Left,* I described the outburst of Yuri Zhukov, one of the best-known Moscow commentators, in *Pravda* on May 30, 1968. He lashed out in fury against Marcuse, Cohn-Bendit, and all the other "werewolves" whose activities, he said, were contributing to the impending defeat of the French Communist Party.

For the Kremlin this was a highly unwelcome form of competition, since the New Left's vehement antiauthoritarianism damaged the prestige of the U.S.S.R. among the young generation abroad and forced Communist parties around the world into a defensive position. In addition, it was seen as causing a worldwide trend toward the right by creating shock and fear among the general population. To be sure, the New Left also made trouble for many Western governments, and it worked for some of the same objectives as Moscow—in its opposition to the Vietnam war, for example. To the best of my knowledge, however, the Kremlin did not create the New Left and has not aided it, but has, of course, tried to make use of it as a means for drawing young radicals into youth organizations closely connected with Communist parties, so far without much success.

Peking as godfather of the New Left—that sounded more plausible, because a very active part of the New Left called itself Maoist and, at times, waved the Little Red Book aloft. In reality, Peking only once demonstratively took note of the New Left: Between May 21 and 26, 1968—according to Chinese sources—20 million Chinese marched to show their support for the rebellion in France. Peking did not go beyond the claim of intellectual paternity: "The overwhelming victories of the Great Proletarian Cultural Revolution of China have imbued the peoples of various countries with revolutionary will and fired them with courage for battle and victory."[3] In its reports of foreign news, the Chinese press mentioned many countries as having student rebellions; in the *Peking Review* alone, thirty or more were noted before the year was out. Looking back on 1968, this journal declared that "the students were in the front line of the revolutionary struggle."[4]

But the Chinese never identified themselves with any one of the New Left groups—most likely because there were none which they fully controlled; perhaps also because they were confused by the chaotic sectarianism on the extreme Left abroad. For the same reason, they never acknowledged any of the New Left leaders as their own men. When they singled out one young man by name, they did not risk anything by praising him; the Czech student Jan Palach, who made a flaming sacrifice of himself as a protest against the Soviet invasion, was safely dead.[5]

While working at the University of California in Berkeley on my monograph *Peking and the New Left,* I was frequently asked whether Peking's hand could be discovered in the American New Left. I had not found it, but I decided to ask the FBI. On my way back to Europe, I struggled through the labyrinth of the FBI building in Washington until I found a specialist on Maoist groups. All he would tell me was that he suspected connections with Peking, without having any proof, apart from the fact that many Maoist bookshops throughout the country were making some money by selling brochures and magazines imported cheaply from China. In Tokyo, I had a similar experience in 1973, while interviewing the man in the Ministry of the Interior who had to keep watch over radical student groups. He said that he lacked "hard evidence" of Peking's financing of such groups, though it was known that firms doing business with China occasionally supported Japanese Maoists with money. He was not aware of any particular interest on Peking's part in the Japanese New Left, and had even heard that radical leftist youngsters, when visiting China, had been admonished not to behave too violently and instead to be dedicated students. For Japanese terrorists the Chinese had nothing but sharp criticism. And while no political party in Japan was willing to support Maoist students, pro-Moscow Communist students were frequently getting assistance from the Japan Communist Party. I met only a few students who listened regularly to the broadcasts from Radio Peking (and Radio Tirana).[6]

If not agents, and if not secret finances, what made Maoism a world movement during the sixties? It was China's Great Proletarian Cultural Revolution, which began in August 1966 and became known to the world more or less by early 1967—that is, at the time when the far more modest youth revolution in the West was approaching its climax. Until then, China had been mainly a matter of interest for the experts. Now the sparks of the Chinese explosion went flying from one campus to the next.

Whatever had happened so far in the West now palled when compared with the news of revolution in China. What a revolution! In Peking, so one was told, 13 million young people, high-school and university students in the main, had marched past Mao at the Gate of Heavenly Peace, waving their Little Red Books. After that they had flooded out over the giant country and its three-quarter-billion population with Mao's instructions in their ears: "Make revolution!" It was to be a revolution against the bureaucracy that had established itself after the Communist victory in the autumn of 1949—against a Communist bureaucracy that had turned itself into a new upper class, a new Establishment. The 13 million young people swept these "new capitalists" from their seats of power and put dunce caps on their heads. Hierarchies crumbled; factory and school directors lost their jobs; workers, peasants, and youngsters took over; Shanghai was transformed into a "commune like the Paris Commune of 1871" (soon to disappear, however, in the waves of the revolution). And high above stood the towering figure of a man who, within a quarter of a century, had risen from unknown guerrilla to leader of the most populous state on earth, and who now, though in his seventies, instead of resting on his laurels had set in motion a powerful new revolution. This was the way it looked at that time, as seen from Berkeley, Paris, or Berlin. And everybody was aware that this upheaval in China was a gigantic affront to the authoritarian and highly militarized Soviet Union—proof of how seriously Mao and his Red Guards took their own brand of Communism.

According to Peking, 10 million copies of the Little Red Book, in twenty-two languages, went out into the world within the short time between the beginning of the Cultural Revolution and the end of 1968.[7] I had first seen copies of the plastic-bound booklet in Hong Kong late in the summer of 1966 in Maoist shops. Soon it was to be found all over the West. It was, however, a symbol rather than a catechism. Never in those years did I hear students in America or in other countries quote from the Little Red Book when they wanted to make a point. (After the death of Lin Piao in September 1971 the Little Red Book was quietly withdrawn because it had been connected with his name.) It was not this small book that made students in the West display Maoist posters in their dormitories and carry Mao portraits during their demonstrations; rather, it was the exciting idea that a vast country was being pushed into a great revolution in order not to become stale and petrified. Gradually it became clear that Mao indeed wanted the unceasing conflict of contradictions; that he wanted one renewed revolution after another as the driving force of history, a revolution which he did not try to channel (as did the men in the Kremlin) but to which he intended to give free rein; that he believed in eternal change and evolution, in the waxing and waning of all things, including Communist parties and even including China. Years later, in October 1975, during the state visit of German Chancellor Helmut Schmidt, whom I accompanied, Mao mentioned the names of four Germans who had profoundly influenced him: Hegel, Marx, Engels, and—Haeckel. Ernst Haeckel, now all but forgotten, was a German biologist-philosopher of the Darwinist school, and his Die Welträthsel (1899; an English translation was published in 1901 under the title The Riddle of the Universe) had been extremely popular among German intellectuals before the First World War. Haeckel taught the eternal evolution of matter, with man but a brief moment in the course of billions of years. In 1958 Mao, in one of his speeches, echoed Haeckel, whom he must have read while a young library assistant in Peking. Mao said:

The universe, too, undergoes transformation, it is not eternal. Capitalism leads to socialism, socialism leads to communism, and communist society must still be transformed, it will also have a beginning and an end, [...] it cannot remain constant. [...] There is nothing in the world that does not arise, develop, and disappear. Monkeys turn into men, mankind arose; in the end, the whole human race will disappear, it may turn into something else, at that time the earth itself will also cease to exist. The earth must certainly be extinguished, the sun too will grow cold.[8]

A man with such breathtaking perspectives was able to influence Western youth far more than Brezhnev, Kosygin, Gromyko, or Soviet marshals with a hundred medals on their chests.

Later there were disappointments: The Chinese Army took over, millions of young Red Guards were sent to the countryside more or less forcibly, and Mao received with great honors the man most hated by the New Left, Richard Nixon. Soon the Maoists in the West became just one extreme Left sect among many others. But the memory of the Great Proletarian Cultural Revolution remained bright; it affected the campus even though the knowledge of it was but vague. Our Maoists seem to survive Mao.

The direct influence of Havana on the New Left, especially in the United States, is undisputed. This was not true at the start. When Fidel Castro came to power in January 1959, little notice was taken on the then quiet U.S. campus. In October 1962 young Americans identified themselves with President John F. Kennedy when, much to Castro's dismay, he forced the removal of Soviet missiles from Cuba. It was only later that the Castro legend was to become political dynamite. The American Maoists were the first to see this possibility. Notwithstanding Washington's prohibition of visits to the island, they organized excursions to Cuba.[9] A student travel office, not obviously Maoist, organized the trips, the first one being in the summer of 1963; the visitors had to fly via Paris and Prague to Havana, and return home the same way.

Since the Cuban government paid a large part of the expenses, the whole excursion, including the flight and the stay in Cuba, cost each visitor only $100. By that time, the process of bureaucratization in Cuba had begun, and the long-haired leftists from the United States did not like everything they saw; yet many of them returned as enthusiasts. Some later became prominent members of the Left radical movement. Although the trips were to be abandoned within a year because of the troubles they caused with U.S. authorities, they contributed to the rise of a pro-Cuban sentiment. As the unrest among young Americans increased, so did their sympathy with Castro; for some he more or less took the place of the late John F. Kennedy, and many saw Cuba's new order as a desirable model for America.

Castro had everything to offer that the New Left wanted: He was young (about twenty-six when he attacked the Moncada barracks, thirty-two when he took power). The fighter-comrades who later became his cabinet members were more or less his age and with few exceptions were young intellectuals, often students—corresponding closely with the picture of the revolutionary elite that had emerged in the works of authors such as C. Wright Mills. Contrary to the textbooks of Marxism-Leninism, Castro had started not with theory (in which he never believed very much) but with action—and he had won by relying on spontaneity, sacrifice, and enthusiasm. He had proved that a very small revolutionary elite which believed in its mission could produce a popular and widely accepted government. Last but not least, Castro kept his distance from the Soviet Union, which was still burdened with the memory of Stalin and the invasion of Hungary (1956). Thus, Castro seemed to be the ideal revolutionary—and still more his friend, comrade, and emissary, Che Guevara, the dead hero from whom no disappointments were to be feared. Castro's popularity grew as the war in Vietnam increased critical sentiment within the United States and abroad against "American imperialism." In the summer of 1968 the German SDS sent thirty-nine of its members to a training camp in Cuba and dispatched a delegation to take part in the celebration of the Cuban national holiday.

There was disappointment, to be sure, when Cuba became a satellite of Moscow, but that development did not occur until the beginning of the seventies. In the midst of the sixties, when the New Left emerged in the West, there was no one among living leftists with whom it could identify more easily than the Cuban leader. Yet Castro's influence was surely not strong enough to explain the campus rebellion around the globe. There were other, more powerful, reasons.

MORATORIUM

Discontent with academic conditions was not a new thing in the universities in America and other countries. It was somewhat stronger during the sixties, but was not itself the main cause of student unrest.[10]

Everyone knows that we are experiencing a population explosion and that the proportion of young people grows especially fast. At the moment, three quarters of a billion people between fifteen and twenty-four years of age live on our planet, and among them the number of university and college students has grown dramatically, as can be seen in the following table.

COLLEGE STUDENTS THROUGHOUT THE WORLD
(By continents)

	1950	1960	1972
Africa	71,000	192,000	603,000
America (North and South)	2,657,000	4,292,000	12,179,000
Asia (excluding U.S.S.R. and China)	1,146,000	2,131,000	6,839,000
Europe (excluding U.S.S.R.)	1,280,000	2,061,000	5,857,000
Oceania	55,000	102,000	315,000
U.S.S.R.	1,247,000	2,396,000	4,630,000
Total	6,456,000	11,174,000	30,423,000

Note: In this table the Soviet Union is treated as a continent; the People's Republic of China is not included.
Source: Data taken from *UNESCO, Statistical Yearbook, 1966*, pp. 47–50; *1974*, pp. 89 f.

In the year 1950—historically speaking, this was yesterday—there were 6.5 million students in colleges and universities around the world; in 1972, 30.4 million young people were getting a college or university education. On the average they spent about 50 percent more time in the process than did earlier student generations. Half a century ago I finished my university studies in four years (three in Germany, one in the United States) and received the Ph.D. degree; today I would need between six and eight years. If we take, to simplify matters, an average of five college and university years per student, then the 30.4 million young people are spending a total of 152 million years in the universities. Some decades ago, a million of them studied four years, a total of only 4 million university years, or 2.6 percent of the present figure. These 152 million years are the truly new phenomenon of our time. They mean a profound and perhaps not sufficiently understood change in the social structure of mankind.

This change becomes even clearer when compared with earlier, pre-academic phases of human development. The phase between childhood and one's first job was very brief in primitive society; without much transition the child became a helper of the adults in hunting and farming. Often this transition was condensed into a brief act. The initiation was the opening to the next phase in the life of the individual. The study of initiation rites, begun by the French Jesuit Joseph-François Lafitau in the early eighteenth century among American Indians, has been developed systematically during recent decades; scholars have found that the rites symbolically preempted important aspects of the transition from childhood to adulthood, condensing a process of many years into an experience lasting a few weeks or even days.

Boys and girls were made to experience their transition dramatically and even painfully (sometimes through surgical operations). The intense interest the entire tribe took in the initiation indicated that it was considered a means for preserving stability. Especially the men wanted, whether consciously or unconsciously, to shorten the period of adolescence, and thereby the duration of youthful rebelliousness connected with it, by giving the boys a quasi-adult status as early as possible. If the initiations were tampered with by outside influences (by missionaries, for example, who defamed them as pagan), there could be serious disturbances to the relationship between the young and their parents, if not to the entire tribe.[11]

As civilization developed, the duration of adolescence increased, as did the number of initiation rites. In the West, we had until recently a whole lot of them—in Germany, for example, a cone-shaped box of candy on the first day of school, the first long pants on the day of confirmation, the ceremony of the first dancing lessons, the transition from apprentice to journeyman, high-school graduation, commencement, acceptance into a fraternity, acquisition of an academic degree, engagement before marriage. They all served to structure the lengthening period between childhood and the first job, clearly visible steps that led the individual deeper into existing society, thereby decreasing the clash of generations.

Within the short span of my lifetime, many of these Western rites have lost much of their significance; for example, academic gowns have become rare even on special occasions in German universities. Compared with a few generations ago, rites have gone out of fashion. They no longer serve, as they once did, to bring structure and order into the violent fluidity of adolescence; as a result, the natural forces of unrest remain unbridled and, in extreme cases, become devastating.

By this I do not want to say that the prolongation of adolescence should be considered merely a negative phenomenon. On the contrary, it also has a positive function in the evolution of young people. This has been stressed in the work of an eminent American psychologist and psychiatrist of adolescence, Erik H. Erikson, of whom we shall hear more when we come to the inner causes of youth unrest.

Erikson uses the key word "moratorium" for this period in the life of the young, and explains what he means by it with great clarity in his book about the young Martin Luther. The quiet years in the monastery were Luther's moratorium, a period of time in which childhood had been left behind and the future personality had not yet been formed, when Luther could mature and grow into the man he was to become.

This moratorium (from the Latin *mora*—deferment, pause), this time of waiting and maturing prior to the beginning of professional life, not only prepares a person for a future profession; it also gives time for thinking about oneself, one's character, one's plans. Never before have so many young people had such a long moratorium as our students today.

There are many examples of the moratorium being used for the purpose of self-analysis. One of them we found in the diary of the Berlin Commune 2; another I take from a letter recently written to me by a girl studying to become a social worker. During the previous semester she had read about psychoanalysis and group dynamics, she wrote, adding: "I have thereby been often confronted with my own neurotic conflicts. I feel that I no longer grow, that I have become rigid and inflexible. I am afraid of being carried away by my own feelings, and yet I would like very much to be spontaneous." And so on. This girl and many other students, both female and male, would not have had the time and stimulation to think so intensely about themselves if they had gone from school to full-time job immediately, without the moratorium.

This interval provides the young with the opportunity of looking at their peers, at society, at their environment in general. How this opportunity is being used can be seen from the rapid expansion of what one might call "problem subjects" at the universities. At New York University in 1958 there was one student of psychology to two students of history; in 1975, one student of history to four of psychology. In my student days, political science did not exist as a subject in German universities, and sociology was studied only by few. According to the UNESCO *Yearbook* for 1973, there are now 1.5 million students of the social sciences in sixteen countries (the United States and West Germany included). These sciences are, by their nature, critical: They measure present realities against the exalted ideas of the great thinkers and find the former wanting. The students, to take an example, learn what those thinkers have said about the ideal of equality; they compare it with what they see, they are disgusted, and they rebel. Kathleen Cleaver, in a TV interview in July 1976, said precisely this about the process of her radicalization at Oberlin College.

In addition, there is the snowball effect. Thousands of young people discover through their studies the weaknesses, problems, and mistakes (some say crimes) of society and, because they are young, feel called upon to act. Through them still others hear about the problems that make these studies so interesting, and thus additional thousands are encouraged to take up political science and sociology. It has been stated repeatedly that the students of these subjects were heavily represented among the militant leftists. In West Germany, among students of psychology, political science, and sociology, 31.7 percent, 33.5 percent, and 49.2 percent respectively were considered "very radical" in 1968. By contrast, the corresponding figures for students of biology and physics were only 19.0 and 23.6 percent, respectively.[12]

The general public finds the students' disputations and demonstrations barely comprehensible. It all sounds disturbing and dangerous, partly because of the jargon they use—who knows how many future Weathermen or SLA people might be among these students? Thus the gap grows between those within and those outside the campus. The Athenians knew what they were doing when they condemned Socrates to death; he had taught their sons to think and thus to question.

DÉTENTE INSTEAD OF COLD WAR

None of the causes mentioned so far can completely account for the dramatic change that took place on the campus in the sixties. What else had happened? In the fifties the Western world was sure of itself. At least its role was clear, as was the image of the enemy, and the Red bloc in the East. From East Berlin to Canton, even to Hanoi, more than a billion people—this was the big danger which threatened the nations of the West and against which they had to stick together. Those fifties were the days of Senator Joseph McCarthy and the House Committee on Un-American (i.e., Communist) Activities. But before the end of the decade, the image of the enemy began to lose its clear contours: President Eisenhower was host to Khrushchev (1959), and the "spirit of Camp David" promised reconciliation, coexistence, détente. This spirit was still to go through difficult periods of trial, what with the Berlin Wall (1961) and the Cuban crisis (1962), but the one side continued to talk with the other, the "hot line" was installed between Washington and Moscow, and the hottest of all armament problems was tackled with the agreement on the prohibition of aboveground nuclear testing. Obviously the two superpowers understood that in an era characterized by a "balance of terror" there did not exist any alternative to détente. Soon West Germany was taking its first step (1966) toward the treaties that would lead by the end of the decade to the full development of Bonn's *Ostpolitik*.

The Soviet giant also seemed no longer quite so threatening after the first cracks appeared in the Red monolith when—after the autumn of 1958—the symptoms of a serious quarrel with China became increasingly visible. Mao's Great Leap Forward unquestionably was also a leap away from the Moscow road. In October 1961 the quarrel could no longer be concealed; Chou En-lai left Moscow in a huff before the end of the Soviet Communist Party Congress. The Red world was now deeply split, and even in the Communist parties of Western Europe, which until then unhesitatingly had followed Moscow's lead, centrifugal forces were at work. After the leader of the largest Communist Party in the West, Italy's Palmiro Togliatti, proclaimed in his political testament (1964) the separate sovereignty of Communist parties, there were no longer just two centers in world affairs, the United States and the Soviet Union, but several. Even the Communist world had become polycentric.

As the image of the foreign enemy and the fear of McCarthy faded, the critical eyes of the young in the West turned from the distant U.S.S.R. to conditions in their own countries. To be sure, there was the mystique of Kennedy—but then he was murdered. As a guest at Harvard I happened to be in the same room with Henry Kissinger and some other faculty members when the news came over the radio. I shall never forget their shocked expressions, or the shock for many days to come in the faces of all Americans.

The glamour of the young president, the optimism he exuded, the willingness of the young to be carried away by his words ("Ask not what your country can do for you, ask what you can do for your country")—all this was suddenly gone. The young people who had been ready to storm into a bright future with Kennedy found themselves alone, without perspectives, dismayed and bereft of confidence in America, no longer willing to consider the defects of the country as passing phenomena. In those weeks of deep despondency a word was heard more and more often, and heard also in Western Europe, a word which was applied to everything (one's own future, one's country, the world as a whole), and it was . . . *shit*.

Those who had earlier criticized the American way of life, the Western consumer mentality, and who had not been listened to, now found support. During the Eisenhower era the sit-ins of the South, the fight for the Bancroft strip in Berkeley, would not have caused national excitement. What had then motivated small groups of extreme leftists was now suddenly mobilizing the campus. The Vietnam war, accepted earlier as part of the defense of freedom, was now condemned as an imperialist intervention against a foreign country. The structure and system of America had become questionable. Did Americans really still live in God's Own Country? No, No, No! Thus criticism turned first to rejection, then to open rebellion. In the United States this rebellion broke out less than a year after Kennedy's death, and shortly afterward in other Western countries, sparked everywhere by inner causes which had hardly been noticed before.

25
RED DIAPERS, JEWISH MOTHERS

THE American language is, like the Chinese, ingenious about putting old words to pithy new uses. Those who heard a few years age for the first time about the existence of "barefoot doctors" in China could guess that these were people without proper training in medicine who looked after the sick in the villages. And if one reads about "red diaper children," one can understand (with the aid of just a word or two of context) that these are young people who grew up as sons and daughters of left-wing, usually communist-minded (if not Communist) parents.

Jonah Raskin—in the story of his youth—has described just such a life story.[1] His parents, themselves children of Jewish immigrants from Eastern Europe, continued to live with the fear of pogroms in their bones. They were left-wingers, and atheists as well, without being members of the Communist Party, and brought up their children in a middle-class Left Jewish environment in Brooklyn, where the father was a lawyer. The execution of Ethel and Julius Rosenberg in 1953—condemned as betrayers of atomic secrets to the Soviet Union—made a profound impression on the Raskins. They lived in permanent dread of the FBI; the mere purchase of a copy of the Communist *Daily Worker* and later its destruction were deeds done with fear and trembling. After the paper was read, it was cut in small pieces and flushed down the toilet; even this was not the end of the drama, because at one time the drain was clogged and a plumber had to be called. In short, according to Jonah, in those years his parents and their friends were "neurotically paranoid in their fears of seen and unseen FBI agents."

After Stalin's condemnation by Khrushchev, the Raskin parents were disillusioned, unhappy, and without a political home, but they remained non-Party communists. When Jonah married in 1964, the wedding party sang the *Internationale*. His wife also came from a Left Jewish immigrant family.

In 1968, during the "Battle of Morningside Heights," young Raskin's sympathies were entirely with the SDS. But in order not to endanger his position as a professor at a nearby university, he participated only stealthily in the events at Columbia. This weighed on his conscience, and to prove himself he joined a demonstration along Fifth Avenue and smashed several windows at Saks, for which he was arrested and beaten. Time and again, personal and political matters converged for him, as for so many of his age-group. When he learned that his wife—during a trip to Cuba—had taken up with another man, he made the classic statement: "Your affair sours the revolution for me." The marriage was dissolved. The wife went over to the Weatherpeople, and Jonah was himself by then a member of SDS, but at the price of further pangs of conscience because, unexpectedly, a large part of the New Left had moved to a pro-Arab, anti-Israel position. He summarizes his and his friends' experiences in these words:

> In the sixties, the children of thirties radicals pushed their middle-aged parents into politics again. Maybe the parents were at first unwilling to march or protest again after so many years. But by demanding that their parents demonstrate, the children were applying their parents' own original values. In a true, historical sense they were thanking the old Leftists who kept alive the sparks of the thirties in the cold, cold fifties.

Many Americans look back nostalgically to the golden Eisenhower years. But for people on the Left these were above all the years of Joe McCarthy, "the Ice Age," or, as Raskin says, "the hour of the mole."

Numerous young people of the New Left have come from families of the Old. But they are not the rule. A German sociologist found that protesting young people came, in the majority, from homes with a "central philosophy of life," of "universalistic principles" (he mentions Trotskyism as an example).[2] Klaus Allerbeck summarizes American and German research in this connection by saying: "Those students are most likely to be radicals who can be radicals with the least amount of conflict between them and their parents."[3]

When talking with New Left people, I often asked about the political attitude of their parents; in the answers I have found a confirmation of the red (or pink) diapers hypothesis. Notions absorbed in the family have a long-term effect; they gradually become a channel into which the passions flow, once the young person has developed a strong political interest of his own. Pink then turns into red, red into deep red.[4]

This is true not only of the Left. In periods of excitement, young people easily try to surpass the political tendencies of their parents. Bruno Bettelheim, who knew the Germany of the twenties and the America of the sixties, wrote that during the rise of Hitler it was largely the children of conservative parents who served as the avant-garde of right-wing extremism; they

> felt a need to lay their bodies on the line for nationalist ideas their parents had only luke-warmly held. [...] In many ways rebellion represents a desperate wish by youth to do better than their parents in exactly those beliefs in which parents seem weakest.[5]

The opposite is also possible. For many children of right-wing parents—in Germany, and in Japan also—the pendulum swung far to the left. Under the influence of defeat, shame for the misdeeds of the fallen regime, and Americanizing reeducation, many of these young people had become, by the sixties, fanatical proponents of extreme democratization, or even turned into left-wing radicals. ("One of my nephews is with the Maoists," a member of an old noble family in Germany wrote in answer to a private poll I took.)

And what about the liberals? The liberal parents and the overwhelmingly liberal university faculty—in fact, the entire liberal section of the upper middle class—were torn and confused. Fundamentally, the young people demanded nothing except the realization of those ideals which their parents, their teachers, their social class had taught them to consider the essence of the American spirit. To that extent, the old generation sympathized with the young rebels while simultaneously being shocked by their vulgar methods. Yet, after all, these were their children, and the courage with which the rebels fought for their convictions, risking nightsticks and jail, impressed these adults and caused them to feel guilty for not having acted the same way when they were young.

Jonah Raskin's story is interesting for another reason. Himself the son of a lawyer, he had early discovered what was to puzzle

303

many observers later on: While the well-to-do students were radical, the poor ones were conservative and against the revolution. Whenever I asked young left-wing radicals about the social position of their fathers, the answer corresponded usually with what young Raskin had noticed and many sociological studies had found: The New Left and the entire left-wing movement of our time was made up predominantly of sons and daughters of families with good or high incomes. These were the ones who joined radical groups on the campus, who demonstrated, occupied buildings, and fought in the streets, while the sons and daughters of lower-income families wanted to study, graduate, and move on quickly into professional life and comformism.

To rebel against prosperity is easy, if one lives in the midst of it. Those, on the other hand, who are still in the process of getting there wish the creation and preservation of conditions that will help them along the road to wealth; they are more likely to follow politicians of the Right than of the Left. In polls of young people at the height of the campus unrest it was found that sympathy with George Wallace was expressed by far more nonstudents (25 percent) than by those enrolled in schools (7 percent). On the campus, in turn, the pro-Wallace vote was lowest in the schools of the social sciences and liberal arts (5 percent) and highest in the schools of engineering (17 percent). The sympathy with Wallace, who was regarded as a man of the Right, shrank as prosperity and liberal education increased.[6] Research in other countries produced similar results. For example, in Japan, the higher the position of the father, the more likely was left-wing involvement among the children.[7]

JEWISH MOTHERS

One last fact about Raskin is worth keeping in mind: He is Jewish. The high proportion of young Jews in America's extreme Left is obvious, and Jews themselves have discussed it frankly.

Much instructive material on this subject was presented in 1975 at Columbia's Research Institute on Political Change, in a seminar on radicalism in which I participated. I am indebted to one of the speakers, Stanley Rothman, a professor at Smith College, for data from a not-yet-published paper, and also to the journalist Stephen D. Isaacs for his book on the role of the Jews in American political life, which devotes a whole chapter to "Jews as radicals."

In 1967 a survey of "radical students" (a term not always uniformly interpreted) found that Jews comprised 61 to 66 percent of radicals in and around Chicago, 65 percent at Harvard University, 83 percent at Berkeley, and 93 percent at the University of Michigan. At the same time, Jews comprised a large proportion of the younger faculty; as a rule they felt a special attachment to Jewish students, many of whom belonged to the New Left.[8]

Left-wing tendencies of Jewish intellectuals are nothing new—from Marx through Trotsky and Rosa Luxemburg to Herbert Marcuse and Daniel Cohn-Bendit. The preponderance of Jews among the early Bolsheviks (before Stalin "liquidated" them) was frequently mentioned in Hitler's anti-Soviet and anti-Jewish propaganda. But rarely has Jewish radicalism been quite so apparent as in the New Left of the sixties. There are many Jews also among the dissidents in the Soviet Union (though some of them are not Jews: Solzhenitsyn, Sakharov, Bukovsky). Whenever the antiauthoritarians turn against totalitarianism (against the real one in the East, against the largely imagined one in the West), Jews are always present in remarkable percentages.

The reasons for this have been the subject of a great deal of thinking, especially among Jews. Here are some of the reasons most often mentioned (many of which are also controversial):

(1) The memory of the genocide inflicted by Hitler on the Jews, and hence their determination to attack everything that smacks remotely of fascism. As if by magic, Angela Davis was transformed into a Jewess on the road to Dachau (as Isaacs comments) and the war in Vietnam into Hitler's extermination campaigns.[9]

(2) Centuries of life in the ghetto, where the Jews, excluded from many professions, were occupied with interpretation of the Torah and the Talmud. This study demanded strenuous training of the mind and created a long intellectual tradition.

(3) The sufferings of their own people, which made them more sympathetic with and understanding of the sufferings of other people, especially other minorities (radical student groups or homosexuals, for example).

(4) The urge to find universalistic ideas in order to secure, once these ideas have been generally accepted, leadership for the Jewish minority over the non-Jewish majority. Rothman writes in his paper:

[The Jews'] supposed identification with the "underdogs" of the society is based less on identification with their suffering than upon a desire to use these [underprivileged] groups as a means for undermining the establishment. [...] In short, the aim of the Jewish radical is to estrange the Christian from society as he feels estranged from it.

(5) The preference for intellectual and dialectical contests, because of the Jews' lack of numbers and opportunity for success in other kinds of contests.

(6) The particularly strong cohesion of the family as defense against a hostile environment, with the result that the frequently left-liberal ideas of the parents have more time to affect the children (not to mention the close ties of young Jews to their mothers—the "Jewish mother" has a prominent place in recent American literature).

The Jews within the ranks of the New Left were thrown into a tragic and almost dead-end conflict after the Six-Day War between Israel and the Arabs in 1967. Their sympathy for the State of Israel, imbibed with their mother's milk, became a problem at the very moment when Israel, no longer weak and pitiable, began to show signs—to a remarkable extent—of a power policy emphatically refuted by the New Left. Israel had acted highly nationalistically and militaristically—in the vocabulary of the New Left, even imperialistically—inasmuch as it had taken pieces of territory from other states and was rejecting resolutions by the United Nations that it should evacuate them. As the New Left came into ever stronger opposition against American foreign policy, it began to look upon Israel as a tool of American imperialism and took the side of the Third World, which included millions of anti-Israel Arabs. Cohn-Bendit describes graphically, in the first chapter of his *Le Grand Bazar,* this spiritual torment in his own life; he replaced his former Jewish identity with a left-wing radical identity because he found Israel "fascistoid" and the young Israelis behaving like a new master race—he uses the Nazi word *Herrenrasse.*

Finally there emerged, much to the disappointment and pain of young Jews in the New Left, a conflict between them and the radical blacks, whom they had supported so energetically throughout the sixties, considering them their dependable allies. As the blacks fought the civil rights struggle more and more on their own, they displayed an increasing resentment of their erstwhile young white allies, who frequently were Jews. When bloody riots and fires exploded in black ghettos, the effects were felt by small Jewish merchants and craftsmen who had lived

there before the blacks came and had remained as unloved landlords and moneylenders. Jews who held high positions in American finance, politics, and communications media appeared to
many blacks as personifications of the hated Establishment. New
frictions emerged when thousands of blacks, especially young
ones, attached themselves to a new sect, the Black Muslims,
which turned them against all whites, whether Christians or
Jews. Stokely Carmichael exclaimed in a speech (1968): "We will
fight to wipe it [i.e., Zionism] out wherever it exists, be it in the
Ghetto of the United States, or in the Middle East." The newspaper *Black Power* (predecessor of the *Black Panther*) published
these lines in 1967:

> We're gunna burn their towns and that ain't all,
> We're gunna piss upon the Wailing Wall [. . .]
> That will be ecstasy, killing every Jew we see
> in Jewland.[10]

In the same year, one of the best-known black poets, LeRoi Jones,
who later changed his name to Imamu Baraka, published a poem
which attacked the Jews—a "dangerous germ culture"—in terms
rivaling those in the notorious Nazi *Stürmer*.[11]

It is easy to imagine the embarrassment and anguish this unexpected hostility brought upon Jews in the New Left. Still, the
majority remained under its Red flags. Conflicts of this kind explain in part why the most fanatical, Bernardine Dohrn among
them, joined the terrorist underground.

26
TEACHERS AND GURUS

IT may still be too early to name all the intellectual ancestors of the New Left; its ideas have been taken from many sources. For this chapter, however, I have selected seven men because of their considerable role in inspiring and teaching the young, thus contributing to the events of the sixties. What makes them especially interesting to a German observer is that six of them left Germany (or Austria) because of Hitler. Most of their works I have read first in English, some of them years before they were available in German.

FRANKFURT IN AMERICA: HORKHEIMER, ADORNO, AND MARCUSE

Max Horkheimer. Born in 1895, the son of a factory owner in Stuttgart, Germany, Horkheimer was one of the co-founders of the Institut für Sozialforschung (Institute for Social Research) at Frankfurt in 1923, and after 1930 was its director and driving force. The institute, one of the most influential academic creations of Weimar Germany in the field of social studies, soon had an international reputation. In 1933, when Hitler came to power, Horkheimer went to Switzerland; he lost his professorship in Frankfurt, and the institute was shut down by the Nazi authorities. In the following year Columbia University, in New York, offered him a haven; in 1941 he moved to southern California. His professorship was reestablished in Frankfurt in 1949. Shortly after the institute was reopened, Horkheimer became rector (president) of Frankfurt University. He retired to the south of Switzerland in 1958 and died there in 1973.

Theodor W. Adorno. Born in 1903, Adorno was the son of a Frankfurt wine merchant. He studied music in Vienna under Alban Berg, but returned to Frankfurt in 1928 and devoted himself primarily to the study of philosophy. He was a close friend of Horkheimer, although at that time he was not yet a member of the Institute for Social Research. He moved to England early in the Hitler period, and in 1938 to the United States. There he joined Horkheimer, whom he followed to California and, after the war, back to Frankfurt. He was appointed deputy director of the institute. In the autumn of 1969 he died of heart failure.

Herbert Marcuse. Born in 1898 in a well-to-do Berlin family, Marcuse studied philosophy under Heidegger, then one of the leading lights in Germany. In 1933 he became a member of the Frankfurt institute's branch in Geneva, and in 1934 he arrived in New York. Marcuse was the first among the institute's members to publish a book in English. This was his *Reason and Revolution,* which appeared in 1941 (German edition, 1962). It did not arouse much interest—1941 was the year of Pearl Harbor. During the war, Marcuse worked in Washington as a specialist on Germany in the Office of Strategic Services, a predecessor of the CIA, and for this he was later to be reproached repeatedly, especially by Soviet writers; he also did wartime work in the State Department. While at the Russian Research Institute of Columbia University he collected material for a critical analysis of the Soviet system, *Soviet Marxism,* published in 1958 (German edition, 1964). In 1954 he became a professor at Brandeis University, and in 1965 at the San Diego campus of the University of California.

All three of these men were Marxists. During the thirties and forties their Marxist position did not attract much notice in America, whose intellectuals at that time were mainly concerned with antifascism—that is, with fighting Nazism and, to a lesser extent, Italian Fascism—and in this respect American liberals and the three Germans were in full agreement. After the Second World War, during the height of the Cold War, America was no place to propagate Marxist ideas. The three Germans led rather withdrawn scholarly lives, glad to have found a quiet asylum; their names were known only to specialists. Horkheimer's *Eclipse of Reason* (1947) made no great splash. Adorno's *Minima Moralia* appeared only in German (1951); his main work, *The Authoritarian Personality* (1950), written with three co-authors, was carried along by the already declining antifascist wave and found a wider audience. Marcuse's philosophical publications and his book on Soviet Marxism at first became known mainly among specialists in philosophy and sovietology.

The breakthrough for the three men, especially for Marcuse, came in the sixties. Suddenly there was on the American campus a lively demand for books critical of the country's regime and society. The three men of the Frankfurt School were right there to offer proof that fascism was also a threat in the United States. They had started as critics of Hitler's National Socialism (which had a particular significance for them, as Jews), but life in America had widened their horizon and here they probed, with the aid of the "critical theory," industrial society in general (including that of the Soviet Union). If fascism was a product of mass society in industrialized countries, was it not incipient also in America?

H. Stuart Hughes, professor at Harvard and author of various books on the history of intellectual relations between Europe and America, believes that the three immigrants' experience of the American way of life decisively affected their thinking.

> In Europe it had been possible for intellectuals to protect their own lives from the inroads of popular culture. Shielded by the ramparts of traditional status and respect, they had been able to keep at a safe distance the grosser and more offensive manifestations of mass taste. With the move to America, these walls collapsed; a flood of vulgarity struck the new arrivals in the face. And, correspondingly, their mood became more embattled: what in Europe had been no more than "vague disdain" in the United States turned into an "elaborate loathing."[1]

Surrounded by a mass society where everybody was willing to do what all the others did, these men detected forms of social coercion which they believed might accomplish what Hitler had brought about by the threat and use of violence. Having seen symptoms of this evil also in the Communist East, they now looked for its roots beyond both capitalism and Communism, and found them in the *Verwaltete Welt* ("administered world") of today.

In the new climate of unrest, the books of the three men—so far more or less unnoticed—acquired popularity. *The Authoritarian Personality* proved especially seminal. When the research for this book was begun at the height of the war in 1944, anti-Semitism was still considered the most fertile ground for the growth of the authoritarian personality. But the rebels of the sixties adopted its theses for criticizing not only German but also American society. The book strengthened their arguments against the oppressive and coercive "fascistoid" character of present Western civilization. The New Left thus took many of its cues from a book which had been written two decades earlier on the basis of the European—and particularly the German—situation.

Proper understanding was also difficult because Adorno and his collaborators had to take into consideration the strong anti-Marxist attitude in America at the time when the book appeared in 1950. Consequently, they did not unfold the banner of Marxist socialism, nor did they frontally attack American society. Rather, by using their critical theory, they assaulted, anonymously as it were, the philosophy of pragmatism which dominated thinking in America.[2] In their earlier *Dialectic of Enlightenment,* Horkheimer and Adorno had shaken another pillar of the American way of life, the "culture industry." The products of Hollywood and other manifestations of American mass culture seemed to them a huge deception, an instrument for controlling the masses, a dangerous symptom of the decline of the human race into new barbarism. But years were to pass before the works of the men from Frankfurt were printed in large editions. The *Dialectic of Enlightenment,* first published in German in a small and almost unnoticed edition at Amsterdam in 1947, only appeared in a regular German edition in 1969, in English in 1972.

Thus the subterranean influence of these books among American and German intellectuals in the fifties, and among the cadres of the New Left on both sides of the Atlantic in the sixties, is all the more surprising. Martin Jay has described the history of the Frankfurt School and its strong influence in America; his bibliography lists fifty-nine English titles about the institute and its members, not counting their own books.[3]

The new teachings of the three men, while contradictory in many instances to the intellectual tradition of America, consorted well with the urges of rebellious youth. But this did not save Adorno from a sad fate. (Horkheimer, as we have seen, had retired in time.) Discarded by the radicals as an old fogy and bourgeois liberal who had remained far behind their rapid advance, Adorno was not spared the spectacle of his Frankfurt seminar—this temple of critical theory—being renamed Spartacus Seminar and occupied by leftist students. At one time, while his lectures were being seriously disrupted, some girls, in a defiant and provocative gesture, bared their breasts.

What the young people inherited from the Frankfurt School was the conviction that the leading forces in the various Western countries—a combination of business and government—had succeeded in completely manipulating and controlling the people by continuously arousing their desire for ever new consumer goods and by bending their minds in the desired direction with the help of the culture industry. Thus, any true individuality had been destroyed.

In the work of these authors the students found also a definition of their own place and role. Science itself, they learned, had become a decisive factor in production, and as a result the scholar's status was reduced to that of a proletarian, but a proletarian potentially more powerful than the worker (because society needed science and technology for the further development of economy and production) and therefore better able to change that society. This thought contributed to the confidence of the young intellectuals. During the radical phase of the rebellion Herbert Marcuse became its most influential intellectual promoter on both sides of the Atlantic. More strongly then Horkheimer and Adorno, he had linked Marxist sociology with the perceptions gained in psychology and, especially, psychoanalysis.

Marcuse's main thesis is this: If man is unfree with regard to exterior (political and social) forces, he is also unfree internally. Inner bondage grows, paradoxically, at the same pace at which man seems, in our prosperous society, to acquire more freedom because of growing income and shorter working hours. But this freedom is deceptive; man now feels that he needs ever more consumer goods, and to obtain these he becomes ever more dependent on those who produce them. Thus, instead of becoming freer with the help of more productivity, he in fact becomes less so.[4]

When youth exploded, the name of Marcuse was suddenly on everyone's lips. The number of books and articles written about him surpasses by far that of his own publications. In Soviet magazines alone, sixteen lengthy articles were published about him between 1968 and 1972.[5] One of his theses proved extraordinarily powerful—the thesis, hitherto unknown to a large audience, that the proletariat had been fully integrated into capitalist society and thus had lost its revolutionary potential. Marcuse developed

312

this thesis especially in his *One-Dimensional Man* (U.S. edition, 1964; German edition, 1967). Briefly Marcuse's argument is as follows: By a variety of oppressive measures man has become so manipulated that he can only move in one single direction, in one dimension; as a result he is no longer able to observe himself and the world and to contemplate his place in it. In modern industrial countries, high productivity and high living standards have created a situation in which hardly anybody wishes to change the regime by revolution, fearing that any such change might impair his own standard of living. Hence there exists a "collusion of business and labor."[6] The working class can be a revolutionary power only as long as it opposes the existing social order, and this the working class no longer does. Therefore the qualitative difference between it and the other classes had disappeared, together with its ability to create a qualitatively different society.[7] Because the proletariat is no longer a class capable of destroying capitalist society and replacing it by a better one, class struggle as Marx envisaged it has become a thing of the past.

If the proletariat no longer could play this role, on whom was one to put the hope for a revolution? According to Marcuse, on the "outcasts and outsiders, the exploited and persecuted of other races and other colors, the unemployed and the unemployable."[8] This hope did not sound very convincing, the less so as it was written on the book's next-to-last page, as if it were an afterthought. Although the students were not mentioned by Marcuse in this catalogue of potential revolutionaries, they found in his writings a historical and philosophical legitimation for their rising, and felt it was their task to take up the flag that the workers had abandoned and to carry it into battle. Later, Marcuse did assign to the students the role of a revolutionary avant-garde, especially in the first chapter of his *Counterrevolution and Revolt* (1972). There he describes the university as an institution for the training of "counter-cadres," ready to fight the existing system. He also names the methods to be employed in this fight: "unlimited general strike, the occupation and taking over of factories, government buildings, centers of communication and transportation, in coordinated action."[9]

Marcuse has, by his teachings, contributed to the "elitist" attitude noted in the New Left by many observers. He allots to the students an important task: to bring the "true" consciousness (which they are more likely to possess than others) to the masses, who are still captives of the "false" consciousness, and thus help the masses understand their "true" needs.[10] During an interview with *L'Express* (Paris) in the summer of 1968, Marcuse quoted John Stuart Mill's advice that educated people ought to have privileges on the basis of which they could direct the sentiments, behavior, and ideas of the uneducated masses. When asked whether they might lack the experience of public life necessary for political leadership, Marcuse answered: "Just because the students and intellectuals do not know their way through what is called politics today, they are the avant-garde. Under present-day conditions, political experience means nothing except experience in a deceitful and bloody game."[11]

Empty Hands. Many young people on the Left agree with Marcuse's diagnosis of the proletariat's integration into modern industrial society. But where does this leave them? If the "outcasts and outsiders," including the students, are too weak in numbers and weapons, who is their great ally? The "masses"? These can only be mobilized if they see a concrete aim for which they would be willing to risk life and limb. "Marcuse and his followers," according to a critical analysis at the height of the revolt, "have nothing to offer but the will to make revolution; they can clench their fists, but their hands are empty."[12]

Marcuse's hands were empty when students in West Berlin expected him to give them clear directions. In a four-day discussion at the Free University with professors and students in 1967, Marcuse was urged repeatedly to say what should be done after the overthrow of the regime—to name "concrete alternatives." The statement which he had made two years earlier (that "the society of the future [is] beyond definition and determination")[13] was not considered satisfactory. And now Marcuse himself was practicing the Great Refusal: It would not be scientific, he explained, to give "institutional recipes" at this time. When one of his Berlin colleagues wondered why Marcuse had not offered a "concrete program" to show "how political demands might be realized and positive political demands articulated and formulated," Marcuse merely expressed negatively what the future society should *not* have, namely, colonial wars, fascist dictatorships, underprivileged citizens. "This is all negatively formulated," he admitted, "but you have to be a *Vollidiot* [full idiot] not to see that a negative formulation includes the positive."[14]

If Herbert Marcuse was the "father" of the student rebellion, he has grown old with his child. In *Counterrevolution and Revolt* he is still angry with the Establishment and with society in general; he still demands the mobilizing of theoretical and practical reason for the purpose of change. But he also understands that *"the revolutionary force* which is destined to terminate this violence [i.e., the violence of the Establishment] *does not exist today."* [Emphasis supplied.] Therefore the "space of operation open to the militant Left is reduced to rigid limits," and this "force must be controlled and contained by the movement itself. Action directed toward vague, general, intangible targets is *senseless;* worse, it augments the number of adversaries." The slogan of the "hot summer" in France, he thinks, "led to idiotic actions of sabotage and destruction, mostly to the detriment not of the ruling class, but of the 'people.' " Therefore, he urges that the Left "learn how to *regroup after defeat* [...] to sustain the long process of education." And finally, in the last sentence of the book, comes the message hardest for youth to swallow: "The next revolution will be the concern of generations and 'the final crisis of capitalism' may take all but a century." [Emphasis supplied throughout.][15] In the German edition, "take all but a century" becomes "last longer then a century."

As the campus quieted down, the students' interest in Marcuse faded. I visited him at San Diego in the spring of 1973, when he was in his mid-seventies. The quiet and amiable old gentleman whom I found in his study had just a few years before been one of the most controversial figures in the intellectual and political life of America. An idol and guru of the Left, he had seemed to others a dangerous seducer of the young, an enemy of the country that had offered him asylum in bad times, whose hospitality he rewarded by inciting the young and employing people like Angela Davis. Now, as we crossed the campus on our way to lunch, the students barely noticed him.

C. WRIGHT MILLS AND THE "POWER ELITE"

The man who furnished empirical and historical support for the New Left theoreticians was neither a refugee from Germany nor a disciple of Marx and Freud. Charles (usually just C.) Wright Mills was a Texan of English and Irish Catholic heritage who used to say that his grandfather was dispatched in the true Wild West manner by a bullet. His first degrees were acquired at the University of Texas; he obtained a doctorate in sociology and anthropology in 1941 at the University of Wisconsin, and then taught at Columbia. In the fifties, he visited Europe, including

Eastern Europe and the Soviet Union, in 1960, Cuba. He died of heart failure in 1963, forty-six years old.

Although Mills had studied Marx, his research took him on a different road; he started not from economic but from sociological data, which led to studies of the holders of power in America. He evaluated data on 1,464 business leaders born after 1570 and deceased prior to 1936, 495 leading politicians since 1776, and 406 trade-union leaders.[16] From such individual studies he formed a collective portrait in *The Power Elite* (1956). Statistically, this book did not reveal anything sensational; as was to be expected, it showed that the larger part of the power elite came from the upper middle classes. Yet the main thesis had a strong impact because it clashed with the traditional picture held by Americans in the Eisenhower years. Contrary to the general assumption, Mills found that America did not have true pluralism, not a multitude of rival groups checking and balancing each other; rather, it had the power elite on the one hand, the mass society on the other. The mass society was steered by an elite of its own, but this was so splintered that it was unable to oppose the larger power elite, which operated in unison.

Mills came to a conclusion similar to that of Marcuse on the question of who, within the mass society, should lead the fight against the power elite: the intellectuals. They *should* lead, he maintained, but they did not do so; therefore he accused them of indolence, even of readiness to lend support to the power elite. In the end he put his hope on youth, on the New Left. His book (unlike Marcuse's early publications) came into wide notice right away because of its criticism of the power elite and, even more, of the intellectuals. Thus it helped prepare the ground for Marcuse.

ERIK H. ERIKSON AND THE CRISIS OF IDENTITY

Our next scholar from Germany is the psychologist Erik H. Erikson. We met him briefly when speaking about the importance of the "moratorium" in the life of young people. This man, who founded the modern "identity theory," was himself a bundle of confused identities. Erikson, born in 1902, the son of a Dane and a Jewess in Frankfurt, never knew his father, who left the young wife before their son was born. Erikson's mother soon married a pediatrician in Karlsruhe, Dr. Homburger, a devout Jew whom the boy took for his natural father. Later he learned that the identity in which he had grown up was not true. To the Jewish friends of his parents, the blond boy was a Gentile; to his schoolmates, a Jew. During the First World War he wanted to be a partriotic German, like most German Jews at that time, yet other Germans took him for a Dane (and Denmark, officially neutral, was in sentiment on the side of Germany's enemies). Who was he? A Jew? A German? A Dane? Having become estranged from mother and stepfather, he changed his name. Calling himself Erik H. Erikson (Erik's son) he made himself in a way his own creation: I the son of I (though in the middle initial his stepfather Homburger remained).[17]

After finishing the gymnasium in Karlsruhe, Erikson led, during the twenties, the life of a Bohemian artist (he sketched and especially like to print woodcuts). Those were the years of the second blossoming of the German youth movement (the first had come in the decade before the war), and Erikson partook of its spirit. On his *Wanderschaft* (the German word which he uses in his autobiography),[18] he carried Angelus Silesius and Lao-tse, Nietzsche and Schopenhauer in his knapsack.

After seven such years he became a teacher in a small private school in Vienna. There he met Anna Freud, daughter and assistant of the great psychoanalyst, through whom he entered the circle of her father. When he married, he took a wife from a distant continent, a Canadian girl. After Hitler came to power in 1933, the Eriksons moved first to Denmark and then to the United States, where on arriving Erikson called himself an immigrant from Denmark, thus separating himself from the flood of Jewish refugees from Germany. He now had to learn a language which previously he had barely known. When working as a psychoanalyst among children of the Sioux and Yurok tribes, he again encountered "his" problem: They were no longer Indians but not yet U.S.–Americans.

Small wonder that Erikson was constantly plagued by the question "Where do I really belong?" He lived, as he put it himself, on the "border line between neurosis and adolescent psychosis."[19] Almost all his books reflect this central problem of his life.

Intense preoccupation with himself made Erikson aware of the importance of his seven years of vagabondage. During that time he had enjoyed a prolonged adolescence without any obligations, a "moratorium," as he was to call it, a period of waiting, and he understood what this meant for the development of young people. Later on he was to study and describe in a much-read book young Luther's "moratorium" (the time in the monastery) on the road to identity. Identity and moratorium—these themes have dominated Erikson's work.

Erikson came to the conclusion that the study of identity was "as strategic in our time as the study of sexuality was in Freud's."[20] This may be an exaggeration, but nobody doubts that he himself had found, after long uncertainty, his identity. The shock of not being the *son* of Homburger receded as he became the *father* of a widely accepted new theory, that of identity. Young Luther had found his identity in his violent spiritual struggle against his great enemy, the Pope (in which process he converted half of Europe to Protestantism); in a similar way Erikson transcended his identity crisis by making his contemporaries identity-conscious. Erikson's doctrine is constantly being confirmed all around us. Millions of blacks in the United States have become different people since they began to accept and even to confirm their black identity ("Black Is Beautiful"). Whatever else the differences may be between the Chinese of 1920 and those of today, the decades of Maoism have given them a new identity.

ERICH FROMM AND WILHELM REICH

Erich Fromm, born in 1900 in Frankfurt, came from the school of psychoanalysis, like Erikson, and has been close to the Institute for Social Research in his native city, like the first three men discussed in this chapter. Later he freed himself from both these influences. After Hitler came to power, Fromm emigrated to America. His *Escape from Freedom* appeared in 1941, just at the time when Americans were trying to understand what Hitler was all about. Fromm compared Luther's and Hitler's impact on the masses; prior to the success of each, he said, a world had fallen apart (medieval Germany in the case of Luther, imperial Germany in the case of Hitler) and the firm values once existing in that world had vanished—people were desperately seeking security in submission to a new idea. Protestantism, according to Fromm, was the answer to the needs of people in the sixteenth and seventeenth centuries who had lost their bearings and had to find their way through a new and unaccustomed world. Approximately the same thing happened to the Germans when their bourgeois world collapsed during and after the First World War; they were ready to submit to a new authority if it would offer them security and an end to doubt. Many young people understood Fromm's message as a warning that other nations too, including America, could in a similar situation choose escape from freedom and flight into fascism.

Wilhelm Reich was born in 1897 of Jewish parents in Galicia, then part of Austria-Hungary.[21] In 1911 his mother committed suicide, apparently after his father had learned through the boy about the mother's affair with his tutor. The father died in 1914. Reich fought on the Austrian side in the war and afterward went to Vienna, where he studied medicine, turned to psychoanalysis, and, touched by the poverty of many of the patients he met, studied Marxism and founded in 1928 a socialist society for sexual counseling and research. In 1930 he moved to Berlin and joined the Communist Party. He was expelled shortly before Hitler came to power because the Party, in its search for respectability, was afraid that Reich was compromising it by his loud preoccupation with sexual issues. Next he lost his membership in the International Society for Psychoanalysis because its leaders feared being compromised by his Communist taint.

Reich emigrated, first to Scandinavia and in 1939 to the United States. We have heard earlier about his ideas on sex and their influence in the mid-sixties.

Now he was occupied, predominantly and to the point of mania, with the search for a central life-energy which could be scientifically measured; he called it the orgone and established a private research institute in Maine to pursue his theory. Accused of quackery, he refused to appear in court and was condemned to two years' imprisonment. He died in 1957 while in prison. A few years later, his disgrace forgotten, Reich had become the guru of the sexual revolution.

Leaving Mills aside, one can see in the arrival of these six men on the American youth scene and in their impact on America (and from there back to Germany and other countries) a remarkable example of the interplay and migration of ideas and actions across the borders of countries and even continents. Here, without wanting to or knowing it, Hitler contributed to the rise of the New Left.

27
ANARCHISM AND PURE DEMOCRACY

ONreturning from Paris in May 1968, I gave my students in Aachen an analysis of the political philosophies I had noted among the French rebels. Beginning with anarchist ideas, which I had found particularly prominent, I briefly sketched the development of anarchism, beginning, as we do with so many subjects, "The ancient Greeks. . ." for it is from them that we took not only the word (*an*, not; *arche*, government, rule; hence *anarchia*, nongovernment, nonrule), but also the idea. The first anarchist thinker, Zeno, believed that a harmonious society without any kind of rule from above was desirable and possible. From Zeno I continued on down the line to the anarchists of the nineteenth and twentieth centuries, quoting passages from the writings of Max Stirner, Pierre-Joseph Proudhon, Mikhail Bakunin, Piotr Kropotkin, Henry Thoreau.

While speaking, I noticed growing unrest, saw surprised faces, questioning eyes, eager note taking. During the ensuing discussion the students confessed that previously they had had little knowledge about anarchism and were amazed to find so many anarchist ideas, which they now identified as such, corresponding with their own revolutionary thinking. They were especially fascinated to discover in the writings of the nineteenth-century anarchists many formulations that helped them to clarify the uneasiness they had felt with regard to Marxism and Soviet Communism.

In France the anarchist tradition had never quite disappeared.

ANARCHISM AND PURE DEMOCRACY

The students there were thus somewhat ahead of their German comrades; the small but powerful book on anarchism by Daniel Guérin, for example, was published in France in 1965, but did not appear in a German edition until the spring of 1968. Even in Paris, however, few of the students who spray-canned anarchist slogans on the walls of the university had read any of the anarchist classics; they had come to anarchism not through study but spontaneously. Their most effective spokesman, Daniel Cohn-Bendit, thought at the time that "perhaps" some of the rebels had read Bakunin. Yet the ideologues in the Soviet Communist orbit regarded Cohn-Bendit and most adherents of the New Left (together with Mao's followers) as anarchists. Wolfgang Harich, one of the leading ideologues of East Berlin, accused Cohn-Bendit specifically of anarchism and wrote sarcastically: "This nice old granny [i.e., anarchism] is now almost a hundred years old, but with the new Paris makeup of 1968 on her wrinkles, she looks almost young, especially since she continues to consider sex to be more important than politics."[1] As anarchism has never been victorious in any country, it has in the course of time been completely overshadowed by the far more successful rival ideology of Marx and Lenin. For decades people neither knew nor thought much about it. Now, just a few years after the Paris May, one may find books on anarchism in most libraries and in cheap paperback editions.

Today it is no longer possible to reconstruct the thoughts that were rumbling in the brains of the Paris students ten years ago. If they had been polled then, the result would, I think, have been surprising: If asked to name their favorite *ideologues,* they would have mentioned Marx, Engels, and Lenin infinitely more often than Bakunin or Kropotkin, who might not have come up at all. But if they had been given a list of political *doctrines* of leading left-wing ideologues, without the names attached, I suspect that the students would have marked with approval the teachings of the anarchists far more frequently than those of other ideologues.

For those who are interested in the struggle of ideas, it is fascinating when ideas are personified in historical figures, especially if these persons, as was the case with Karl Marx and Mikhail Bakunin, have actually met and clashed in real life—a spectacle worthy of a playwright's pen. The fight between these two men and the ideas they represented was all the more exciting because they had the same aim and the same enemy.

Their lifelong struggle confirms what we know from intellec-

321

tual history (from the Thirty Years' War, for example): The sharpest conflicts are fought between those who wish to realize the same ideas but are going along totally different roads. Bakunin, with his impetuous yet magnanimous nature, was more inclined to speak out frankly. (If no other source is given, I am referring to the Stuke edition of Bakunin's works,[2] translation and emphases are mine.) In a letter of January 1872, Bakunin wrote about Marx, "He wants what we want, the total triumph of economic and social equality, but . . ."

It was this "but" that separated the two men and their two worlds. The sentence continued: "[Marx wants this triumph] in the state and *through state power,* through the dictatorship of a very strong and so to speak despotic provisional government, which means, through the negation of freedom. His economic ideal is the state as the single owner of land and of any kind of capital." Bakunin himself and his friends continued to want the same, but

> *through the liquidation of the state* and of everything that can be called legal rights and what, according to us, constitutes the permanent negation of the human right. We want the reconstruction of society [. . .] not from above down, with the help of some kind of authority and of socialist officials, engineers, and other public scholars—but from below up through the free federation of workers' associations, free from the yoke of the state.

In reading these words, one should remember not only Marx (and Engels), but also Lenin, Stalin, and Brezhnev. Then one will agree with the words of Bakunin that directly followed: "As you see, there could hardly be two theories more opposed to each other than our theories are." Marx and his successors could have answered: We too wish the state and its apparatus to wither away. But only later, because after the victory of the revolution we need at first a strong state.

We have now reached the decisive point of the controversy. Bakunin was convinced that freedom must be granted during the revolution and after the revolution, *immediately and at any price,* because otherwise it would be lost for a long, long time. If the revolutionaries prior to their victory established a firm authoritarian organization, then the society to be established after the revolution would also become authoritarian. In the statement of a group close to Bakunin it was said: "How can an egalitarian and free society emerge from an authoritarian organization? That is impossible. Our group, the embryo of the future human society, must be even now the true image of our principles of freedom and federation and must discard every principle which leads to authority and dictatorship."[3]

Bakunin coined this powerful sentence in 1866: "Put the most sincere Democrat on the throne; if he does not leave it immediately he will become infallibly a scoundrel." Bakunin did not leave behind a systematic theoretical structure. But increasingly he hammered into the brains of friends or foes his fundamental thesis about rule leading to misrule. He demanded the abolition of any "centralizing and domineering state," the "absolute destruction of every state, every church, of all religions, political, bureaucratic, legal, financial, police, economic, university, fiscal institutions." Bakunin understood quite rightly that there lurked within Marxism the danger of an "authoritarian system of oppression"; he prophesied that Marx's communism (which Bakunin called "state communism") could transform all workers into "wage workers of the state" because this kind of communism, "instead of diminishing state power would increase it by concentrating all power in the hands of the state." He was enough of a visionary to predict "that the system of Marx [...] would lead to the rule of an intelligent minority which alone is able to comprehend the complicated issues unavoidable as a result of centralization, and consequently to the slavery of the masses and to their exploitation through this intelligent minority." Many of these ideas can be found in the speeches and writings of the two leading rebels of 1967 and 1968, Dutschke and Cohn-Bendit. And did not Kuroń and Modzelewski say the same thing, decades after the establishment of a Communist regime in their native Poland?

One is reminded of the long feud between the two Red giants, the Soviet Union and China, when Bakunin in his letter "To the Spanish Brothers" argues that Marx's system would lead "directly to the establishment of new big nation states, which are separate and necessarily rivals and enemies of each other," and that it would end in "the negation of internationalism." Isn't that exactly what happened on both sides of the Sino-Soviet border?

Freedom! Bakunin urged it ceaselessly. In a letter of 1868 he warned: "Nothing that is alive and human can exist outside of freedom. A socialism which expels freedom from its midst, and which does not accept freedom as the sole creative principle and foundation, would lead us back directly to slavery and bestiality."

"NONSENSE," MARX SAID

Bakunin's writings are full of maxims such as these: "We are the natural enemies of such revolutionaries—future dictators, rule makers, and brow beaters [who], even before the revolution has produced a good and healthy disorder, are scheming about how to end it and how to put a muzzle on the people; [who] would again condemn the masses to discipline, immobility, and death by handing them over to slavery and exploitation by a new quasi-revolutionary aristocracy. [. . .] The revolution, as we understand it, must destroy completely and from the first day the state and all state institutions." Freedom is "the uprising of the human individual against *any* divine human, against *any* collective and individual authority."[4]

"Nonsense," Marx said to all this.[5] But those who remember the outbreak of antiauthoritarian sentiment among the rebels of the sixties can understand that for many of them Bakunin's "nonsense" struck a very responsive chord.

What Bakunin was against is clear—but what was he for? He refused a binding answer categorically, and he did it again in the name of freedom. Bakunin thought that to set up rules and regulations for the development of the revolution, as Marx did, constituted "interference with the wealth and spontaneity of life which enjoys endless possibilities; and what is worse, such rules would be in contrast to the very principle of freedom." And this: "I hate communism because it is the negation of freedom."[6] He bitingly attacked the "dilettantes and philistines of science" who insisted that "without a well-prepared plan of construction one should not be destructive," and he also attacked those who invented all kinds of plans, "only the devil knows for whom and why."

All this did not prevent Bakunin from sketching in rough outline a picture of the future life among free people, of their labor and wages. He envisaged the factories as belonging to the workers employed there (i.e., not to the state, as in Soviet Communist countries), and these workers as organizing themselves in local associations, several of them uniting into larger ones, and so on upward. He also thought about the formation of locally elected councils (in Russian, *soviety*) which would unite in ever higher territorial councils up to the council for the whole country. One might interject: This is what Lenin also wanted! But the fact is that Lenin emasculated the Russian soviets the moment they had shown themselves capable of a life of their own. He submitted them to the dictatorship, not of the proletariat, but of his highly disciplined party and police.

Were one to examine Bakunin's blueprints in greater detail, one would find many contradictions. We can omit these from our discussion because for the youth of the sixties the appeal of anarchism lay not in one detail or another, but in its overpowering call for freedom, for struggle against all authorities—a call rarely sounded with such vigor either before or afterward. It was this antiauthoritarian tone which captivated the young people and made them overlook some of Bakunin's macabre predictions.

Bakunin, while appreciating the role of young rebels as the avant-garde of a better future, was quite aware of the dangers involved should they claim leadership on this road. He warns of "circles" in which they might band together, and we certainly know many groups (down to the Weathermen and the Baader-Meinhof gang) whom Bakunin could have had in mind. He wrote, not without sarcasm, in 1869 (almost a century before the epidemic fragmentation of groups on the extreme Left) of

circles which consisted exclusively of young doctrinaire conspiratory socialists and bookish revolutionaries who intoxicate themselves in their self-conceit and in their mostly empty although passionate words, who are caught not in actions but in words and who [...] are condemned to powerlessness, because strength and actions one can find only among the people and there is a gap between them and the people. These are our cabinet revolutionaries, the supporters of a strong state and of future dictators, the lovers and spokesmen of a youth which stands outside the ranks of the people [...]. They play at revolution but have absolutely no means to start one [...]. They are not lacking in plans; their plans are full of passion, their self-deception and arrogance tremendous, but their strength is zero.

"So far, so good," some readers might say. "Quite a man, this Bakunin. Then why is the world so nervous about him and the anarchists?" The answer is simple, and those who know the history of Europe in Bakunin's day do not have to search far for it. Bakunin was a man of more than revolutionary words. Whenever he saw a chance to promote an uprising—in Russia (where he called on his adherents to unite with robbers) and in Germany, Austria, France, Italy—he was right there, a powerful speaker, a formulator of programs, a fighter on the barricades. During the rebellion in Saxony in May 1849 he was arrested and twice condemned to death. He escaped execution because the tsar demanded his extradition and then commuted his sentence to seven years in prison.

Since the great hours of revolt were rare, Bakunin recommended other means for normal times ("poison, dagger, the noose, etc."—the "etc." meaning primarily the bomb), because "the revolution sanctifies everything that is done in this struggle. The field is open!" He approved the use of violence against the state of Napoleon III and his officials "from the mayors to the judges, to the clergymen, and down to the foresters."[7] One may well doubt that Bakunin was actually ready to kill a forester with his own hands. But violence as such corresponded to his temperament, which was boundless—and anarchistic. It was a personal confession when in an 1842 article, "The Reaction in Germany," he wrote the famous words: "The joy of destruction is a creative joy."

"DAGGER, RIFLE, DYNAMITE"

Prince Piotr Kropotkin, Bakunin's countryman, was called "the gentle revolutionary." He spent three years behind bars in France because of words only. But his words were unmistakable and echo to this day. He appealed to the students: "Go on studying at the expense of society—but do not let them make you into instruments of exploitation!" Of parliaments he said that they had become the instruments of the rulers, and that therefore it was necessary to snatch freedom from them by "extraparliamentary agitation."[8] In the choice of methods Kropotkin did not remain much behind Bakunin. In his review *Le Révolté* (1880), he wrote: "Our action must be the permanent revolt, by word and writing, *by dagger, rifle, dynamite* . . . all that is outside of legality is good for us." [Emphasis supplied.] He also called to the proletarians: "In a world such as ours you cannot be considered as decent men by everybody. Either one is a thief, murderer, arsonist on the side of the oppressors and gluttons, or one is a *thief, murderer, arsonist* on the side of the oppressed, exploited, suffering and hungry. [Emphasis supplied.] It is up to you, you undecisive, fainthearted cowards, to make the choice."[9]

There were plenty of determined people at the anarchist congress in London in 1881. Their resolution: "Legality must be left behind in order to carry our actions into illegal territory."[10] Many had not waited for this call; we know that Bakunin's and Kropotkin's fatherland was resounding with bomb explosions, and that one tsar was assassinated during the same year. In the rest of Europe, crowned heads and state presidents were also trembling.

The German emperor, Wilhelm I, who had survived two attempts on his life, would have been the victim of a third (at the dedication of a national monument in 1883) if rain had not extinguished the fuse of a bomb. The assassin, a printer by the name of August Reinsdorf, explained his action to the court as a true anarchist: "For a noble purpose [the liberation of mankind] the individual must be prepared to fall; the end justifies the means." He called his attempt "propaganda by action" and ended: "I have nothing more to say, do what you like. If I had ten heads, I would with joy put them on the block for the same cause."[11]

Reinsdorf was not alone. His friend Johann Most, who at that time lived in America, regretted in the anarchist paper *Freiheit* that the attempts on the emperor's life had failed; otherwise, "this would have been the most glorious event in the history of our country."[12] Most was later to change his mind about terrorism; but even in 1883, he and Reinsdorf should have known who would actually profit from terrorist actions. Five years earlier, when an attempt was made on the life of Wilhelm I, forcing the old gentleman for many months into a painful convalescence, the population was enraged and Parliament passed a severe antisocialist law.

Much damage was done to the cause of anarchism in 1869 when a young Russian admirer of Bakunin, Sergei Nechayev, had one of his own terrorist group killed for not unconditionally obeying orders. This event was used by Dostoevski as material for *The Possessed* (1872), a novel which increased the abhorrence for anarchist conspirators. When in 1894 the anarchist Emile Henry threw a bomb into the Café Terminus in Paris, killing two people and injuring twenty, the reaction was one of loathing.

The anarchists hoped to weaken and eventually to destroy the existing power machine of the state by constantly threatening its representatives, large and small; they tried through provocations to force the government to hit back brutally and then unleash a counterterror which would make it hated among the people. But the hope of winning a nation for the revolution by bombs and by declarations about the "joy of destruction" has not been fulfilled. Neither the upper and middle classes nor the working class will have anything to do with terrorists. The only accomplishment of the anarchists has been to prepare the ground for others, for people like Lenin or Mussolini.

This weakness of the anarchists was constantly pointed out by their bitterest enemies, the Marxists. Bakunin was Marx's most serious rival—even in his own family. Both sons-in-law of Marx were anarchists for a considerable period; in November 1882,

327

Marx expressed his disgust in a letter to Engels: "Longuet as the last Proudhonist and Lafargue as the last Bakunist, *que le diable les emporte* [may the devil take them]."[13] The deeply rooted aversion of the anarchists for any disciplined organization of their supporters (which would re-create within their own ranks the hated rule from above) put them at a disadvantage in their quarrel with the Marxists. They battled constantly on two fronts: not only on the Right, against the government, but also on the Left, against the Marxists, and in the process they were always pulverized. In two revolutionary eruptions of our time, Marx defeated Bakunin: in the Russian Revolution, when Lenin "liquidated" his erstwhile anarchist allies, and in the Spanish Civil War, when the pro-Moscow Spanish Communists won out over the Spanish anarchists, only to be beaten in turn by Franco.

There is no need to speak in detail about other leaders of classic anarchism, just a few words about an Italian and a German anarchist.

Enrico Malatesta, the Italian anarchist who outlived all the classic anarchists, said in his eulogy for Lenin: "His aim was right, but he became a tyrant and smothered the Russian Revolution. During his life we have not venerated him, in his death we cannot grieve for him. Lenin is dead, long live liberty."[14] Instead of liberty there came Stalin, and liberty has not come to life in Bakunin's land to this day.

The leading German anarchist, Max Stirner, refused to be a political leader. His motto was *Mir geht nichts über mich* ("For me nothing is more important than myself"). And even if he had wanted to, he could not have been a leader of German workers. They prefer order to anarchism and like solid men at their head, such as the longtime socialist leader August Bebel, and solid organizations, such as the Social Democratic Party. As a result, the German workers were heartily disliked by Bakunin, who never had a kind word for these non-anarchists.

Anarchism found its most fertile ground in the country which Bakunin had reached only by letters and messengers—Spain. Large and durable anarchist organizations were founded there in close connection with the trade unions. The other countries with anarchist traditions are Portugal, France, Italy, Argentina, and Bulgaria.

The age-old dilemma of freedom versus order was solved neither by the anarchists nor by the Marxist Communists. The first offered freedom without order, the latter the opposite. We know from Russia what happens when those who win bring discipline without freedom. Mao has seriously tried to keep discipline while dispensing with fixed hierarchies. But his is a special case, and judgment would be premature.

The absence of domination of the many by the few is an old and noble ideal of mankind; it has sparked more than one religious or political movement. But our task cannot be, in the name of this ideal, to undermine and overthrow by violence the democratic system, which guards, though imperfectly, our liberties and is still the best in existence, despite obvious flaws. Rather, we must combat the growing general trend in mass society toward manipulative and oppressive measures, toward controlling people's lives, and must widen that area of life which is free of domination.

PURE DEMOCRACY?

Those among the young rebels who understand that anarchy is not a viable state structure are by no means satisfied with the existing one. They have demanded and they still demand a democracy which they describe by the adjectives "true," "pure," "primary," "direct," or "participatory." Among these, "direct" and "participatory" best suggest what they have in mind. Every member of the community should participate directly in each one of its decisions; in principle, there should be no administrative body between the will of the citizens and the realization of that will. This would be democracy in its pure form.

Personally I have experienced this kind of democracy only once, between the autumn of 1945 and the summer of 1946, at Kiangwan camp, a few miles outside Shanghai. In this camp, at the end of the Second World War, 350 Germans residing in the great city were interned (myself among them) until the U.S. troop transport ship *Marine Robin* took us to Germany.

Kiangwan camp was administered by Nationalist Chinese officials and guarded by Chinese soldiers, but apart from that we took care of ourselves. The entire inner conduct of the camp, even the kitchen, was in our own hands. All decisions were made by the camp community as a whole. There were questions to be solved all the time—the purchase of provisions, hygiene, school (there were many families among us)—and as the entire community could not be in constant session, it elected a camp council consisting of seven persons, each of whom had his or her special tasks. But this camp council was not a "representative" body in the sense that it had power of its own and could decide matters in place of the other camp members. The seven council members lived in cramped quarters together with all the others, in constant contact with those who had elected them. The council's activities were "transparent," well known to all the others, and constantly discussed by one and all. The frequent meetings, open to every inmate, including teenagers, were usually visited by a majority of the internees; they came if for no other reason than the lack of other entertainment.

During the last weeks before our departure for Germany, meetings were held every few days, sometimes several meetings on a single day, because of the large number of questions the internees had to settle among themselves and also with the Chinese camp administration on the one hand and the U.S. military authorities responsible for our transportation on the other. In addition to our group, practically all the Germans formerly resident elsewhere in China were now brought to Shanghai. For the captain and the military commander of the *Marine Robin,* its crew, and the platoon of soldiers as a guard, it was an unaccustomed matter to be transporting thousands of civilians—men, women, and children—over the thousands of miles from East Asia to Western Europe. Naturally, it was not their intention to make the month-long voyage a pleasure trip for the Germans, yet they did not want to have more trouble with this operation than was necessary, and they were willing to accept our cooperation in preparing for and carrying it out in an orderly manner.

Even today, from the perspective of more than three decades, I find that our camp's tiny "direct democracy" stood the test. Many of the best ideas for the solution of arising problems came from the meetings. No doubt it was a big help that many professions were represented among the internees and that, where the children were concerned, we had the benefit of the mothers' experience.

Our method of self-government had satisfied the Chinese camp officers so much that they suggested to the commander of the *Marine Robin* that it be practiced also during the trip to Bremerhaven. Thus, the direct democracy of our "Shanghai 350" was extended to the rest of the Germans who were being shipped home. There was, of course, no room on board big enough to hold plenary meetings of some 3,500 people, but the commander let us use the public address system; thus, the questions which had to be discussed could be piped to all holds of the ship, where they were debated in smaller groups until, finally, clear majority opinions were reached.

In later years, as I met former Kiangwan internees in Germany or overseas, they emphasized how much they liked to remember

330

that painful year in the camp and on the troop ship, when they had been bolstered by the knowledge that they were participating in the decisions on all questions concerning them. The kind of democracy that developed at Kiangwan spontaneously and without any political science textbooks created a feeling of satisfaction among those who experienced it.

Of course, our direct democracy was favored by the fact that all of us had only one aim: We wanted to get back to Germany with our families in good health, the belongings in our few suitcases intact. To be sure, differences of opinion arose among the repatriates on some questions, but under the guns of the Chinese first and the Americans afterward, our options were limited. There would have been serious disagreement if some of the internees had advocated seizing the camp commander or the captain as hostages! But we had no such crazies among us. Thus, there was no basis for the formation of "parties" with sharply divergent opinions.

Ours was a very modest model of a pure democracy, but it functioned, and thereby it demonstrated the conditions under which a pure democracy can be expected to function. First, the number of the participants must be small (350 in Kiangwan was the ideal figure, 3,500 on the *Marine Robin* a bit too high). Second, the environment must favor the formation and consolidation of the community (there is nothing more uniting than a hostile environment). Third, one must agree in principle about the aim toward which one is moving and also about the road leading there (which excludes serious disturbances by militant minorities). Fourth (and this is especially important), one must have sufficient time for extended discussions. Direct democracies based on these four conditions have existed in the American and German SDS organizations, among students who occupied university buildings—where they not only held their meetings with hardly an interruption, but also ate and slept—and in the kibbutzim, which as defense and work villages with an elite population meet the four conditions to a high degree.

Jean-Jacques Rousseau has gone down in history as the father of modern democracy. He propagated democracy in its pure form and refused to entertain any idea of separation of powers or the transfer of even part of the plenary assembly's sovereignty to elected representatives. He condemned the English system by explaining that there the citizens were free only on the day on which they cast their votes for their members of Parliament, after which they returned to their habitual servitude. In reality,

England at that time, in its many forms of self-government, was practicing far more democracy then Rousseau knew. The English people, and soon afterward the newborn American nation, had obtained their democracy not so much by reference to grand ideas à la Rousseau, but rather by insisting on quite pragmatic demands, such as "No Taxation Without Representation." It was thus that the British Parliament unseated the Stuarts, with their bent for absolutism, and the English settlers in America acquired their independence.

It was a great American, Thomas Jefferson, who, more than others, insisted on instituting participatory democracy by dividing the country into small autonomous "wards," where people were sufficiently close to know each other and to rule themselves. The wards, which he called elementary republics, and the higher units—the county republics, the state republics, and the republic of the Union—were to form a gradation of authorities, very much like the system of soviets was meant to be but never was. It was also Jefferson who exclaimed in his famous statement in a letter from Paris, November 13, 1787: "God forbid we should ever be twenty years without such a rebellion" as the one that had just occurred in Massachusetts, for "the tree of liberty must be refreshed from time to time, with the blood of patriots and tyrants," this blood being its "natural manure." Thus Jefferson anticipated Russia's soviets of 1905 and 1917 as well as Mao Tse-tung's idea about the need for frequent revolutions *after* the victory of the Revolution in order to prevent the petrification of the postrevolutionary structure.

But the United States was little known on the European continent in those faraway times. It was not from America but from England that the greatest German reformer of the nineteenth century, Freiherr von Stein, received his inspiration for bringing about the renewal of Prussia (and the eventual defeat of Napoleon) through the granting of self-government in the lower levels of administration as the first step toward a German democracy. The process that he started was not completed. The democratic system established in 1919 suffered from structural weakness, and also from the fact that it was looked upon by very many Germans as having been imposed on them by the victorious enemies at the end of the First World War.

"ALL POWER TO THE SOVIETS!"

After the First World War, when the Left was looking for a viable new system to substitute for the existing one, again it was a foreign model that attracted German thinking. This time the model was taken from Russia. The soviets (councils) had arisen spontaneously in the unsuccessful revolution of 1905 and had helped Lenin come to power in the Bolshevik Revolution of 1917. The idea was that the soviets, elected by the people of individual factories, villages, and army units, would combine step-by-step in higher and higher councils up to the Supreme Soviet. But when Lenin ejected all non-Bolshevik delegates from the Fifth Soviet Congress, on June 9, 1918, the soviets at all levels were turned into obedient instruments of the Communist Party. There were attempts to revitalize them, the most effective in 1921 when the sailors of Kronstadt (the fortress island in the Baltic) demanded free elections of soviets. But their revolt was overthrown, and at the Party congress in March, Lenin restored the Party's monopoly of power. "We do not need any opposition," he said, "we are tired of it." After this there remained only the name. The world still speaks of "the Soviets," but this term refers to the persons who run the U.S.S.R. or else the population as a whole, for the original soviets, including the Supreme Soviet, are nothing but a façade.

But although the soviets in the U.S.S.R. were discredited for being merely tools in the hands of the all-powerful totalitarian Party, the ideal of democracy by council was adopted and hotly debated by at least part of the New Left in the sixties. The question was whether the soviets could be restored to their original function as an organ of direct democracy. The tradition of the Kronstadt sailors inspired a group of West Berlin anarchists who called a "Kronstadt Congress" in 1971, exactly fifty years after that last heroic rising in the cause of freedom in the Soviet Union. The young rebels of 1971 repeated the accusation of the Kronstadt rebels: "Lenin has said that Communism is Soviet power plus electrification [a famous Lenin dictum], but the people have found out that Bolshevik Communism means rule by [Party-appointed, not elected] commissars and by firing squad!"[15] And they declared: "For us Kronstadt is not history but an example for the future."[16]

The search for a democracy of the council type is one of the forms in which the yearning for a direct democracy manifests itself, and is characteristic of the young generation. We are surrounded by the discontent and doubts felt by many young people all over the world when they think about our present political and social systems. Therefore, even those who have no sympathy with this model can consider it as a hopeful sign that democracy in its pure (that is, direct) form is one of the desires of the young—most of whom know that direct democracy has so far proved impracticable yet have continued their search for its viability. The fact that they did so during the sixties in forms repulsive to the older generation should not prevent us from taking these yearnings into account when thinking about the future of our political system. Our system is the best of those that have been tried so far. But there is no guarantee that it will withstand the storms of the coming decades without the input of new ideas and new passions.

28
INNER CAUSES

IF we are to understand and judge fairly the developments of the past decade and a half, and perhaps even ponder a therapy in case of recurrence, it seems to me that we can best proceed by considering the restlessness of youth in the light of the restlessness of the epoch into which this generation was born.

CONTINUITY BROKEN

Every day we hear that we live in a time of crisis, of a radical break in mankind's history; in fact, of a break in the sequence of time, of a *Zeitbruch*. The thought is not farfetched, when we compare our time with those periods of the past when the river of history, after having flowed calmly for centuries, perhaps for millennia, suddenly enters the whirlpools, rapids, or waterfalls that we call revolutions. The Dutch historian Johan Huizinga—in a book also written at a time of change (during the First World War)—describes one such revolution, the turn from the Middle Ages to modern times. It is surprising and even somewhat disquieting to find, across half a thousand years, so many similarities. At that time too, people "lived in a continual mental crisis" and felt insecure and threatened; its atmosphere was expressed in the verses of Eustache Deschamps, a French poet of the fourteenth century:

> La fin approche, en vérité ...
> Tout va mal.

WHENCE?

Here is what Huizinga writes about the thinking of the later Middle Ages:

> If the medieval mind wants to know the nature or the reason of a thing, it neither looks into it, to analyze its structure, nor behind it, to inquire into its origin, but looks up to heaven, where it shines as an idea.[1]

This seems curiously familiar when we remember the thought structure of today's left-wing ideologists, except that it was prerational thinking, while we see much that is postrational in the youth of today.

Are we living through a period similar to the late Middle Ages, a similar break in continuity, this time in the Industrial Revolution? I believe so. In fact, the process of change from a feudal agrarian to a modern industrial society has been constantly accelerating during the last two centuries, acquiring finally a pace that makes us experience quantitative changes (e.g., in the speedup from a horse to a Mars rocket) as if they were changes in quality, and these bring forth fright and insecurity along with the exaltation of conquering nature.

For many, this acceleration is a daily experience, thanks to some 300 million automobiles rushing with tremendous speed over an ever more complicated web of roads. The nervous tension to which millions of people are exposed day after day when they enter a freeway that is full of fast cars and when they intently scan the road signs (one mistake and there might be no chance of correcting it for another 10 miles)—all this would have seemed impossible and surely unbearable to former generations. In America alone more than 55,000 people were killed in motor vehicle accidents in 1973 (38,000 in 1960).

Another example: Only a few decades ago, you knew what was going on in the world, if you knew it at all, through newspapers; it took time for them to get the news from afar, to print and to deliver it to you. Now you see the news within hours, if not live, and often even in color, on your TV screen. You are right there when murder is committed, and you stand behind the Rhodesian soldiers, looking down the barrels of their guns straight toward their targets.

Each of us can name sources of tension all around us, and we know that as a result of these tensions, doubts are growing concerning the value of progress. These doubts have been emphatically confirmed in the report of the Club of Rome with its programmatic title *Limits of Growth*.[2]

PROGRESS WITH A CLOVEN HOOF

"Even the ancient Greeks," to use this phrase once more, felt at times doubtful about progress and prosperity. Their earliest hero of progress, Prometheus, who brought fire to mankind, was punished by the gods; Icarus crashed when, in his first flight, he came too close to the sun. Among the ancient philosophers, Diogenes "in the barrel" has become the personification of happy frugality—the man who threw away his cup when he noticed a boy drinking with his cupped hands, and who was so content in his poverty that he had only one wish when Alexander the Great paid him a respectful visit: "Just move out of the way of the sun." "There is nothing more powerful than man," sings the chorus in Sophocles' *Antigone*, but the word *deinos*, translated as "powerful," is ambivalent; it means "dreadful" and "sinister" as well.

During the Christian Middle Ages, people's curiosity did not go beyond the word of God as interpreted by the Church; to study the unknown and to improve on nature seemed presumptuous. "God hates the innovators," a Belgian clergyman wrote in the eleventh century. The Renaissance inspired immortal works of art, but Leonardo da Vinci's magnificent technical designs remained on paper. The belief in progress as something wonderful and desirable is a child of the eighteenth century, when epochal discoveries in science and technology coincided with the conviction held by men of the Enlightenment that there were no limits to the capabilities of human reason.

Only gradually was the euphoric optimism of the Western nations corroded by doubt (the first signs of pessimism were evident as a result of the First World War, "when the lights went out over Europe"). Doubt appeared earliest among the Germans, with their sense of tragedy, and only much later in America, the "land of unlimited possibilities." In America it was the young generation that turned critical, while the older people still dreamed of the bigger and better things that the American Way of Life seemed to hold in store. Beginning with the Beatniks, an important section of young America moved in the direction of cultural pessimism. Paul Potter, one of the most talented leaders of the American New Left and president of SDS at its height in 1964–1965, called progress an enemy and the bloodiest of all bloody altars on which man sacrificed men; he blamed progress for dehumanizing human beings by coupling them with machines. The notion was seriously discussed in America that the disadvantages of progress might outweigh its advantages.

Philip E. Slater goes one step further: Whatever was taken as progress on the road to a better future turned out to be the opposite. The automobile, so enthusiastically praised, in reality destroyed community life in America, and any "progress" (he puts this word in quotes), though greeted as a chance for overcoming the problems created by earlier progress, did nothing but produce new problems.[3] The psychologist Bruno Bettelheim discovered disadvantages even in that symbol of progress, the dishwasher: For some couples, he wrote, it had eliminated the only thing which they still did together—the dishes.[4]

Those who decry progress today hold a political philosophy which until recently was the strongest supporter of progress, namely, the liberal and socialist ideology. In this respect the New Left (in the widest sense of the word) is different from the old Left, which still believes in progress. The captains of capitalism, who satisfy the constantly growing appetite of the population by increasing production, are also believers, as are the leaders in the Soviet Communist state, who need progress because they have promised their people someday to "catch up with and overtake" the prosperous Western world.

Yet the realization has grown greatly, throughout the world, that progress cannot be left entirely unto itself, that it must be controlled, planned, and limited. The shock of the OPEC decision drastically to increase oil prices has awakened people to the problem. The publications of the Club of Rome are being read and discussed vehemently;[5] in Germany a book with the provocative title *Ein Planet wird geplündert* (A Planet Is Being Plundered) recently remained for months on the best-seller lists,[6] and in February 1977, tens of thousands marched near Hamburg to prevent the construction of a nuclear power plant. Problems of pollution and environmental control have become, within a few years, the daily bread of politicians and administrators on all levels.

All this is not enough, say the rebels. All major technical problems have been solved. Progress therefore is no longer needed, and a walk on the moon nothing but a desperate attempt to find something for science and technology to do—though both are now working more for the disadvantage than for the good of mankind. The real tasks of future decades must be found not in the technological but in the human and social fields. (The last explains the enormous expansion of university subjects such as psychology, sociology, education, and political science, and the attention being given to topics such as transcendental meditation.)

Charles A. Reich, professor at Yale, found a name for this new attitude in his highly controversial best-seller, *The Greening of America*. He calls it Consciousness III, which differs from Consciousness II of the fathers and grandfathers, and from Consciousness I of still more distant generations. He considers the discrepancy between what is and what might be an overwhelming fact in the life of Consciousness III youth, and perhaps the single most important one, while the older generation accepts this discrepancy as given and takes it for granted. The Consciousness III generation, he thinks, wishes the reconstitution of the natural environment and the spiritual forces damaged and lost through concentration on material progress (for which he holds the Consciousness II attitude responsible).[7] In contrast to the scholarly prognosis of Daniel Bell, who also envisages the end of industrial society,[8] the book of Reich is not an analysis based on research of the past and present but rather a vision of the future. Like many of his enthusiastic young readers, Reich is not interested in history. If you have Consciousness III, you have purged yourself from the sins of your fathers by participating in revolutionary activities, and then history has nothing to teach you. This, incidentally, helps to explain the decline of the study of history, once the pride of scholarship, in schools and universities around the world. In America, in connection with the Bicentennial, I noticed some revival of interest in this discipline, at least in the history of the American nation. But I doubt that we shall see the return of history to its preeminence in the academic curricula of our time.

AGAINST WEALTH ...

Since time immemorial, the dream of conquering poverty and achieving abundance has been closely linked to the conviction that with the fulfillment of this dream the problems of mankind would be solved. In many modern industrialized countries of the West, including Japan, this dream has come true for an extraordinarily large part of the population, especially in America and Germany. But has this solved our problems? Has happiness entered our homes?

Warnings also have been voiced throughout history. All great religions deprecate Mammon; ancient legends, as well as the poetry and philosophy of all ages, do not speak highly of material wealth. Ortega y Gasset, the great Spaniard, warned in 1930 of prosperity's dangers for man.[9] But it was always a minority which felt that way. In an essay published in 1956, the sociologist David Riesman described American students, on the basis of a poll, as a "well-tempered generation," totally adjusted, satisfied with themselves and their country and mainly interested in earning a pile of money; these young people, he felt, were no danger to society; they would not blow up anybody, neither others nor themselves. Yet it was precisely this—blowing up others and themselves—that some young people from prosperous and even wealthy homes were doing a few years later. Instead of enjoying their prosperity, they felt bad about it, even despised it, and considered themselves, because they were middle- or upper-class, as morally inferior to the poor, to the blacks, to the hungry Third World.[10] Business career and success, status symbols and high consumption—these were no longer desired but rather declined. Particularly the sons and daughters from the upper class, from the Establishment, took this negative position. "You have to grow up in Scarsdale to know how bad things really are," a student said sarcastically to Kenneth Keniston.[11] When New York was still the empress of the world's cities and the envy of other nations, Jack Kerouac, in 1951, believed it to be in the grasp of "absolute madness," a city "with its millions and millions hustling forever for a buck among themselves, the mad dream—grabbing, taking, giving, sighing, dying, just so they could be buried in those awful cemetery cities beyond Long Island City."[12]

What had been admired throughout American history as "keen competition" and as "natural selection" of the best was now called a "rat race." A German writer, far removed from leftist thinking, wrote in 1974:

> Competition changes the character of people who participate in it. The restlessness developed in one's job continues after one leaves the place of work; it has corroded the soul. After work, people seek not repose, but diversion. Unremittingly, man remains under the influence of the propulsion which he has integrated as a result of competition.[13]

... AND AGAINST THE ACHIEVEMENT SOCIETY

Here we have it, even in the words of a conservative writer: the pressure exerted on everybody, making each one crave achievement, making all submit to what the Left ideologists damn as instruments of domination and oppression. Once you have become imbued with the drive for achievement, you have neither time or strength for, nor interest in, fighting the existing system. The advertisement of goods of consumption, accomplished by an ever more efficient sales pitch, is the whip that stings people into an unceasing drive for achievement. It seduces people into ever new demands which they can only satisfy by still greater achievement, thus turning them through *Konsumterror,* as the German students say, into slaves of the system.

The most influential voice criticizing the prosperous society of our time is still that of Herbert Marcuse. To him, the people are corrupted by prosperity and *Konsumterror;* he even asks the question of whether it makes much sense to preach liberation to the members of a society which, more than any before it, has been able to banish poverty, reduce the hardship of work and the length of the working day, and raise the standard of living. These people seem no longer able to recognize their own situation, having been deformed by abundance to the point of defending their own slavery.[14]

Prosperity, the dream of mankind, deforming the human race? Renunciation of comfort and wealth to avoid such deformation? Is this all that is left to us? Some critics tell the young rebels reproachfully that they condemn the Achievement Society and its prosperity while—with the left hand, so to speak—they cash the monthly check from home, provided by their families from work done within the society. They get their tactics from Gandhi, their idealism in the philosophy class, and their money from Daddy, said the University of Michigan student paper in the spring of 1968.[15] This was surely true of many who applauded when Janis Joplin asked the Lord, in one of her songs, to buy her a Mercedes-Benz.

Some unabashedly declared that there was no better use for Daddy's money than investment in their revolution. But we should not forget that many young people were in earnest when they challenged the high value attached to wealth by their elders.

"ALIENATION"

Since the time of Karl Marx, "alienation" has been one of the key words in the critique of society. The capitalist system produced a fundamental change in human existence which Marx explained as follows. This system separates the laborer from the product of his labor (of which he produces only a tiny part) and robs him of any influence on the production process (which, as a craftsman prior to industrialization, he had still understood and directed). He is unhappy in his work because he cannot freely develop his physical and intellectual energy; thus, both mind and body are ruined. The worker is, in Marx's inimitable phrase, *ausser der Arbeit bei sich and in der Arbeit ausser sich* (himself, when not at work; when at work, not himself). And thus: "The more the laborer labors, the more powerful becomes the foreign world of objects which he produces, and the poorer he becomes himself, the less his inner world belongs to him."[16] The economy, which is now split by this division of labor, appears to the workers as "a foreign power which lies beyond themselves, of which they do not know the whence and whereto, which they no longer control, which on the contrary now passes through a peculiar [. . .] sequence, independent of men's wishes and tricks."[17]

Thus man in his most important activity, in work, is pulled away from his true destiny, namely his self-realization according to his own desire: He becomes alienated. This thought, which is not foreign to humanist tradition, captivates young people more than the rigid structure of dogmatic Marxism, because now that they have finally found themselves after much struggle and pain, after the storms of puberty, they feel "strange" in the world of adults and especially in the world of work, and are threatened by the danger of becoming estranged, "alienated" from their environment and from themselves. They find confirmation of this sentiment in Marx, in the young Marx in particular, as well as encouragement to active resistance against society (unless they choose to withdraw from it in hippie manner).

It is this mood to which they allude, often unconsciously, whenever they explain any discomfort or uneasiness they may feel as "alienation," thereby extending the limits of this term to a questionable extent. When I ask students on both sides of the Atlantic to define what they mean when calling themselves alienated, they usually answer, "Everything is shit" (or the equivalent). But even in serious publications the term "alienation" has been used very loosely, in a very general way—for example, when a student group in Japan simply said it had a feeling of alienation which it wanted to overcome.[18] A former Harvard student, giving his description of the sixties, wryly wrote that "alienation is a contagious disease spread by late nights and meaningless discussions."[19]

One reason for confusion as to the meaning of the term is that it is applicable both to the process of *becoming* alienated (as described by Marx), which is a subject for sociology, and to the condition of *being* alienated, which belongs to the field of psychology. There have even been suggestions for replacing the word with another one[20] (the Hungarian Marxist Georg Lukács recommended *Verdinglichung,* which indicates that man is "becoming a thing"). But "alienation" has taken root. Paul Potter gave this impressive definition of alienation:

> Those incredible things we call our minds do not really belong to us. The belong to our parents and Oedipus and Richard Nixon and the Pentagon and all the corporation presidents.[...] Even our neuroses are not our own. They belong emphatically to our parents. What is ours (as much as anything can be) is anger and humiliation and shame. What is ours is the sense of emptiness. [...] What is very much ours is a terrible need to fill that emptiness. Let me call that need the need to love.[21]

"Alienated" man had found his place in world literature long before the term as such had come into use. Hamlet certainly was alienated, so was Hermann Hesse's "Steppenwolf," but never before has alienation been felt by so many people as such an important feature of their lives as in our century. As the feeling of alienation has spread, the concept has become associated with senselessness and absurdity. The continuous success of the "theater of the absurd" allows the conclusion that the audience finds its own attitude toward life expressed there.

Students ought to be much less alienated than workers; they themselves select their field of study, and they plan it—more or less—in the way they want it. But they are more conscious of their alienation. Sometimes one might think that they do everything they can to *become* alienated. For example, with increasing frequency they insist on dividing labor, which is considered to be the chief source of alienation—they write their papers, even their dissertations, not by themselves but together with others. Some even seem to enjoy alienation. One young man of the New Left wrote that it was "wonderful" to feel alienated.[22] In one of his books, Kenneth Keniston has an entire chapter on alienated students, based on a poll at Harvard. His conclusion: Alienation means "an explicit rejection of what are seen as the dominant values of the surrounding society."[23] Those who feel alienated reject reality by turning their backs on it (Marcuse's Great Refusal), or seek to meet it on the barricades. Everywhere they see the same enemy, "society"—in reality, modern civilization.

To many this civilization appears as a man-devouring Moloch, a bureaucratic machine in which man (Kafka's Josef K. is the best example) is helpless—alienated, atomized, twisted, deformed, and robbed of his natural speech, the most important instrument of communication. Such Kafkaesque visions might be far removed from everyday life, but the feeling of powerlessness against surrounding forces does exist among young people in many variations and degrees of consciousness, and it may condense to the danger point if hundreds of thousands, perhaps millions, of young people are shut off from satisfying vocations through no fault of their own. Those among them who still believe in changing the world by taking part in the changing of society, but find no chance of doing so, can easily end up on the road to violence in their search for true identity.

"IDENTITY"

In the same way as "alienation," "identity" has within a few years become a key word in many languages. You can read or hear it every day: The Shah of Iran has emphasized that his country will keep its identity in spite of modernization; Pope Paul VI has lamented the identity crisis of the priesthood; West Berlin, a Western island in a Red sea, is concerned about its identity; an acquaintance even told me that his terrier, which he had put in a kennel for the duration of a lengthy voyage, suffered a lengthy "identity crisis" afterward. Erik Erikson coined the term when he gave psychiatric treatment during the Second World War to young men who were shell-shocked. They no longer knew who they were and had lost their "ego identity."[24]

Here, as before, only the word is new, not the phenomenon. Remember Phaeton in Greek mythology: His mother has told him that Helios, the sun god, is his father. But Phaeton has doubts and suffers because of them. He asks Helios to lend him the sun chariot for one day as proof of his paternity. Reluctantly, Helios agrees. But Phaeton is not able to master the horses, and Zeus kills him by lightning before the runaway chariot can set the earth on fire. Thus, an identity crisis leads to death.

In our days, the most advanced resources of surgery and pharmacology are being put into the service of the identity search. Women who doubt their identity are being turned into men; Doris Richards, a physical education teacher for girls in a high school in

Emeryville, California, was turned into Steve Dain. And vice versa: Dr. Richard Raskind, a top-ranking tennis player in New York, played in a women's tennis tournament under the name of Dr. Renee Richards a year after sex change.

Erikson's warnings must be taken seriously. "In the social jungle of human exisence," he contends, "there is no feeling of being alive without a sense of identity," and "identity confusion" has grave consequences for young people:

> Youth after youth, bewildered by the incapacity to assume a role forced on him by the inexorable standardization of American adolescence, runs away in one form or another, dropping out of school, leaving jobs, staying out all night or withdrawing into bizarre and inaccessible moods. [...] To keep themselves together they temporarily overidentify with the heroes of cliques and crowds to the point of an apparently complete loss of individuality [which helps to explain] the appeal of simple and cruel totalitarian doctrines.

Erikson's "negative identity" supplies insight into the diagnosis and therapy of youthful opposition. The young person, to remain true to himself, "would rather act shamelessly in the eyes of his elders, out of free choice, than be forced into activities which would be shameful in his own eyes, or in those of his peers."[25] The less the young think they are understood by the adult environment, the greater is the danger. Some of them will succumb to their identity crisis

> in all manner of neurotic, psychotic, or delinquent behavior; others will resolve it through participation in ideological movements passionately concerned with religion or politics, nature or art. Still others [...] eventually come to contribute an original bit to an emerging style of life: the very danger which they had sensed has forced them to mobilize capacities to see and say, to dream and plan, to design and construct, in new ways.[26]

Everybody has to face his identity crisis by himself. But in former days one was helped in this painful process by traditions, institutions, and authorities with whom one could identify; today these are all undergoing their own crises. The family has shrunk to just parents and children; it is often brittle and sometimes broken; what was firm before (*my* grandparents, *my* parents, *my* brothers and sisters) has been weakened. Professional morale is

345

dwindling: "In the old days I knew I was a railway man, and I was proud to be one," a German train conductor told me the other day. "But now? Everything disintegrates." The Fatherland and "My Country, Right or Wrong"? This value also has lost its glamour, not only in Germany, where it perished in flame and shame, but in the Western world as a whole, where few people are willing to use patriotic terms and slogans they would have recited some decades ago. European unification? This started out as the great identifier for young Europeans, but something that stumbles along so painfully is hardly strong enough to enlist young people. Religion? To be sure, the struggle between Protestants and Catholics, which yesterday had irritated, even repelled the young, has been alleviated (save for Ireland); but now they hear of deep contradictions within the churches themselves, even within the Catholic Church, concerning the substance of faith (going as far as a "God is dead" theology) and the church's message to the world. For many young people on the move, the established churches are too much a part of the Establishment.

What we have heard with regard to America in an earlier chapter is true also, if less extremely, of Germany. California's "Children of God" are Germany's *Gotteskinder,* and Sun Myung Moon too has quite a few German followers. A German author, in his book about the Jehovah's Witnesses, claims that in the Federal Republic alone there are millions of people with some kind of religious mania, who are trying to satisfy their needs outside the established churches.[27] Another author, himself a Protestant preacher, tells of a girl who would have "rather a Jesus Freak revolution than yawningly boring church services." After the painful progression from Marx and Mao via Buddha or Krishna (and drugs), youth has arrived, he thinks, at the point where the world is still in order, with Jesus as the guru of gurus.[28]

One thing is certain: Many young people are searching, and quite a few of them try unconventional roads. On the other hand, it appears that conservative and fundamentalist preachers who do nothing but preach the "word of God" attract youth more than those who modernize the Bible and thereby put it in question.[29]

The growing instability of human relations (with and without marriage vows) has intensified a dangerous problem: loneliness. There are the lonely people of one of the most popular Beatle songs, "Eleanor Rigby." And Janis Joplin, a singer famous the world over, cried out: "Nobody loves me!" She faced, as her biographer puts it, "the yawning chasm of painful loneliness."[30]

346

Many students fear that someday they may be superfluous because there might not be enough jobs for the armies of university graduates. If they study liberal arts, they are apprehensive that, in what Zbigniew Brzezinski, formerly of Columbia University, called the technotronic age, they will be outdated, discarded, shunted off. Such fears add to the anxiety over identity and create the strong desire for finding a sheltering roof—perhaps an identity for two in a one-to-one relationship, or collective security in a fraternity or a political organization. Since nothing creates closer ties than facing the same enemy, many prefer groups which stand in opposition to society.

Groups of all kinds take over the sheltering function which the family once exercised. Their activities can be varied; they can offer sport, music, backpacking, adventures (which might turn violent if the group tends in this direction). But they offer the greatest satisfaction if they transmit to their members the idea that they all serve one great purpose. The desire to do so is unbroken in most young people who have not yet been caught by the routine of holding a job, making money, taking care of a family. How could they understand and value a society which is unable to show them great and exciting aims!

After the Columbia riots in 1968, one psychologist concluded that some students had found in clashes with the police a radical remedy for their spiritual unease. Those who had been unhappy about their bashfulness and lack of strength had found in these collective actions unexpected strength within themselves.[31] A former Harvard student, one of the leaders in the struggle against the Vietnam war, later asked himself whether he had really been so concerned about peace in Vietnam, or had been motivated primarily by the wish to prove that he, a middle-class student, was not afraid of jail.[32] A critical observer remarked that some radicals, unable to sort out things for themselves, tried to destroy whatever they could so that the troubles suffered by the world would be comparable to their own.[33]

A young Harvard student said that he was resentful about American society because it had let him grow up without belief in values. "If I had been brought up in, say, Nazi Germany—that is, presupposing I wasn't Jewish—they'd have given me an absolute set of values to believe in, and maybe I wouldn't be sitting here like this now."[34] This surprising statement might make it easier for young Germans to understand why Hitler was able to win over the German universities even before he came to power. An Austrian historian who did much for the psychological analysis of National Socialism has warned of the danger of a psychological vacuum; "unemployment of the soul" he called "a social phenomenon of the first order."[35]

The spiritual nourishment which the young get from the older generation they often call stones instead of bread. "While the world is about to blow up," a professor says in a not-yet-published novel by a former Berkeley student, "we send the students into the nuclear reactor lab so that they can blow it up even sooner."[36] Many youth groups consider their officially proclaimed ideology as secondary and know little of the main writings of their revolution. "We learn from deeds, not from books," one can hear them saying. Their boisterous, wild activism is blind and often an escape reaction. One American SDS girl explained that she would cease to exist the moment she stopped fighting and frankly confessed that she and her friends would not know what to do if the university administration were to grant all their demands, leaving them nothing to protest against and forcing them again to face themselves.[37]

Everybody who has seen, if only on TV, a rock band in action (or surveyed the battlefield after the concert) knows that enthusiasm can turn into senseless, raving violence. At no time has patience been a virtue of youth. But no youth before has been quite as much an "instant generation" as the one today. Bob Dylan spoke for many when he said: "Yesterday does not exist. Tomorrow does not come. There is only today. Or nothing."[38] And Janis Joplin is thus described by her friend: "She wanted to have everything! Everything at once, every minute. If something was beautiful five minutes ago but not now, it was shit!"[39]

The inability to wait, the desire to have "everything at once," no matter what—psychologists like to trace this back to the parents' (especially the mother's) habit of satisfying speedily every wish of their children. David Riesman said of the impatiently demanding and rioting students of the late sixties that they had once been the babies who always had to be picked up right away when they cried.[40] But there is more to it than blind mother love. It is not easy to talk young people out of their instant-attitude if they live under the shadow of the atom bomb and of the population explosion, surrounded by gloomy pessimists.

"Most explanations of the student movement and of concrete cases of unrest are as controversial as the phenomena which they

348

are supposed to explain." This is the conclusion of a young German sociologist who studied the American and German literature on the unrest of the past ten to fifteen years.[41] None of the explanations are completely new—neither the break in continuity, nor the criticism of progress and prosperity, not even the alienation and the identity crises—although the words themselves sound new. What is really new and has not occurred before in history is the coincidence of these factors, reinforcing each other, at a time when each of them happened to be reaching a climax. Another new factor is the extremely wide area in which these tensions could be experienced. Never before had so many young people, for so long a period of time, the chance to think, to develop, to criticize.

IV

WHITHER?

The worldwide unrest of youth in the sixties—was it a temporary fever, like measles, which one gets through infection, accompanied by high temperatures and a frightening red rash that passes quickly and leaves no traces, except lifelong immunity? Or was it more like a recurring disease, such as malaria, which suddenly breaks out and disappears after a short time, leaving the patient exhausted, only to flare up again a few years later? Or was it, still worse, like a kind of multiple sclerosis, which knows periods of remission but which paralyzes new parts of the nervous system each time it returns, finally leading to a terminal condition which—following Oswald Spengler—might be called Decline of the West?

Less than a decade after the "year of the students," it is still too early for a final assessment. But a hiatus has been reached. Whether one wishes to call it "the end of the protest movement,"[1] or speak of the "stranded Left" unable to free itself of its dreams,[2] or settle for the milder formulation of the "aging of the New Left,"[3] there is no doubt of one thing: The big wave has roared by, leaving many rivulets behind. The time seems long past when the SDS in Germany was thought to be near its goal, "to overthrow the dictatorship of the bourgeoisie by the armed people's war and to replace it by the dictatorship of the proletariat."[4]

The tremors, to be sure, have not disappeared completely: At Stanford, I saw 294 students arrested on May 9, 1977, in connection with a protest meeting against apartheid in South Africa; and in Berkeley, I watched the arrest of 56 students on June 2, 1977, for the same reason. (On the Santa Cruz campus of the University of California, on May 27, the number of students arrested was even higher—401.) But these were rather polite affairs, and the campuses were barely affected.

Indeed, the rebellion of the sixties is over and done with. But what has become of those who were part of it? And what is the meaning of their rebellion for us today?

29
SCATTERED FAR AND WIDE

WHAT became of those vast hordes that jumped on the world stage in the sixties and are now all but forgotten?

As far as the hippies are concerned, a careful and interesting study has been made by the Berkeley Center for Drug Use (an affiliate of the Wright Institute in that same city), continuing the work done previously by the Haight-Ashbury Research Project. In the course of the research, 250 "flower children" were studied during the height of the hippie movement, as well as during the following years. Needless to say, it proved most difficult to follow the fate of these constantly moving people, some changing their addresses up to five times a year. Yet it was possible to keep track of more than half of the original group over a period of ten to thirty months. The following data are taken from a prepublication draft of a book by Stephen M. Pittel and Henry Miller and from an article summarizing some of the Center's findings.[1]

SOME "RE-ENTER," OTHERS NOT
The authors of the study have found a significant trend toward what they call a "re-entry" into American society: a "moving back toward mainstream American mores." Drug use, for example, has significantly decreased. So has involvement with the drug subculture as gauged by participation in drug dealing; the number of people who have turned on some other person to drugs for the first time has gone down from 81 percent at the beginning to 35 percent at the end of the study. The use of LSD has been abandoned by 82 percent.

The study distinguishes between the "Re-entry," "Semi Re-entry," and "Non Re-entry" groups (numbering 54, 44, and 31 persons, respectively), in accordance with the degree of their reintegration into American society. Here are examples of each of the three groups. Re-entry: A young man lived two years in Haight-Ashbury, took on a number of jobs, including that of a forest worker, then entered the army, where he was being trained in electronics and preparing himself for a job. Semi Re-entry: A twenty-five-year-old woman lived with her man and a small daughter in a community in Berkeley, mainly on welfare, earning a few dollars by baby-sitting or similar chores and occasionally supported by her parents. Non Re-entry: A young man still lived near the hippie scene, close to Golden Gate Park, used hard drugs, made his living as a drug pusher, and declined his father's offer to return to the family business.

Not unexpectedly, the researchers found that those hippies who had been closer in their upbringing and personality to basic American values and traditions were more likely to re-enter than those who had been deviants even before they came to Haight-Ashbury. For the re-enterers, hippiedom was a phase of their personal development from teenager to adult; for those on the other extreme it was a more or less permanent way of life. It was found that the re-enterers had come from less disturbed homes and had better relations with their parents (in this connection the relationship with the father proved especially important). Moreover, they were more stable in their relationships to the other sex, had higher IQ's, were psychologically healthier, were more independent-minded, and possessed a higher degree of self-confidence.

But—and this is an equally significant part of the findings—all three groups have remained skeptical of American society. Lumping those who "agree" and "strongly agree" together, we find that the following statements were affirmed by percentages given in parentheses:

"American society is in many ways a repressive society" (92 percent); "No one has the right to claim total possession of any property; material goods should be shared with those who need them" (80 percent); "By dehumanizing society, science and technology have done more harm than good" (71 percent); "In government today there is no one you can really trust" (70 percent). But when it comes to doing something about it, the percentage figures are considerably smaller: "The way things are today in the U.S., I'd like to emigrate to another country" (42 percent); "This country would be better off if there was a real revolution" (35 percent).

The groups as a whole, in the words of the authors, take a "dim view of some of society's treasured institutions and assumptions. Anywhere from half to almost all of them believe that people are basically selfish, that the world is a potentially brutal place, that schools are irrelevant and that children may suffer at their parents' hands. Moreover, they are unwilling to achieve efficiency at the expense of human values and they disparage competition to keep them on their toes." In contrast to American society as a whole, only 10 percent view themselves as Protestant, Catholic, or Jewish (that is, as members of established religions), while 47 percent indicate a preference for Eastern and other religious sects, and 43 percent have no religious preference at all. Their interest in politics is minute: 84 percent consider themselves uninvolved. Only 16 percent report an increase in political activity, and it is unclear exactly what this means; in context, however, one can assume that this involvement is mostly negative as far as the political and social system of the country is concerned.

Their more positive judgments are reserved for the family. Only 31 percent are in favor of replacing the nuclear family by another system; only 27 percent think that under present conditions "no one should bring children into the world." In their attitudes toward sex the study found that they are "neither quite so preoccupied with sex nor quite so radical in their sexual politics as it once seemed."

A number of such follow-up studies have appeared lately; the one which came to my attention most recently is that by Medved and Wallechinsky. It describes the fate of the class of 1965 of the Palisades High School (near Los Angeles), which in January 1965 was the subject of a *Time* cover story. The book includes thirty-one portraits but no generalizations. One can appreciate why: the development of the thirty-one respondents (including the editors of the book) has been too divergent, ranging from a quarterback on the football team who has become a Hollywood masseur to the gang leader of "The Saracens" who has built a million-dollar business empire.

THE BERKELEY REBELS

Six years after the events on the "26-foot strip" a study was made concerning the fate of some of the main actors.[2] Here is what it found:

Brian Turner was the man who sat at a table with brochures

and signature sheets for SNCC, the one whom the university administration decided to make an example of. Turner was expelled from the university (later he was readmitted); he also spent forty-five days in jail because he had participated in the Sproul Hall sit-in. Since then, his radical views have hardened. While preparing his dissertation in anthropology in New York, he participated in many protest actions. He didn't want simply to sit within his four walls writing books and papers because that way, he felt, he was supporting "one of the worst regimes history knows" (he meant the Nixon administration).

Mario Savio, twenty-one years old in 1963 and, much to his surprise, overnight the leader of the Free Speech Movement, had married Suzanne Goldberg, one of the prominent students in the FSM. He had spent four months in jail in 1967 because of a sit-in, had run—unsuccessfully—for a seat in the California legislature, and had finally left the radical movement. The couple has children. Savio has held various jobs, all in Berkeley. These included positions in the city department of health, in a bar, and in a bookshop.

Jack Weinberg, who entered the history of the sixties with his "Don't trust anyone over thirty," had himself crossed this ominous borderline in 1970. He too had remained a radical, and was working as a journalist on a left-wing weekly in Los Angeles.

Steve Weissman, one of the tacticians of FSM, had remained an activist. After his FSM experience he worked as an SDS cadre at Stanford, founded a center for left-wing students, and joined *Ramparts*.

Mike Rossman, one of the most radical in 1964, author of the much-discussed Rossman report about the alleged repression of students by the university administration, at first continued his studies in mathematics, but dropped out two weeks before the end of the summer term in 1966. He wandered over to the Scene, lived with girl friend and child in a Berkeley commune, and earned his money with occasional work, including lectures and articles on group therapy and ecology. "I have learned," he explained, "to live outside the institutional framework and to do whatever I like."

Matthew Hallinan joined the Communist Party. One could not guess his past ("he looked like a teller of the Chase Manhattan Bank"), but he did have a bust of Lenin in his apartment. He lamented the generation gap, by which he meant the gap between the student generation of his day and the present one. He saw no indication of a mass movement such as existed in the sixties.

Art Goldberg and his sister Jackie, both once active in FSM, lived together in Los Angeles, she a teacher in a black suburb, he a lawyer working for the radicalization of the National Lawyers Guild.

Manuel G. Abascal, whom I mention last, although among the 814 arrested in the great Sproul Hall sit-in he had appeared first alphabetically, explained that he was primarily interested in leading a life exemplary for others, by which he hoped to do more good than by forcing other people to do things they did not want to. He did not think that he would ever become more radical than that. Most of all, he would like to emigrate.

The interviewer of the former Berkeley activists reached the conclusion that none of them had turned into a typical middle-class American, and none was likely to do so in the future. There is much to be said in support of this judgment, at least of its first part. When David Chadwick—once a SNCC member, later an SDS man—became abbot of the Zen Monastery Tassajara in Carmel Valley, he explained how he had gotten there: one day, when he felt sick and tired of political activities, he had looked under "Zen" in the telephone directory and had found this place. The opposite road was traveled by Sam Brown. Once a leading organizer of marches against the Vietnam war, he joined the Democratic Party, became treasurer of the state of Colorado, administering a quarter of a billion dollars, and eventually worked in the Carter Administration.

OTHER VIPS OF THE SIXTIES

David Harris, former husband of Joan Baez, who had been briefly in the South with SNCC, had been president of the Stanford student body in 1966, and had spent, as one of the leading draft resisters, two years in prison, ran as a Democrat for the U.S. Congress in 1976. He lost but did rather well—getting 60,000 votes to the incumbent's 120,000. I heard him make a campaign speech in a church not far from Stanford. Among those who asked questions at the end of the talk were a number of pacifists. Harris was cautious, avoiding words from the vocabulary of the sixties and arguing calmly, even about rearmament. His book, which appeared during the election campaign, describes his experience behind bars and is an outcry against the prison system, but otherwise unpolitical.

Tom Hayden, once president of SDS and the author of the Port Huron Statement, had still higher ambitions. He ran for one of the two senatorial seats from California (but was defeated by the

Democratic incumbent in the primary). Those who did not remember the early days of the SDS had known Hayden for a number of years only as the husband of Jane Fonda. But his attempt to win the Democratic senatorial nomination brought him back into the limelight. He did not use any socialist slogans, nor did he think of a third party; in America, he said, it was wiser to work through the existing two-party system. When attacked for his radical views in the sixties, as he was at a meeting in Palo Alto, his rebuttal was: "The radicalism of the sixties has become the common sense of the seventies," which of course is only partially true, and "We made a mistake then—we came ten years too early."

The "Black Panthers" were not a student organization, but they have passionately moved the young people, not only the black ones and not only in America; there was in Frankfurt, Germany, in 1970, a "Black Panther Solidarity Committee" which demanded Bobby Seale's release from prison; among the members of the committee were Daniel Cohn-Bendit and one of the former presidents of the German SDS, Karl Dietrich Wolff. March 6, 1971, was declared "International Solidarity Day for Bobby Seale" in a number of countries. Seale, released soon afterward, ran for mayor of Oakland, California (the Panthers' capital), in the spring of 1973; among nine candidates he obtained 20 percent of the vote and an honorable second place.

Still more remarkable was the development of another Black Panther leader, Eldridge Cleaver, whose volume of letters and essays, *Soul on Ice* (1968), sold more than 2 million copies in America alone. Arrested after a shoot-out in Oakland in 1968, he jumped bail, fled to Cuba and Algeria, and visited during the following years a number of Communist states, including the Soviet Union and North Korea. He lived in Paris from 1973 until late in 1975, when he returned to America, where he was again arrested and, in August 1976, once more released on bail. The statements which he made in print and in TV interviews were an astonishing proof of changing times. He attacked the Communists for having established the most oppressive regime history had ever known, called for a strong America, and even urged efforts for the destruction of the totalitarian Soviet regime. He dates his change of heart from that day in February 1972 when Mao Tse-tung was welcoming and shaking hands with President Richard Nixon.[3]

Joan Baez is still on the road with her concerts, singing about nonviolence (she appeared with great success in September 1976 at a rally in New York which protested against the repressive regime in Chile) but more often about love, her son, and Bob Dylan, with whom she has been on several tours again. Dylan himself, after a period of withdrawal, has been heard more frequently in the past two years; he has been on a fifty-concert tour, with his Rolling Thunder Revue, and on September 14, 1976, he appeared with Joan Baez on a TV show. He has had a house built for himself and his family above the cliffs of Malibu in southern California; according to an Associated Press story it looks "like a Disneyland attraction that got lost on its way to Fantasyland, part ranch house, part castle." He is believed to be a deeply religious man; in one of his interviews he said, "The highest form of song is prayer."[4] A recent book about him, by Stephen Pickering, has the subtitle *A Portrait of the Jewish Poet in Search of God*; it is meant to be a "midrash" (commentary on a holy text) and makes him out to be a Hasidic sage.

Allen Ginsberg continues his writing of poetry; he was reading poems on a tour with Dylan in 1976, once to a crowd of 27,000 people, and is codirector of the Kerouac School of Disembodied Poetics at the (Buddhist) Naropa Institute in Boulder, Colorado. In an interview in 1976 he regretted the sixties rhetoric he participated in and helped coin. "All that screaming about 'Kill the Pigs' is the wrong mantra," he said, explaining that kind of political activism as a "manifestation of ego and anxiety,"[5] Ginsberg recently attacked his old friend and co-smoker Timothy Leary at a public meeting. Leary, the drug apostle from Harvard, had escaped from prison, first to Algeria, later to Switzerland, but he too returned and went to jail, to be released later. From mindblowing he is now "into" space migration, together with a group which calls itself SMI^{2}LE (from Space Migration Increased Intelligence and Life Extension). He prefers not to speak about his past. About Eastern religions he said: "Nothing good has come out of Asia since the Japanese camera."[6] His former friends have accused him of "singing" on them; one, Richard Alpert, his closest associate in the psychedelic days at Harvard has become, after two visits to India in 1967 and 1971, a popular guru who calls himself Ram Dass (servant of Rama).[7] Charles Reich has given up his chair at the Yale Law School and retired to San Francisco. His new book, *The Sorcerer of Bolinas Reef,* is mainly about the greening of Charles Reich and his very personal hang-ups. Stephen Gatkin, once a radical in the Bay area, went with his followers to Tennessee to run The Farm, mentioned in Chapter 20.

There are many indications that the students of the radical years have carried over some attitudes into their professional lives of the seventies. The young lawyers on the West Coast are showing an increased involvement in cases of a social and political nature, for example, those of draft resisters who accepted the clemency program offered by President Gerald Ford, political defendants such as Angela Davis, and drug dealers; they also defend producers of porno films (from whose cases they can make the most money).[8] In France, among the country's 5,000 judges, about 2,000 belong to the traditional organization (union des magistrats), while 1,000, mostly the younger ones, have joined the left-wing *Syndicat de la Magistrature,* formed in the days of the Paris May; in cases of labor conflict they are making life so hard for the employers that the latter are protesting against the administration of law in France, which they say is becoming a matter of class struggle.[9]

In 1974, *Business Week* polled many enterprises about their experiences with employees who graduated during the restless sixties. It was found that they differed from those of the fifties. They were difficult but not eccentric, intelligent, critical, willing to take a new look at things, full of unorthodox and not always practicable suggestions, but not "anti-business." On the other hand, the number of left-leaning professors of economics is said to have risen in the United States from a mere fifteen or twenty in 1962 to almost a thousand in 1975.[10]

THE LEFT WING IN EUROPE

For Europe we do not have biographical material in such abundance. Daniel Cohn-Bendit runs a bookshop in Frankfurt and has worked, for a while, with preschool children. In 1975 he published a book under the appropriate title *Le Grand Bazar,* first in French and, a year later, in a revised version in German (from which I make the following translation). It is amusing and revealing; with remarkable honesty Cohn-Bendit describes his intellectual and spiritual collapse in 1968, which occurred before the month of May was even over:

I had lost my ability to intervene politically. [...] I had completely lost orientation. When I arrived in Germany [a few days later] I was empty. [I now had] a personal interest in remaining a celeb-

rity, a material interest; I liked the "high life." [Cohn-Bendit uses
the English term to characterize his life as the lionized ex-leader of
the Paris May.] I could no longer speak extemporaneously, not
even about the May. I became a weak speech-machine. [. . .] I went
to Sardinia with an actress. We lived there two weeks in an expensive hotel. [. . .] We wanted to have fun. [. . .] Until 1969 I behaved
truly like a bureaucrat who can afford, on the basis of his name, a
pleasant and useless life.

"I would not do this again," he writes, looking back on these flings
during the first year after the Paris May. But he is not too happy
about what he has accomplished since, either. He tried, with
scant success, to revolutionize the workers of the Opel automobile
plant in Rüsselsheim (near Frankfurt); after two years he found
that he and his friends were politically weaker then they had
been when they started their work in the plant. The preschool
work became a bore, the superprogressive education methods employed there disillusioned him. Although he seems to have enjoyed the "erotic character" of flirting with five-year-old girls, he
came to the conclusion: "I am against antiauthoritarian education if that means that the kids do whatever they like."

But Cohn-Bendit did not lose his antiauthoritarian contempt
for the Soviet Union. In words almost as strong as those of
Dutschke, he attacks Soviet Communism, which to him is not
very different from bourgeois society in the West. The Soviet
Communists' own abominable behavior, he explains, is responsible for the anti-Communism existing in the world. Moscow is
trying to fool the world into believing that there is a soviet democracy, a democracy of labor (and other) councils, while in reality these were destroyed long ago. Coining a bitter metaphor, he
says that the Moscow leaders use the fire of the revolution, which
they themselves extinguished, like coastal pirates who light fires
along the shore to attract benighted ships in search of a port, so as
to wreck and rob them upon arrival. Next to Moscow he dislikes
East Berlin, Moscow's most loyal satellite, which to him exudes
the "boredom of a Sunday afternoon in a provincial town without
the glittering bourgeois luxury of European cities."[11]

Among the German rebels, Rudi Dutschke spent some time in
England following the attempt on his life in 1968. He has since
moved to Denmark, where he lives with his American-born wife
and two children in the university town of Aarhus. His study on
Lenin earned him the doctoral degree in 1974. His income consists of lecture fees and unemployment money paid by the West

German government. Hans Jügen Krahl, called the "outstanding theoretician of the German New Left" by a competent German observer, [12] was killed in an automobile accident. Bernd Rabehl, once a leading SDS man, co-founder and ideologue of West Berlin's Commune 1, became an assistant professor of political science at the Free University of Berlin. Others are active in radical organizations, some are in prison or underground, some have died in shoot-outs with the police or by suicide. One former SDS leader, after studying literature, runs a publishing business. Many have withdrawn from politics.

The so-called "fundamental experience of impotence" of the sixties has had its effect. The majority of those who were ready for solidarization have gone their own ways; the activists have remained hopelessly split among themselves. The terrorists, of course, see to it that they are not forgotten; they are only a tiny minority, but it is exactly the feeling of not being understood by anybody and of being forsaken by yesterday's friends that stimulates their will to prove themselves in front of the entire world. Smuggled letters found in the cells of the Baader-Meinhof people show how far removed they are from a sense of reality. [13]

Some veterans of the sixties have been attracted by the pro-Moscow Communist groups; they hope to find intellectual security in organizations which have a strict discipline and an undisputed dogma about which there can be no quarrels once an issue has been authoritatively interpreted from above. For those in Germany who, after years of emotional involvement with the New Left, desire peace and quiet and have turned conservative, yet still wish to preserve the revolutionary bravado of yesterday, the pro-Moscow Communist Party (DKP) and its youth organizations (such as Spartacus on the campus) offer themselves as havens of refuge. However, in the long run many converts find it difficult to submit to the sterile rigidity of this orthodoxy.

Radicalism in the German university has generally declined. For this there are three main reasons. First, the baby boom of the early fifties produced such a big wave of university applicants that—for the first time in German peacetime history—strict admission rules are being enforced on high-school graduates (who formerly could enter a university without further ado); competition for the admission has become very tough and absorbs many energies. Second, the recession in the mid-seventies has shrunk the job market. The results of university examinations have become important in getting jobs; consequently, students are working harder and have less time for political activities. Third, since the outbreak of terrorist activities the German government has tightened admission rules for civil service jobs (which are the ultimate destination of many students; e.g., for almost all who prepare themselves as schoolteachers), and the record of the applicant as to disruptive political activities during his university years is one of the criteria taken into consideration. In 1976 (before the issue had come up for more than a very few), I found students deeply concerned, some outright afraid, and on the whole anxious to accommodate themselves, stay quiet, and not participate in oppositional student activities that might negatively affect their position in the competition for the shrinking number of civil service jobs now available. This is a case of backlash about which nobody can be happy.

The public in West Germany had been disturbed by reports of growing numbers of young left-wing teachers in German schools. Many of them had taken seriously Rudi Dutschke's advice (when the decline of the student rebellion became clear) about "the long march through the institutions." This meant one should desist from outright revolutionary activity and rather, after finishing the university, enter professional careers (including, of course, teaching), thus changing society by working "through its institutions."

IN JAPAN THE IMPRINT IS DEEP BUT FADING

No country has been shaken by student unrest more severely or over a longer period than Japan. There, too, the unrest has quieted down. But what about those who were in the thick of it a decade and more ago? What happened to the "Ampo generation" (as it is still being called, in view of its focus—the struggle against the U.S.-Japan Security Treaty)?

We are fortunate in having a fine follow-up study by a young American scholar, Ellis S. Krauss, who in 1969 and 1970 "revisited" the Japanese radicals.[14] This he did by trying to find as many radicals as possible who had been studied in 1962 by Professor Kazuko Tsurumi (referred to in Chapter 14) and by analyzing the answers given then and now to the same questions.

Professor Krauss subdivided his respondents into several categories according to their political views and found the activists of 1962 little changed since graduation. "Most are still left-wing and many exceedingly so," he says, adding: "In orientation and behavior, most are alienated, antitreaty, and politically participant, [... wishing] to change the capitalist system." (The percentage of anticapitalists among the activists remained almost the same; it was 78 percent in 1962, 75 percent in 1970.) Greater maturity had not diminished the activists' idealism; on the contrary, the proportion of those who would be "willing to sacrifice their personal happiness to change the system" had increased from 18 to 54 percent.

In one respect the activists had changed—in their attitude toward Marxism. Krauss distinguishes between "total Marxists" (who think Marx was and is right in everything he wrote), "eclectic Marxists" (who have abandoned some Marxist tenets and held onto others), and "non-Marxists." By comparing Professor Tsurumi's and his own results he found that, among those attracted to Marxism, in 1962 two-thirds were "total Marxists," whereas in 1970 two-thirds were "eclectic Marxists." Krauss sees the reason for this change in the strength of the capitalist system, which surprised the respondents; beginning in the late fifties it had brought an unexpected and spectacular rise in the prosperity of the Japanese people, producing the famous slogan"Jimmu irai" (Never since Jimmu), meaning that never since the days of the legendary emperor Jimmu had the Japanese been so well off as during the sixties. When asked whether they expected "a great change in the social system of Japan," 94 percent of the active and the less active radicals said yes in 1962. But by 1970 the very same people had changed their minds dramatically; only 26 percent gave an affirmative answer.

While students who had been less involved in the movement were turning toward conservatism, toward adjustment to the social order, and into lucrative jobs, the former activists tended to find work in education, research, or writing.

It must be said that the number of Krauss's respondents is small, only fifty-three, but I am inclined to take his findings seriously, inasmuch as they correspond to my own impressions during frequent visits to Japan during the sixties and seventies.

SUMMARY

If what we have found so far is condensed into a simplified scheme, it becomes evident that the survivors of the youth rebellion fall into four categories.

There are the *terrorists*, several hundred of them over the world, organized in small, tightly knit, conspiratorial groups, some of them linked together on an international scale, partly financed by Libya, as Colonel Qaddafi admitted during the Fifth Nonaligned Conference at Colombo in August 1976. Their sympathizers—whose numbers may have dwindled lately because of revulsion against their murderous actions—are of great importance to the terrorists, as a screen behind which the terrorists stay invisible until the moment they strike. The terrorists know that without such support they are hopelessly isolated. Only in some countries of South America are social conditions so bad that the terrorist "fish" still find sufficient "water" to swim in; elsewhere they operate in the name of one or another of the various national liberation groups such as the Palestinians fighting against Israel, or the blacks against the whites in southern Africa.

Much larger is the number of *activists* who continue their radical political efforts without going underground. For some of them this is a full-time job. Others follow more or less normal professions, mainly to earn enough money for their own sustenance.

The third group, larger yet, consists of people who are the *long marchers* of whom Dutschke has spoken. Some have entered existing political parties, or are involved in helping certain causes (such as the fight against nuclear power plants), or individual candidates for election to public office (here the "children's crusade" for Eugene McCarthy in 1968 comes to mind). Very many decide to go into professions where they can work as—to use a German term—"multiplicators," primarily as teachers in schools and colleges, where they are making themselves felt increasingly, but also as preachers, journalists, or actors. Bookselling helps in the "multiplication" of political ideas; I mentioned Cohn-Bendit's bookshop in Frankfurt and might add the name of Ira Sandperl, who sees to it that one of the best shops on the West Coast (near Stanford University) is always supplied with books on subjects close to his heart, such as nonviolence, pacifism, and psychology.

There remains the fourth category. It is in numbers—though not in importance—certainly by far the largest group, consisting of those *who have left the movement*, whose involvement in the student revolt, even if a passionate one, turned out to have been not more than a phase in their transition from boy to man, from girl to mature woman, a way to overcome "alienation," to find one's own "identity." For those who have since entered the Establishment, the memory of the rebellious years might be embarrassing, but most shrug it off as one of the many ways to "sow wild

365

oats" when one is young and boisterous. Many even enjoy, as Günter Grass predicted, talking about the youthful adventures that are now well behind them. Some, who may not be aware of it, were molded by their experience; to this day I find that Germans of my age who went through the Youth Movement of the twenties have retained unmistakable characteristics—their way of shaking hands, their facial expressions when greeting each other, their lively interest in certain topics of conversation, in the poets and writers of those days (Hermann Hesse for one), in old folk songs, and, in the case of women, a predilection for simple adornments, not too different from what the street people have been selling lately on the sidewalks in many countries.

So much for the people who survived. What else has remained? In what ways did the young rebels actually change the world which all of them wanted to improve and some, as a first step toward this aim, to destroy?

The observer, especially if he belongs to the older generation, notices one phenomenon above all. The personal way of life has been changed, in some areas and in some countries quite remarkably. The hippies have affected the fashions; even the great fashion dictators of Paris had to adopt some of their trends. The relationship between the sexes has become far more free and liberal than ever before in Western history; young unmarried couples live together without popular outcry, premarital sex having been condoned even by the wife of President Ford. The "back to nature" movement, which might have come anyway for ecological reasons, has been greatly speeded up by the fierce aversion of many young people to the city and its many evils. Drugs are still "in," unfortunately. Here the widespread permissiveness may be relatively undangerous if it is confined to the ritual of passing a joint around; but marijuana can be just the beginning and may eventually lead to heavier stuff, in the end to addiction. This aspect of permissiveness may prove to be the worst in the long run.

More changes are evident. Fundamental problems of a social and political kind, which formerly occupied only a very small segment of the population, have been dramatized by the youth revolt and have thus been pushed into the consciousness of large numbers of people—how to save our earth from destruction, how to make democracy more direct, how to promote social justice beyond the mere application of the letters of the law, how to improve the relations between majorities and minorities, and how to better the prisons. The political discussion of topics previously considered settled or taboo has been mightily advanced. Marxism is—to varying degrees in different countries—embedded in much of the new thinking, often unconsciously. But, in general, youth today takes Marx and his ideas with a larger grain of salt than the Left of yesterday did (and does), or the Soviet Union does today. The widespread skepticism about reason and logic, although bound to have come as a backlash against the exaggerated confidence in science and technology, prominent in the first phase of the Industrial Revolution, was intensified by youth's desire to look for truth and fulfillment in sentiments rather than in rationality, and by its drive toward the irrational.

It has been said for decades that the religion of many adults was not Christianity but, rather, success and prosperity.[15] If this is true, then it may be said that anti-materialism of the young has a religious aspect.

America's engagement in Vietnam would be over by now anyway; but undoubtedly the violent opposition of hundreds of thousands of young people against the continuation of the war accelerated the process of American withdrawal, with all its many ramifications. In itself, this is an indication of the impact which the youth revolt has had on world affairs.

Many politicians left their positions because of pressure from the young; more than one government trembled, and some governments fell. The young have, by their skepticism about the state and its officials, about government in general, damaged governmental authority by challenging the state directly and by refusing to cooperate and to identify with it.

The youth revolt has not succeeded in changing the political and economic structure of the West or of Japan, much less of that of the Communist countries, but it did succeed, to an extent unthinkable during the first stirrings of the Beatniks, in changing style and outlook. If it was a revolution, as I think it was, it was a moral and cultural revolution.

30
CONCLUSION

WHAT will be said about the youth unrest of the sixties in the history books fifty years hence? Will it appear as old rubbish on the refuse heap of history, covered by more rubbish deposited since? Or as yeast that has entered into the dough from which the bread of the future will be baked? None of us today will insist that in the slogans, activities, communal forms, and life-styles of this rebellious youth the model of the future society has been pre-formed. But many may agree that there are symptoms of the future development of society, smoke signals indicating "which way the wind blows."

The millions studying on the campuses of the world since the days of the "angry young men" have been touched, in one way or the other, by the unrest they witnessed. These millions are going to be with us for several decades—with us of the older generation who had experienced so much before they came on the scene, and also with the next generation, which perhaps is facing a less stormy adolescence. They will be among us—a few as open or camouflaged revolutionaries, and very many with questions on their minds which we must face and, if we can, answer. These living witnesses and bearers of the unrest are a daily challenge to our society, and the unrest itself, which we can now look back on as a more or less completed phase of our recent past, is not settled just because—for how long?—law and order have been restored. "The heroes are tired," some say mockingly at the end of a turbulent period, satisfied with themselves because they kept clear of the vortex. But others may come along to ask still more impatiently, to demand more urgently, and perhaps to attack more furiously if we ignore the challenge, if we deny the answer because we never quite understood the unrest.

Of the factors which seriously affected the course of the rebellion, one has been eliminated—the war in Vietnam. But this was by no means the triggering event, and it directly affected only the American youth, and that not before the summer of 1967. While the Vietnam war was receding into history, one more development helped to quiet the young generation: the worldwide economic recession, which began in the early seventies but was greatly exacerbated by the oil boycott of 1973–1974 and its aftermath. Jobs became scarcer; one had to study harder to obtain them and work harder to keep them. This calming effect of the economic recession may disappear as the economy gets back into stride. Emerging from its shadow, the young people may find that many of the issues for which they fought in the sixties are still with them, again requiring their involvement. If, on the other hand, the upswing of the mid-seventies should prove to have been deceptive and the boom of the fifties and sixties but a brief and unusual moment in history, if unemployment on a large scale should be here to stay as a permanent feature of a civilization with unlimited productivity but limited resources, then the demand for a new social order along "socialist" lines might become loud and pressing.

TREMORS AND QUAKES

It is a moot question whether our civilization will adapt itself within this century to the tremendous scientific and technological changes of our epoch. (I do not expect that it will; these changes have not yet run their course, and every day new events take us by surprise, demanding ever new reactions and new changes.) The break in the continuity of our civilization, from which came insecurity, alienation, and identity crises with all the consequences described above, this *Zeitbruch,* seems to me the true source of the rebellion. This break has not disappeared, nor has the danger that an atomic catastrophe might destroy our civilization—although the danger has receded in our everyday thoughts (because we have learned to "live with the bomb"), it has, in fact, increased with the growing number and sophistication of atomic weapons and the proliferation of the potential for their production.

After the unrest of the sixties and early seventies has become a

369

thing of the past, new tremors along the generational fault line must be expected—in other forms but from similar causes. For people, like myself, who were born as optimists, this is no reason for alarm: They know that creative tension between old and new keeps people and nations on the alert and their blood in circulation. Those who avoid such confrontation or try to prevent it completely by force (the Batistas, Salazars, and Francos, the last tsars, and also the Brezhnevs) must pay for this someday. A condition of stability and peace, which most of us desire for our own nations and for the world, is not identical with rigidity. On the contrary, it presupposes flexibility and readiness to change.

"Tremors"—the term should not be unexpected in a book which largely was written in northern California, an area that is endangered seismologically and where in 1906 a tremendous earthquake laid waste a great city. This danger is caused by a mighty north-south fissure, hundreds of miles long, the San Andreas Fault, to the west of which the earth moves northward a half inch or so every year. Along most of the fault this gigantic process is turned harmless by hundreds of small tremors every year (most of which are noticeable only on very sensitive seismographs); they constantly release the tension without causing damage because they prevent it from building up to a danger point. It is only where these tremors do not occur, as in a part of the Bay Area, that a destructive earthquake might happen. In fact, a whole army of scientists is trying to find ways and means for producing small tremors in this area—artificially—in order to prevent the accumulation of destructive tensions.

The dynamism of modern scientific and technological development can well be compared to the overwhelming power of these tectonic forces. They too continuously produce—in the social and political field—tensions which discharge in catastrophes (i.e., revolutions) if they are not released every so often by timely changes (i.e., reforms). To help bring about such changes, such solutions of existing tensions, is in my opinion the true function of youthful unrest. Hence it is necessary, even though it often takes annoying and sometimes abhorrent forms.

SHAPE OF THINGS TO COME?

Youth itself does not offer us any clear information about where it intends to go. Not only is it too impetuous, too absolute in its demands, too abstract in its thinking to do this; it also refuses even to indicate the outlines of the future it aspires to. The explanation the young people give for their behavior is simple and sounds logical. How could we, they say, design plans for a world which no one has seen yet? Would this not be like drawing maps for a country that no one has ever visited before? We would have to make our plans for the future, they continue, on the basis of experience in the world surrounding us today, and this we shall not do, because we want to escape this world, not remain tied to it, not continue the present interminably. And even if we were to describe the utopia of the radically different world which we want to build after the overthrow of the present order, we would violate our fundamental precept of spontaneity, manipulating in advance those who in that crucial hour of change will be called upon to act—in other words, we would be doing exactly that for which we reproach all rulers up till now.

How then are we to find out the direction humanity will take? At all times artists have proved to be equipped with particularly sensitive antennae for what was coming, for disturbances of all kinds, both in their own spiritual sphere and in social and economic areas. The great Swiss psychologist C. G. Jung, Freud's pupil and antagonist, considered works of art to be bridges to a yet unseen coast, expressions of things which are real but still unknown. The prophetic aspect of the arts, he said, is often understood only much later. If a poet who has been out of fashion suddenly is rediscovered, then this happens, according to Jung, because the consciousness of the public has now caught up with the level the artist had attained much earlier; as a symbol his vision had been there all along, but fresher eyes were needed to discover it, for old eyes only see what they are accustomed to. This sounds as if Jung had spoken about the surprising Hesse renaissance of the last ten or fifteen years; in reality these ideas were expressed in a lecture in 1922.[1]

Long before the First World War and the collapse of the second German empire, Friedrich Nietzsche predicted "growing darkness and an eclipse of the sun, the like of which the earth might never have witnessed before."[2] To be sure, after the first great gloominess, the Germans experienced, in the Weimar Republic, a new flowering of literature—but who, except for some specialists, knew then and appreciated Kafka, who drew, still in the twenties, the pictures of an anonymous administrative machinery in whose soulless nets helpless people were to be caught and tortured, a machinery which at that time had hardly begun to emerge? At the same time the German Expressionists covered canvas upon canvas with the colors of a chaos that lay still in the future. Three years ago, among the works of the late Max Ernst at New York's Guggenheim Museum, I saw *Le Massacre des Innocents,* the visionary painting in which he showed (in 1920!) the atmosphere of Auschwitz—two decades before that camp was established. The author Heinrich Mann (brother of Thomas Mann) once wrote: "If literature does not know in advance what a society and a century can become, then no one does." This is true not only of literature but of art in general.

We do not have to assign prophetic faculties to youth; enough that it looks at the world with new and fresh eyes. To admit this is difficult for the older generation. The present book has been written in the hope that it will help in building bridges across the generation gap. Therefore, in this last chapter, a double question must be asked: Which tendencies for the future can be discerned or at least foreseen from the character of the youth rebellion? And what are we to say about them?

NEW PROFILE

An American or British author would use other terms than I shall; but perhaps I can succeed in explaining what I mean by making a comparison with the young people of my student days in the Germany of the twenties. As Gallup polls did not exist then, not even in America, the country of the polls, memories must be used. I find five main differences between my student generation and the present one.

First: In spite of all youthful obstinacy, we were, in the twenties, far more conscious of history, far more embedded in traditions. Among ourselves we avoided most of the conventional forms, but it did not bother us if others complied with them, though we knew that very many did this only for show; they were, we felt, fundamentally hypocrites, practicing what amounted to a "double standard." Today's youth, in contrast, denounces all hypocrisies and thus asserts a single standard, not only for itself but also for its elders. It does this in the spirit of an unusually generous tolerance toward the private (not the political!) behavior of its age-group and under the widely accepted motto "Do your thing!" This attitude manifests itself in a wide variety of clothes, hairstyles, and sexual attitudes, and in the almost suicidal experiments with drugs. Stand on your head, streak naked through the streets, make love while others are watching, bring your baby or your dog to class—do your thing! You can call this absolute honesty, though it be absolute disregard of others.

Second: Fifty years ago we were oriented very much toward achievement; the ideal of equality did not have a high priority for us. *Suum cuique* (To each his deserts)—this motto of the Prussian kings seemed self-evident and correct. Inequality of achievement and therefore of living standards was taken for granted. If someone agitated for equality, he was surely a failure. Equality of chances—of course; we thought that it truly existed in our country, and our American peers were of the same opinion, with their slogan "From rags to riches." Failures could not count on sympathy. Youth today, on the other hand, considers equality to be one of the most urgent ideals. "To each the same" might be their motto now. Correspondingly, the attitude toward the ideal of justice has changed. For us, justice was the correct application of the law. For the young of today, justice is what enhances equality, including that of minorities. In my youth, hardly anyone outside the legal profession was interested in the penal system or in prison reform; those who lived along the edge of society (homosexuals, for example) had to shift for themselves. Today's young radicals feel a strong tie with all the outsiders of society: the blacks, the prisoners, the homosexuals, the drug addicts, the handicapped, even the mentally retarded—in a word, with the underpriviledged and, collectively, with the Third World.

Third: We were passionate patriots and judged the peoples of Europe and the world by one criterion—whether they were for or, as we Germans were, against the Treaty of Versailles. Those others who were against the treaty were few in number—the Austrians, the Hungarians, the Bulgarians, the Turks (who all lost territories after their defeat); the South Tyroleans (who had been handed to Italy against their wish); and, strangely enough, the Chinese (who opposed the forced concessions to Japan). The Indians, to be sure, were not against the treaty, but they were against the rule of the British, who favored it, and so were with us. The fact that the Soviets, for reasons of their own, had repudiated the order imposed on Europe at Versailles was for many of us, including the officers of the then minute German army, more important than their being Bolsheviks and atheists. How different it is today! National sentiments have evaporated, most of all for the young Germans. For today's young radicals the world does not consist of their nation's friends and foes, but of "oppressors" and "oppressed." Hence the enthusiasm for Ho Chi Minh and the murdered Lumumba; hence the rocks thrown at American embassies; hence, also, since the Soviet invasions of Hungary (1956) and Czechoslovakia (1968), the lack of sympathy with the U.S.S.R. I do not think that the young today are more "socialist" than those of the twenties. The "socialist yearning" which was frequently mentioned then exists for many now, but in those days the Soviet economic system with its "planned economy" was believed to be an alternative to capitalism. Today, most young people, including those on the Left, know that Soviet socialism is essentially a rather inefficient state capitalism, and that planned economy is identical with monopolistic bureaucracy. Hence their unceasing search for new economic and political forms.

Fourth: We were not afraid of a strong state. On the contrary, we demanded it; this too explains why the weak Weimar Republic was little loved, and why the young went in droves to Hitler and to the Communists. The value of freedom was only understood after Hitler destroyed it. In the field of economy, many were impressed by big dimensions—giant ocean liners, giant laboratories, giant industrial plants (only in the Youth Movement was some criticism voiced). Today, youth is frightened by the ever growing corporations and factories, by organizations of all kinds, and depressed by the prospect of becoming an even smaller cog in an ever greater machine. When Columbus, in the service of the Spanish queen, started his venture into the unknown, he was, in planning and execution, his own master. But the first men on the moon? They knew that the computer had it all figured out in advance, the exact time and the exact spot of their landing. Only for brief moments did they act on their own; everything else had been practiced for months, as if it were for a ballet—even the kangaroo hops that amused us on our TV screens. There are countless other examples of our lack of independence. Therefore we must understand the urge of the young protesters to be spontaneous, to "do your thing," their yearning for the "happening," for breaking out of an always calculated system—if need be with the help of drugs, or by force.

Fifth: In principle the old German youth movement was for women's equality; the *Wandervogel* and many other youth groups had girls and boys alike in their ranks. But the traditional attitude concerning the roles of the sexes was largely intact. To marry and to have many children in the loving care of the mother—that was the general desire, too obvious even to talk about. Not so today. The feminist movement has changed the outlook of millions in the young generation; the ongoing "birth strike" in my country (which puts Germany among the countries with the lowest birth rates in the world) is one of the—one might say "natural"—consequences. The dream of a matriarchal society no longer sounds queer, but in my student days it had rarely been voiced; one of the exceptions was Gerhard Hauptmann's novel *Die Insel der grossen Mutter* (The Island of the Great Mother, 1924). But now one young (male) reader of my book's German edition has written to me that the end of the throw-away society and the beginning of the ecological era (both mentioned in Chapter 7) were welcome steps away from our male-oriented age; women, by their very nature in favor of conserving and storing, were the proper leaders for a society that had reached the "limits of growth."

And, finally, sixth: My generation, certainly its great majority, knew (more correctly, thought it knew) what it was living for. The meaning of life, of course, was not the same for all, but it was simple and clear, whatever the position. For some (a long time before Hitler appeared on the stage) it meant the restitution of honor and greatness to the defeated and humiliated Fatherland, for others the building of a communist paradise through world revolution under Moscow's leadership. Everything in between these two positions was increasingly crushed and absorbed. Today, the German Fatherland has lost its magnetic attraction, as has the Soviet Union its glory as "the Fatherland of all toilers." Success in one's profession, which gave purpose to former generations, is being discounted today as egotistical; those who experience it often have to fight a bad conscience rather than enjoy a proud satisfaction. The shrinking numbers of those who accept unquestioningly what the established churches say about life's purpose make it understandable also why the questions of the young are so urgent and sometimes desperate, and the answers they find often so curious, if not bizarre. And yet, a young generation that was not searching for life's purpose would be devoid of life and a victim of premature withering.

What has been said so far does not mean that youth today acts in accordance with the ideas it voices. Few actually work among the underprivileged, and many of those who are willing to put their ideals into practice do this selectively, which means within their own groups. But though the actual proving of good intentions may be rare, no one can doubt that American or German youth of the seventies differs from that of the fifties. Thus it seems

permissible to project the development of the last two decades a
bit into the future, and to assume that these young people's image
of the future affords us some glimpses of the features of the "new
man."

REBUTTAL

Let me add some thoughts of my own. Though they may seem
"conservative" to some younger readers, they have been checked,
over these decades, with newly emerging realities and experiences, and also with the ideas of the young themselves. Often they
have been modified or replaced accordingly.

We can coexist as citizens of one state and as nations of one
world in a dignified manner only if we succeed in achieving a
canon of values and behavioral norms that is understandable to
all and acceptable to most. On this road, all declarations, even
those of Helsinki in 1975, are milestones if they proclaim human
rights and regulate international behavior, though unfortunately
some of them will not truly be lived up to for quite some time to
come. Even voluntary organizations such as Amnesty International, blithely overlooked by the dictatorships, are important as
bearers of hopes held by what is probably a majority of the thinking people in many countries, including those in the East.

It is, of course, not enough to search for values only in politics
and in international fields; we must do it also in individual
human relationships. If we were to do this by insisting simply on
the restoration of yesterday's norms, we could be sure of failure.
Youth would not accept this, least of all in the field which for
many is topic number one: The broken taboos in the relationship
between the sexes cannot be restored. But there is one principle
on which agreement should be possible—that each one who enters
a relationship, in whichever form, takes upon himself a responsibility toward the partner. Sex merely for the purpose of satiating
an urge hurts the dignity and integrity of the other.

My second point concerns the reproach hurled by the rebellious
young against the adults' glorification of achievement and
performance—of the work ethic. This problem cannot be solved by
cutting through it with a sword, as Alexander the Great did with
the Gordian knot.

We do have in the Western world the facts of overproduction
and the efforts of even sharper salesmanship to sell what is being
produced by arousing new demands; at the same time, we have
begun to feel the pinch of the "limits of growth." This explains

why many countries have a high unemployment rate, with which we will have to live. The fear of ending up unemployed is a dampening factor for young people when they think about their future careers; it encourages them to opt for the hippie way of life. This makes sense, in a way, for society too: If there will be, from now on, close to 10 million unemployed in the United States and Germany together, some of them might just as well be happy-go-lucky hippie types who buy a decaying farm somewhere in the wilderness, where they then live a primitive but contented life, far away from the sad slum homes of so many of our unemployables today. It so happens that the aversion for what we would call normal work coincides with a phase of structural unemployment. It is hard to blame young people when they refuse to join what they call the "rat race" at a time when many millions go without work anyway. The time when you *had* to work in order to stay alive has passed. Nowadays you *do* stay alive if you don't work; in fact, you can live quite pleasantly if you reduce your demands to the hippie or commune level.

On the other hand, we must face the tremendous task, unimaginable three or four generations ago, of feeding and housing some 4 billion people today, some 5 or 6 billion tomorrow. We must even raise the living standards of those who are still far behind in the comforts of life, in order to prevent them from feeling underprivileged, abused, exploited, and desperate enough to attack like so many locusts our islands of prosperity. This forces the industrialized nations to produce more and more, to have first-rate scientists, technicians, managers, foremen, and workers who can carry out this gigantic assignment and find new sources of energy, food, and raw materials, and new methods to preserve nature's precarious equilibrium. Thus, we are likely to face a paradoxical situation: We shall have to insist on high performance and the work ethic while there will be, at the same time, millions of people who are idle either by choice or by necessity. Densely populated countries with few, if any, raw materials will not be able to exist if a majority of their people take up the hippie life-style. We cannot possibly abandon the achievement society as an antiquated form of life. But those who champion this kind of society will have to get used to the arguments of those who have nothing but scorn for it. Some people advocate the spreading of work more thinly, so as to abolish unemployment by simply reducing the number of working hours per week. But such dilution could be tolerated only within modest limits, at least under present psychological conditions. Maybe someday humanity will be able to get along without a work ethic; it does not now.

In this entire field we are on totally new ground. Hitherto we have looked on idleness as a vice or as a temporary emergency in a time of recession. Now we must find ways and means of bringing about what one might call creative idleness, and in this respect, I say without irony, the young will be a great help. The urge to find their identity, so strongly developed among them, can be satisfied more easily in creative idleness than in the misery of unemployment.

We must also try to find ways which would lead away from that scourge of modern times, alienation (which Charlie Chaplin so brilliantly exposed in his aptly named film *Modern Times*). By removing the worker far from the finished product, to which he contributes but a minute part, the conveyor belt has become the symbol of alienation. But can we go back to the days preceding Henry Ford? Hardly. Some factories, most notably a Swedish automobile plant, are experimenting with new production methods which would dispense with the conveyor, but we are still far from a solution.

One of the strongest aversions we have met among the young is that toward authority. Here too the Gordian solution cannot be applied. At present, as a result of the fears created during the economic depression, youth accepts the authority of its elders far more readily than in the sixties; but I doubt that young people will revert to the docility of the Eisenhower years. Youth will also voice its demand that authority, to be respected, must be based on the personal merits of those who exercise it, not on positions achieved behind closed doors; and, no doubt, authority of merit is preferable to authority of the *ex officio* kind. But in mass societies there just are not enough people with such endowments; hence, authority of office must be respected too. No modern state can exist without an efficient bureaucracy, which by its nature is largely anonymous and faceless; for this reason alone it will remain unable to exercise the personal authority that, at least in the ideal case, elected officials possess.

The dangers inherent in submission to personal authority only became evident in the thirties with the rise of Mussolini and Hitler. Modern democracy is entitled to demand its citizens' respect for the leadership of their personally elected representatives, to whom they must then entrust the employment of a nonelected but efficient bureaucracy.

Terrorists must be subjected to the order achieved by the consensus of elected representatives. The terrorists could be reminded of the words written by their Russian predecessors. After an American president, James Garfield, was shot by an assassin and died in September 1881, a declaration was published on October 23 of that year in the terrorist paper *Narodnaya volya* (People's Will) by young Russians whose bombs had killed Tsar Alexander II. They protested "in the name of Russian Revolutionaries against all such deeds of violence as that just committed in America." They rejected terrorism in such a country:

> In a land where the citizens are free to express their ideas, and where the will of the people does not only make the law but appoints the person who is to carry the law into effect, in such a country political assassination is the manifestation of a despotic tendency identical with that to whose destruction in Russia we have devoted ourselves. Despotism, whatever may be the parties or whoever may be the individuals that exercise it, is always blameworthy, and force can be justified only when employed to resist force.[3]

It will take patient persuasion to bring our radical New Left to understand this attitude. This will only be possible by our adopting a truly democratic attitude, by refraining from treating our present order as taboo, as something unchangeable, and by listening judiciously to young voices demanding change.

Obviously youth faces one particular difficulty: It is moving in an unknown territory without convincing models. The heroes of the twenties and thirties are gone, some of them in disgrace and shame. Newer ones have faded or lost their credibility. Moscow erected a disappointing oppressive monopoly bureaucratism; Mao shook hands with Nixon and was succeeded by matter-of-fact pragmatists; Castro became the Kremlin's satellite. The radiant Kennedy, who summoned America and the entire West to new frontiers, was murdered and had no one to take his place. There are no road signs in unknown lands.

The realization is growing that we are all in a new land where the old rules and maps are of little use, in a twilight where we cannot yet see the shape of things to come. To find our way through the unknown we need—on a world scale, not just in the West—the discriminating experience of the old as well as the taboo-breaking courage of the young.

NOTES ON SOURCES

THE books and articles mentioned in abbreviated form in the following notes on sources are given with all necessary publication data in the bibliography under the name of their authors or editors.

1 START WITH A HOWL

1. Charters, *Kerouac*, p. 21.
2. Kerouac, *On the Road*, pp. 173 f.
3. Gilbert Millstein, *New York Times*, November 5, 1957.
4. Cook, *Beat*, p. 6.
5. *Nugget*, October 1960; quoted in Charters, *Kerouac*, pp. 361, 403.
6. Cook, *Beat*, p. 65.
7. Kramer, *Ginsberg*, p. 86.
8. Cook, *Beat*, p. 108.
9. Cook, *Beat*, pp. 111 f.
10. Kramer, *Ginsberg*, pp. 106, 112.
11. Cook, *Beat*, p. 7.
12. Snyder, *Earth House Hold*, p. 105.
13. *New York Times*, November 16, 1962; quoted in Charters, *Kerouac*, p. 169.
14. Charters, *Kerouac*, p. 396.
15. Holbo and Sellen, *Eisenhower*.
16. William H. Whyte, Jr., *The Organization Man* (New York, 1956; 471 pp.).
17. Sloan Wilson, *The Man in the Gray Flannel Suit* (New York, 1955; 344 pp.).
18. Holbo and Sellen, *Eisenhower*, pp. 13, 1, 8.
19. Cook, *Beat*, p. 88.

20. Charters, *Kerouac,* pp. 246, 346, 365, 403.
21. Ibid., p. 364.
22. Cook, *Beat,* p. 152.
23. J. R. Taylor, *Anger,* pp. 9, 39 ff., 44.

2 DEVILS AND ANGELS

1. Unless stated otherwise, the quotations are from Thompson, *Hell's Angels,* pp. 153, 188, 283, 316 ff., 334.
2. See Buttons, *The Making of a President* (London, 1971; 158 pp.).
3. Jody A. Steuer, "Fear and Loathing in Tuolumne," *San Francisco Sunday Examiner and Chronicle,* August 29, 1976.
4. This and the following quotations are from Bacciocco, *New Left,* pp. 35, 59, 66, 69.
See also Lauter and Howe.

3 SDS AND FSM

1. C. Wright Mills, "Letter to the New Left," *New Left Review,* no. 5, September/October 1960; frequently reprinted, e.g., in Long, *New Left,* pp. 14–25.
2. The archivists of the Hoover Institution let me use these now rare documents, of which they have typed and mimeographed copies: *The Port Huron Statement* (New York [1962]; 52 pp.; 25¢); Tom Hayden, *Student and Social Action* (San Francisco, [1962]; rev. 1965; 13 pp.; 10¢); R. Alan Haber, *Students and Labor* (New York, 1962; 19 pp.; 10¢); America and the New Era (New York [1963], 30 pp.; 15¢).
3. Tom Hayden, A Movement of Many Voices (Ann Arbor, Mich., 1964/65).
4. Quoted in Sale, *SDS,* pp. 22, 166; see also Lipset and Wolin, Berkeley, pp. 37–60.
5. Quoted in Bacciocco, *New Left,* p. 151.
6. See Lipset and Wolin, *Berkeley,* pp. 66–81.
7. See Ibid., pp. 99–199 (chronology of events in Berkeley, September 10, 1964, to January 4, 1965).
8. Sale, *SDS,* p. 163.
9. In this and the preceding paragraphs I drew on Bacciocco, *New Left,* pp. 156 f.
10. Nathan Glazer, "'Student Power' in Berkeley," in Morton et al., *Youth,* pp. 275–279.
See also Adelson, Draper, Heirich, Lipset and Wolin, Miller, Wolin; on California State: Fullerton, Epstein; on Columbia: Avorn, Kahn, Kunen; on Kent: Casale, Davies, Eszterhas, Stone, Taylor et al., Warren; on San Francisco State: Barlowe, Kay Boyle, Karagueuzian, Robert Smith et al.

4 VIETNAM AND THE STUDENTS

1. Sale, *SDS*, pp. 186, 220.
2. Harrington, *Fragments*, p. 145.
3. Staar, *1976 Yearbook*, p. 521.
4. Staar, *1975 Yearbook*, p. 560.
5. Hurwitz, *Marching*, p. 103.
6. See *Statutes at Large, 1967*, vol. 81, Washington, D.C., 1968, p. 102; and *Congressional Quarterly, Weekly Report*, February 23, 1968, pp. 369–374.
7. Kelman, *Push*, pp. 118 f.
8. Theodore H. White, *The Making of the President 1968* (pb: New York, 1970; 570 pp.), pp. 127 f.
9. Sale, *SDS*, pp. 635–638.
10. Lipset, *Rebellion*, pp. 44 f.
11. Bryan, *This Soldier*, p. 87.
12. Lipset, *Rebellion*, pp. 52–58.
See also Richard Boyle, Ferber, Waterhouse

5 DISINTEGRATION AND END

1. Yankelovich, *Changing Values*, p. 64; Sale, *SDS*, pp. 457, 713.
2. *New Left Notes*, December 18, 1967; quoted in Sale, *SDS*, pp. 393, 710.
3. Sale, *SDS*, p. 395.
4. *Time*, May 9, 1969.
5. *Chronicle of Higher Education*, April 6, 1970; *Public Opinion Quarterly*, Fall 1970; quoted in Sale, *SDS*, pp. 547, 720.
6. Full text also in Jacobs, *Weatherman*, pp. 51–90.
See also Bugliosi, St. John.

6 UNDERGROUND

1. Sale, *SDS*, p. 411 (see also p. 711).
2. Ibid., p. 615.
3. For the quotations from the Flint meeting see Sale, *SDS*, pp. 627 f.
4. Dellinger, *More Power*, p. 152.
5. See Powers, *Diana*.
6. Raskin, *Weather Eye*.
7. *New York Times*, January 14, 1975, pp. 14 f.
8. Stern, *With the Weathermen*, pp. 220 f., 239, 255.
9. Raskin, *Weather Eye*, pp. 92–100.
10. Bryan, *This Soldier*, p. 119.
11. See also Bacciocco, *New Left*, p. 26.
12. Bryan, *This Soldier*, pp. 323 f.
13. Belcher and West, *Patty*, pp. 318–347.
14. Michener, *Kent State*, pp. 447–455.
15. Sale, *SDS*, p. 590.

16. See Vogelsang, *Long Dark Night.*
17. Mailer, *Armies,* pp. 211 f.
18. Theodore Roszak, "The Disease Called Politics," in Paul Goodman, ed., *Seeds of Liberation,* (New York, 1965); quoted in Vogelsang, *Long Dark Night,* p. 167.

7 NEW INTERESTS

1. *Newsweek,* January 20, 1975, p. 69.
2. Quoted in Wendell Robert Carr's Introduction in Mill, *The Subjection of Women* (Cambridge and London, 1870; 101 pp.), p. xiii.
3. Jane Adams, "On Equality for Women," *New Left Notes,* January 1967.
4. See Freeman, *Politics; Women.*
5. Evelyn Goldfield et al., "A Woman is a Sometime Thing," in Long, *New Left,* p. 201.
6. Hendin, "Psychoanalyst."
7. Leni Wildflower, in Preface in Potter, *A Name,* p. xiv ff.
8. Lucinda Franks, "The 4-Year Odyssey of Jane Alpert: From Revolutionary Bomber to Feminist," *New York Times,* January 14, 1975.
9. *New York Times,* May 7, 1975.
10. Virginia Lee Warren, "This Day of Liberation: They Study How to Please Their Men," *New York Times,* August 28, 1975, p. 14.

8 TURNING INWARD

1. Ellwood, *One Way,* pp. 59–63.
2. Ward, *Far-Out Saints,* pp. 137–153.
3. James J. Gill, S.J., "A Jesuit Psychiatrist on the Jesus Revolution," *Intellectual Digest,* April 1972, pp. 85 ff.
4. Harriet Van Horne, "The Jesus Movement," *New York Post,* January 17, 1972, p. 34.
5. "Rallying for Jesus," *Life,* June 30, 1972, p. 43.
6. Ellen Graham, "Transcendent Trend," *Wall Street Journal,* August 31, 1972; *Congressional Record,* May 6, 1974, no. 62, pp. 7105–7109.
7. *San Francisco Chronicle* and *San Francisco Examiner,* October 13, 1975.
8. Edward B. Fiske, "Parents vs. Religious Communes," *New York Times,* March 5, 1973, p. 1; *Newsweek,* March 12, 1973, p. 44; *International Herald Tribune,* November 25, 1974, p. 7.
9. Jerry M. Flint, "Rise in Occultism Viewed as Revolt Against Science," *New York Times,* September 10, 1972.
10. *Newsweek,* April 9, 1973, p. 91.
11. Sun Myung Moon, *New Hope: Twelve Talks* (Washington, D.C., 1973; 103 pp.), p. v.
12. Quoted in Lee Sannella, *Kundalini:—Psychosis or Transcendence?* (in press).
13. Beth Ashley, "Sikh Community Movin' On," *Independent Journal* (San Rafael, Calif.), May 8, 1975, p. 13.

14. Michael Grieg, "Inner Peace Puts Sex on Shelf," *San Francisco Chronicle,* October 4, 1975, p. 12.
15. W. E. Barnes, "Jerry Brown," *San Francisco Sunday Examiner and Chronicle,* November 16, 1975., p. 3.
See also Casebeer, Holzer, Metzner, Schurmacher.

9 THE GERMAN SDS, ITS ENEMIES AND ALLIES

1. Hager, *Rebellen von Berlin,* pp. 26–35.
2. Hermann, *Revolte,* pp. 40 f.
3. Benneter et al., *Februar 1968,* p. 9.
4. Ibid., pp. 42 f.
5. Ibid., p. 97.
6. Günter Grass, in Litten, *Eine verpasste,* pp. 9–11.
See also Ahlberg, Grossmann and Negt, Oelinger; on Berlin: Larsson, Nevermann.

10 RUDI DUTSCHKE

1. Marcuse, *One-Dimensional Man,* p. 257.
2. Marcuse, "Repressive Tolerance," in Wolff, *Critique,* p. 123.
3. Günter Bartsch, "Die Situationisten," *Osteuropa* (Aachen), April 1976.
4. Dutschke, in Bergmann et al., *Rebellion,* p. 45.
5. Dutschke, *Versuch,* pp. 317, 321 f., 328 f., 333 f.
6. Dutschke, *Sowjetunion,* pp. 11 f., 301.
7. Dutschke, in Bergmann, *Rebellion,* p. 76.

11 STUDENT AND WORKER

1. Marcuse, *One-Dimensional Man,* pp. xii, 2, xiii.
2. Ibid., p. 257.
3. H. O. Smith, *Japan's First,* p. 77.
4. *Der Spiegel,* no. 36 (1973), pp. 23 f.
5. Sale, *SDS,* p. 525.
6. Marcuse, *Counterrevolution,* p. 5.
7. Kukuck, *Student,* esp. pp. 103–115, 127–150, 174–189.
8. H. E. Brand, in *links* (Offenbach), no. 70 (October 1975), pp. 15–17.
9. Schneider, *Die lange Wut,* pp. 51 f., 57 f., 60 f., 77, 80, 84–86, 91 f., 255 f., 95.
10. Rudolph zur Lippe, "Objektiver Faktor Subjektivität," *Kursbuch,* no. 35 (April 1974), p. 3.
11. Quoted in Allemann, *Macht,* p. 209.

12 ENTER THE THIRD WORLD

1. Bergmann et al., *Rebellion,* pp. 64, 63, 67–69.

NOTES ON SOURCES

2. *Kursbuch,* no. 9 (June 1967), pp. 181–199.
3. *Kursbuch,* no. 13 (June 1968), pp. 1–17.
4. Fanon, *Wretched,* p. 311.
5. Bergmann et al., *Rebellion,* p. 91.
6. Rabehl, in Bergmann et al., *Rebellion,* pp. 151–177, esp. 164 f.
7. Kunen, *Strawberry Statement,* p. 155.
8. Gregor, *Fascist,* p. 351.

13 THE GERMAN TERRORISTS

1. Bundeskriminalamt, *Baader-Meinhof-Report,* p. 12.
2. Riemeck, in Meinhof, *Dokumente,* p. 105.
3. Ibid., p. 105.
4. *konkret,* no. 14 (1968).
5. Röhl, *Fünf Finger,* p. 285.
6. Riemeck, in Meinhof, *Dokumente,* pp. 106 f.
7. *Der Spiegel,* no. 27 (1972), p. 71.
8. Röhl, *Fünf Finger,* p. 419.
9. *Der Spiegel,* no. 24 (1972), p. 24.
10. Bookhagen, *Versuch* [Kommune 2], p. 48.
11. *Der Spiegel,* no. 21 (1975), p. 39.
12. *Der Spiegel,* no. 24 (1972), p. 22.
13. *Der Spiegel,* no. 37 (1972), p. 62.
14. Brückner, *Gewalt,* pp. 43 ff.
15. Ibid., p. 101.
16. Quoted in *Frankfurter Allgemeine Zeitung,* June 10, 1972.

14 WITH HELMET AND GEBABO

1. Dowsey, *Zengakuren,* pp. 215 ff.
2. H. D. Smith, *Japan's First,* pp. 27, 66, 215, 217 f.
3. Ibid., p. 263.
4. Battistini, *Postwar,* p. 149.
5. Tsurumi, *Social Change,* p. 332.
6. *Newsweek,* May 6, 1974, p. 25.
7. Ian Gorman, "Japan Troubled by Its Leftists," *New York Post,* June 26, 1972.
8. Steinhoff, "Portrait."
9. Most of the figures are taken from Passin, "Changing Values," as is the sample from the comedy.
See also Bowen, Duke, and "University and Society."

15 GUERRILLAS

1. See Debray, *Revolution.*
2. Labrousse, *Tupamaros,* p. 47.
3. Abraham Guillén, *La Angonía del Imperialismo* (Buenos Aires, 1957), and *El Imperialismo del Dólar* (Buenos Aires, 1952; 702 pp.).

385

4. Hodges, Introduction to Guillén, *Philosophy*.
5. Guillén, *Estrategia de la Guerrilla Urbana* (Montevideo, 1966; 133 pp.); excerpts in Guillén, *Philosophy*, pp. 229–302.
6. Guillén, *Philosophy*, pp. 11, 19 f., 39 f.
7. Ibid., p. 251.
8. German text in Alves, *Zerschlagt*.
9. Jackson, *People's Prison*.
10. Quoted in Gebhardt, *Guerillas*, pp. 60–65.
11. Ibid., p. 135.
12. Allemann, *Macht*, pp. 11, 383 f.; on Lamarca, see p. 307.
13. Ibid., p. 359.
14. C. Johnson, *Autopsy*, pp. 88 f.
15. See Tophoven, *Politik*.
16. Guevara, *Complete Bolivian Diaries*, pp. 151, 202.
See also Gilio, Goldenberg, Huberman.

16 THE YEAR OF THE STUDENTS

1. Statera, *Death*, p. 105.
2. Ibid., p. 170.
3. See Carlson, *Hötorgskravallerna*.
4. Hartley, *State of England*, pp. 73 f.
5. Sedgwick, "Varieties," pp. 53 f.
6. Widgery, *The Left*, p. 513.
7. Sedgwick, "Varieties," pp. 63 f.
8. Levin, *Pendulum Years*, p. 253.
9. Fisk, "Student Unrest," pp. 82 f.
10. University of Essex, *Report*.
11. Ibid., p. 26.
12. See bibliographies in B. Brown, *Protest*, and Schnapp, *French Student Uprising*.
13. Roland Bacri, *Canard Enchaîné*, May 3, 1965; quoted in Claassen, *Rebellion*, p. 127.
14. See Peters, *Kunst*.
15. B. Brown, *Protest*, p. 14.
16. Cohn-Bendit, *Obsolete Communism*, p. 62.
17. *Observer*, London, May 10, 1970.
18. Theo Sommer, in *Die Zeit*, June 7, 1968.
19. *Neue Zeit*, June 8; *Neue Zeitung*, June 14; *Express*, August 1, 1968.
20. *Neue Zürcher Zeitung* (foreign ed.), June 1, 1968, p. 17.
21. *Die Zeit*, July 12, 1968, p. 16.
22. *New York Times*, January 15, 1975.
23. See Poniatowska, *La Noche*; Roberto Blanco Moheno, *Tlatelolco, Historia de una Infamia* (Mexico City, 1973; 286 pp.); Juan Miguel de Mora, *Tlatelolco 68* (Mexico City, 1973; 178 pp.).
See also on Belgium: Studenten; on Canada: Daniels, Harding, Reid, Roussopoulos; on Finland: Silius-Broo; on France: Bourges, Claassen, Glucksmann, Richard Johnson, Lefebvre, Priaulx, Singer, Touraine; on Great Britain: Crouch, Jacko, Kidd, Martin, Neville, Parkin; on Hong

Kong: Ta Kung Pao; on India: Altbach, Cormack, Desai, Gupta, Kakar, Mehta, Neelsen, Singh; on Iran: Arasteh; on Latin America: Silvert, David Smith; on Netherlands: Coenjaarts, Tuynman; on Puerto Rico: Liebmann.

17 UNDER RED FLAGS

1. "Feniks," in *Grani* (Frankfurt), December 1962, pp. 87–190.
2. Ibid., p. 179.
3. Ibid., p. 87.
4. Ibid., p. 178.
5. Ibid., p. 151.
6. Ibid., pp. 124, 143.
7. See Gerstenmaier, *The Voices.* The Samizdat Archive of Radio Liberty, Munich, comprises more than 15,000 pages.
8. Raina, *Krise,* p. 70.
9. Text in *Survey,* no. 68 (July 1968), pp. 114 f.
10. See Kuroń and Modzelewski, "Open Letter."
11. "Jun-Lipanj 1968 Dokumenti," *Praxis* (Zagreb), nos. 1–2 (1969).
12. Ibid., pp. 62 f.
13. Goldenberg, *Kommunismus,* pp. 352 f., 599.
14. *Peking Review,* February 9, 1976, pp. 11–13.
15. Yeung Cheng, "Vom Rotgardisten zum Revolutionären Marxisten," *Die Internationale,* October 1974, pp. 139–146.
16. Mikhail Demidov, in *Literaturnaya gazeta* (Moscow), October 2, 1974, p. 11.
17. Arkadi Vaksberg, in *Literaturnaya gazeta* (Moscow), October 15, 1975, p. 12.
18. Ochlies Wolf, *Selbstmorde und Selbstmordentwicklung in Osteuropa* (Cologne: Bundesinstitut für ostwissenschaftliche und internationale Studien, November 1975; 46 pp).
19. Vladimir Tendryakov, *Die Nacht nach der Entlassung* (Frankfurt, 1975), p. 10.
20. *Polityka,* August 30, 1975.
See also on China: Chang, Chow; on Cuba: Carbajal; on the U.S.S.R.: Feldbrugge, Lewytzkyj, Reddaway, von Tarnow, Tökes; on Eastern Europe in general: Neuburg, Stafford.

18 THE SCENE

1. Hollstein, *Untergrund.*
2. Kaiser, *Underground;* Berke, ed., *Counter Culture;* Schwendter, *Theorie.*
3. Kreuzer, *Boheme.*
4. Bonn, *Unter Hippies;* J. D. Brown, ed., *Hippies;* B. Wolfe, *Hippies.*
5. *Frankfurter Allgemeine Zeitung,* November 13, 1975.
6. Rubin, *Do It!* pp. 122, 126 f., 249, 256.
7. Abbie Hoffman, *Woodstock Nation.*

NOTES ON SOURCES

8. Abbie Hoffman, *Revolution*, p. 68.
9. Jeff Nyghtbyrd, "The Many Noses of Abbie," *San Francisco Examiner*, December 5, 1975, p. 1.
10. See Tom Wolfe, *Radical Chic*.
11. James E. Tinen, "On Campus Chronicle," *Nutshell* (Berkeley) 1975/76, pp. 18–22.
12. J. W. Aldridge, *Country*, p. 107.
13. Landy, *Underground Dictionary*.
14. Röhl, *Fünf Finger*, p. 280.
15. Michener, *Kent State*, pp. 221–225.
16. Hans Weigel, *Die Leiden der jungen Wörter: Ein Antiwörterbuch* (Zurich, 1974).
17. *Newsweek*, December 8, 1975, p. 14.
18. See Bugliosi and Gentry, *Helter Skelter*.
19. Eisen, ed., *Altamont*, pp. 217, 70.
See also Baacke, Foss, Neville, Wigginton; on runaways, Bock and English, Cervantes; on hippies, Coulter, Hopkins, Yablonsky; on language, Koplin, Weigt, Weiss, *Schlagwörter*.

19 THE CAMPUS

1. Lurie, *War*, p. 337.
2. UNESCO, *Statistical Yearbook, 1966*, pp. 252 f.; *1974*, pp. 425, 446.
3. Marcuse, *Ende der Utopie*, p. 80.

20 THE COMMUNE

1. Mehnert, *Youth*, pp. 159–186.
2. *New York Times*, December 17, 1970.
3. *San Francisco Chronicle*, February 12, 1970.
4. Fairfield, *Communes USA*, pp. 169 f.
5. Heinlein, *Stranger*.
6. Fairfield, *Communes USA*, p. 317.
7. Houriet, *Getting Back*, p. 40.
8. Fairfield, *Communes USA*, pp. 264 f.; Houriet, *Getting Back*, p. 103.
9. Houriet, *Getting Back*, p. 19.
10. Ibid., p. 39.
11. Mehnert, *Youth*, pp. 136–158.
12. Fairfield, *Communes USA*, pp. 180 f.
13. Houriet, *Getting Back*, pp. 28 f.
14. Melville, *Communes*, pp. 236 f.
15. Fairfield, *Communes USA*, pp. 46, 173, 245, 286.
16. Rothchild and Wolf, *Children*, pp. 19, 71, 27 f., 49, 170, 179, 9, 207
17. Schwartz, "Why Communes Fail," p. 220.
18. Fairfield, *Communes USA*, pp. 190, 193–196.
19. *New York Post*, August 6, 1971.
20. See Bookhagen, *Versuch* [Kommune 2].
See also Atcheson, Darin-Drabkin (kibbutz), Diamond, Feil, Hedgepeth and Stock, Roberts, Sundancer, Ungers and Ungers (history of U.S. communes), Veysey.

21 SEX AND DRUGS

1. Röhl, *Fünf Finger*, p. 83.
2. Baxandall, ed., *Sex-Pol*, pp. 251–274.
3. Alexander Borin, "An Exciting Affair," *Literaturnaya gazeta* (Moscow), February 5, 1975, p. 12.
4. Reich, *Sexual Revolution*, p. 12.
5. Baxandall, ed., *Sex-Pol*, pp. vi, xxvi.
6. Röhl, *Fünf Finger*, pp. 257 f., 289.
7. Robinson, *Freudian Left*, p. 201.
8. See Erica Jong, *Fear of Flying* (New York, 1974; 311 pp.).
9. James Smith, and Lynn Smith, eds., *Beyond Monogamy*, p. 30.
10. Bea Pixa, "Now We're Hearing It for Chastity," *San Francisco Sunday Examiner and Chronicle*, September 21, 1975.
11. *San Francisco Chronicle*, June 8, 1975.
12. Hunt, *"Sexual Behavior,"* 1975, esp. chap. 3 and Epilogue.
13. Hunt, *"Sexual Behavior,"* 1973.
14. Barbara Schirge, in *Schwarzwälder Bote*, July 21, 1972.
15. Blum, *Students*, p. 97.
16. Houriet, *Getting Back*, p. 131.
17. Blum, *Horatio*, p. 284.
18. *Die Zeit*, September 17, 1971, p. 49.
19. *Stuttgarter Zeitung*, July 21, 1973, p. 24.
20. *Für Dich* (East Berlin), no. 34 (August 1968), pp. 20–22.
See also: Sex, O'Neill, Sorensen, Teal; drugs, Braden (LSD), Cuskey, Hendin, Nowlis.

22 ESPERANTO OF THE ROCK GENERATION

1. Ralph J. Gleason, "The Children's Crusade," in McGregor, ed., *Bob Dylan*, p. 173.
2. Neil Hickey, "A Voice Still Blowin' in the Wind," *TV Guide*, September 11–17, 1976, pp. 3–8.
3. Most biographical data and quotations are from Scaduto, *Dylan*.
4. McGregor, *Bob Dylan*, p. 2.
5. Scaduto, *Dylan*, p. 327.
6. Bugliosi and Gentry, *Helter Skelter*, pp. 238–246.
7. Aldridge, *Beatles*, pp. 109–111.
8. See Friedman, *Buried Alive*.
9. This interview was published as a brochure; see Baez, *Joan*, pp. 33, 21.
10. See Neil Hickey, "A Voice Still Blowin' in the Wind," *TV Guide*, September 11–17, 1976, pp. 3–8.
11. John F. Scott, "The Sounds of the Tuned-in Generation," in Levitt and Rubinstein, *Youth*, pp. 342–355.
12. Michael Lydon, "Rock for Sale," in Eisen, ed., *Age of Rock*, vol. 2, p. 53.
13. Felix Belair, Jr., *New York Times*, November 6, 1955.
14. A. A. [Nirumand], "Zur Kritik der Progressiven Intelligenz in Deutschland," in *Kursbuch*, no. 9 (June 1967), p. 188.
15. Dollase et al., *Rock*, pp. 44, 204.

23 THE ROAD TO VIOLENCE

1. David Abrahamsen, *Our Violent Society* (New York, 1972; 298 pp.).
2. Marx and Engels, *Gesamtausgabe* (East Berlin, 1962), vol. 20, p. 171; Lenin, *State and Revolution* (1917), toward the end of chap. 1.
3. Stepniak, *Underground Russia* (New York, 1892) pp. 32, 257.
4. Bernard Pares, "Reaction and Revolution in Russia," in *The Cambridge Modern History* (Cambridge, 1910) vol. 12, pp. 294–345, 304 ff.
5. Valentin Gitermann, *Geschichte Russlands* (Hamburg, 1947), vol. 3 (679 pp.), pp. 615–620.
6. David Fromkin, "The Strategy of Terrorism," *Foreign Affairs*, July 1975, pp. 683–698.
7. Baez, *Joan*, pp. 20 f.
8. Arendt, *On Violence.*
9. Debray, *Revolution*, p. 84.
10. *Report . . . History of Violence*, pp. 596–730.
11. Steinhoff, "Portrait."
12. Hacker, *Aggression*, pp. 359–366.
13. *New York Times*, March 30, 1975.
14. Birch Bayh, "On Combating School Violence," *New York Times*, July 18, 1975.
15. Leamer, *Paper Revolutionaries*, p. 49.
16. *Report . . . History of Violence*, p. 579.
17. Ortega y Gasset, *Wesen*, p. 145.
18. Abbie Hoffman, *Woodstock*, p. 52 f.
19. Both quotations in Lipset, *Rebellion*, p. xxi.
See also Bienen, Coute, Joll, Müller-Borchert, Tophoven; Eisen (Altamont), Schober.

24 NOTHING NEW UNDER THE SUN?

1. Plato, *The Republic*, ed. Henricus Stephanus, pp. 562–565.
2. Quoted in Erikson, *Challenge of Youth*, pp. 139 f., 213–215.
3. *Peking Review*, no. 21 (May 24, 1968), pp. 17–24; no. 22 (May 31, 1968), pp. 9–17.
4. Ibid., December 31, 1968.
5. Ibid., February 11, 1968.
6. See Schlomann and Friedlingstein, *Maoisten*, pp. 40–56.
7. *Peking Rundschau*, no. 2 (1969), pp. 3 f.
8. Mao Tse-tung, "Talks at the Chengtu Conference (March 1968)," in Schram, *Chairman Mao*, p. 110.
9. Luce, *New Left*, pp. 81–103; *New Left Today*, pp. 54–65.
10. Allerbeck, *Soziologie*, p. 238.
11. See Popp, *Initiation.*
12. Allerbeck, *Soziologie*, p. 154.

25 RED DIAPERS, JEWISH MOTHERS

1. Raskin, *Whale*, passim.

2. Erwin K. Scheuch, in Langguth, *Protestbewegung*, p. 13.
3. Allerbeck, *Soziologie*, pp. 103, 108
4. Similar observations are in Keniston, *Youth*, pp. 273 ff.; Lipset and Altbach, *Students*, p. 497.
5. Quoted in Lipset, *Rebellion*, pp. 81 f.
6. Lipset and Raab, *Unreason*, pp. 367, 369.
7. Parkin, *Middle Class*, p. 166.
8. Isaacs, *Jews*, p. 106.
9. Ibid., p. 103.
10. Chertoff, *New Left*, p. 179.
11. Ibid., p. 247.
See also Hentoff (on black anti-Semitism).

26 TEACHERS AND GURUS

1. Hughes, *Sea Change*, pp. 137 f.
2. Ibid., p. 153.
3. See Jay, *Dialectical Imagination*.
4. *Freud in der Gegenwart: Ein Vortragszyklus der Universitäten Frankfurt und Heidelberg zum 100. Geburtstag, Frankfurter Beiträge zur Soziologie*, vol. 6 (Frankfurt, 1957; 447 pp.).
5. See Mehnert, *Moscow*, pp. 58–70.
6. Marcuse, *One-Dimensional*, p. xii.
7. Marcuse, "Perspektiven des Sozialismus in der industriell entwickelten Gesellschaft," *neue kritik*, August 31, 1965, p. 11 ff.
8. Marcuse, *One-Dimensional*, p. 256.
9. Marcuse, *Counterrevolution*, p. 53.
10. Marcuse, *One-Dimensional*, pp. xiii, 4.
11. Marcuse, *Über Revolte*, pp. 38, 28.
12. Edith Eucken-Erdsiek, "Die Hoffnungslosigkeit des Dr. Marcuse," in *Frankfurter Allgemeine Zeitung*, August 3, 1968.
13. Marcuse, "Repressive," p. 87.
14. Marcuse, *Das Ende*, pp. 66, 88, 116–118.
15. Marcuse, *Counterrevolution*, pp. 53, 134.
16. See the collection of Mills's articles in Horowitz, *Power*.
17. Marshall Berman, "Life History and the Historical Moment," *New York Times Book Review*, March 30, 1975, pp. 1 f., 22.
18. Erikson, *Life History*, p. 26.
19. Ibid., pp. 17–47.
20. Ibid., p. 43.
21. Rycroft, *Reich*, p. 7.

27 ANARCHISM AND PURE DEMOCRACY

1. Wolfgang Harich, "Zur Kritik der revolutionären Ungeduld," *Kursbuch* (Frankfurt), no. 19 (December 1969), p. 110.
2. Stuke, ed., *Bakunin*, pp. 770 f., 19, 24, xiii, 7, 807, 727, 86 f., 89, 4 f., 102, 8 ff., 96.
3. Krämer-Badoni, *Anarchismus*, p. 152.

4. Bakunin, *Dieu et l'état* (1871); quoted in Rammstedt, *Anarchismus*, p. 45.
5. Marx and Engels, *Werke*, vol. 18, p. 637.
6. Valentin Gitermann, *Geschichte Russlands* (Hamburg, 1947), vol. 3, p. 225.
7. Krämer-Badoni, *Anarchismus*, p. 67.
8. Ibid., pp. 236 f.
9. Ibid., p. 242.
10. Ibid., pp. 243 f.
11. Ibid., p. 21.
12. Ibid., p. 30.
13. Ibid., pp. 43 f.
14. Ibid., p. 233.
15. *Izvestiya* (Kronstadt), March 9, 1921; quoted in Bartsch, *Anarchismus*, p. 204.
16. *tu was*, October 1971, p. 14; quoted in Bartsch, *Anarchismus*, p. 204.

28 INNER CAUSES

1. Johan Huizinga, *Herfsttijd de Middeleeuwen*, (Leiden, 1919). English translation: *The Waning of the Middle Ages* (London, 1924; 328 pp.), p. 195.
2. See Meadows et al., *Limits*.
3. Slater, *Pursuit*, pp. 129–131.
4. Bettelheim, *Informed Heart*, p. 49.
5. E. G. Oltmans, *On Growth*.
6. Gruhl, *Planet*.
7. Reich, *Greening*, esp. chap. 9; also Nobile, *Con III*.
8. See Bell, *Post-Industrial Society*.
9. José Ortega y Gasset, *The Revolt of the Masses* (pb.; New York, 1957).
10. Raskin, *Whale*, p. 19.
11. Keniston, *Youth*, p. 313.
12. Kerouac, *On the Road*, pp. 89 f.
13. Pentzlin, *Kinder*, pp. 43–46.
14. Cooper, ed., *Dialectics*.
15. *Time*, May 3, 1968.
16. Marx, "Ökonomisch-philosophische Manuskripte," in *Marx-Engels-Gesamtausgabe* (Berlin, 1932), pt. 1, vol. 3, pp. 83 ff.
17. Ibid., vol. 5, pp. 23 f.
18. Tsurumi, *Social Change*, p. 383.
19. Kelman, *Push*, p. 88.
20. See Israel, *Alienation*; Schacht, *Alienation*.
21. Potter, *Name*, p. 45.
22. Raskin, *Whale*, p. 67.
23. Keniston, *Youth*, p. 174.
24. Erikson, *Identity*, pp. 16 f.
25. Ibid., pp. 130, 132 f., 172, 129.
26. Erikson, *Luther*, p. 14.

27. Knaut, *Propheten*, p. 193.
28. Geppert, *Wir Gotteskinder*, pp. 13, 175.
29. Kelley, *Why*.
30. Friedman, *Buried*, pp. 155, 348.
31. Hendin, "Psychoanalyst."
32. Hurwitz, *Marching*, p. 215.
33. Bettelheim, in *San Francisco Examiner and Chronicle*, March 2, 1969.
34. Kelman, *Push*, p. 101.
35. Friedrich Heer, "Arbeitslose Seelan," in *Deutsche Zeitung/Christ und Welt* (Bonn), October 17, 1975, p. 2.
36. Robert Grudin, "The Ghost of Folly" (unpublished novel).
37. Bettelheim, in *Encounter*, September 1962, p. 37.
38. Scaduto, *Dylan*, p. 205.
39. Friedman, *Buried*, p. 150.
40. *Time*, May 3, 1968.
41. Allerbeck, *Soziologie*, p. 131.
See also on alienation: Gilmour, Josephson, "University and Society"; on identity: Levita.

INTRODUCTION TO PART IV: WHITHER?

1. Langguth, *Protestbewegung*.
2. Leszek Kolakowski, *Der Revolutionäre Geist* (pb.; Stuttgart, 1972; 99 pp.).
3. Abosch, "Altern."
4. *SDS-Info*, December 22, 1969, p. 4; quoted in Langguth, *Protestbewegung*, p. 55.

29 SCATTERED FAR AND WIDE

1. Stephen M. Pittel and Henry Miller, "Dropping Down" (Wright report), prepublication draft (Berkeley, 1976) and summary report in *San Francisco Chronicle*, July 3, 1975, p. 16.
2. Wade Green, "Where Are the Savios of Yesteryear?" *New York Times*, July 17, 1970, pp. 6–9, 35–37.
3. Eldridge Cleaver, interview with Curtis Taylor, *Rolling Stone*, August 11, 1975, pp. 40–48, 60–64.
4. Neil Hickey, "A Voice Still Blowin' in the Wind," *TV Guide*, September 11–17, 1976, pp. 2–8.
5. Louise Billotte, "Ginsberg Reflects," *Berkeley Barb*, September 3–9, 1976.
6. Dean Calbreath, "Tim Leary: A Caterpillar Reaches for Outer Space," *Berkeley Barb*, August 13–19, 1976.
7. Richard M. Levine, "The Pizza and the Path," *Rolling Stone*, April 22, 1976, pp. 42–47, 76–85.
8. Cate Coleman, "The Movement Lawyers Today," *San Francisco Sunday Examiner and Chronicle*, August 10, 1965, pp. 22–27.

NOTES ON SOURCES

9. Klaus Arnsperger, "Rebellen in der Richterrobe," *Süddeutsche Zeitung* (Munich), December 5, 1975, p. 31; Klaus Huwe, "Justitia mit der roten Brille," *Deutsche Zeitung/Christ und Welt* (Bonn), December 26, 1975, p. 8.
10. William Trombley, "Rise of Radical Economists," *International World Tribune*, January 5, 1975.
11. Cohn-Bendit, *Der grosse Basar*, pp. 51–55, 123, 140, 72, 74.
12. Langguth, *Protestbewegung*, p. 23.
13. Bundesministerium des Innern, ed., *Dokumentation*.
14. Krauss, *Japan's Radicals Revisited*.
15. Frederic Hunter, "Religious Ferment in America," *Christian Science Monitor*, November 12, 1974, p. 7.

30 CONCLUSION

1. C. G. Jung, "Über die Beziehungen der analytischen Psychologie zum dichterischen Kunstwerk" (1922), quoted from C. G. Jung, *The Spirit in Man, Art, and Literature*, ed. G. Adler et al. (Princeton, 1971).
2. Friedrich Nietzsche, *Fröhliche Wissenschaft*, in *Werke*, pt. 1, vol. 5 (Leipzig, 1895).
3. Quoted in Thomas G. Masaryk, *The Spirit of Russia* (London, 1919), vol. 2, p. 545.

SELECTED BIBLIOGRAPHY

THIS is a bibliography of books, with only a few articles included. Paperbacks are marked "(pb)." Books that carry sizable bibliographies are indicated by the abbreviation "(bibl.)." In the case of translations into English, the original title with place and year of publication is usually given in brackets. The German original of this book lists additional titles, especially from non-English languages.

Abosch, Heinz. "Das Altern der Neuen Linken." *Neue Rundschau,* no. 2 (1974), pp. 193–213.

Adelson, Alan. *SDS: Profile.* New York, 1972. 276 pp.

Adorno, Theodor W., et al. *The Authoritarian Personality.* New York, 1950. 990 pp.

Ahlberg, René. *Akademische Lehrmeinungen und Studentenunruhen in der Bundesrepublik.* Freiburg/Breisgau, 1970. 84 pp.

——— *Ursachen der Revolte: Analyse des studentischen Protestes.* Stuttgart, 1972 (pb). 91 pp.

Aldridge, Alan, ed. *The Beatles Songbook.* Munich, 1971 (pb). 206 pp.

Aldridge, John W. *In the Country of the Young.* New York, 1971 (pb). 128 pp.

Ali, Tariq, ed. *The New Revolutionaries: A Handbook of the International Left.* New York, 1969. 319 pp.

Allemann, Fritz René. *Macht und Ohnmacht der Guerilla.* Munich, 1974. 532 pp.

Allerbeck, Klaus R. *Soziologie radikaler Studentenbewegungen: Eine vergleichende Untersuchung in der Bundesrepublik Deutschland und den Vereinigten Staaten.* Munich, 1973. 272 pp. (bibl.).

Altbach, Philip G. *A Select Bibliography on Students, Politics, and Higher Education.* Cambridge, Mass., 1970. 65 pp. (bibl.).

SELECTED BIBLIOGRAPHY

Alves, Marcio D. *Zerschlagt die Wohlstandsinseln der Dritten Welt.* Hamburg, 1971 (pb). 118 pp.

"American Youth: Its Outlook Is Changing the World." *Fortune* (special issue), January 1969, 161 pp.

Andelin, Helen B. *Fascinating Womanhood.* Santa Barbara, Calif., 1965; quoted from New York, 1975 (pb). 343 pp.

Annals of the American Academy of Political and Social Science. Vol. 395: *The Students Protest.* Philadelphia, May 1971. 277 pp. (bibl.).

Anthony, Earl. *The Time of the Furnaces: A Case Study of Black Student Revolt.* New York, 1971. 131 pp.

Aptheker, Bettina. *The Academic Rebellion in the United States: A Marxist Appraisal.* Secaucus, N.J., 1972. 218 pp.

Arasteh, A. Reza. *Faces of Persian Youth: A Sociological Study.* Leiden, 1970. 268 pp.

Archer, Margaret Scotford, ed. *Students, University and Society: A Comparative Sociological Review.* London, 1972. 280 pp.

Arendt, Hannah. *On Violence.* New York, 1969. 106 pp.

Aron, Raymond. *The Elusive Revolution: Anatomy of a Student Revolt.* New York, 1969. 200 pp. [*La Révolution introuvable.* Paris, 1968.]

Asinof, Eliot. *Craig and Joan: Two Lives for Peace,* New York, 1971. 245 pp.

Atcheson, Richard. *The Bearded Lady: Going on the Commune Trip and Beyond,* New York, 1971. 365 pp.

Ausubel, David P. *Theory and Problems of Adolescent Development.* New York, 1954. 580 pp. (bibl.).

Avorn, Jerry L., ed. *Up Against the Ivy Wall: A History of the Columbia Crisis.* 2d ed. New York, 1970. 307 pp.

Baacke, Dieter. *Beat—die sprachlose Opposition.* 2d ed. Munich, 1970. 239 pp. (bibl.).

——— *Jugend und Subkultur.* Munich, 1972. 205 pp. (bibl.).

Baader, Andreas, et al. *Vor einer solchen Justiz verteidigen wir uns nicht: Schlusswort im Kaufhausbrandprozess.* Frankfurt-Main, 1968. 27 pp.

Bacciocco, Edward J. *The New Left in America: Reform to Revolution, 1956 to 1970.* Stanford, 1974. 300 pp. (bibl.).

——— *New Left Monthly Report.* Stanford (Hoover), 1970–1973 (mime.).

Baez, Joan. *Daybreak.* 12th ed. New York, 1973 (pb). 191 pp.

——— *Joan.* Chicago [n.d.] (pb). 47 pp.

Bakunin, Mikhail. *see* Stuke, H.

Barlow, William, and Peter Shapiro. *An End to Silence: The San Francisco State College Student Movement in the '60s.* New York, 1971. 330 pp.

Barschel, Uwe, et al. *Was wir wünschen: Junge Bundesbürger über die Zukunft ihres Staates.* Cologne, 1974. 310 pp.

Bartsch, Günter. *Anarchismus in Deutschland, 1965–1973.* Hannover, 1973. 423 pp.

——— *Schulen und Praxis des Anarchismus.* Troisdorf, 1974. 239 pp.

SELECTED BIBLIOGRAPHY

Battistini, Lawrence H. *The Postwar Student Struggle in Japan.* Tokyo, 1956. 167 pp.
Baxandall, Lee, ed. *Wilhelm Reich Sex-Pol: Essays, 1929–1934.* New York, 1972 (pb). 377 pp.
Beatles; *See* Aldridge, Alan.
Beck, Heinrich. *Machtkampf der Generationen? Zum Aufstand der Jugend gegen den Autoritätsanspruch der Gessellschaft.*2d ed. Frankfurt/Main, 1973 (pb). 107 pp. (bibl.).
Bednarik, Karl. *Die unheimliche Jugend.* Vienna, 1969. 142 pp.
——— *Der junge Arbeiter von heute—ein neuer Typ.* Stuttgart, 1953 (pb). 158 pp.
Belcher, Jerry, and Don West. *Patty/Tania.* New York, 1975 (pb) 347 pp.
Bell, Daniel. *The Coming of Post-Industrial Society.* London, 1974. 507 pp.
——— *The End of Ideology.* Glencoe, Ill., 1960. 416 pp.
Bell, Daniel, and Irving Kristol, eds. *Confrontation: The Student Rebellion and the Universities.* New York, 1968. 191 pp.
Benneter, Klaus-Uwe, et al. *Februar 1968 Tage die Berlin erschütterten.* Frankfurt/Main, 1968. 123 pp.
Berger, Peter L., and Richard John Neuhaus. *Movement and Revolution: On American Radicalism.* Garden City, N.Y., 1970. 240 pp.
Bergmann, Uwe, et al. *Rebellion der Studenten oder Die neue Opposition: Eine Analyse.* Hamburg, 1968 (pb). 188 pp.
Berke, Joseph, ed. *Counter Culture: The Creation of an Alternative Society.* London, 1969. 416 pp.
Berner, Wolfgang. *Der Evangelist des Castroismus-Guevarismus: Régis Debray und seine Guerilla-Doktrin.* Velbert, 1969. 82 pp.
Bettelheim, Bruno. *The Informed Heart.* Glencoe, Ill., 1960. 309 pp.
——— "Obsolete Youth? Towards a Psychograph of Adolescent Rebellion." *Encounter,* September 1969, pp. 29–42.
——— "The Problem of Generations" in Erikson, *Challenge,* pp. 76–109.
Bienen, Henry. *Violence and Social Change: A Review of Current Literature.* 2d ed. Chicago 1970. 119 pp. (bibl.).
Birmingham, John, ed. *Our Time Is Now: Notes from the High School Underground.* New York, 1970 (pb). 273 pp.
Blaine, Graham B., et al. *Emotional Problems of the Student.* Garden City, N.Y., 1966 (pb). 283 pp.
Blum, Richard H., et al. *Horatio Alger's Children: The Role of the Family in the Origin and Prevention of Drug Risk.* London, Washington, and San Francisco, 1972. 327 pp. (bibl.).
——— *Students and Drugs. Drugs II: College and High School Observations.* San Francisco, 1970. 399 pp. (bibl.).
Bock, Richard, and Abigail English. *Got Me on the Run: A Study of Runaways.* Boston, 1973. 237 pp.
Bonn, Gisela. *Unter Hippies.* Düsseldorf, 1968. 157 pp. (bibl.).
Bookchin, Murray *Post-Scarcity Anarchism.* Berkeley, 1971. 288 pp.
Bookhagen, Christl, et al. *Versuch der Revolutionierung des*

397

bürgerlichen Individuums: Kollektives Leben mit politischer Arbeit verbinden! [Kommune 2]. Berlin, 1969. 311 pp.

Bourges, Hervé, ed. *The French Student Revolt: The Leaders Speak.* New York [1968]. 112 pp. [*La Révolte étudiante—les animateurs parlent.* Paris, 1968.]

Bowen, Roger Wilson. "The Narita Conflict." *Asian Survey,* July 1975, pp. 598-615.

Boyle, Kay. *The Long Walk at San Francisco State.* New York, 1970 (pb). 150 pp.

Boyle, Richard. *The Flower of the Dragon: The Breakdown of the U.S. Army in Vietnam.* San Francisco, 1972. 282 pp.

Braden, William. *The Private Sea: LSD and the Search for God.* 2d ed. New York, 1968 (pb). 212 pp.

Breines, Paul, ed. *Critical Interruptions: New Left Perspectives on Herbert Marcuse.* New York, 1970. 188 pp.

Brown, Bernard E. *Protest in Paris: Anatomy of a Revolt.* Morristown, N.J., 1974. 240 pp. (bibl.).

Brown, Joe David, ed. *The Hippies.* New York, 1967. 220 pp.

Brückner, Peter, and Barbara Sichtermann. *Gewalt und Solidarität. Zur Ermordung Ulrich Schmückers durch Genossen: Dokumente und Analysen.* Berlin, 1974. 103 pp.

Bryan, John. *This Soldier Still at War.* New York, 1975. 341 pp.

Brzezinski, Zbigniew. *Between Two Ages: America's Role in the Technetronic Era.* 4th ed. New York, 1972. 334 pp.

Bugliosi, Vincent, and Curt Gentry. *Helter Skelter: The True Story of the Manson Murders.* New York, 1974. 502 pp.

Bundeskriminalamt, Sonderkommission Bonn und Bundesamt für Verfassungsschutz. *Aus den Akten . . . , Der Baader-Meißhof-Report: Dokumente—Analysen—Zusammenhänge.* Mainz, 1972. 245 pp.

Bundesministerium des Innern, ed. *Dokumentation über Aktivitäten anarchistischer Gewalttäter in der Bundesrepublik Deutschland.* [Bonn, n.d.] 165 pp.

Bundesministerium des Innern. Referat Öffentlichkeitsarbeit, ed. *Die Studentenunruhen.* Bonn, 1969 (pb). 64 pp.

——— *Erfahrungsbericht über die Beobachtungen der Ämter für Verfassungsschutz im Jahre 1968.* Bonn, 1969 (pb). 152 pp.

——— Betrifft: Verfassungsschutz 1969/70. *Rechts- und Linksradikale Bestrebungen, Spionageabwehr, Sicherheitsgefährdende Bestrebungen von Ausländern.* Bonn. *1969/70,* 72 pp.; *1971,* 122 pp.; *1972,* 160 pp.; *1973,* 152 pp.; *1974,* 139 pp.; *1975,* 145 pp.

Califano, Joseph A. *The Student Revolution: A Global Confrontation.* New York, 1970. 96 pp.

Calvert, Greg, and Carol Neiman. *A Disrupted History: The New Left and the New Capitalism.* New York, 1971. 176 pp.

Carbajal, Ladislao Gonzalez. *El Ala Izquierda Estudiantil y Su Época.* Havana, 1974. 528 pp.

Carey, Gary. *Lenny, Janis and Jimi.* New York, 1975 (pb). 299 pp.

Carlson, Sören. *Hötorgkravallerna i Stockholm: Hösten 1965.* Stockholm, 1967. 65 pp.

Casale, Ottavio M., ed. *The Kent Affair: Documents and Interpretations.* Boston, 1971. 260 pp.

Casebeer, Edwin F. *Hermann Hesse.* 2d ed. New York, 1973 (pb). 206 pp. (bibl.).

Caserta, Peggy. *Going Down with Janis: Janis Joplin's Intimate Story.* 4th ed. New York, 1974 (pb). 267 pp.

Caute, David. *Frantz Fanon.* New York, 1970 (pb). 116 pp.

Centre Europeén de Documentation et d'Information (CEDI). *La Révolte de la Jeunesse: Compte-rendu de la XVIIIième réunion internationale du CEDI.* Madrid, 1969. 196 pp.

Cervantes, Lucius F. *The Dropout: Causes and Cures.* Ann Arbor, Mich., 1969. 244 pp.

Chang, Parris H. *Radicals and Radical Ideology in China's Cultural Revolution.* New York, 1973. 103 pp.

Charters, Ann. *Kerouac: A Biography.* New York, 1974 (pb). 416 pp.

Chertoff, Mordecai S., ed. *The New Left and the Jews.* New York, 1971. 322 pp.

Chomsky, Noam. *American Power and the New Mandarins.* New York, 1969. 404 pp.

Chow Tse-tsung. *The May Fourth Movement: Intellectual Revolution in Modern China.* Cambridge, Mass., 1960. 486 pp.

Claassen, Emil-Maria, and Louis-Ferdinand Peters. *Rebellion in Frankreich: Die Manifestation der europäischen Kulturrevolution 1968.* Munich, 1968 (pb). 153 pp.

Cleaver, Eldridge. *Post-Prison Writings and Speeches.* New York, 1969. 211 pp.

Cockburn, Alexander, and Robin Blackburn, eds. *Student Power: Problems, Diagnosis, Action.* Harmondsworth, 1969 (pb). 378 pp.

Coenjaarts, H. F. M. G. *Buitenparlementaire oppositie en de universiteit.* Meppel, 1972. 227 pp. (bibl.).

Cohen, Mitchell, and Dennis Hale. *The New Student Left: An Anthology.* Boston, 1967. 339 pp.

Cohn-Bendit, Daniel. *Der grosse Basar.* Munich, 1975. 174 pp. [*Le Grand Bazar.* Paris, 1975.]

Cohen-Bendit, Daniel, and Gabriel Cohen-Bendit. *Obsolete Communism: The Left Wing Alternative.* New York, 1968. 255 pp. [*Le Gauchisme.* Hamburg, 1968.]

Coleman, James, et al. *Youth: Transition to Adulthood.* Chicago, 1974. 193 pp. (bibl.).

Commission on Obscenity; *see Report of the Commission on Obscenity. . . .*

Conant, Ralph W. *The Prospects for Revolution: A Study of Riots, Civil Disobedience, and Insurrection in Contemporary America.* New York, 1971. 289 pp. (bibl.).

Cook, Bruce. *The Beat Generation: The Tumultuous '50s Movement and Its Impact on Today.* New York, 1971. 248 pp.

Cooper, David, ed. *Dialectics of Liberation.* London, 1968.

Cormack, Margaret. *She Who Rides a Peacock: Indian Students and Social Change.* Bombay, 1961. 264 pp.

Cox Commission; *see Report of the Fact-Finding Commission . . . .*

SELECTED BIBLIOGRAPHY

Coyne, John R. *The Kumquat Statement.* New York, 1970. 213 pp.
Crawley, Harriet. *A Degree of Defiance: Students in England and Europe Now.* London, 1969. 207 pp.
Crick, Bernard, and William A. Robson, eds. *Protest and Discontent.* Harmondsworth, 1970 (pb). 220 pp.
Crouch, Colin. *The Student Revolt.* London, 1970. 251 pp.
Cuskey, Walter R., et al. *Drug-Trip Abroad: American Drug-Refugees in Amsterdam and London.* Philadelphia, 1972 (bibl.)

Dahl, Robert A. *After the Revolution? Authority in a Good Society.* 2d ed. New Haven, 1971. 171 pp.
Daniels, Dan, ed. *Quebec/Canada and the October Crisis.* Montreal, 1973. 134 pp.
Davies, Peter, et al. *The Truth About Kent State: A Challenge to the American Conscience.* New York, 1973. 241 pp. (bibl.).
Debray, Régis. *Revolution in the Revolution? Armed Struggle and Political Struggle in Latin America.* New York, 1967 (pb). 126 pp. [*Révolution dans la révolution?* Paris, 1967.]
DeConde, Alexander, ed. *Student Activism: Town and Gown in Historical Perspective.* New York, 1971. 342 pp. (bibl.)
Dector, Midge. *Liberal Parents, Radical Children.* New York, 1975. 248 pp.
Dellinger, Dave. *More Power Than We Know: The People's Movement Toward Democracy.* Garden City, N.Y., 1975. 326 pp.
Desai, B. G. *The Emerging Youth.* Bombay, 1967. 199 pp. (bibl.)
Deutsches Jugendinstitut München. *Bibliographie Studentenunruhen: Dokumentation.* Munich, 1968. 71 pp.
Devlin, Bernadette. *The Price of My Soul.* London, 1969 (pb). 206 pp.
Diamond, Stephen. *What the Trees Said: Life on a New Age Farm.* New York, 1971. 182 pp.
Divale, William Tulio, and James Joseph. *I Lived Inside the Campus Revolution.* New York, 1970. 253 pp.
Dollase, Rainer, et al. *Rock People oder Die befragte Szene.* Frankfurt/Main, 1974 (pb). 262 pp. (bibl.)
Domhoff, G. William, and Hoyt B. Ballard. *C. Wright Mills and the Power Elite.* Boston, 1968. 278 pp.
Dowsey, Stuart, ed. *Zengakuren: Japan's Revolutionary Students.* Berkeley, 1970. 269 pp. (bibl.).
Drachkovitch, Milorad M. "The 'New Left' in the USA: Critical Appraisal," *Western Politica,* vol. 1 (1966).
Draper, Hal. *Berkeley: The New Student Revolt.* New York, 1965 (pb). 246 pp.
Duke, Benjamin C. *Japan's Militant Teachers: A History of the Left-Wing Teachers' Movement.* Honolulu, 1973. 236 pp.
Dutschke, Rudi. *Versuch, Lenin auf die Füsse zu stellen: Über den halbasiatischen und den westeuropäischen Weg zum Sozialismus.* Berlin, 1974. 384 pp.
———— *See also* Bergmann et al.
Dutschke, Rudi, and Manfred Wilke, eds. *Die Sowjetunion, Solschenizyn und die westliche Linke.* Hamburg, 1975 (pb). 317 pp.

Dylan, Bob. *Song Book.* New York, 1975. 143 pp.
—— *See also* Pickering.

Eckstein, George Günther. *USA: Die neue Linke am Ende?* Munich, 1970 (pb). 110 pp. (bibl.).
Edwards, Harry. *Black Students.* New York, 1970. 234 pp. (bibl.).
Ehrenreich, Barbara, and John Ehrenreich. *Long March, Short Spring: The Student Uprising at Home and Abroad.* New York, 1969. 189 pp. (bibl.).
Ehrlich, John, and Susan Ehrlich, eds. *Student Power, Participation and Revolution.* New York, 1970. 254 pp.
Eisen, Jonathan, ed. *The Age of Rock: Sounds of the American Cultural Revolution.* Vol. 1: New York, 1969, 388 pp. Vol. 2: New York, 1970, 339 pp.
—— *Altamont: Death of Innocence in the Woodstock Nation.* New York, 1970 (pb). 271 pp.
Eisenberg, Dennis, and Elli Landau. *Carlos: Terror International.* London, 1976 (pb). 285 pp.
Eisenstadt, S. N. *From Generation to Generation: Age Groups and Social Structure.* Glencoe, Ill., 1956. 257 pp.
Ellson, Hal. *Blood on the Ivy.* New York, 1970 (pb). 220 pp.
Ellul, Jacques. *De la révolution aux révoltes.* Paris, 1972.
Ellwood, Robert S. *One Way: The Jesus Movement and Its Meaning.* Englewood Cliffs, N.J., 1973. 150 pp.
Epstein, Cy. *How to Kill a College: The Story Behind the Revolution at California State College, Fullerton.* Los Angeles, 1971. 201 pp.
Erikson, Erik H. *The Challenge of Youth.* New York, 1965 (pb). 340 pp. [Original title: *Youth, Change and Challenge.* New York, 1961.]
—— *Dimensions of a New Identity.* New York, 1974. 125 pp.
—— *Identity, Youth and Crisis.* New York, 1968. 336 pp.
—— *Life History and the Historical Moment.* New York, 1975. 283 pp.
—— *Young Man Luther: A Study in Psychoanalysis and History.* New York, 1958. 288 pp.
Estrada, Jacquelyn, ed. *The University Under Siege.* Los Angeles, 1971. 280 pp.
Eszterhas, Joe, and Michael E. Roberts. *Thirteen Seconds: Confrontation at Kent State.* New York, 1970. 308 pp.

Fairfield, Richard. *Communes Europe.* San Francisco, 1972. 239 pp.
—— *Communes USA: A Personal Tour.* Baltimore, 1972. 400 pp. (bibl.).
Fairfield, Richard, ed. *The Modern Utopian: Communes Japan.* San Francisco, 1972. 134 pp.
—— *Utopia, USA.* San Francisco, 1972. 231 pp.
Fanon, Frantz. *The Wretched of the Earth.* New York, 1968 (pb). 316 pp. [*Les Damnés de la terre.* Paris, 1961.]
—— *See also* Caute; Geismar; Gendzier; Zaher.
Farber, Thomas. *Tales for the Son of My Unborn Child: Berkeley, 1966–1969.* New York, 1971. 211 pp.

SELECTED BIBLIOGRAPHY

Feldbrugge, F. J. M. *Samizdat and Political Dissent in the Soviet Union.* Leyden, 1975. 255 pp.

Ferber, Michael, and Staughton Lynd. *The Resistance.* Boston, 1971. 300 pp.

Feuer, Lewis S. *The Conflict of Generations: The Character and Significance of Student Movements.* New York, 1969. 543 pp.

Fisk, Trevor. "The Nature and Causes of Student Unrest." In Crick and Robson, *Protest and Discontent,* pp. 78–85.

Flacks, Richard. *Conformity, Resistance, and Self-Determination: The Individual and Authority.* 2d ed. Boston, 1973. 360 pp.

Foss, Daniel. *Freak Culture: Life-Style and Politics.* New York, 1972. 218 pp.

Foster, Julian, and Durward Long, eds. *Protest! Student Activism in America.* New York, 1970. 596 pp.

Foxfire Book, The, see Wigginton.

Fraktionerung des amerikanischen SDS, Die. Berlin, 1970. 279 pp.

Franklin, H. Bruce. *Back Where You Came From: A Life in the Death of the Empire.* New York, 1975. 219 pp.

Freeman, Jo. *The Politics of Women's Liberation: A Case Study of an Emerging Social Movement and Its Relation to the Policy Process.* New York, 1975. 268 pp. (bibl.).

Freeman, Jo, ed. *Women: A Feminist Perspective.* Palo Alto, Calif., 1975. 487 pp.

Friedenberg, Edgar Z. *Coming of Age in America: Growth and Acquiescence.* 1963; quoted from New York, 1965 (pb), 300 pp.

—— *The Vanishing Adolescent.* Boston, 1959. 144 pp.

Friedenberg, Edgar Z., ed. *The Anti-American Generation.* New Brunswick, N.J., 1972. 277 pp.

Friedman, Myra. *Buried Alive: The Bibliography of Janis Joplin.* New York, 1973, quoted from New York, 1974 (pb), 395 pp.

Friedrich, Walter. *Jugend Heute: Theoretische Probleme empirische Daten pädagogische Konsequenzen.* 2d ed. [East] Berlin, 1967. 200 pp. (bibl.)

Fromkin, David. "The Strategy of Terrorism." *Foreign Affairs,* July 1975, pp. 683–698.

Fromm, Erich. *The Anatomy of Human Destructiveness.* New York, 1973, 521 pp.

—— *Escape from Freedom.* New York, 1941. 305 pp.

—— *The Sane Society.* New York, 1955. 370 pp.

Fuchs, Lawrence H. *Family Matters: Why the American Family Is in Trouble.* New York, 1972. 266 pp. (bibl.)

Fyvel, T. R. [pseud. for R. J. Feiwel]. *The Insecure Offenders: Rebellious Youth in the Welfare State.* London, 1961. 347 pp.

Gans, Herbert J. *More Equality.* New York, 1973. 261 pp. (bibl.).

Gebhardt, Hermann P. *Guerillas: Schicksalsfrage für den Westen. Die lateinamerikanische Revolutionsbewegung.* Stuttgart, 1971. 168 pp. (bibl.).

Geismar, Peter. *Fanon: A Biography.* New York, 1971. 214 pp. (bibl.).

Gendzier, Irene L. *Frantz Fanon: A Critical Study.* New York, 1973. 300 pp.

Geppert, Hans J. *Wir Gotteskinder: Die Jesus-People-Bewegung.* Gütersloh, 1972. 187 pp. (bibl.).

Gerassi, John, ed. *The Coming of the New International: A Revolutionary Anthology.* New York, 1971. 610 pp.

Gerstenmaier, Cornelia. *The Voice of the Silent.* New York, 1972. 587 pp. [*Die Stimme der Stummen.* Stuttgart, 1971.]

Gerzon, Mark. *The Whole World Is Watching: A Young Man Looks at Youth's Dissent.* New York, 1969; quoted from New York, 1970 (pb), 320 pp. (bibl.).

Ghosh, S. K. *The Student Challenge Round the World.* Calcutta, 1969. 254 pp. (bibl.).

Gilio, Maria Esther. *The Tupamaro Guerillas.* New York, 1972. 204 pp.

Gilmour, Robert S., and Robert B. Lamb. *Political Alienation in Contemporary America.* New York, 1975. 198 pp.

Ginsberg, Allen. *Howl.* San Francisco, 1956.

—— *Planet News.* San Francisco, 1968.

—— See also Kramer.

Glaser, Hermann. *Radikalität und Scheinradikalität: Zur Sozialpsychologie des jugendlichen Protests.* Munich, 1970. 176 pp.

Glazer, Nathan. *Remembering the Answers: Essays on the American Student Revolt.* New York, 1970. 311 pp.

Glucksmann, André, et al. *Stratégie de la révolution en France 1968.* Paris, 1968. 132 pp.

Goldenberg, Boris. *Kommunismus in Lateinamerika.* Stuttgart, 1971. 639 pp. (bibl.).

Goodman, Paul. *Growing Up Absurd: Problems of Youth in the Organized Society.* New York, 1956; quoted from New York, 1960 (pb), 296 pp.

Graubard, Stephen R., and Geno A. Ballotti, eds. *The Embattled University.* New York, 1970. 451 pp.

Greenfield, Jeff. *No Peace, No Place: Excavations Along the Generational Fault.* Garden City, N.Y., 1973. 286 pp.

Gregor, A. James. *The Fascist Persuasion in Radical Politics.* Princeton, 1974. 472 pp.

Grossarth-Maticek, Ronald. *Anfänge anarchistischer Gewaltbereitschaft in der Bundesrepublik Deutschland.* Bonn, 1975. 80 pp. (bibl.).

Grossman, Heinz, and Oskar Negt, eds. *Die Auferstehung der Gewalt: Springerblockade und politische Reaktion in der Bundesrepublik.* Frankfurt/Main, 1968. 187 pp.

Gruhl, Herbert. *Ein Planet wird geplündert.* 3d ed. Frankfurt/Main, 1976. 375 pp.

Guérin, Daniel. *Anarchism: From Theory to Practice.* New York, 1970. 166 pp. [*L'anarchisme.* Paris, 1965].

Guevara, Ernesto [Che]. *The Complete Bolivian Diaries of Che Guevara and Other Captured Documents.* Edited by James Daniels. New York, 1968; quoted from New York, 1969 (pb). 330 pp.

SELECTED BIBLIOGRAPHY

Guevara, Ernesto [Che]. *Guerrilla Warfare.* New York, 1961. 127 pp. [*La Guerra de Guerrillas*], 1960.

—— *Reminiscences of the Cuban Revolutionary War.* New York, 1968. 287 pp.

—— *See also* James, Lavan, Sinclair.

Guillén, Abraham. *Philosophy of the Urban Guerrilla: The Revolutionary Writings.* Edited by D. Hodges. New York, 1973. 305 pp. (bibl.).

Gupta, Chandra R., ed. *Youth in Ferment.* Delhi, 1968. 153 pp.

Habermas, Jürgen, *Antworten auf Herbert Marcuse.* Frankfurt/ Main, 1968 (pb). 160 pp. (bibl.)

—— *Toward a Rational Society: Student Protest, Science and Politics.* Boston, 1970. 132 pp.

—— *See also* Negt.

Hacker, Friedrich. *Aggression: Die Brutalisierung der modernen Welt.* Hamburg, 1973 (pb). 426 pp. (bibl.).

Häckel, Erwin, and Wolfram Elsner. *Kritik der Jungen Linken an Europa.* Bonn, 1973. 160 pp.

Hager, Jens. *Die Rebellen von Berlin: Studentenpolitik an der Freien Universität. Eine Dokumentation.* 2d ed. Cologne, 1967. 194 pp.

Harding, James, and Dimitrios Roussopoulos. "The New Left in British Columbia—Towards A Revolutionary Youth Movement." *Our Generation* (London) 7, no. 2 (June 1970), pp. 21–59.

Harrington, Michael, *Fragments of the Century: A Social Autobiography.* New York, 1973. 246 pp.

Hartley, Anthony. *A State of England.* London, 1963. 255 pp.

Hayden, Tom. *The Love of Possession Is a Disease with Them.* Chicago, 1972. 134 pp.

—— *Rebellion and Repression.* New York, 1969. 186 pp.

—— *Rebellion in Newark: Official Violence and Ghetto Response.* New York, 1967. 102 pp.

—— *Trial.* New York, 1970 (pb). 68 pp.

Hedgepeth, William, and Dennis Stock. *The Alternative. Communal Life in New America.* New York, 1970. 191 pp.

Heinlein, Robert A. *Stranger in a Strange Land.* New York, 1961.

Heirich, Max. *The Spiral of Conflict.* Berkeley, 1964; New York, 1968. 502 pp. (bibl.).

Hendin, Herbert. "A Psychoanalyst Looks at Student Revolutionaries." *New York Times Magazine,* January 17, 1971.

Hentoff, Nat, ed. *Black Anti-Semitism and Jewish Racism.* 2d ed. New York, 1972. 237 pp.

Hermann, Kai. *Die Revolte der Studenten.* Hamburg, 1967. 155 pp.

Hitpass, Josef. *Radikale Minderheit—Schweigende Mehrheit: Zur Verhaltensgestalt der studentischen Jugend.* Osnabrück, 1974. 152 pp. (bibl.).

Hitpass, Josef, and Albert Mock. *Das Image der Universität: Studentische Perspektiven.* Düsseldorf, 1972. 135 pp. (bibl.).

Hodges, Donald C. *See* Guillén.

Hoffman, Abbie. *Revolution for the Hell of It.* New York, 1968. 231 pp.

404

Hoffman, Abbie. *Woodstock Nation.* New York, 1969. 153 pp.

Hoffman, Nicholas von. *We Are the People Our Parents Warned Us Against.* Chicago, 1968. 279 pp.

Holbo, Paul S., and Robert W. Sellen, eds. *The Eisenhower Era: The Age of Consensus.* Hinsdale, Ill., 1974. 176 pp.

Hollstein, Walter. *Der Untergrund: Zur Soziologie jugendlicher Protestbewegungen.* Neuwied, 1969. 180 pp. (bibl.).

Holz, Hans Heinz. *Utopie und Anarchismus: Zur Kritik der kritischen Theorie Herbert Marcuses.* Cologne, 1968. 134 pp.

Holzer, Hans. *The Witchcraft Report.* New York, 1973 (pb). 222 pp.

Hope, Marjorie. *The New Revolutionaries.* 2d ed. Boston, 1970. 409 pp. (bibl.).

Hopkins, Jerry, ed. *The Hippie Papers: Notes From the Underground Press.* New York, 1968 (pb). 222 pp.

Horowitz, David, et al., eds. *Counterculture and Revolution.* New York, 1972. 203 pp.

Horowitz, Irving Louis, ed. *Power, Politics and People: The Collected Essays of C. Wright Mills.* New York, 1963. 657 pp. (bibl.).

Houriet, Robert. *Getting Back Together: Account of Revolutionary Life Styles.* New York, 1971; quoted from New York, 1972 (pb), 408 pp.

Howe, Irving, ed. *Beyond the New Left.* New York, 1970. 249 pp.

Huberman, Leo, et al. *Régis Debray and the Latin American Revolution: Essays.* New York, 1968. 138 pp.

Hughes, H. Stuart. *The Sea Change: The Migration of Social Thought, 1930–1965.* New York, 1975. 283 pp.

Hunt, Morton. "Sexual Behavior in the 1970s." *Playboy* (October 1973), pp. 85–88, 194–207.

——— *Sexual Behavior in the 1970s.* New York, 1975 (pb). 395 pp. (bibl.).

Hurwitz, Ken. *Marching Nowhere.* New York, 1971. 216 pp.

Hyman, Sidney. *Youth in Politics: Expectations and Realities.* New York, 1972. 436 pp.

Institut International d'Études sur l'Éducation (IIEE). *Bulletin.* Brussels (monthly).

Isaacs, Stephen D. *Jews and American Politics.* Garden City, N.Y., 1974. 302 pp. (bibl.).

Israel, Joachim. *Alienation: From Marx to Modern Sociology.* Boston, 1971. 358 pp. (bibl.). [*Fremmedgørelse.* Copenhagen, 1970.]

Jacko, Keith, Caroline Cox, and John Marks. *Rape of Reason: The Corruption of the Polytechnic of North London.* London, 1976 (pb). 148 pp.

Jackson, Geoffrey. *People's Prison.* London, 1973. 221 pp.

Jacobs, Harold, ed. *Weatherman* [San Francisco] 1970. 519 pp.

Jacobs, Paul, and Saul Landau. *The New Radicals: A Report with Documents.* New York, 1966 (pb). 333 pp.

James, Daniel. *Ché Guevara: A Biography.* London, 1970. 382 pp.

Jay, Martin. *The Dialectical Imagination: A History of the Frankfurt School and the Institute of Social Research, 1923–1950.* Boston, 1973. 382 pp. (bibl.).

Johnson, Chalmers. *Autopsy on People's War.* Berkeley, 1973. 118 pp.

Johnson, John J. *Continuity and Change in Latin America.* Stanford, 1964. 282 pp.

Johnson, Richard. *The French Communist Party Versus the Students: Revolutionary Politics in May–June 1968.* New Haven, 1972. 215 pp. (bibl.).

Joll, James, *The Anarchists.* London, 1964. 303 pp.

Josephson, Eric, and Mary Josephson, eds. *Man Alone: Alienation in Modern Society.* 13th ed. New York, 1971 (pb). 588 pp. (bibl.).

Kadushin, Charles. *The American Intellectual Elite.* Boston, 1974. 395 pp. (bibl.).

Kahn, Roger. *The Battle for Morningside Heights: Why Students Rebel.* 2d ed. New York, 1971. 254 pp.

Kaiser, Rolf-Ulrich. *Underground? Pop? Nein! Gegenkultur! Eine Buchcollage.* Cologne, 1969 (pb). 224 pp.

Kakar, Sudhir, and Kamla Chowdhry. *Conflict and Choice: Indian Youth in a Changing Society.* Bombay, 1970. 177 pp. (bibl.).

Karagueuzian, Dikran. *Blow It Up! The Black Student Revolt at San Francisco State College and the Emergence of Dr. Hayakawa.* Boston, 1971. 196 pp.

Kelley, Dean M. *Why Conservative Churches Are Growing: A Study in Sociology of Religion.* New York, 1972. 184 pp.

Kelman, Steven. *Push Comes to Shove: The Escalation of Student Protest.* 2d ed. Boston, 1970. 287 pp.

Keniston, Kenneth. *The Uncommitted: Alienated Youth in American Society.* 4th ed. New York, 1974 (pb). 434 pp. (bibl.).

——— *Youth and Dissent: The Rise of a New Opposition.* New York, 1971. 403 pp.

Kennan, George F. *Democracy and the Student Left.* Boston, 1968. 239 pp.

Kerouac, John. *On the Road.* New York, 1957. 310 pp.

——— *The Dharma Bums.* New York, 1958. 244 pp.

Kerr, Clark. *The Uses of the University.* Cambridge, Mass., 1964. 140 pp.

Kidd, Harry. *The Trouble at L.S.E. 1966–1967.* London, 1969. 189 pp.

Killmer, Richard L., et al. *They Can't Go Home Again: The Story of America's Political Exiles.* Philadelphia, 1971. 118 pp.

Kittler, Glenn D. *The Jesus Kids and Their Leaders.* New York, 1972 (pb). 237 pp.

Kleeman, Susann. *Ursachen und Formen der amerikanischen Studentenopposition.* Frankfurt/Main, 1971 (pb). 229 pp. (bibl.).

Klein, Alexander, ed. *Natural Enemies??? Youth and the Clash of Generations.* Philadelphia, 1969. 533 pp.

Knaut, Horst. *Propheten der Angst: Berichte zu psychopathologischen Trends der Gegenwart.* Percha, 1975 (pb). 231 pp. (bibl.).

Kopkin, Raimund. *Sprachführer durch die Revolution.* Munich, 1968 (pb). 128 pp. (bibl.).

SELECTED BIBLIOGRAPHY

Kramer, Jane. *Allen Ginsberg in America.* New York, 1968; quoted from New York, 1970 (pb), 202 pp.

Krämer-Badoni, Rudolf. *Anarchismus: Geschichte und Gegenwart einer Utopie.* Vienna, 1970. 288 pp.

Krauss, Ellis S. *Japan's Radicals Revisited.* Berkeley, 1974. 192 pp. (bibl.).

Kreuzer, Helmut. *Die Boheme: Beiträge zu ihrer Beschreibung.* Stuttgart, 1968. 435 pp. (bibl.).

Kukuck, Margareth. *Student und Klassenkampf: Studentenbewegung in der BRD seit 1967.* Hamburg, 1974. 278 pp. (bibl.).

Kunen, James Simon. *The Strawberry Statement: Notes of a College Revolutionary.* New York, 1969. 150 pp.

Kuroń, Jacek, and Karol Modzelewski. "An Open Letter to the Communist Party Members." In Jacek Kuroń, et al., *Revolutionary Marxist Students in Poland Speak Out: 1964–1968.* New York, 1968. 96 pp.

Labrousse, Alain. *Les Tupamaros: Guérila urbaine en Uruguay.* Paris, 1971. 201 pp.

Landy, Eugene E. *The Underground Dictionary.* New York, 1971 (pb). 200 pp.

Langguth, Gerd. *Protestbewegung am Ende: Die Neue Linke als Vorhut der DKP.* Mainz, 1971. 348 pp. (bibl.).

Laqueur, Walter. "Reflections on Youth Movements." In Chertoff, ed., *The New Left,* pp. 54–76.

——— *Young Germany.* New York, 1962 (pb). 253 pp.

Larsson, Bernard. *Demonstrationen. Ein Berliner Modell. Fotos und Texte.* Berlin, 1967. 179 pp.

Lauter, Paul, and Florence Howe. *The Conspiracy of the Young.* New York, 1971. 399 pp.

Lavan, George, ed. *Che Guevara Speaks: Selected Speeches and Writings.* 1967; quoted from New York, 1968 (pb), 159 pp.

Leamer, Laurence. *The Paper Revolutionaries: The Rise of the Underground Press.* New York, 1972. 220 pp. (bibl.).

Leary, Timothy. *Jail Notes.* New York, 1970. 154 pp.

Lee, Calvin B. T. *The Campus Scene, 1900–1970: Changing Styles in Undergraduate Life.* New York, 1970. 178 pp.

Lefebvre, Henri. *L'irruption de Nanterre au sommet.* Paris, 1968. 178 pp.

Levin, Bernard. *The Pendulum Years: Britain and the Sixties.* London, 1970; quoted from London, 1972 (pb). 442 pp.

Levinson, Sandra, ed. *Venceremos Brigade: Diaries and Letters.* New York, 1971. 421 pp.

Levita, David J. de. *The Concept of Identity.* Paris, 1965. 209 pp.

Levitt, Morton, and Ben Rubinstein. *Youth and Social Change.* Detroit, 1972. 410 pp.

Lewis, Roger. *Outlaws of America: The Underground Press and Its Context.* Harmondsworth, 1972 (pb). 204 pp.

Lewytzkyj, Borys. *Die linke Opposition in der Sowjetunion: Systemkritik Programme Dokumente.* Hamburg, 1974. 191 pp. (bibl.).

Lewytzkyj, Borys. *Politische Opposition in der Soujetunion, 1960–1972: Analyse und Dokumentation.* Munich, 1972 (pb). 337 pp. (bibl.).
Liebert, Robert. *Radical and Militant Youth: A Psychoanalytic Inquiry.* New York, 1971. 257 pp.
Liebmann, Arthur. *The Politics of Puerto Rican University Students.* Austin, 1970. 205 pp. (bibl.).
Lipset, Seymour Martin. *Rebellion in the University.* Boston, 1971. 310 pp.
Lipset, Seymour Martin, ed. *Student Politics.* New York, 1967. 403 pp.
Lipset, Seymour Martin, and Earl Raab. *The Politics of Unreason: Right-Wing Extremism in America, 1790–1970.* New York, 1970. 547 pp.
Lipset, Seymour Martin, and Philip G. Altbach, eds. *Students in Revolt.* Boston, 1971. 561 pp. (bibl.).
Lipset, Seymour Martin, and Sheldon S. Wolin, eds. *The Berkeley Student Revolt: Facts and Interpretations.* Garden City, N.Y., 1965 (pb). 585 pp.
Litten, Jens. *Eine verpasste Revolution? Nachruf auf den SDS.* Hamburg, 1969. 97 pp.
Long, Priscilla, ed. *The New Left: A Collection of Essays.* 2d ed. Boston, 1970. 475 pp. (bibl.).
Lothstein, Arthur, ed. *"All We Are Saying . . ." The Philosophy of the New Left.* New York, 1971. 381 pp.
Löwenthal, Richard. *Der romantische Rückfall.* Stuttgart, 1970 (pb). 88 pp.
Luce, Phillip Abbott. *The New Left.* New York, 1966. 214 pp.
——— *The New Left Today: America's Trojan Horse.* Washington, D.C., 1971. 164 pp.
Lukas, J. Anthony. *Don't Shoot—We Are Your Children!* New York, 1968. 461 pp.
Lurie, Alison. *The War Between the Tates.* New York, 1975 (pb). 350 pp.

Maas, Henry S., and Joseph A. Kuypers. *From Thirty to Seventy: A Forty-Year Longitudinal Study of Adult Life Styles and Personality.* 2d ed. San Francisco, 1975. 240 pp. (bibl.).
McFadden, Michael. *The Jesus Revolution.* New York, 1972 (pb). 212 pp.
McGregor, Craig, ed. *Bob Dylan: A Retrospective.* New York, 1972. 407 pp.
MacIntyre, Alasdair. *Herbert Marcuse.* New York, 1970. 95 pp.
Maddox, Robert James. *The New Left and the Origins of the Cold War.* Princeton, 1973. 169 pp.
Mailer, Norman. *The Armies of the Night: History as a Novel—The Novel as History.* New York, 1968 (pb). 320 pp.
Malcolm, Henry. *Generation of Narcissus.* Boston, 1971. 266 pp.
Malcolm X [Malcolm Little]. *The Autobiography of Malcolm X.* Edited by Alex Haley. New York, 1965. 455 pp.
Marcuse, Herbert. *Counterrevolution and Revolt.* Boston, 1972. 138 pp.

Marcuse, Herbert. *Das Ende der Utopie. Herbert Marcuse diskutiert mit Studenten und Professoren der FU Berlin.* Berlin, 1967. 151 pp.
—— *Eros and Civilization: A Philosophical Inquiry into Freud.* Boston, 1955. 277 pp.
—— *An Essay on Liberation.* Boston 1969. 91 pp.
—— *One-Dimensional Man: Studies in the Ideology of Advanced Industrial Society.* Boston, 1964. 266 pp.
—— "Repressive Tolerance." In Wolff, *Critique,*
—— *Soviet Marxism: A Critical Analysis.* New York, 1958. 271 pp.
—— *Über Revolte, Anarchismus und Einsamkeit: Ein Gespräch.* Zürich, 1969 (pb). 48 pp. [Also, in *L'Express,* 1969.]
—— *See also* Breines; Habermas, *Antworten*; Holz; MacIntyre; Robinson; Stark; Vivas
Martin, David, ed. *Anarchy and Culture: The Problem of the Contemporary University.* London, 1969. 212 pp.
Mead, Margaret. *Culture and Commitment.* Garden City, N.Y., 1970. 113 pp.
Meadows, Dennis, et al. *The Limits to Growth.* London, 1973. 218 pp.
Medved, Michael, and David Wallechinsky. *What Really Happened to the Class of '65?* New York, 1976. 285 pp.
Mehnert, Klaus. *Amerikanische und russische Jugend um 1930.* Stuttgart, 1973. 297 pp.
—— *Moscow and the New Left.* Berkeley, 1975. 275 pp. (bibl.).
—— *Peking and the New Left.* Berkeley, 1969. 156 pp.
—— *Youth in Soviet Russia.* London, 1933. 270 pp.
Mehta, Prayag, ed. *The Indian Youth: Emerging Problems and Issues.* Bombay, 1971. 194 pp.
[**Meinhof, Ulrike**]. "Das Konzept Stadtguerilla." In Schubert, *Stadtguerilla,* pp. 103–124.
Meinhof, Ulrike. *Dokumente einer Rebellion: 10 Jahre konkret-Kolumnen.* Hamburg, 1972. 111 pp.
Melville, Keith. *Communes in the Counter Culture: Origins, Theories, Styles of Life.* New York, 1972. 256 pp. (bibl.).
Mendel, Gérard. *La Crise de générations.* Paris, 1969. 254 pp.
Methvin, Eugene H. *The Riot Makers: The Technology of Social Demolition.* 2d ed. New Rochelle, N.Y., 1971. 586 pp.
Metzner, Ralph. *Maps of Consciousness: I Ching—Tantra—Tarot—Alchemy—Astrology—Actualism.* New York, 1974. 160 pp.
Michener, James A. *Kent State: What Happened and Why.* New York, 1971. 559 pp.
Miles, Michael W. *The Radical Probe: The Logic of Student Rebellion.* New York, 1971. 311 pp.
Miller, Michael V., and Susan Gilmore, eds. *Revolution at Berkeley: The Crisis in American Education.* New York, 1965 (pb). 348 pp.
Mills, C. Wright. *The Power Elite.* New York, 1956. 423 pp.
—— *See also* Domhoff; Horowitz.
Molnar, Thomas. *La Gauche vue d'en face.* Paris, 1970. 152 pp.
Morgan, Thomas B. *Among the Anti-Americans.* New York, 1967. 211 pp.

Müller-Borchert, Hans Joachim. *Guerilla im Industriestaat: Ziele, Ansatzpunkte und Erfolgsaussichten.* Hamburg, 1973. 182 pp.
Mungo, Raymond. *Famous Long Ago: My Life and Hard Times with Liberation News Service.* 2d ed. Boston, 1970. 202 pp.

Nathan, John. *Mishima: A Biography.* Boston, 1974. 300 pp.
National Advisory Commission on Civil Disorders; *see Report of....*
National Commission on Marihuana and Drug Abuse; *see Report of....*
National Commission on the Causes and Prevention of Violence; *see Reports of... or to....*
Neelsen, John Peter. *Student Unrest in India: A Typology and a Socio-Structural Analysis.* Munich, 1973. 101 pp. (bibl.)
Negt, Oskar, ed. *Die Linke antwortet Jürgen Habermas.* Frankfurt/Main, 1969. 211 pp.
Neuburg, Paul. *The Hero's Children: The Post-War Generation in Eastern Europe.* New York, 1973. 383 pp. (bibl.).
Nevermann, Knut. *Der 2. Juni 1967. Studenten zwischen Notstand und Demokratie—Dokumente zu den Ereignissen anlässlich des Schah-Besuchs.* Cologne, 1967. 151 pp.
Neville, Richard. *Play Power: Exploring the International Underground.* London, 1970; New York, 1971 (pb). 325 pp.
Newfield, Jack. *A Prophetic Minority.* New York, 1967 (pb). 158 pp.
Niederhoffer, Arthur. *Behind the Shield: The Police in Urban Society.* Garden City, N.Y., 1969 (pb). 263 pp.
Nirumand, Bahman. *Persien, Modell eines Entwicklungslandes oder Die Diktatur der Freien Welt.* 6th ed. Hamburg, 1967. 155 pp.
Nobile, Philip, ed. *The Con III Controversy: The Critics Look at "The Greening of America."* New York, 1971 (pb). 273 pp.
Nowlis, Helen H. *Drugs on the College Campus.* Garden City, N.Y., 1969 (pb). 144 pp.

Oelinger, Josef. *Die Neue Linke und der SDS: Die politische Theorie der revolutionären Opposition.* Cologne, 1969 (pb). 220 pp. (bibl.).
Oltmans, Willem L., ed. *On Growth.* New York, 1974. 493 pp. [*Grenzen aan de groei.* Utrecht, 1973.]
O'Neill, Nena, and George O'Neill. *Open Marriage: A New Life Style for Couples.* 3d ed. New York, 1973 (pb). 286 pp. (bibl.).
Ortega y Gasset, José. *Das Wesen geschichtlicher Krisen.* 2d ed. Stuttgart, 1951. 145 pp. [*Esquema de la crisis y otros ensayos.* Madrid, 1942.]
Osborne, John. *Look Back in Anger.* New York, 1956. 96 pp.

Paetel, Karl O., ed. *Beat: Eine Anthologie.* 2d ed. Hamburg, 1968. 300 pp. (bibl.).
Parkin, Frank. *Middle Class Radicalism: The Social Bases of the British Campaign for Nuclear Disarmament.* Manchester, 1968. 207 pp.

SELECTED BIBLIOGRAPHY

Passin, Herbert. "Changing Values: Work and Growth in Japan."
Asian Survey, October 1975, pp. 821–850.

Pentzlin, Heinz. *Die Kinder des Wohlstands: Herausforderung der
Jugend?* Osnabrück, 1974. 82 pp.

Peters, Louis F. *Kunst und Revolte: Das Politische Plakat und der
Aufstand der französischen Studenten.* Cologne, 1968. 151 pp.

Pickering, Stephen. *Bob Dylan Approximately: A Portrait of the
Jewish Poet in Search of God.* New York, 1975. 204 pp.

Poniatowska, Elena. *La Noche de Tlatelolco: Testemonios de historia oral.* 24th ed. Mexico, 1975. 281 pp. (33 pp. pictures).

Popp, Volker, ed. *Initiation.* Frankfurt/Main, 1969. 182 pp. (bibl.).

Potter, Paul. *A Name for Ourselves: Feelings About Authentic Identity, Love, Intuitive Politics, Us.* New York, 1971. 238 pp.

Powell, William. *The Anarchist Cookbook.* New York, 1971. 160 pp.

Powers, Thomas. *Diana: The Making of a Terrorist.* Boston, 1971.
225 pp.

President's Commission on Campus Unrest; see *Report of
. . . .*

President's Commission on Law Enforcement; see *Report by
. . .*

Priaulx, Allan, and Sanford J. Ungar. *The Almost Revolution:
France 1968.* New York, 1969 (pb). 177 pp.

Rader, Dotson. *I Ain't Marchin' Anymore.* New York, 1969 (pb). 160
pp.

Raina, Peter K. *Die Krise der Intellektuellen: Die Rebellion für die
Freiheit in Polen.* Olten, 1968. 128 pp.

Rammstedt, Otthein, ed. *Anarchismus. Grundtexte zur Theorie
und Praxis der Gewalt.* Cologne/Opladen, 1969. 168 pp. (bibl.).

Rand, Ayn. *The New Left: The Anti-Industrial Revolution.* New
York, 1971 (pb). 204 pp.

Rapoport, Roger, and Laurence J. Kirshbaum. *Is the Library
Burning?* New York, 1969 (pb). 180 pp.

Raskin, Jonah. *Out of the Whale: An Autobiography.* New York,
1974. 216 pp.

Raskin, Jonah, ed. *The Weather Eye: Communiques from the
Weather Underground, May 1970–May 1974.* New York, 1974. 124 pp.

Reddaway, Peter, ed. *Uncensored Russia: The Human Movement
in the Soviet Union. The Annotated Text of the Unofficial Journal "A
Chronicle of Current Events"* [nos. 1–11]. London, 1972. 499 pp.

Reich, Charles A. *The Greening of America.* New York, 1970. 399
pp.
——— *See also* Nobile.

Reich, Wilhelm. *The Function of the Orgasm.* 2d ed. London, 1968.
[Amsterdam, 1965. 206 pp.]
——— *The Sexual Revolution.* New York, 1945. [*Die sexuelle Revolu-
tion.* Copenhagen, 1936; quoted from Frankfurt/Main, 1966 (pb), 269
pp.]
——— *See also* Baxandall; Rycroft.

Reid, Tim, and Julian Reid, eds. *Student Power and the Canadian Campus.* Toronto, 1969. 226 pp.

411

SELECTED BIBLIOGRAPHY

Report by the President's Commission on Law Enforcement and Administration of Justice. The Challenge of Crime in a Free Society. New York, 1968 (pb). 814 pp.
Report of the Commission on Obscenity and Pornography. Washington, D.C., 1970. 646 pp. [Also New York, 1970 (pb). 700 pp.]
Report of the Fact-Finding Commission Appointed to Investigate the Disturbances at Columbia University in April and May 1968 [Cox Report]. New York, 1968 (pb). 222 pp.
Report of the National Advisory Commission on Civil Disorders [Kerner Report]. 13th ed. New York, 1968 (pb). 609 pp.
Report of the National Commission on Marihuana and Drug Abuse. New York, 1972 (pb). 233 pp.
Report of [or to] the National Commission on the Causes and Prevention of Violence. Assassination and Political Violence. New York, 1970 (pb). 752 pp. (bibl.).
—— *The History of Violence in America.* New York, 1969 (pb). 822 pp.
—— *Law and Order Reconsidered.* New York, 1970 (pb). 659 pp.
—— *The Politics of Protest* [Skolnick Report]. New York, 1969 (pb). 419 pp.
—— *Rights in Conflict* [Walker Report]. New York, 1968 (pb). 362 pp.
—— *To Establish Justice, To Insure Domestic Tranquility.* New York, 1970 (pb). 277 pp.
Report of the President's Commission on Campus Unrest [Chairman William W. Scranton]. Washington, D.C., 1970. 537 pp. [Also New York, 1971 (pb). 537 pp.]
Report of the White House Conference on Youth, April 1971. Washington, D.C. [n.d.]. 310 pp.
Riesman, David, et al. *The Lonely Crowd.* New Haven, 1950. 386 pp.
Rimmer, Robert H. *The Harrad Experiment: A Novel.* New York, 1968 (pb). 312 pp. (bibl.).
—— *The Harrad Letters to Robert H. Rimmer.* New York, 1969 (pb). 160 pp.
—— *Proposition 31.* New York, 1969 (pb). 285 pp. (bibl.).
Roberts, Ron E. *The New Communes: Coming Together in America.* Englewood Cliffs, N.J., 1971. 144 pp.
Robinson, Paul A. *The Freudian Left: Wilhelm Reich, Geza Roheim, Herbert Marcuse.* New York, 1969. 252 pp.
Rockefeller, John D. *The Second American Revolution: Some Personal Observations.* New York, 1973. 189 pp.
Röhl, Klaus Rainer. *Fünf Finger sind keine Faust.* Cologne, 1974. 456 pp.
—— *Die Genossin: Roman.* Vienna, 1975. 324 pp.
Roszak, Theodore. *The Making of a Counter Culture: Reflections on the Technocratic Society and Its Youthful Opposition.* Garden City, N.Y., 1969 (pb). 303 pp. (bibl.).
—— *Where the Wasteland Ends: Politics and Transcendence in Postindustrial Society.* Garden City, N.Y., 1973 (pb). 451 pp.

Rothchild, John, and Susan Wolf. *The Children of the Counterculture.* Garden City, N.Y., 1976. 207 pp.
Roussopoulos, Dimitrios J., ed. *The New Left in Canada.* 2d ed. Montreal, 1971. 152 pp. (bibl.).
Rubin, Jerry. *Do It! Scenarios of the Revolution.* New York, 1970. 256 pp.
Rycroft, Charles. *Wilhelm Reich.* London, 1971. 105 pp.

Sale, Kirkpatrick. *SDS: The Rise and Development of the Students for a Democratic Society.* New York, 1974 (pb). 752 pp.
Salisbury, Harrison. *The Shook-up Generation.* New York. 1958.
Scaduto, Anthony. *Bob Dylan: A Biography.* New York, 1973 (pb). 351 pp.
Schacht, Richard. *Alienation.* Garden City, N.Y., 1971 (pb). 285 pp.
Schelsky, Helmut. *Die skeptische Generation: Eine Soziologie der deutschen Jugend.* Düsseldorf, 1963. 409 pp. (bibl.).
Scheuch, Erwin K. *Haschisch und LSD als Modedrogen: Wunschdenken und Tatsachen.* Osnabrück, 1970. 73 pp.
Scheuch, Erwin K., ed. *Die Wiedertäufer der Wohlstandsgesellschaft: Eine kritische Untersuchung der "Neuen Linken" und ihrer Dogmen.* Cologne, 1968. 222 pp.
Schlomann, Friedrich-Wilhelm, and Paulette Friedlingstein. *Die Maoisten: Pekings Filialen in Westeuropa.* Frankfurt/Main, 1970. 300 pp.
Schnapp, Alain, and Pierre Vidal-Naquet. *The French Student Uprising, November 1967–June 1968: An Analytical Record.* Boston, 1971. 654 pp. (bibl.). [*Journal de la commune étudiante: textes et documents, Novembre 1967–Juin 1968.* Paris, 1969.]
Schneider, Michael. *Die lange Wut zum langen Marsch: Aufsätze zur sozialistischen Politik und Literatur.* Hamburg, 1975. 355 pp.
Schober, Siegfried, ed. *Let It Bleed: Die Rolling Stones in Altamont—Berichte und Photos.* Munich, 1970 (pb). 138 pp.
Schram, Stuart. *Chairman Mao Talks to the People: Talks and Letters, 1956–1971.* New York, 1974. 352 pp.
Schubert, Alex. *Stadtguerilla: Tupamaros in Uruguay—Rote Armee Fraktion in der Bundesrepublik.* Berlin, 1974. 124 pp.
Schurmacher, Emile C. *Witchcraft in America Today.* New York, 1970 (pb). 176 pp.
Schwartz, Ed. "Why Communes Fail: For Those Who Hadn't Known They Did." In Fairfield, *Utopia.*
Schwendter, Rolf. *Theorie der Subkultur.* Cologne, 1971. 363 pp. (bibl.).
Searle, John. *The Campus War. A Sympathetic Look at the University in Agony.* New York, 1971. 242 pp.
Sedgwick, Peter. "Varieties of Socialist Thought." In Crick and Robson, *Protest and Discontent,* pp. 37–67.
Silius-Broo, Harriet. *Studentrörelsen och funktionalism.* Åbo, 1972. 90 pp. (mimeo., bibl.).
Silvert, K. H. "The University Student [in Latin America]." In Johnson, *Continuity and Change,* pp. 206–226.
Sinclair, Andrew. *Che Guevara.* London, 1970.

413

Singer, Daniel. *Prelude to Revolution: France in May 1968.* New York, 1970. 434 pp.

Singh, Amar Kumar. *Indian Students in Britain: A Survey of Their Adjustment and Attitudes.* Bombay, 1963. 208 pp. (bibl.).

Skinner, B. F. *Walden Two.* New York, 1962 (pb). 320 pp.

Slater, Philip. *The Pursuit of Loneliness: American Culture at the Breaking Point.* 7th ed. Boston, 1972. 154 pp.

Smith, David H. *Latin American Student Activism.* Lexington, Mass., 1973. 169 pp.

Smith, Henry Delwitt. *Japan's First Student Radicals.* Cambridge, Mass., 1972. 341 pp.

Smith, James R., and Lynn G. Smith, eds. *Beyond Monogamy: Recent Studies of Sexual Alternatives in Marriage.* Baltimore, 1974. 336 pp.

Smith, Robert, et al. *By Any Means Necessary: The Revolutionary Struggle at San Francisco State.* San Francisco, 1970. 370 pp.

Snyder, Gary. *Earth House Hold: Technical Notes and Queries to Fellow Dharma Revolutionaries.* New York [n.d.]. 143 pp.

Sokoloff, Boris. *The Permissive Society.* New Rochelle, N.Y., 1971. 254 pp.

Sontheimer, Kurt, et al. *Der Überdruss an der Demokratie: Neue Linke und alte Rechte—Unterschiede und Gemeinsamkeiten.* Cologne, 1970. 208 pp.

Sorensen, Robert C. *Adolescent Sexuality in Contemporary America: Personal Values and Sexual Behavior, Ages Thirteen to Nineteen.* New York, 1973. 549 pp.

Spender, Stephen. *The Year of the Young Rebels.* New York, 1969 (pb). 186 pp.

Spranger, Eduard. *Psychologie des Jugendalters.* 25th ed. Heidelberg, 1957. 321 pp.

Staar, Richard F., ed. *1975 Yearbook on International Communist Affairs.* Stanford, 1975. 678 pp. *1976 Yearbook* .... Stanford, 1976. 636 pp.

Stafford, Peter. *Sexual Behavior in the Communist World: An Eyewitness Report of Life, Love and the Human Condition Behind the Iron Curtain.* New York, 1967. 287 pp. (bibl.).

Stark, Franz, ed. *Revolution oder Reform? Herbert Marcuse und Karl Popper: Eine Konfrontation.* Munich, 1971. 48 pp.

Statera, Gianni. *Death of a Utopia: The Development and Decline of Student Movements in Europe.* New York, 1975. 294 pp.

Statistisches Bundesamt, ed. *Statistisches Jahrbuch für die Bundesrepublik Deutschland 1974.* Stuttgart, 1974. 567 + 136 pp.

Steininger, Alexander. *Literatur und Politik in der Sowjetunion nach Stalins Tod.* Wiesbaden, 1965. 236 pp. (bibl.).

Steinhoff, Patricia G. "Portrait of a Terrorist." *Asian Survey* 16 (September 1976), pp. 830–845.

Stent, Gunther S. *The Coming of the Golden Age: A View of the End of Progress.* Garden City, N.Y., 1969. 146 pp. (bibl.).

Stern, Fritz. *The Politics of Cultural Despair.* Berkeley, 1963. 367 pp. (bibl.).

SELECTED BIBLIOGRAPHY

Stern, Susan. *With the Weathermen: The Personal Journal of a Revolutionary Woman.* Garden City, N.Y., 1975. 374 pp.

St. John, Jeffrey. *Countdown to Chaos.* Los Angeles, 1969. 202 pp.

Stone, I. F. *The Killings at Kent State: How Murder Went Unpunished.* 3d ed. New York, 1971 (pb). 158 pp.

Studenten Vakbeweging. *Ervaringen uit twee jaar stridj toe Leuven.* Louvain [n.d.]. 129 pp.

Stuke, Horst, ed. *Michail Bakunin, Staatlichkeit und Anarchie und andere Schriften.* Frankfurt/Main, 1972. 885 pp. (bibl.).

Sundancer, Elaine. *Celery Wine: The Story of a Country Commune.* Yellow Springs, Ohio, 1973. 176 pp.

Ta Kung Pao, ed. *The Upheaval in Hong Kong.* Hong Kong, 1967. [Unpaginated.]

Tannenbaum, Abraham J., ed. *Alienated Youth.* New York, 1969. 167 pp.

Tarnow, Alexander von. *Demokratie in der Illegalität: Die "Chronik der laufenden Ereignisse"—Ein Untergrund—Informationsblatt in der Sowjetunion.* Stuttgart, 1971. 191 pp.

Taylor J. R. *Anger and After: A Guide to the New British Drama.* London, 1962. 391 pp.

Taylor, Stuart, et al. *Violence at Kent State, May 1 to 4, 1970: The Students' Perspective.* New York, 1971. 195 pp.

Teal, Donn. *The Gay Militants.* New York, 1971. 355 pp.

Teodori, Massimo, ed. *The New Left: A Documentary.* Indianapolis, 1969. 501 pp. (bibl.).

Thompson, Hunter S. *Hell's Angels: A Strange and Terrible Saga.* 11th ed. New York, 1974 (pb). 348 pp.

Thoreau, Henry David. *On the Duty of Civil Disobedience.* 1849.

Tökes, Rudolf L., ed. *Dissent in the USSR: Politics, Ideology, and People.* Baltimore, 1975. 453 pp.

Tophoven, Rolf. *Politik durch Gewalt: Guerilla und Terrorismus heute.* Bonn, 1976. 173 pp.

Touraine, Alain. *The May Movement: Revolt and Reform. May 1968—The Student Rebellion and Workers' Strikes—The Birth of a Social Movement.* New York, 1971. 373 pp. [*Le Mouvement de mai ou le communisme utopique.* Paris, 1968.]

Tsurumi, Kazuko. *Social Change and the Individual: Japan Before and After Defeat in World War II.* Princeton, 1970. 441 pp.

—— *Student Movements in 1960 and 1969: Continuity and Change.* Tokyo [n.d.]. 55 pp.

Tucker, Robert, W. *The Radical Left and American Foreign Policy.* Baltimore, 1971. 156 pp.

Tuynman, Hans. *Ich bin ein Provo: Das permanente Happening.* Darmstadt, 1966. 169 pp. [*Full Time Provo.* Amsterdam, 1966.]

UNESCO. *Statistical Yearbook, 1966.* Paris, 1968. 505 pp.

—— *Statistical Yearbook, 1973.* Paris, 1974. 788 pp.

Ungers, Lieselotte, and O. M. Ungers. *Kommunen in der Neuen Welt, 1740–1971.* Cologne, 1972 (pb). 102 pp. (bibl.).

415

SELECTED BIBLIOGRAPHY

University of Essex. *Report of the Annan Enquiry.* 1974. 38 pp.
"University and Society." *Journal of Social and Political Ideas in Japan* (special issue) 5, nos. 2–3 (Tokyo, 1967), 364 pp.
U.S. Department of Commerce, ed. *Statistical Abstract of the United States, 1974.* Washington, D.C., 1974. 1028 pp.
U.S. News and World Report. *Communism and the New Left: What They're Up To Now* (special issue). New York, 1969. 222 pp.

Veysey, Laurence. *The Communal Experience: Anarchist and Mystical Counter-Cultures in America.* New York, 1973. 495 pp.
Vivas, Eliseo. *Contra Marcuse.* New York, 1971. 236 pp.
Vogelsang, Sandy. *The Long Dark Night of the Soul: The American Intellectual Left and the Vietnam War.* New York, 1974. 249 pp. (bibl.).

Wallerstein, Immanuel, and Paul Starr, eds. *The University Crisis Reader.* Vol 1: *The Liberal University Under Attack.* New York, 1971 (pb). 558 pp. Vol. 2: *Confrontation and Counterattack.* New York, 1971 (pb). 515 pp.
Ward, Hiley H. *The Far-Out Saints of the Jesus Communes.* New York, 1972. 192 pp.
Warren, Bill, ed. *The Middle of the Country: The Events of May 4th as Seen by Students and Faculty at Kent State University.* New York, 1970 (pb). 160 pp.
Waterhouse, Larry G., and Mariann G. Wizard. *Turning the Guns Around: Notes on the GI Movement.* New York, 1971. 224 pp.
[Weather Underground.] *Prairie Fire: The Politics of Revolutionary Anti-Imperialism.* New York, 1974. 152 pp.
Weigt, Peter, ed. *Revolutionslexikon: Taschenbuch der ausserparlamentarischen Aktion.* Frankfurt/Main, 1968. 64 pp.
Weiss, Andreas von. *Die Neue Linke: Kritische Analyse.* Boppard a.Rh., 1969. 331 pp. (bibl.).
——— *Schlagwörter der Neuen Linken: Die Agitation der Sozialrevolutionäre.* Munich, 1974 (pb). 246 pp. (bibl.).
Weyer, Hartmut. *MSB Spartakus: Von der studentischen Protestbewegung zum Klassenkampf.* Stuttgart, 1973. 132 pp. (bibl.).
Wheelis, Allen. *The Quest for Identity.* New York, 1958. 250 pp.
White, George Abbot, and Charles Newman, ed. *Literature in Revolution.* New York, 1972. 640 pp.
White House Conference on Youth, see *Report of . . . .*
Widgery, David. *The Left in Britain 1956–68.* London, 1976 (pb). 549 pp. (bibl.).
Wigginton, Eliot, ed. *The Foxfire Book.* Garden City, N.Y., 1972. 384 pp. *Foxfire 2.* Garden City, N.Y., 1973. 410 pp.
Wolf, Leonhardt, and Deborah Wolf, eds. *Voices From the Love Generation.* Boston, 1968. 283 pp.
Wolfe, Burton H. *The Hippies.* New York, 1968 (pb). 207 pp.
Wolfe, Tom. *Radical Chic & Mau-Mauing the Flak-Catchers.* New York, 1970. 153 pp.
Wolff, Robert Paul, et al. *A Critique of Pure Tolerance.* Boston, 1965. 123 pp.

SELECTED BIBLIOGRAPHY

Wolin, Sheldon S., and John H. Schaar. *The Berkeley Rebellion and Beyond: Essays on Politics and Education in the Technological Society.* New York, 1970 (pb). 158 pp.

Yablonsky, Lewis. *The Hippie Trip: A Firsthand Account of the Beliefs and Behaviors of Hippies in America.* New York, 1968. 368 pp.
Yankelovich, Daniel. *The Changing Values on Campus: Political and Personal Attitudes of Today's College Students.* New York, 1972. 246 pp.
——— *The New Morality: A Profile of American Youth in the 70's.* New York, 1974. 166 pp.

Zaher, Renate. *Kolonialismus und Entfremdung: Zur politischen Theorie Frantz Fanons.* Frankfurt/Main, 1969. 112 pp. (bibl.).
Zorza, Richard. *The Right to Say "We": The Adventures of a Young Englishman at Harvard and in the Youth Movement.* London, 1970. 213 pp.

INDEX

INDEX

Bell, Daniel, 10, 98, 339
Berg, Rev. David, 79
Berkeley, California, 25–26, 199–200
Berkeley, University of California at, 25–31, 69, 305
Berkeley Center for Drug Use, 353
Berry, Chuck, 264
Bettelheim, Bruno, 303, 338
Black Muslims, 59, 307
Black Panther Party, 21, 45, 54, 58, 68, 358
Blum, Richard A., 247
Bolivia, 141–143
Bookchin, Murray, 225
Boudin, Kathy, 50
Brandt, Willy, 37
Brazil, 143–146, 148
Brewster, Ben, 161
Brezhnev, Leonid, 102, 189, 322
Brodsky, Yosif, 181
Brown, Edmund G., Sr., 28
Brown, Edmund G. (Jerry), Jr., 85
Brown, H. Rap, 21
Brown, Sam, 357
Brzezinski, Zbigniew, 347
Buckley, William F., Jr., 11
Bugliosi, Vincent, 259
Bukovsky, Vladimir, 181, 305
Bulgaria, 328
Bureaucracy, 101–102, 185, 192, 291, 378
Business Week (magazine), 360

Caen, Herb, 9
California, University of (Berkeley), 25–31, 69, 305
Calvert, Greg, 40
Cambodia, 36, 37
Camara, Dom Helder, 146
Campaign for Nuclear Disarmament, 157
Cambridge University, 161, 165
Camus, Albert, 269
Capitalism, anti-, 192–193
Carlos (Ilich Ramírez Sánchez), 122
Carmichael, Stokely, 21, 68, 281, 307
Carr, Gordon, 165
Carter, Jimmy, 252
Cash, Johnny, 80
Castalia Foundation, 246

Castro, Fidel, 104, 141–143, 148–149, 188–189, 293–294, 379
Central Intelligence Agency (CIA), 64, 141
Chadwick, David, 357
Chaplin, Charlie, 378
Chessman, Caryl, 54
Chiang Ching, 190
Children of God, 79–81, 346
Children of the Counter Culture, The (Rothchild and Wolf), 230–231
Chile, 114
China
  attitudes toward, 46, 102, 103
  communes in, 222
  Cultural Revolution in, 190–191, 291–293
  marriage in, 240
  New Left and, 290–291
  1968 events in France and, 290
  Sino-Soviet split, 299
Christian Democrats
  Germany, 91
  Italy, 153
Civil rights movement, 18–21, 26, 54
Clausewitz, Karl von, 116
Cleaver, Eldridge, 358
Cleaver, Kathleen, 298
Cleveland, Brad, 27
Club of Rome, 337, 338
Cockburn, Aexander, 161
Cohn-Bendit, Daniel, 102, 112, 152, 160, 166, 274, 289, 306, 321, 323, 358, 360–361
Cold War, 298–299, 309
Colleges, *see* Universities and colleges
Collins, G. Mansfield, 16
Columbia University, 37, 48, 62, 281
Commando Holger Meins, 122
Commune 1 (K1; Germany), 207, 362
Commune 2 (K2; Germany), 120, 233–236
Communes
  Chinese, 222
  German, 233–236
  United States, 74–76, 223–233
  See also Kibbutzim
Communist Party
  Brazil, 144
  China, 190

420

INDEX

Red Army Fraction, 119
Red Guards, 190–191
Reich, Charles A., 339, 359
Reich, Wilhelm, 166, 239–240, 242,
  318–319
Reinsdorf, August, 327
Religion and religious cults, 71–74,
  76–85, 286, 346, 355, 367
Remiro, Joe, 53, 55
Republic (Plato), 288
Reuther, Elizabeth, 85
Revolutionary Peoples Army (ERP),
  143
Revolutionary Peoples Vanguard
  (UPR), 143, 146
Revolutionary Youth Movement
  (RYM), 42
Rhee, Syngman, 174
Rhodesia, 159
Riesman, David, 11, 340, 348
Rock music, 250–264
  *See also specific musicians and
  groups*
Robbins, Terry, 43, 50
Rodewald, Fritz, 119
Röhl, Klaus Rainer, 117, 238, 240, 248
Rolling Stones, 213
Rome, University of, 154
Rosenberg, Ethel, 301
Rosenberg, Julius, 301
Rossman, Mike, 356
Rothchild, John, 224, 230
Rothman, Stanley, 304, 305
Rotolo, Suze, 253
Rousseau, Jean-Jacques, 331–332
Rubin, Jerry, 207–208
Rudd, Mark, 43, 48–50, 281
Russia (prerevolutionary), 268–270, 333
  See also Union of Soviet Socialist
  Republics

Samuel, Ralph, 157
San Francisco, California, 7, 201
San Francisco State College, 215
Sandperl, Ira, 365
Sartre, Jean-Paul, 112–113
Sato, Eisaku, 132, 136
Savio, Mario, 27–29, 356
Saxbe, William, 52
Schmidt, Helmut, 292

Schneider, Michael, 108–109
Scott, John F., 262–263
Seale, Bobby, 58, 358
Sedgwick, Peter, 158
Senegal, 170–171
Sex, 237–246, 286, 355, 376
  in communes, 233, 234
  premarital, 243–246, 366
  Reich on, 239–240
Sheng-wu-lien, 191
Siddhartha (Hesse), 206
Sinclair, Upton, 22
Sit-ins, 18–19, 21, 26, 28, 277–278
Situationist International, 100
Sjöman, Vilgot, 238
Skinner, B. F., 255
Slater, Philip E., 338
Sloman, Albert, 160, 163
Snyder, Gary, 5, 8–10
Social Democratic Party (Germany), 13,
  92–93, 96, 100, 118
Social Democratic University Union
  (SHB; Germany), 96
Socialist German Student Alliance
  (SDS), 22, 94, 95, 100, 103, 106,
  110, 120, 294, 331
Socialist Party (United States), 33
Socialist Workers Party (United
  States), 34
Sociological jargon, 212
Solidarity (periodical), 158
Soltysik, Patricia, 53, 55
Sophocles, 337
Sorbonne University, 167, 170
Soul on Ice (Cleaver), 358
South Africa, 114
South Korea, 31, 174–175
Soviet Marxism (Marcuse), 100, 241,
  309
Soviets, 324, 332–333
Spain, 96, 152–153, 328
Spartakus, 95–96, 102, 362
Spock, Benjamin, 99
Spranger, Edward, 287
Spreti, Count Karl von, 144
Springer, Axel, 92
Stalin, Joseph, 177, 222, 240, 305
Stein, Freiherr von, 332
Steppenwolf (Hesse), 206, 343
Stern, Susan, 52

426

Stevenson, Adlai, 10
Stewart, Michael, 278
Stirner, Max, 328
Stockholm, Sweden, 202
Student League for Industrial
  Democracy, 22
Student Nonviolent Coordinating
  Committee (SNCC), 19–22, 28, 356,
  357
Students for a Democratic Society
  (SDS), 31–33, 58, 106, 302, 331,
  337
  disintegration of, 40–46
  origins of, 22–25
  women and, 66–68
Studies on the Left (periodical), 23
Suzuki, D. T., 84
Sweden, 154–155
Switzerland, 172
Symbionese Liberation Army (SLA),
  51–57

Taylor, John Russell, 12
Teach-ins against Vietnam War, 32,
  278
Television, 275–276, 336
Tendryakov, Vladimir, 195
Terror, 267–268, 277
Terrorism, 57
  anarchism and, 326–327
  in Germany, 116–123
  mass, 267–268
  recent incidents of, 271–274, 362,
    364–365
  in Russia (prerevolutionary), 268–270
  See also specific terrorist groups
Teufel, Fritz, 93, 207
Third World, 110–115, 138, 265–266,
  306, 373
  students in, 217–218
Tho, Le Duc, 36
Thompson, E. P., 157
Thompson, Hunter S., 16, 17
Tito, Marshal, 187–188
Todai (Tokyo University), 127–130,
  132, 133, 278
Toffler, Alvin, 65
Togliatti, Palmiro, 299
Tokyo, 199
Torres, Camilo, 145–146

Transcendental meditation (TM), 73,
  80, 85
Trotsky, Leon, 63
Trotskyists, 96, 131, 143, 158, 164
  in United States, 34–37, 45
Tshombe, Moïse, 90, 93, 110
Tsurumi, Kazuko, 363–364
Tupamaros, 143, 145–148
Turner, Brian, 355–356

Unification Church, 82
Union of Soviet Socialist Republics
  (U.S.S.R.), 13, 24, 33, 109, 131,
  134, 188, 222, 289–290, 294, 299,
  305, 333, 361, 374, 375
  Dutschke's attitude toward, 100–103
  youth unrest in, 177–182
Universities and colleges, 26–27, 194,
  214–221, 237–238, 362–363
  See also specific student groups
Universities and Left Review, 157
Uruguay, Tupamaros in, 143, 145–148

Vienna, University of, 171
Vietnam War, 32–39, 45, 92, 93, 110,
  112, 154–155, 278
Violence, 99, 265–267, 275–276
  See also Terrorism
Vladimirov, A., 179

Wallace, George, 304
Walls, Rufus, 68
Warsaw Institute of Technology, 183
Watts, Alan, 84
Wealth, 339–340
  See also Prosperity
Weatherman, 269, 270, 325
  SDS and, 43–44
  underground, 47–52
Weinberg, Jack, 28, 356
Weissman, Steve, 41, 356
Weisstein, Naomi, 67
West Berlin, 89–90, 92–94
Widgery, David, 158
Wilkerson, Cathlyn, 50
Wilhelm I, Kaiser, 326–327
Williams, Raymond, 157
Wolf, Susan, 224, 230
Wolfe, Tom, 208
Wolff, Karl Dietrich, 358

INDEX

Women's Lib, 66–70, 242, 374–375
Woodstock Festival, 260
Work ethic, 12, 378
Worker Student Alliance, 41–42
Workers (proletariat)
  campus, 59
  German, 328
  guerrillas and, 146
  Marcuse on, 58–59, 105–108, 312–314
  Marx on, 342
  1968 events in France and, 167–170
  in Poland, 184–185
  students and, 41–42, 58–59, 104–109
World Christian Liberation Front, 78

Wretched of the Earth, The (Fanon), 49, 112

Yeung Cheng, 191
Yevtushenko, Yevgeny, 13, 178
Yippies, 207–208
Young Socialist Alliance, 34
Yoyogi, 129–131, 135
Yugoslavia, 103, 185–188

Zen Buddhism, 84
Zengakuren, 134–135
Zeno, 320
Zhukor, Yuri, 289